I-Ching C

Government Internet C
and International Law

Kölner Schriften zum
Internationalen und Europäischen Recht

Cologne Studies
in International and European Law

herausgegeben von/edited by

Prof. Dr. Stephan Hobe

Band/Volume 26

LIT

I-Ching Chen

Government Internet Censorship Measures and International Law

LIT

This book is printed on acid-free paper.

Bibliographic information published by the Deutsche Nationalbibliothek
The Deutsche Nationalbibliothek lists this publication in the Deutsche Nationalbibliografie; detailed bibliographic data are available on the Internet at http://dnb.d-nb.de.

ISBN 978-3-643-91051-6 (pb)
ISBN 978-3-643-96051-1 (PDF)
Zugl.: Köln, Univ., Diss., 2018

A catalogue record for this book is available from the British Library.

Zweigniederlassung Zürich 2018
Klosbachstr. 107
CH-8032 Zürich
Tel. +41 (0) 44-251 75 05
E-Mail: zuerich@lit-verlag.ch http://www.lit-verlag.ch

Distribution:

In the UK: Global Book Marketing, e-mail: mo@centralbooks.com
In North America: Independent Publishers Group, e-mail: orders@ipgbook.com
In Germany: LIT Verlag Fresnostr. 2, D-48159 Münster
Tel. +49 (0) 2 51-620 32 22, Fax +49 (0) 2 51-922 60 99, e-mail: vertrieb@lit-verlag.de

e-books are available at www.litwebshop.de

Acknowledgement

I am grateful to many people who have assisted me during the preparation of this book and I have been very fortune to benefit from the generosity of them as well as the support of a number of institutions. Particular thanks to Prof. Dr. Stephan Hobe for his guidance and support throughout the project. As my doctoral supervisor, Prof. Hobe's help was invaluable for preparing the manuscript. His insightful comments and willingness to endlessly debate the issues inspired many of the ideas that appear in the book.

Thanks also to Prof. Dr. Chia-Jui Cheng for his encouragement during the years of my doctoral research. I am fortunate to have such a mentor to guide me to the right direction of life. I am grateful to Prof. Dr. Bernhard Kempen for his precious opinions in the final stages of completing this book. Thanks to all those who assisted me more generally in my research of the Institut für Luftrecht, Weltraumrecht und Cyberrecht at the University of Cologne. I would also like to thank Verein der Freunde und Förderer des Instituts für Luft-und Weltraumrecht an der Universität zu Köln for the financial support in publishing the book.

Thanks to my dearest friends who have always been a great source of support and lightened my life in many different ways. Love and gratitude above all to my parents, Cheng-Hua Chen and Pi-Wu Hsiung, who supported me with an extraordinary combination of unconditional love and unwavering belief throughout the project. Their encouragement was the motivation that kept me going. I am indebted to them in so many ways to list. This book is dedicated to my parents.

I-Ching Chen

Cologne, Germany

2018

Summary Contents

Contents

List of Abbreviations

APEC	Asia-Pacific Economic Cooperation
CCP	Chinese Communist Party
CESCR	Committee on Economic, Social and Cultural Rights (UN)
CITES	Convention on International Trade in Endangered Species
CNNIC	China Internet Network Information Center
CPBR	Consumer Privacy Bill of Rights
CPC	Central Product Classification
DNS	Domain Name Server
DPD	Data Protection Directive
DPI	Deep Packet Inspection
DSB	Dispute Settlement Body (WTO)
DSU	Understanding on Rules and Procedures Governing the Settlement of Dispute (WTO)
ECHR	European Convention on Human Rights
ECtHR	European Court of Human Rights
ECJ	European Court of Justice
ECOSOC	Economic and Social Council (UN)
ECPA	Electronic Communication Privacy Act
EUCFR	European Union Charter of Fundamental Rights
FTC	Federal Trade Commission
GATS	General Agreement on Trade in Services
GATT	General Agreement on Tariffs and Trade
GDPR	General Data Protection Regulation
GNI	Global Network Initiative
GPS	Global Position System
GSP	General System of Preferences
HRC	Human Rights Committee
IACHR	Inter-American Convention on Human Rights
ICCPR	International Covenant on Civil and Political Rights
ICESR	International Covenant on Economic, Social and Cultural Rights
ICP	Internet Content Provider
ICT	Information and Communication Technology
ICJ	International Court of Justice
IIS	Internet Information Service
IMF	International Monetary Fund
ISP	Internet Service Provider

ITA	Information Technology Agreement
ITO	International Trade Organization
MFN	Most Favoured Nation
MIIT	Ministry of Industry and Information Technology
MMPA	Marine Mammal Protecting Act
NCFC	National Computing and Networking Facility of China
NGO	Non-Governmental Organization
NSF	National Science Foundation
OAS	Organization of American States
OECD	Organization for Economic Co-Operation and Development
OHCHR	Office of the High Commissioner for Human Rights
PPM	Process and Production Method
PTA	Preferential Trade Agreements
RTA	Regional and Bilateral Trade Agreement
SPS Agreement	Agreement on Sanitary and Phytosanitary Measures (WTO)
TBT Agreement	Agreement on Technical Barriers to Trade (WTO)
TEFU	Treaty on the Functioning of the European Union
TRIPS	Agreement on Trade-Related Aspects of Intellectual Property Rights (WTO)
UDHR	Universal Declaration of Human Rights
UN	United Nations
UNCLOS	United Nations Convention on the Law of the Sea
UNCTAD	United Nations Conference on Trade and Development
UNESCO	United Nations Educational, Scientific and Cultural Organization
UNHRC	United Nation Human Rights Council
UPR	Universal Periodical Review
URL	Universal Resource Locater
US	United States
USTR	United States Trade Representative
VCLT	Vienna Convention on the Law of Treaties
WFOE	Wholly Foreign Owned Enterprise
WPDR	Working Party on Domestic Regulation
WPPS	Working Party on Professional Services
WTO	World Trade Organization

Introduction

This is true liberty, when free-born man,
Having to advise the public, may speak free,
Which he who can, and will, deserves high praise,
Who neither can, nor will, may hold his peace;
What can be juster in a state than this?
Euripid. Hicetid[1]

The expansion of the Internet in the late 1980s and early 1990s brought hopes to people that this new communication technology would erode the traditional territorial authorities and evolve its own system of government. Proponents of Internet freedom believed the geographical borders in the physical world were irrelevant to the virtual world and the new boundary made by binary code 1 and 0 could create more decent and freer societies than those built upon dirt, concrete, and capital.[2] The early Internet architects and pioneers considered the Internet to represent an anti-authoritarian or a non-hierarchical sphere, whose development could only be led and shaped by a self-organized community.[3] For them, the nature and origin of the Internet were based on the ideology that it should be treated as a global commons and no traditional sovereign state could assert jurisdiction over this borderless space.[4]

Early notions of an open self-governed Internet are mostly discredited.[5] On the one hand, the functions of the Internet today are much broader than was the case two decades ago. In those days, people mainly used the Internet to participate in online communities on a common platform. Nowadays, however, the Internet is integrated into nearly every aspect of modern human life. Individuals depend on it for communication, education, entertainment, trade, information, socialization, and political affiliation. Considering the magnitude and the depth

---

[1] John Milton and Edward Arber, *Areopagitica: a speech of Mr. John Milton for the liberty of unlicens'd printing, to the Parliament of England ...: London, printed in year 1644*, London:
publisher not identified (1869).
[2] Julian Dibbell, *My Tiny Life, Crime and Passion in a Virtual World*, New York: Henry Holt and Company (1998), p. 12.
[3] *See* David R. Johnson and David Post, *Law and Borders – The Rise of Law in Cyberspace*, Stanford Law Review, Vol.48, No.5 (1996), pp. 1365-1402.
[4] *See* Timothy S. Wu, *Cyber Sovereignty? – the Internet and the International System*, Harvard Journal of Law & Technology, Vol.10, No.3 (1997), p. 648.
[5] *See* Jack Goldsmith and Tim Wu, *Who Controls the Internet? Illusions of a Borderless World*, New York: Oxford University Press (2006), pp. 65-85.

of the influence of the Internet, especially since the advent of the Web 2.0,[6] what happens on it has a significant consequence in the real world. The changes brought about by this innovative technology have triggered the need for regulatory responses to each layer.

On the other hand, due to the substantial economic, political, and social implications of the Internet, nation states are enthusiastic to participate in its governance. The term 'Internet sovereignty' has been interpreted as being opposite to its original concept, that is, a regime that is independent of all territorial governments. Both democratic and authoritarian states have proclaimed sovereign autonomy over the Internet to maintain societal stability, ensure economic growth, and protect national security. Additionally, the idea that the borderless nature of the Internet makes it impossible to be regulated has been proven naïve. As an artificial creation resting upon tangible infrastructure and human involvement, the Internet is certainly subject to the control of nation states. Countries have implemented various mechanisms to monitor and intercept the information flow either within their territories or at the borders. As Jack Goldsmith and Tim Wu asserted, "behind the mists and magic of the Internet lies an older and stronger order whose relevance remains inescapable."[7]

Still, why is the Internet so different from other communication technologies, such as the telegraph or satellites, and why is Internet censorship important in the international sphere? These two questions are two sides of the same coin. It is undeniable that we are living in an information- and knowledge-based economy and society and such information or knowledge is gradually traveling through a single platform, i.e., the Internet.[8] Unlike any other medium, the Internet enables people to seek, receive, and impart information of all kinds instantaneously and inexpensively on a global level. The interoperability of information on the Internet facilitates comprehensive economic activities in both goods and services. The Internet has evolved as a critical instrument for individuals to express themselves and to share ideas. The Internet and the social media have become a vital intermediate tool for political reforms. Any re-

---

[6] The meaning of Web2.0 has evolved over time. However, the essential definition of the term is used to describe the second generation of the World Wide Web, whereby it moved from static HTML pages to a more interactive and dynamic web platform. Instead of emphasizing one-way conversation, Web 2.0 focuses on the Internet user's abilities to collaborate and share information online through social media, live-streaming videos and blogging.

[7] Jack Goldsmith and Tim Wu, *Who Controls the Internet? Illusions of a Borderless World*, New York: Oxford University Press (2006), p. ix.

[8] *See* Tim Wu, *The Master Switch – The Rise and Fall of Information Empires*, New York: Alfred A. Knopf (2010), pp. 5-7.

strictions on Internet-related activities, therefore, would have an adverse impact on international trade as well as individuals' fundamental rights and freedoms.

As a result, the increasingly sophisticated censorship activities conducted by governments on the Internet have created new concerns about international trade issues and human rights violations. Internet censorship measures could constitute barriers to international trade owing to the fact that most Internet services are provided as commercial activities.[9] The inherent global nature of the Internet means that any restriction of online activities imposed by one country might have a direct economic effect on the competitive advantages of others. From a human rights perspective, disproportionate restrictions on people's online behaviors can severely constrain people's enjoyment of rights on the Internet. While a nation may claim the right to regulate within its territory, the trans-border nature of the Internet easily leads to extra-territorial implementation of national regulations.

In the absent of a coherent legal response at the international level, the purpose of this study is to consider the boundaries of a nation's sovereign rights on the Internet through its international commitments and obligations. Internet governance is a controversial political debate as well as an economic and cultural argument. Any attempt to conceptualize the diverging and competing values of a given society is complicated and contested.[10] Nevertheless, for greater legal consistency and certainty in the governance of the Internet, the focus should be on the international cooperation within international institutions.

The book, therefore, is aimed at finding out to what extent the government's Internet censorship measures could constitute violations of international rules in both the trade and human rights regimes. The principles of the World Trade Organization (WTO), especially those of the General Agreement on Trade in Services (GATS), will be examined. The WTO, as an international organization with more than 160 members, is the most suitable forum to address the new challenges in digital trade. The WTO shapes a general and increasingly universal framework for almost all trade relations with Member States, and its remarkable dispute settlement system provides a rule-oriented enforcement instrument to settle disputes peacefully between parties. In the context of Internet censorship, the essential issue is whether WTO law, in both substantive and procedural mechanisms, is flexible enough to accommodate the commercial activities on the Internet.

---

[9] *See* Brian Hindley and Hosuk Lee-Makiyama, *Protectionism Online: Internet Censorship and International Trade Law,* ECIPE Working Paper, No.12 (2009).

[10] *See* Thomas Cottier, *Multilayered Governance, Pluralism and Moral Conflict*, Indiana Journal of Global Legal Studies, Vol.16, No.2 (Summer 2009), pp. 647-679.

Due to the heterogeneity of the foundations of human rights,[11] the assessment of the human rights and their relationship to Internet censorship will be based on the rights codified in the positive national, regional and, international laws, such as declarations, covenants and conventions, as well as human rights norms that have obtained the status of international customary law. Whereas numerous essential rights are affected by Internet censorship measures, the analysis will focus on the discussion of individuals' freedom of expression and the right to privacy in the online world. Nevertheless, the overall enforcement system of international human rights is ineffective and relatively weak compared to the dispute settlement system under the WTO legal framework. As a result, the ultimate purpose of the book is to assess whether Internet censorship is found to in violation of international human rights, and whether the WTO adjudicating bodies have the competence to apply and interpret WTO rules in conformity with human rights norms and principles.

Nevertheless, the linkage between the WTO and human rights is not self-evident but, rather, needs to be examined from different perspectives and angles. Chapter 1 first provides some important aspects of the establishment of the WTO and the formation of modern international human rights. The rationale and conceptual justice of the two regimes will be illustrated. After giving an outline of the historical background, Section II of Chapter 1 examines whether, in practice, there is space for human rights assessment under the legal framework of the WTO.

While the term 'human rights' is nowhere to be found in any of the WTO agreements and human rights cannot be brought in front of a WTO panel as an independent claim, nowhere do WTO agreements explicitly contract out the

---

[11] *See* Philip Alston, *Core Labour Standards' and the Transformation of the International Labour Rights Regime*, European Journal of International Law, Vol.15, No.3 (2004), pp. 457-521 (483-483). The author explains that because of the 'heterogeneity and seeming irreconcilability', the current established international and regional human rights regimes "have steadfastly resisted the designation of a limited core of rights which are considered hierarchically superior, or deserving of chronological priority, to other human rights in the accepted overall catalogue of rights." Kenneth Roth, a prominent human rights advocate, also argued "the international human rights movement, in my view, has no choice but to rest on a positive-law justification for its work. That is, unless there are concrete and broadly understandable reasons to deviate from existing law, we must defend human rights law largely as written if we are to have any legitimacy and force to our work. That law, of course, codifies civil and political as well as ESC rights."

(Kenneth Roth, *Defending Economic, Social and Cultural Rights: Practical Issues Faced by an International Human Rights Organization,* Human Rights Quarterly, Vol. 26, No.1 (2004), pp. 64-73 (64).)

general international law concerning human rights. Many human rights or environmental advocates have criticized the fact that the WTO agreements undermine the ability of Member States to pursue other important policy values.[12] The fragmentation of international law inevitably leads to frictions between the objectives of trade and human rights. Nonetheless, under the modern international legal system, it is impossible to apply international trade rules without contemplating legal standards from other international laws, including human rights. Pursuant to Article 31 of the Vienna Convention on the Law of Treaties (Vienna Convention), treaty interpretation should be conducted in good faith and, in interpreting a treaty provision, all other international legal obligations that the parties have adhered to must be considered.[13] Therefore, the role of the WTO should not only be considered with limited domain of trade liberalization, but also with its collective purposes of promoting global welfare and maintaining sustainable development. Chapter 1 examines possible interpretative choices a panel might have to incorporate vital public interests within a dispute settlement proceeding and addresses the issue of reconciliation of free trade and other social values.

If a link is found between the trade and human rights regimes, Chapter 2 considers the connection between government Internet censorship measures and human rights protection. The Internet has created unprecedented opportunities for people to seek, receive, and impart information. As communication technologies evolved, so did the modalities by which public and private entities monitor, filter and, control online activities. In other words, technological innovation does not unconditionally guarantee the protection and promotion of human rights.[14]

Over the past decade, the debate on fundamental rights and freedoms on the Internet has been taken seriously among scholars, human rights campaigners,

---

[12] *See* Thomas Cottier, Joost Pauwelyn, and Elisabeth Bürgi, Linking Trade Regulation and Human Rights in International Law: An Overview. In: Thomas Cottier, Joost Pauwelyn, and Elisabeth Bürgi (eds.), *Human Rights and International Trade*, New York: Oxford University Press (2005), pp. 1-26.

[13] United Nations, Vienna Convention on the Law of Treaties (VCLT), 1155 U.N.T.S. 331; 8 ILM 679 (23 May 1969), p. 331. Article 31 (1) of the VCLT regulates:

> A treaty should be interpreted in good faith in accordance with the ordinary meaning to be given to the terms of the treaty in their context and in the light of its object and purpose.

Article 31(3) (c) further stipulates:

> There shall be taken into account, together with the context:
>
> (c) Any relevant rules of international law applicable in the relations between the parties.

[14] *See* William Dutton, Anna Dopatka, Michael Hills, Ginette Law, and Victoria Nash, *Freedom of Connection – Freedom of Expression: The Changing Legal and Regulatory Ecology Shaping the Internet*, Oxford Internet Institute, UNESCO (19 August 2011).

and policy makers. If the Internet is an important tool for development and for exercising human rights, or if Internet freedom is a human right *per se*, what kind of legal framework from the formalized international human rights treaties can be applied to the unique characteristics of the Internet? Assuming that international human rights law remains equally applicable to new communication technologies, individuals should be able to enjoy the same quality of protection of their rights and freedoms online as the same rights they have offline. Section I of Chapter 2, therefore, examines the current human rights legal framework for the protection of freedom of expression and the right to privacy. Whereas the international community has stated its commitments to both rights in various international and regional declarations, covenants and conventions, the dynamic nature of the Internet has raised the question of whether the current human rights instruments are sufficient to address the protection of those rights in the digital age.

Additionally, Chapter 2 contemplates legitimate restrictions on people's fundamental rights on the Internet. Like most values in modern democratic society, freedom of expression and the right to privacy are not absolute but subject to various limitations. Because of cultural diversity, the substantive scope of limitations is different from country to country. Although a nation might enjoy a certain margin of appreciation in determining the extent of interference in individual's rights with other policy objectives, such discretion is not unfettered. As General Comment 34 to Article 19 of the International Covenant on Civil and Political Rights (ICCPR) states, "the relation between right and restriction and between norm and exception must not be reversed."[15] Thus, restrictions on online behavior should be implemented proportionally and in accordance with the standards and norms of international human rights law.

Section II of Chapter 2 further addresses whether the new information technologies bring about new threats to human rights. Freedom of expression is critical for ensuring accountability and transparency of good governance in a democratic society, and the right to privacy is essential for personal dignity and self-determination. Still, the diverse threats to both rights online have emerged from ongoing revelations of Internet censorship and mass surveillance mechanisms conducted by both governmental and private entities. Since the right to privacy could be seen as an enabler of other fundamental human rights, including freedom of expression, Section II observes the new types of interference to individuals' right to a reasonable expectation of privacy on the Internet. The central issue of privacy protection in the digital age is the precise relationship

---

[15] Human Rights Committee, *General Comment No. 34 Article 19: Freedoms of Opinion and Expression*, U.N. Doc. CCPR/C/GC/34 (12 September 2011), para. 21.

between the right to privacy and personal data protection. Since a harmonized international data protection system does not exist yet,[16] Section II looks into the existing legal frameworks to evaluate the extent to which data protection principles are guaranteed as a part of the established human right to privacy.

The purpose of Chapter 3 is to assess whether the WTO rules are relevant or sufficiently flexible to adapt to the technological evolution in the digital age. While the technological advances enhanced international trade in all aspects, the same technologies revealed the illusionary uncontrolled nature of the Internet.[17] Internet-related goods and services are usually provided in a commercial form, and the Internet market is lucrative for online business. The revenue of those Internet companies normally relies on user fees or online advertisements.[18] Internet censorship measures that intercept the access to a Member's domestic market could constitute barriers to trade and violate the Member's substantive obligations under the WTO. Although the WTO was negotiated before the widely use of the Internet, this does not imply that WTO rules are irrelevant for digital trade. On the contrary, substantial evidence can be found in the WTO jurisprudence for connecting WTO law with electronic commerce and with future technological evolution.

Section I of Chapter 3 explores an overview of the relations between digital trade and the WTO. The roles of both the GATT and the GATS in Internet-related commercial activities are considered. Notwithstanding most digital trade debates emphasize trade in services, the regulations on trade in goods are significant with respect to digitally delivered products. The importance of trade in goods is reflected in the discussion of whether specific digital products should be considered as goods or services. Furthermore, since digital trade is often associated with transactions that do not encompass tangible goods and almost all commercial activities on the Internet involve some online data-processing or computer-based services, the GATS inevitably occupies a prominent role in assessing whether WTO rules remain relevant in the digital age.

To examine the applicability of WTO law to digital trade, section II and Section III of Chapter 3 present a critical case review of two recent disputes

---

[16] *See* Toby Mendel, Andrew Puddephatt, Ben Wagner, Dixie Hawtin, and Natalia Torres, *Global Survey on Internet Privacy and Freedom of Expression*, United Nations Educational, Scientific and Cultural Organization (2012).

[17] *See* Lawrence Lessig, *Code and Other Laws of Cyberspace*, New York: Basic Books (1999); see also Jack Goldsmith & Tim Wu, *Who Controls the Internet? Illusions of a Borderless World*, New York: Oxford University Press (2006).

[18] *See* Brian Hindley and Hosuk Lee-Makiyama, *Protectionism Online: Internet Censorship and International Trade Law*, ECIPE Working Paper, No.12 (2009).

brought before the WTO judiciary bodies: *US – Gambling*[19] and *China – Audiovisual Products*[20]. Both cases concerned Internet-related measures adopted by Member States. The lack of an explicit legal framework encompassing digital trade rules within the context of the WTO is mainly due to the fact that, during the Uruguay Round, only a few negotiators foresaw the significant impact of E-commerce on international trade and regulatory policies. The cases provided in Sections II and III shed some light on several controversial issues concerning the application of the WTO agreements to trade in digital goods and cross-border electronically delivered services. Importantly, Chapter 3 also assesses the justification of public moral and public orders in connection with government Internet censorship measures under WTO general exception clauses.

Chapter 4 presents a case study of China. To determine the extent to which Internet censorship mechanisms adopted by nation states violate international legal norms and standards, China represents an important case study on several grounds. First of all, having 688 million Internet users at the end of 2015,[21] China is the country with the largest number of Internet users and has the biggest online business market. Second, whereas the Internet infrastructure and Internet-related services in China have experienced unprecedented growth in terms of scale and quality,[22] China has one of the most oppressive Internet environments in the world. Third, in the name of Internet sovereignty, the Chinese Communist Party (CCP) has tightening up the control over all Internet-related products, services, and infrastructures in the past decade.

Section I of Chapter 4 first provides a background to Internet development in China. The Internet was first officially introduced into China in 1994. Notwithstanding this late beginning, during the past two decades, Internet users and online market have flourished in China. The explosive growth of the Internet and online market does not necessarily indicate the political liberalization of the people and the free market. Following, section II introduces the Internet censorship mechanisms adopted by the Chinese authorities at all levels to monitor and control Internet activities and content. Sophisticated technical surveillance from

---

[19] *United States – Measures Affecting the Cross-Border Supply of Gambling and Betting Services* (cited as *US – Gambling*), WT/DS285.

[20] *China – Measures Affecting Trading Rights and Distribution Services for Certain Publications and Audiovisual Entertainment Products* (cited as *China – Audiovisual Products*), WT/DS363.

[21] China Internet Network Information Center (CNNIC), *37th Statistical Survey Report on the Internet Development in China* (January 2016).

[22] *See* Jyh-An Lee and Ching-Yi Liu, *Forbidden City Enclosed by the Great Firewall: The Law and Power of Internet Filtering in China*, Minn. J. L. Sci. & Tech., Vol.13:1 (2012), pp. 125-151.

the backbone infrastructure of the Internet to the local service providers, in combination with self-censorship and criminalization of online behavior, severely constrain the individual's fundamental rights and access to the Chinese Internet market.

Section III of Chapter 4, therefore, discusses the extent to which China's Internet censorship measures might violate its international human rights obligations. In addition, the section further illustrates the conception of Internet sovereignty. Living in the middle of a transition in which sovereignty seems to be the direction that Internet governance is heading, the debate should no longer be whether nations have a legitimate right to proclaim sovereignty over the Internet, but how to define the boundary between a state's sovereign authority and its international commitments and obligations. The governance of the Internet, a platform with multiple stakeholders, requires new thinking around the concept of state sovereignty.

Lastly, Section IV of Chapter 4 addresses the analysis of whether Chinese Internet censorship measures constitute a barrier to trade within the context of WTO law. Given the compound nature of the issue, Section IV takes the *Google – China* incident as a research baseline. The discussion proceeds to inspect the possibility of a successful WTO challenge to China's Internet related policies. Both general and specific obligations under the GATS are examined. If the measures at issue are in violation of any GATS provisions, Section IV considers whether the Chinese government can justify its measures on the basis of public moral and public orders exceptions set out in Article XIV (a) of the GATS, and whether WTO adjudicating bodies would have sufficient latitude to interpret the terms of general exceptions clause in conformity with international standards of human rights law.

Finally, the conclusion provides some broad reflections and concluding remarks and summarizes the key findings in the previous chapter.

Chapter 1. International Human Rights Law and International Trade Law

Each time a man stands up for an ideal, or acts to improve the lot of others, or strikes out against injustice, he sends forth a tiny ripple of hope, and crossing each other from a million different centers of energy and daring, those ripples build a current that can sweep down the mightiest walls of oppression and resistance.
Robert Kennedy

The international trade and human rights regimes are both post-war phenomena, with the shared vision of contributing to a better, more peaceful world through international cooperation.[1] Nevertheless, as an international trade organization which aims to maximize free trade among member states, the WTO has been criticized for operating in splendid isolation from other international legal systems, including international human rights law.[2] Many environmental protectors and human rights advocates expressed the fear that WTO rules, supported by its dispute settlement and enforcement mechanisms, elevate free trade over other vital social interests.[3] However, it is imperative to contemplate whether the concept of 'free trade' is the dominant ideological notion which has shaped the international trading system over the past two decades. As the UN Committee on Economic, Social, and Cultural Rights has recognized that "trade liberalization must be understood as a means, not an end. The end to which trade liberalization should serve is the objective of human well-being to which the international human rights instruments give legal expression".[4]

---

[1] *See* Robert Howse and Makau Mutua, *Protecting Human Rights in a Global Economy: Challenges for the World Trade Organization*, International Centre for Human Rights and Democratic Development (April 2000); *see* also Caroline Dommen, Safeguarding the Legitimacy of Multilateral Trading System: The Role of Human Rights Law. In: Frederick M Abbott, Christine Greining-Kaufmann, and Thomas Cottier (eds.), *International Trade and Human Rights: Foundations and Conceptual Issues*, University of Michigan: The World Trade Forum, Vol.5 (2006), pp. 121-132.

[2] *See* Thomas Cottier, *Trade and Human Rights – A Relationship to Discover*, Journal of International Economic Law, Vol.5, No.1 (2002), pp. 111-132 (112).

[3] *See* Thomas Cottier, Joost Pauwelyn, and Elisabeth Bürgi, Linking Trade Regulation and Human Rights in International Law: An Overview. In: Thomas Cottier, Joost Pauwelyn, and Elisabeth Bürgi (eds.), *Human Rights and International Trade*, New York: Oxford University Press (2005), pp. 1-26.

[4] UN Economic and Social Council, *Statement of the UN Committee on Economic, Social and Cultural Rights to the Third Ministerial Conference of the World Trade*

While there is little doubt that trade and human rights are complementary to a certain degree, the link of the two regimes at the international level is not self-evident. Section I, therefore, sets out a historical background analysis on the development of international trade and human rights respectively. Section II provides a possible legal framework for the analysis of a human rights approach to international trade law. Nations regularly impose trade sanctions or provide trade incentives either to protect human rights of their citizens or to improve human rights situations in other countries. However, a human rights-related trade measure could be discriminatory in nature and applies as a disguised protectionism.[5] As a result, Chapter 1 intends to explore how to deal with human rights issues within the context of the WTO legal system.

The analysis of the space for human rights considerations focuses on the WTO dispute settlement system to determine whether the WTO agreements could be interpreted consistently with other established norms of international law. The jurisdiction of the WTO adjudicating bodies and the applicable law before them are examined. A court might have limited jurisdiction but unlimited sources of applicable law to determine the meaning of the terms in a treaty. Since many WTO provisions are deliberately negotiated in an ambiguous manner for further clarifications, important social values might be adequately addressed in the WTO context through proper interpretative methods.

Organization (Seattle, 30 November to 3 December 1999), UN Doc. E/C.12/1999/9 (26 November 1999), para. 6.

[5] *See* Sarah H. Cleveland, Human Rights Sanctions and the World Trade Organization. In: Francesco Francioni (ed.), *Environment, Human Rights and International Trade*, Oxford and Portland: Hart Publishing (2001), pp. 119-261 (119-203).

I. The Relationship Between WTO Law and Human Rights Law

To search for bridging legal foundations between trade and human rights, an introduction of the historical backgrounds of both regimes is necessary. While the two international legal systems are the outcomes of the perception of promoting world peace after the World War II, it was not until recently that scholars and policy makers have begun to realize that the coordination between trade and human rights is essential in the pursuit of human development and happiness. From the following section, one can perceive that the development of international trade law and the human rights law has significantly modified the way that international law was implemented in centuries. While states might still play central roles in international relations, the focus of the rights to protect shift from the sovereign states to individual human beings. Such a change is reflected in both the preamble to the WTO Agreement and the positive international human rights law.

A. The World Trade Organization

The beginning of this section first illustrates the historical background of the WTO – an international trade organization whose jurisdiction has extended to issues regarding trade in goods, trade in services and trade-related intellectual property rights. The second part of the section provides the rationale of the WTO to examine whether the ultimate purpose of the WTO goes beyond removing barriers to trade among its Member States. As an international trade organization that shapes the legal framework for almost all aspects of global trade, the collective purposes and common ideology of the WTO should be carefully scrutinized.

a. Historical Background (The GATT 1947 & The WTO)

In the aftermath of the World War II, a small group of countries met in Bretton Woods, New Hampshire in the United States and began to negotiate numerous institutions and agreements that would serve as the foundation of the contemporary multilateral economic system.[6] The original purpose of the system, which

---

[6] John H, Jackson, William J. Davery & Alan O. Sykes, Jr, *Legal Problems of International Economic Relations: Cases, Materials and Text (4th Edition)*, St. Paul, MN: Thomason West (2002), pp. 199-207. (These institutions and agreements were developed during a series of conferences beginning near the end of the Second World War,

could be termed as the Bretton Woods system, is to reduce obstacles to international trade and to give effect to the principle of multilateral non-discriminatory trade.[7] One of the factors that led to World War II was the economic mistrust among nations; the Great Depression has been partly blamed for this war, as has the severe reparations policy toward Germany.[8] In the interwar period (1920 to 1940), many nations began enacting protectionist measures which choked off international trade. Nevertheless, World War II brought unilateral protectionism and bilateral trade negotiations to an end. Being acutely aware that an unstable economic environment could easily lead to an unstable political context, political leaders in the United States and elsewhere made statements concerning the significance of establishing postwar economic institutions that would prevent these mistakes from happening again.[9] The Bretton Woods System, incorporating the GATT 1947, World Bank, International Monetary Fund (IMF), and the International Trade Organization (ITO), was designed to avoid economic conflicts and to minimize the impediments to the international trading system.

In 1945, the United States invited a number of nations to enter into negotiations to conclude a multilateral agreement on the reduction of tariffs among participating countries. The United Nations, formed in the same year, contributed to this experience through establishing a particular principle organ, the Economic and Social Council (ECOSOC). At the first meeting in London in 1946, the ECOSOC, under the surveillance of the United Nations, initiated the negotiations of a draft charter for the ITO.[10] The ITO Charter, also called the Havana Charter, was adopted in 1947 and the GATT 1947 was further negotiated for the purpose of establishing a multilateral trade agreement to reciprocally reduce tariffs.[11]

---

extending to the end of the 1940s. In 1944, the Bretton Woods conference itself was held at Bretton Wood in the United States.)

[7] Ibid., p. 200.

[8] *See* Richard N. Cooper, Trade Policy as Foreign Policy. In: Robert M. Stern (ed.), *US Trade Policies in Changing World Economy*, MIT Press (January 1987), pp. 291-336.

[9] *See* United States International Trade Commission, *The Economic Effects of Significant US Import Restraint (Sixth Update)*, Investigation No. 332-325, Publication 4095 (August 2009), pp. 59-115 (US Trade Policy since 1943).

[10] *See* Peter-Tobias Stoll and Frank Schorkopf, *WTO – World Economic Order, World Trade Law*, Max Planck Institute for Comparative Public Law and International Law, Leiden/Boston The Netherlands: Martinus Nijhoff Publishers (2006), pp. 11-14.

[11] *See* John H. Jackson, *Sovereignty, the WTO, and Changing Fundamentals of International Law*, United Kingdom: Cambridge University Press (2006), pp. 91-104.
(The final act of the establishment of ITO was drafted in Havana at the conference from 21 Nov. 1947 to 24 Mar. 1948, cf. p. 5 in the Final Act of the United Nations Conference on Trade and Employment.)

The history of the preparation of the GATT 1947 is entangled with that of the preparation of the ITO Charter. Nevertheless, due to the refusal of the United States to ratify the ITO Charter,[12] the GATT 1947 was brought into force by the adoption of the Protocol of Provisional Application in 1947 without waiting for the ITO Charter.[13] Since the ITO never came into being,[14] the GATT 1947 took on the central role of coordinating national policies in the international trade sphere. From 1948 until the advent of the WTO, the GATT 1947 was the principal international agreement regulating trade relations among nation states. The GATT 1947 has been credited with considerable success in removing barriers to trade in goods and in reducing the economic conflicts among its contracting parties.

Regardless of emerging as a comparatively modest international trade agreement, some of the "birth defects"[15] of the GATT 1947 led to the creation of the WTO in 1995. The participating nations signed the Marrakesh Agreement at the end of the eighth round, the Uruguay Round (1986-1994)[16], of the GATT 1947 negotiations. The Marrakesh Agreement was ratified by a sufficient number of Member States on 15 April 1994[17] and established the WTO in 1995.[18] The Agreement explicitly outlines four important annexes that technically contain

---

[12] *See* Amrita Narlikar, *The World Trade Organization: A Very Short Introduction*, New York: Oxford University Press (2005) (At the end of 1951, the President's office announced that the attempt to obtain approval of the ITO was abandoned. Although other countries could still enforce the ITO without the US, US was economically the strongest country in the world and the initiatives of the agreement came from the US. No country desired to enter an ITO that would not be ratified by the US.)

[13] Protocol of Provisional Application of the General Agreement on Tariffs and Trade, 55 UNTS 308 (1947).

[14] *See* John Jackson, *World Trade and the Law of GATT: A Legal Analysis of the General Agreement on Tariffs and Trade*, Bobbes-Merrill (1969). (The ill-fated ITO was supposed to be the institutional and organizational framework for trade rules, which would have included GATT 1947. Yet when the draft of Havana Charter failed to come into effect, the GATT 1947 had to fill the vacuum.)

[15] *See* John H. Jackson, The Evolution of the World Trading System – The Legal and Institutional Context. In: Daniel Bethlehem, Isabelle van Damme, Donald McRae, and Rodney Neufeld (eds.), *The Oxford Handbook of International Trade Law*, New York: Oxford University Press (January 2009), pp. 31-50.

[16] The eighth and last of the major trade rounds under the GATT was the Uruguay Round, launched at Punta del Este, Uruguay, in 1986, and finally concluded at a ministerial-level final negotiating conference in Marrakech, Morocco, in April 1994.

[17] Final Act Embodying the Results of the Uruguay Round of Multilateral Trade Negotiations, 1867 U.N.T.S. 14, 33 I.L.M. (15 April 1994). [hereinafter Final Act].

[18] WTO Agreement: Marrakesh Agreement Establishing the World Trade Organization, 1867 U.N.T.S. 154, 33 I.L.M 1144 (15 April 1994). [hereinafter Marrakesh Agreement].

thousands of pages of substantive rules. Pursuant to Article II:2 of the Agreement, these annexes are integral parts of the WTO Agreement and are "binding on all Members".[19] Additional agreements which address goods, services, intellectual property issues, and provisions for dispute settlement are within the annexes.[20]

As a single undertaking treaty, the WTO Agreement significantly expanded the mandate and strength of the WTO beyond that of its GATT predecessor. The responsibilities of the WTO are driven toward a further dynamic development of the international trade order.[21]The WTO treaty is one entire unified document implementing the principle of single undertaking to which a nation would be required to accept all obligations of the massive treaty complex in order to become a Member. The Uruguay Round produced a massive expansion of existing global trading rules, with numerous new agreements negotiated. Tariffs schedules under the WTO Agreement are more comprehensive than those under the GATT 1947 in terms of numbers and types of goods covered.[22] Furthermore, the WTO elaborates the non-tariff barrier to trade in two sensitive agreements, the Agreement on the Application of Sanitary and Phytosanitary

---

[19] Ibid., Article II: 1 and Article II:2 stipulate:

> 1. The WTO shall provide the common institutional framework for the conduct the trade relations among its Members in matters related to the agreements and associated legal instruments included in the Annexes to this Agreement.
>
> 2. The agreements and associated legal instruments included in Annexes 1, 2 and 3 (hereinafter referred to as "Multilateral Trade Agreements") are integral parts of this Agreement, binding on all Members.

[20] Annex 1 contains most of the treaty pages. This annex is termed the "Multilateral Agreements," which are mandatory substantive agreements. It is divided into A, B, C three parts.

- Annex 1A: Multilateral Agreements on Trade in Goods
- Annex 1B: General Agreements on Trade in Services
- Annex 1C: Agreements on Trade Related Aspects of Intellectual Property Rights

Annex 2 contains the Dispute Settlement Understandings, a text about 24 pages which governs dispute settlement procedures in some detail.

Annex 3 contains the Trade Policy Review Mechanism, short provisions designed to set up a structure of regulatory structured institutional reviews of each member's trade policies.

Annex 4 contains Plurilateral Trade Agreements, which are supposedly optional.

[21] *See* Peter-Tobias Stoll and Frank Schorkopf, *WTO – World Economic Order, World Trade Law*, Max Planck Institute for Comparative Public Law and International Law, Leiden/Boston The Netherlands: Martinus Nijhoff Publishers (2006), pp. 15-16.

[22] For example, agreements on liberalization commitments in trade in goods in a particular area: the Agreement on Agriculture (AoA) which contains commitments to reduce support for and protection of the agricultural sector in three areas – market access, export subsidies, and domestic support; the Agreement on Textiles and Clothing (ATC) which aims at reducing barriers to trade in the textiles and clothing industries.

Measures (SPS) and the Agreement on Technical Barriers to Trade (TBT). Additionally, the key non-discrimination principles of the GATT 1947, which underline the fundamental objective of international trading systems, are reflected in several WTO agreements.[23]

The negotiation of the Uruguay Round also led to the establishment of the GATS, which sets out a legal framework for the liberalization of trade in services. The GATS consists of a set of general and specific obligations apply to all measures by Members affecting trade in services. With a broad range of measures and some 97 Schedules of services commitments, the GATS has the potential to cover almost all international trade-related services with only a few exceptions.[24] The objective of the GATS is to establish a multilateral framework of principles for trade in services to promote the global economic growth.[25]

Due to the intangible nature of services, however, trade in services, unlike trade in goods, is affected by a variety of domestic regulations instead of by border measures.[26] The internal domestic regulating issues range from qualification and licensing requirement in professional services, safety standards in transportation services, to universal assessment requirements in health and education services. Being aware of possible tensions between trade liberalization in services and national regulatory autonomy, the GATS explicitly recognizes "the

---

[23] For example, the most favored nations principle, which ensures all WTO Members' equality of opportunity to export to or import from other WTO members, can be found in Article II of the GATT and Article II of the GATS; and national treatment obligations, which guarantee WTO Member should not afford protection for domestic goods through internal measures, are stipulated in Article III of the GATT and Article XVII of the GATS.

[24] Article I:3 of the GATS excludes 'service supplied in the exercise of government authority'. These are services that are supplied neither on a commercial basis nor in comparison with other service suppliers.

[25] *See* in general John H. Jackson, William J. Davey, Alan O. Sykes, Jr., *Legal Problems of International Economic Relations: Cases, Materials and Text (Fourth Edition)*, West Group (2002); Markus Krajewski, *National Regulation and Trade Liberalization in Services – The Legal Impact of the General Agreement on Trade in Services (GATS) on National Regulatory Autonomy*, Kluwer Law International (2003); Nicolas F. Diebold, *Non-Discrimination in International Trade in Service – Likeness in WTO/GATS*, Cambridge University Press (2010); and *see* Kern Alexander and Mads Andenas, *The World Trade Organization and Trade in Services*, Leiden; Boston: Matinus Nijhoff (2008).

[26] Aaditya Mattoo and Pierre Sauvé, Domestic Regulation and Trade in Services: Key Issues. In: Aaditya Mattoo and Pierre Sauvé, *Domestic Regulation and Service Trade Liberalization*, World Bank and Oxford University Press (2003), pp. 1-7.

right of Members to regulate, and to introduce new regulations, on the supply of services within their territories in order to meet national policy objectives".[27] Thus, the GATS is aimed at, on the one hand, progressive liberalization of trade in services, while, on the other hand, it upholds the right of a Member to regulate in order to pursue important social values.

A further concurrence as the result of the Uruguay Round was the development of the remarkable dispute settlement and enforcement system, established under the Understanding on Rules and Procedures Governing the Settlement of Disputes (DSU).[28] The dispute settlement system of the WTO is significantly different from other international courts or tribunals. Under the international law, states can only be brought before an international court in cases they have consented to the jurisdiction of that court. Under the WTO legal system, a Member has the right to invoke a dispute settlement proceeding without the approval of the defending party.[29] A WTO panel embraces mandatory exclusive jurisdiction[30]; the dispute settlement reports are automatically adopted through the Dispute Settlement Body (DSB)[31]; and the legal effect of the adopted panel reports is a binding international obligation.[32] Consequently, the WTO dispute

[27] *See* the Preamble of the General Agreement on Trade in Services.

[28] Understanding on Rules and Procedures Governing the Settlement of Disputes Art. 1, Marrakesh Agreement Establishing the World Trade Organization, Annex 2, 1869 U.N.T.S. 401 (15 April 1994). [hereinafter DSU].

[29] Article 4 and Article 6 of the DSU. Article 6.1 of the DSU stipulates:

> 1. If the complaining party so requests, a panel shall be established at the latest at the DSB meeting following that at which the request first appears as an item on the DSB's agenda, unless at the meeting the DSB decides by consensus not to establish a panel.

[30] Article 23.1 of the DSU gives exclusive jurisdiction of the WTO dispute settlement system. The Article regulates:

> When Members seek the redress of a violation of obligations or other nullification or impairment of benefits under the covered agreements or an impediment to the attainment of any objective of the covered agreements, they shall have recourse to, and abide by, the rules and procedures of this Understanding.

[31] Article 16 (4) of the DSU:

> Within 60 days after the date of circulation of a panel report to the Members, the report shall be adopted at a DSB meeting unless a party to the dispute formally notifies the DSB of its decision to appeal or the DSB decides by consensus not to adopt the report. .... This adoption procedure is without prejudice to the right of Members to express their views on a panel report.

[32] *See* John H. Jackson, *The WTO Dispute Settlement Understanding – Misunderstandings on the Nature of Legal Obligation*, The American Journal of International Law, Vol. 91, Issue:1 (Jan. 1997), pp. 60-64.

settlement system has been described as the most influential system of any international tribunals and as the "jewel in the crown" of the WTO.[33]

b. The Rationale of the WTO and Its Relations to International Legal Systems

Essentially, the WTO, as an international trade organization with more than 160 Member States[34], is a forum where countries seek to achieve trade liberalization through a variety of mechanisms, including trade negotiations and dispute settlements.[35] With an extensively covered scope and a mandatory judiciary system, the WTO should act as an influential organization that deals with greater concerns than its trade mandate.[36] Nevertheless, the conundrum of taking into account other essential societal values within the WTO legal system lies in the question of the competence of the WTO. A broad interpretation of the abilities of international institutions often attracts considerable legitimacy debates since the issue is constantly tangled with the concept of state sovereignty and the dispute of the allocation of power.[37] As illustrated in the following section, if the WTO is considered as a branch of public international law and is bound by the obligations under the general rules of international law, the constitutional scope of the WTO should have the sufficient capacity to take into account non-trade social values, including human rights.[38]

i. The Rationale and Conceptual Justice of the WTO

To analyze the rationale of the WTO, it is appropriate to look into the goals and policy objectives of its establishment. According to Article 31 of the Vienna Convention, a treaty "shall be interpreted in good faith in accordance with the

[33] *See* John H. Jackson, *Sovereignty, the WTO, and Changing Fundamentals of International Law*, United Kingdom: Cambridge University Press (2006), pp. 134-145.
[34] As of July 2016, the WTO has 164 Members. Available at https://www.wto.org/english/thewto_e/whatis_e/tif_e/org6_e.htm. (accessed 21 September 2016)
[35] *See* Mitsuo Matsushita, Thomas J. Schoenbaum, Petros C. Mavroidis and Michael Hahn, *The World Trade Organization – Law, Practice, and Policy (Third Edition)*, Oxford University Press, United Kingdom (2015), pp. 11-16.
[36] *See* James Harrison, *The Human Rights Impact of the World Trade Organization*, Oxford and Portland, Oregon: Hart Publishing (2007), pp. 10-14.
[37] *See* John H. Jackson, *Sovereignty, the WTO, and Changing Fundamentals of International Law*, United Kingdom: Cambridge University Press (2006), pp. 128-131.
[38] *See* Henrik Andersen, *Protection of Non-Trade Values in WTO Appellate Body Jurisprudence: Exceptions, Economic Arguments, and Eluding Questions*, Journal of International Economic Law, Vol.18 (16 May 2015), pp. 383-405.

ordinary meaning to be given to the terms of the treaty in their context and in the light of its object and purpose".[39] While the preamble to the GATT 1947 shows that the GATT 1947 is more trade-oriented to keep the peace and to enhance global welfare[40], the preamble to the Marrakesh Agreement indicates the objectives of the WTO are more comprehensive than mere trade liberalization. In recognition of the importance of the continuity of the international trade system, the negotiators of the WTO used most of the GATT 1947 preamble language as the template for the preamble of the Marrakesh Agreement[41] and added more objectives.

The GATT 1947 was negotiated primarily to reduce tariffs among contracting members and was very successful in doing so. Nevertheless, as the world was becoming increasingly interdependent because of the declining costs of information and transportation, the strait function of the GATT 1947 was insufficient to cope with the tensions among nations in terms of various economic interests and societal values. These concerns are reflected in the preamble of the Marrakesh Agreement. It is possible to cogitate from the language of the preamble that while the system of the WTO may be understood as aiming at expanding global prosperity through trade liberalization, its policy objectives are far more complex than the concepts associated with the idea of free trade.[42] In its first recital, the preamble emphasizes several overriding goals, including the increased standard of living; the attainment of full employment; the steady growth of real income and effective demand; and the expansion of production of and trade in goods and services. In pursuing these objectives, the need for preservation of the environment and the needs of developing countries should be taken into account.

Additionally, the preamble further stresses the importance of sustainable economic development and ensuring the respective share in the growth of interna-

---

[39] United Nations, Vienna Convention on the Law of Treaties (VCLT), 1155 U.N.T.S. 331; 8 ILM 679 (23 May 1969), p. 331.

[40] *See* John H. Jackson, *Sovereignty, the WTO, and Changing Fundamentals of International Law*, United Kingdom: Cambridge University Press (2006), pp. 84-90.
The assertion of "keeping the peace" stemmed from the notion that good trade and economic policies are of vital importance to maintaining international peace after WWII. The idea of enhancing global welfare is based on the belief that improving aggregate wealth will eventually reduce the property around the world.

[41] Appellate Body Report, *United States – Import Prohibition of Certain Shrimp and Shrimp Product* (cited as *US -- Shrimp*), WT/DS58/AB/R (12 October 1998), para. 152.

[42] *See* Peter-Tobias Stoll and Frank Schorkopf, *WTO – World Economic Order, World Trade Law*, Max Planck Institute for Comparative Public Law and International Law, Leiden/Boston The Netherlands: Martinus Nijhoff Publishers (2006), pp. 33-40

tional trade of the developing countries, in particular, the least developed countries. At the same time, the preamble expressly refers to the elimination of discrimination in international trade relations. The statement indicates that the objective of the trade order should go beyond merely pursuing the reduction of trade barriers, but including more principled concepts, such as those of equal competitive opportunities.[43] The words used in the WTO preamble, therefore, illustrate that the WTO is not only about trade liberalization but also higher-ranking policy objectives.[44]

The WTO, as a rule-oriented organization, is to provide greater certainty and predictability to the international trading and economic system. Hence, the WTO is not for free trade at any cost.[45] The WTO agreements are full of provisions taking the interests of development into account, and the ultimate purpose of the WTO is to increase the general well-being of all people through providing a secure and predictable multilateral trading system.[46] The goals and the policy objectives of the WTO are not only to protect commercial interests but also to promote world economic development and welfare, to reduce poverty and eventually to keep the world peace.[47] As the UN Committee on Economic, Social, and Cultural Rights has recognized that "trade liberalization must be understood as a means, not an end. The end to which trade liberalization should serve is the objective of human well-being to which the international human rights instruments give legal expression."[48]

---

43 Ibid.

44 *See* Peter Van den Bossche and Werner Zdouc, *The Law and Policy of the World Trade Organization – Text, Cases and Materials*, New York: Cambridge University Press (2013), pp. 82-104.

45 WTO, *Ten Common Misunderstandings about the WTO* (2007). Available at http://www.wto.org/english/res_e/dOload_e/10mis_e.pdf. (accessed 08 August 2011)

46 *See* James Harrison, *The Human Rights Impact of the World Trade Organization*, Oxford and Portland, Oregon: Hart Publishing (2007), pp. 3-13.

47 *See* John H. Jackson, *Reflection on the Trade and Peace Relationship*. In: Padideh Ala'I, Tomer Brounde and Colin Picker (eds), *Trade as Guarantor of Peace, Liberty, and Security? Critical, Empirical and Historical Perspectives*, Washington, DC: The American Society of International Law (2006), pp. 23-32.

48 UN Economic and Social Council, *Statement of the UN Committee on Economic, Social and Cultural Rights to the Third Ministerial Conference of the World Trade Organization (Seattle, 30 November to 3 December 1999)*, UN Doc. E/C.12/1999/9 (26 November 1999), para. 6.

ii. The WTO and Other International Legal Systems

The notion that the WTO is an international organization brings together the two concepts of international law. The first is the natural legal structure of the WTO established under the public international law. At the heart of the WTO are the WTO agreements, which are negotiated and signed by a significant number of nation states. Unlike its predecessor, the WTO Agreement clearly establishes an international organization, which endows it with legal personality[49] and supports it with treaty clauses. The WTO agreements are integrated into a "single undertaking" binding on all Member States. Furthermore, as a legally constituted international organization, the WTO has a plenary ministerial conference, which is mandated to meet every two years, a secretariat, a director general, and a series of sub-bodies, including four councils led by a General Council.[50] In sum, from the legal structural perspective, the WTO is to be considered as a branch of the public international legal system.

The second is the WTO's dispute settlement mechanism, which is required by the contemporary international law. One of the distinctive features of the WTO is its automatic and sophisticated dispute settlement system. The principle of obligations of the states to settle disputes peacefully is enshrined in the United Nations Charter Article VI,[51] and recalled in the General Assembly Declaration on principles of peaceful coexistence, which stated that "all States shall settle their international disputes by peaceful means in such a manner that international peace and security, and justice, are not endangered".[52] The dispute settlement system under the WTO is largely responsible for establishing the rule of law in international trade and bringing the peaceful settlement of disputes

---

[49] WTO Agreement: Marrakesh Agreement Establishing the World Trade Organization, 1867 U.N.T.S. 154, 33 I.L.M 1144 (15 April 1994). Article VIII:1 concerns the status of the WTO and states:

> The WTO shall have legal personality and shall be accorded by each of its Members such legal capacity as may be necessary for the exercise of its functions.

[50] Ibid, Article IV requires the establishment of a Ministerial Conference, a General Council, a Council for Trade in Goods, a Council for Trade in Services, and a Council for Trade-Related Aspects of Intellectual Property Rights. Article VI requires the establishment of a Secretariat of the WTO.

[51] United Nations, *Charter of the United Nations*, 1 UNTS XVI (34 October 1945). Chapter VI: Pacific Settlement of Disputes, Article 33 stipulates:

> 1. The parties to any dispute, the continuance of which is likely to endanger the maintenance of international peace and security, shall, first of all, seek a solution by negotiation, enquiry, mediation, conciliation, arbitrary, judicial settlement, resort to regional agencies or arrangements, or other peaceful means of their own choice.

[52] United Nations, United Nations General Assembly, A/RES/37/10 (15 November 1982). The Assembly is calling for the peaceful settlement of disputes between States.

among its members. As mentioned previously, the jurisdiction of the DSB is compulsory for all members.[53] Most importantly, WTO Members have frequently used the dispute settlement system and the vast majority of the cases have been resolved by peaceful means.[54] The WTO dispute settlement system not only makes the WTO a distinctive organization but also plays an active role in the development of the substantive and procedural content of international law.[55]

Accordingly, the WTO must be regarded as a part of the wider corpus of public international law and therefore must, in substantial circumstances, respond to the general principles of law, customary international law, and other international legal systems. Where is this leading us? Does this mean there is space to apply other legal in a WTO dispute? A detailed analysis relating to the limited jurisdiction of WTO adjudicating bodies and the available WTO applicable law are illustrated in the succeeding Section II when considering the place of human rights considerations under the WTO legal system. It is important to point out here that Article 3.2 of the DSU explicitly regulates panels and the Appellate Body to 'clarify the existing provisions of agreements in accordance with customary rules of interpretation of the public international law'. Furthermore, in *US-Gasoline*, the first WTO dispute, the Appellate Body immediately addressed the question of the relation of international law to the WTO and emphatically pronounced that the WTO system cannot be construed in a 'clinical isolation' of the extensive source of public international law.[56] Consequently, the WTO adjudicating bodies will play a critical role in establishing the links between the WTO law and other fields of international laws.

B. The International Human Rights Law

The attention to human rights is universal and human rights law has modified the way international law was perceived for centuries. One of the most prominent contributions of human rights law is that it altered the traditional under-

---

[53] *See* Joost Pauwelyn, *The Role of Public International in the WTO: How Far Can We Go?*, The American Journal of International Law, Vol.95 (2001), pp. 535-578.

[54] *See* Kara Leitner and Simon Lester, *WTO Dispute Settlement 1995-2013 – A statistical Analysis*, Journal of International Economic Law, Vol.17, Issue: 1 (2014), pp. 191-201.

[55] *See* Donald M. McRae, *The WTO in International Law: Tradition Continued or New Frontier?*, Journal of International Economic Law, Vol.3, Issue:1 (1 March 2000), pp. 27-41.

[56] Appellate Body Report, *United States – Standards for Reformulated and Conventional Gasoline (US -- Gasoline)*, WT/DS2/AB/R (20 May 1996), para. 17.

standing of the concept of state sovereignty, or specifically the Westphalian Sovereignty,[57] and constrained the autonomous power of sovereign states to the extent of protecting internationally recognized human rights.[58] Whereas some political leaders have general concerns that broad applications of the human rights norms and standards inhibit a state's ability to regulate domestic affairs, "continuing demands for self-determination, a broad conception of international peace and security, the collapse of state authority, and the increasing importance of popular sovereignty"[59] all challenge the traditional notion of state sovereignty. To derogate part of the sovereign power to the international institutions for the better development of society as a whole is the main concept of contemporary international relations.

Nevertheless, struggles are real when considering universalism of the human rights norms. Although everyone has a general idea of what human rights should be, the modern conceptions of human rights are not based on the principles that are universally accepted in all civilizations.[60] The divergent understandings of the concept of human rights originated from political difference, cultural diversity, and the evolving nature of human rights in time and space. Cultural relativism posits that rules about morality vary from place to place and a universal application of human rights without deference to cultural traits undermines cultural identity.[61] It is undeniable that cultural diversity is a driving force for the development and needs to be protected and promoted. The ra-

---

[57] A more detailed analysis of the notion of Westphalian Sovereignty will be presented in Chapter 4 when comparing the traditional and modern concepts of sovereignty in the digital age. Generally speaking, Westphalian Sovereignty usually refers to the absolute right of the sovereign states.

[58] *See* Robert Howse and Makau Mutua, *Protecting Human Rights in a Global Economy: Challenges for the World Trade Organization*, International Centre for Human Rights and Democratic Development (April 2000).

[59] ICISS, *The Responsibility to Protect – Research, Bibliography, Background (Supplementary Volume to the Report of the International Commission on Intervention and State Sovereignty)*, International Development Research Centre (2001), p. 8.

[60] *See* Susan Ariel Aaronson and Jamie M. Zimmermann, *Trade Imbalance: The Struggle to Weigh Human Rights Concerns in Trade Policymaking*, New York: Cambridge University Press (2007), pp. 1-31.

[61] *See* Jack Donnelly, *Cultural Relativism and Universal Human Rights*, Human Rights Quarterly, Vol. 6, No.4 (November 1984), pp. 400-419; and *see* also Eva Maria Lassen, Universalism and Relativism. In: Anja Mihr and Mark Gibney, *The SAGE Handbook of Human rights (Volume 1)*, Los Angles: SAGE Publications (2014), pp. 39-55.

tionale for cultural diversity promotion is enshrined in the UNESCO Convention on the Protection and Promotion of the Diversity Cultural Expression.[62]

Yet, the cultural boundaries between one place and another have obscured in the contemporary world, and the common culture of modernity has engulfed all society by virtue of the globalization.[63] The notion of cultural diversity does not give any nation a reason to withdraw from its obligations to respect individuals' inherent dignity and equality which are the roots of modern international human rights. In other words, the assertion of cultural rights should not be in violation of essential human rights and individual freedoms.[64]

The purpose of the book is to understand the interaction between trade and human rights in the information age. Therefore, the human rights assessments are provided on the basis of human rights codified in the positive national, regional, and international human rights law, as well as human rights law that is considered with the status of customary international law. The first part of the section provides a background illustration of the international human rights regimes, notably the Universal Declaration of Human Rights (UDHR), the International Covenant on Civil and Political Rights (ICCPR) and the International Covenant on Economic, Social and Cultural Rights (ICESCR). The second part discusses human rights law and its relationship to customary international law. The main issue is the extent to which human rights law could be treated as part of customary international law that binds all nations regardless of the consents.

a. Positive International Human Rights Law

Not until the 20th century have policymakers around the world begun to recognize the need for the human rights protection at the international level. The

[62] United Nations Educational, Scientific and Cultural Organization is a United Nations agency entrusted with the mandate to promote and coordinate international cooperation in education, science, cultural and communication. The UNESCO Convention on Cultural Diversity was adopted on 20 October 2005 and entered into force on 18 March 2007. The purpose of the Convention is to promote and protect the diversity of cultural expression to strengthen the development of human well-being.
(UNESCO, *The 2005 Convention on the Protection and Promotion of the Diversity of Cultural Expression (Convention on Cultural Diversity)* (adopted on 20 October 2005).)
[63] *See* R.J. Vincent, *Human Rights and International Relations*, New York: Cambridge University Press (1986), pp. 37-57.
[64] *See* JingXia Shi, *Free Trade and Cultural Diversity in International Law*, United Kingdom: Hart Publishing (2013), pp. 32-43.

recognition came from the awareness that people need to be protected from their own governments by granting rights to individuals after the Second World War. During the war, US President Franklin D. Roosevelt set the stage for a vision of how the modern conceptions of human rights should develop at the international level. In his famous Four Freedom speech, Roosevelt stated:[65]

> "In the future days which we seek to make secure, we look forward to a world founded upon four essential human freedoms.
> The first is freedom of speech and expression – everywhere in the world.
> The second is freedom of every person to worship God in his own way – everywhere in the world.
> The third is freedom from want – which, translated into world terms, means economic understandings which all secure to every nation a healthy peace time life for its inhabitants – everywhere in the world
> The fourth is freedom from fear – which, translated into to world terms, means a world-wide reduction of armaments to such a point and in such a thorough fashion that no nation will be in a position to commit an act of physical aggression against any neighbor – everywhere in the world."

Later after the war, though without giving a precise definition, the Charter of the UN included several references to human rights. The promotion and encouragement of respect for human rights and fundamental freedoms were expressed in Article 1(3) of the UN Charter.[66] Under Article 55 and Article 56 of the Charter, UN Member States commit themselves to take a joint or separate action to achieve a higher standard of living; solutions of international economic, social, and health problems; and universal respect for, and observance of, human rights.[67] While the states are only obliged to promote human rights within the context of the UN Charter, the Charter provided a forum for future international human rights developments by endowing the General Assembly and the ECOSOC, which contributed to the adoption of the UDHR in 1948 and the ICCPR & ICESR in 1966. The three documents are often known as 'The International Bill of Rights'.

---

[65] Franklin Delano Roosevelt, The Speech Given to the US Congress (6 January 1941.)

[66] Article 1(3) of the UN Charter stated:

> To achieve international cooperation in solving international problems of an economic, social, cultural, or humanitarian character, and in promoting and encouraging respect for human rights and for fundamental freedoms for all without distinction as to race, sex, language, or religion…

[67] *See* Article 55 & 56 of the UN Charter.

i. The Universal Declaration of Human Rights

The creation of the UDHR marked the foundation of modern notions of human rights. The UDHR was prepared by the Commission on Human Rights and adopted by the UN General Assembly in 1948.[68] As a General Assembly resolution, the UDHR is not legally binding among nation states. Nevertheless, the increasing universality of international human rights norms and standards that are codified within the UDHR has led most scholars to agree that the UDHR has evolved into a part of customary international law.[69] States regularly refer to the UDHR as a guide to fashion their constitutions as well as to formulate domestic and foreign policies.[70] At the International Conference on Human Rights at Teheran, the participants of which included 84 Member States and specialized agencies, regional intergovernmental organizations, and NGOs, adopted the Proclamation of Tehran. The Proclamation stated that the UDHR constitutes "an obligation for members of an international community"[71]. Later on, the UDHR was reaffirmed in the Vienna Declaration and Programme of Action in 1993[72]. Moreover, most of the human rights norms in the UDHR were codified into two binding treaties: the ICCPR and the ICESER.

The relevant human rights under the UDHR include:

> Article 3
> Everyone has the right to life, liberty and security of person.
> Article 7
> All are equal before the law and are entitled without any discrimination to equal protection of the law. All are entitled to equal protection against any dis-

---

[68] UN General Assembly, *Universal Declaration of Human Rights*, A/RES/3/217A(III) (10 December 1948).

[69] *See* Robert Howse and Makau Mutua, *Protecting Human Rights in a Global Economy: Challenges for the World Trade Organization*, International Centre for Human Rights and Democratic Development (April 2000); *see* also Holger Hestermeyer, *Human Rights and the WTO – The Case of Patents and Access to Medicines*, New York: Oxford University Press (2007), pp. 79-83 & 119-120.

[70] Ibid.

[71] United Nations, *Proclamation of Teheran – Final Act of the International Conference on Human Rights*, UN Doc. A/CONF. 32/41 at 3 (13 May 1986). The Proclamation stated

> 2. The Universal Declaration of Human Rights states a common understanding of the peoples of the world concerning the inalienable and inviolable rights of all members of the human family and constitutes an obligation for the members of the international community;

[72] United Nations, *Vienna Declaration and Programme of Action*, UN Doc. A/CONF. 157/23 (25 June 1993).

crimination in violation of this Declaration against any incitement to such discrimination.
Article 8
Everyone has the right to an effective remedy by the competent national tribunals for acts violating the fundamental rights granted him by the constitution or by law.
Article 12
No one shall be subjected to arbitrary interference with his privacy, family, home or correspondence, nor to attacks upon his honour and reputation. Everyone has the right to the protection of the law against such interference or attacks.
Article 17
1. Everyone has the right to own property alone as well as in association with others.
2. No one shall be arbitrarily deprived of his property.
Article 19
Everyone has the right to freedom of opinion and expression; this right includes freedom to hold opinions without interference and to seek, receive and impart information and ideas through any media and regardless of frontiers.
Article 22
Everyone, as a member of society, has the right to social security and is entitled to realization, through national effort and international co-operation and in accordance with the organization and resources of each States, of the economic, social and cultural rights indispensable for his dignity and the free development of his personality.
Article 27
1. Everyone has the right to freely to participate in the cultural life of the community, to enjoy the art and to share in scientific advancement and its benefits.
2. Everyone has the right to the protection of moral and material interests resulting from any scientific, literary, or artistic production of which he is the author.

ii. The International Covenant on Civil and Political Rights

In contrast to the UDHR, the ICCPR is one of the binding international human rights treaties, providing a range of protections for civil and political rights. The context of the ICCPR was adopted in 1966 and entered into force on March 23, 1974.[73] The Covenant is open for ratification by all states and there are currently

[73] UN General Assembly, *International Covenant on Civil and Political Rights*, Treaty Series, Vol. 999 (16 December 1966), p. 171.

74 signatories and 168 State Parties to the ICCPR.[74] The ICCPR has two optional protocols for further rights protections. The first protocol provides individuals opportunities to bring complaints in front of the Human Rights committee.[75] The second protocol is designed to abolish the death penalty for States Parties.[76] The ICCPR is composed of a preamble and 53 Articles. By reaffirming the principles proclaimed in the UN Charter and the UDHR, the preamble of the ICCPR recognizes that "the idea of free human beings enjoying civil and political freedom and freedom from fear and want can only be achieved if conditions are created whereby everyone may enjoy his civil and political rights, as well as his economic, social and cultural rights".[77]

The underlying values of the ICCPR are listed in Article 2, which is based on the notions of fair treatment and non-discrimination. Article 2 of the ICCPR requires State Parties to respect and to ensure the rights within the Covenant to all persons who may be within their territory and to all persons subject to their jurisdiction.[78] Paragraph 2 obliges the State Parties to take necessary steps to give effect to the rights recognized in the Covenant in the domestic order. Failing to comply with the obligations set in paragraph 2 cannot be justified by reference to political, social, cultural, or economic considerations within the States. An individual's right to have accessible and effective remedies, the right to have a fair trial, and the right of equal protection of law could be perceived from paragraph 3 of Article 2. Generally speaking, Article 2 imposes both the negative and positive obligations for States Parties to refrain from violating rights within the Covenant as well as to protect and fulfill an individual's rights.

For the purpose of the book, Article 19 of the ICCPR plays a major role in connecting human rights and trade in the digital age. Article 19 protects individuals' right to freedom of opinion and expression. Whereas more detailed

---

[74] It is worth to note here that China is a State party to the ICCPR without ratification. After the succession to sovereignty over Hong Kong and Macau, the Chinese government has agreed that the ICCPR continues to apply to the territories.

[75] Updated lists of States parties to all the treaties could be found in the Treaty Bodies database of the Office of the United Nations High Commissioner of Human rights. Available at http://indicators.ohchr.org. (accessed 02 February 2015)

[76] UN General Assembly, *Optional Protocol to the International Covenant on Civil and Political Rights*, United Nations, Treaty Series, Vol. 999, p. 171 (19 December 1966).

[77] UN General Assembly, *Second Optional Protocol to the International Covenant on Civil and Political Rights, Aiming at the Abolition of the Death Penalty*, A/RES/44/128 (15 December 1989).

[78] *See* in general UN Human Rights Committee (HRC), *General Comment no. 31 [80], The nature of the general obligation imposed on States Parties to the Covenant*, CCPR/C/32/Rev.1/Add.13 (26 May 2004).

analysis regarding whether the rights guaranteed in Article 19 are sufficient enough to protect fundamental human rights on the Internet will be discussed in Chapter 2, it is noteworthy that the protection of freedom of expression and information is a prerequisite for a good governance not only because it is an essential freedom, but also because it safeguards the legitimacy of a national or international legal system by providing transparency and accountability to the regime embracing such right.[79]

Importantly, most civil and political rights are subjected to permissible limitations.[80] In other words, under certain strictly defined circumstances, the ICCPR allows for State Parties to derogate from the responsibilities within the Covenant. Nevertheless, in general, a State bears the burden of proof in establishing that the restriction on the right must be prescribed by law, the restriction must pursue one of the legitimate aims and it must be necessary to achieve the genuine purpose.[81] The bottom line is that limitations to an individual's rights must be proportionate and not jeopardize the right itself. The derogation must be compatible with the provisions of the treaties relied upon and 'the relation between right and restriction, between norm and exception, must not be reversed'.[82]

iii. The International Covenant on Economic, Social, and Cultural Rights

The ICESCR, as a legally binding international treaty on 165 States, sets a range of rules for protecting and promoting people's economic, social, and cultural rights. The Committee on Economic, Social and Cultural Rights acts as the centerpiece to promote the rights codified in the ICESCR. The Committee is a

[79] *See* Human Rights Committee, *General Comment No. 34 Article 19: Freedoms of Opinion and Expression*, U.N. Doc. CCPR/C/GC/34 (12 September 2011).
[80] Some rights contained in the ICCPR are absolute rights without any derogation. For example: the right to life (Article 6), the right to be free from torture and other ill treatment (Article 7), and the right to be free from slavery and servitude (Article 8).
[81] UN Human Rights Committee (HRC), *Mukong v, Cameroon*, Communication No. 458/1991(21 July 1994), para. 9.7)
[82] UN Human Rights Committee (HRC), *CCPR General Comment No. 27: Article 12 (Freedom of Movement)*, CCPR/C/21/Rev.1/Add.9 (2 November 1999). In paragraph 13, the Committee Stated:

> In adopting laws providing for restriction permitted by article12, paragraph 3, States should always be guided by the principle that the restriction must not impair the essence of the right (cf. article 5, paragraph 1); the relation between right and restriction, between norm and exception, must not be reserved. The law authorizing the application of restrictions should use precise criteria and may not confer unfettered discretion on those charged with their execution.

body of 18 independent experts whose task is to monitor the implementation of the Covenant. The Commitment has the legal mandate to cooperate with the States Parties and other bodies of the UN concerned with economic, social, and cultural rights.[83] Through the General Comments, the Committee has been giving substance to the legal content of the ICESCR. The infrastructure of the ICESCR has long been criticized as being inferior to that of the ICCPR due to the lack of the independent expert body and the absence of positive obligations upon the States Parties.[84] Nevertheless, 23 General Comments conducted by the Committee on Economic, Social and Cultural Rights since 1989 have sufficiently filled the vacuums of the pre-existing non-defined rights.

The general obligations of the ICESCR, which are contained in Article 2, emphasize the progressive realization of the economic, social, and cultural rights. Article 2 states:

> 1. Each State Party to the present Covenant undertakes to take steps, individually and through international assistance and co-operation, especially economic and technical, to the maximum of its available resources, with a view to achieving progressively the full realization of the rights recognized in the present Covenant by all appropriate means, including particularly the adoption of legislative measures.

The terms used in the paragraph attracted criticisms from scholars. For example, the obligations under the ICESCR are progressive rather than immediate and only subject to a State Party's maximum available resources. From the text itself, the mild obligations make it easier for a State to deviate from the rights of the Covenant since it is hard to measure whether the State has progressively exercised its maximum endeavor in promoting the rights.[85] The Committee,

---

[83] *See* Caroline Dommen, Safeguarding the Legitimacy of Multilateral Trading System: The Role of Human Rights Law. In: Frederick M Abbott, Christine Greining-Kaufmann, and Thomas Cottier (eds.), *International Trade and Human Rights: Foundations and Conceptual Issues*, University of Michigan: The World Trade Forum, Vol.5 (2006), pp. 121-132; *see* also UN Office of the High Commissioner for Human Rights, *Review of the composition, organization and administrative arrangements of the Sessional Working Group of the Governmental Experts on the Implementation of International Covenant on Economic, Social and Cultural Rights*, Economic and Social resolution 1985/17 (1985).

[84] *See* Sarah Joseph, *Blame It to the WTO? A Human Rights Critique*, New York: Oxford University Press (2011), pp. 17-29; *see* also Daniel J. Whelan, The Two Covenants and the Evolution of Human Rights. In: Anja Mihr and Mark Gibney, *The SAGE Handbook of Human rights (Volume 1)*, Los Angles: SAGE Publications (2014), pp. 123-144.

[85] Ibid.

however, makes it clear that the full realization of the rights should be taken within a reasonably short time.[86] For example, when considering the relation to access to medicines, progressive realization means "a State is required to be doing better in five years time than it is doing today."[87]

Additionally, the UN General Assembly adopted an Optional Protocol to the ICESCR in December 2008, which entered into force in May 2013.[88] The Option Protocol provides a justiciable legal framework for the economic, social, and cultural rights by offering an individual complaint mechanism. To afford an opportunity for individual complaints ushers the ICESCR into the same legal status as the ICCPR. Article 2 of the Protocol stipulates that "communications may be submitted by or on behalf of individuals or groups of individuals, under the jurisdiction of a State Party, claiming to the victims of a violation of any of the economic, social and cultural rights set forth in the Covenant by the State Party".[89] Article 8 (4) of the Protocol adopts a reasonable standard to examine whether the State Party has taken a range of possible policy measures for the realization of the rights outlined in the Covenant.[90]

Irrespective of the efficacy of the new Optional Protocol, the equal importance of realizing an individual's economic, social and cultural rights to enjoy life as well as his or her civil and political rights should not be underestimated. The UDRH recognizes that both liberty rights (referring to the rights contained in the ICCPR) and distributive rights (relating to the rights included in the ICESCR) are necessary to ensure the inherent dignity and the equal and inalienable rights of all members of the human family.

---

[86] UN Committee on Economic, Social and Cultural Rights (CESCR), *General Comment No.3: The Nature of States Parties' Obligation (Art.2, Para. 1, of the Covenant)*, (14 December 1990), para. 2. The Committee stated:

> Thus, while the full realization of the relevant rights may be achieved progressively, steps towards that goal must be taken within a reasonably short time after the Covenant's entry into force for the State concerned.

[87] UN General Assembly, *The Right of Everyone to the Enjoyment of the Highest Attainable Standard of Physical and Mental Health*, A/61/338 (13 September 2006), para. 55.

[88] UN General Assembly, *Optional Protocol to the International Covenant on Economic, Social and Cultural Rights: Resolution/ adopted by the General Assembly*, A/Res/63/117 (5 March 2009).

[89] Ibid., Article 2.

[90] Ibid., Article 8 (4):

> When examining communications under the present Protocol, the Committee shall consider the reasonableness of the steps taken by the State Party in accordance with part II of the Covenant. In doing so, the Committee shall bear in mind that the State Party may adopt a range of possible policy measures for the implementation of the rights set forth in the Covenant.

b. Customary International Law and Human Rights Law

The question of the relations between human rights law and customary international law is the question of whether human rights could be treated as having the status of customary international law, which is binding on all nations regardless of the consents to the treaties.[91] Article 38(1)(b) of the Statute of the International Court of Justice includes international custom as one of the applicable sources of law to form its opinion on a dispute.[92] It recognized "international custom, as evidence of a general practice accepted as law". In the North Sea Continental Shelf case, the International Court of Justice (ICJ) held that for a customary rule to emerge, two components must be presented: an objective element of state practice and a subjective element of *opinio juris*. The ICJ stated:[93]

> "73. With respect to the other elements usually regarded as necessary before a conventional rule can be considered to have become a general rule of international law, it might be that, even without the passage of any considerable period of time, a very widespread and representative participation in the convention might suffice of itself, provided it included that of States whose interest were specifically affected.
> 77. The essential point to this connection – and it seems necessary to stress it – is that even if these instances of action by nonparties to the Convention were much more numerous than they in fact are, they would not, even in the aggregate, suffice in themselves to constitute the *opinio juris*; – for, in order to achieve this result, two conditions must be fulfilled. Not only must the acts concerned amount to settled practice, but they must also be such, or be carried out in such a way, as to be evidence of a belief that this practice is rendered obligatory by the existence of the rule of law requiring it. The need for such a belief, i.e., the existence of a subjective element, is implicit in the very notion of the *opinio juris sive necessitates. The States concerned must therefore feel that they are conforming to what amounts to a legal obligation.*" (emphasis added)

---

[91] *See* Robert Howse and Makau Mutua, *Protecting Human Rights in a Global Economy: Challenges for the World Trade Organization*, International Centre for Human Rights and Democratic Development (April 2000).

[92] United Nations, *Statute of the International Court of Justice* (18 April 1946). Other sources of international law contained in Article 38 (1) include international convention, the general principles of law recognized by civilized nations, and judicial decisions and teachings of distinguished publicists.

[93] *North Sea Continental Shelf Cases (the Federal Republic of Germany v. Denmark; Federal Republic of Germany v. Netherlands)*, I.C.J. Reports 1969 (20 February 1969).

While the two components are clear for the emergence of a customary international law, the substantive content of each of the elements is controversial. As to the meaning of 'practice,' what acts of a nation are to be counted as practice? Do some nations' acts count as more significant than other nations'? As to the definition of '*opinio juris*', is '*opinio juris*' the tacit consent of states?[94] How can '*opinio juris*' be proven? How can a state believe it is legally bound by a rule of law that is not yet formulated? Due to the uncertainties of the concepts of customary laws and the evolving nature of both customs and human rights, the whole debate of the emergence of customary international law and the status of human rights is controversial and goes beyond the discussion here. As previously mentioned, the human rights assessments are be based on positive law in order to examine the connection between the trade and human rights regimes. Hence, in considering the relation of human rights law to customary international law, the analysis focuses on the legal status of International Bill of Human Rights, especially the UDHR.

The importance of the UDHR in obtaining legal status as customary international law is that the principles and notions of human rights codified within the UDHR will be by definition binding on all nations. The universal binding effect of the UDHR is critical not only for the academic exercise but also for the realization of the rights protected since it provides an alternative source of obligation for the states. Whereas most of the UN universal human rights instruments have been gradually embraced and accepted, not all state nations have ratified all of them.[95] Nevertheless, the argument here is that either from the 'practice' or '*opinio juris*' perspective, the customary status of the UDHR is widely accepted.

The customary status of the UDHR can be indicated by a number of grounds. First, the UDHR is in the widespread use of many international declarations, covenants, and conventions. The evidence could be found in the Declaration of Teheran, Vienna Declaration and Programme of Action in 1993, the ICCPR and the ICESCR. At the Vienna World Conference on Human Rights, 171 participated States agreed that the promotion and protection of all human rights is a legitimate concern of the international community and reaffirmed their com-

[94] *See* in general John H. Jackson, *Sovereignty, the WTO, and Changing Fundamentals of International Law*, United Kingdom: Cambridge University Press (2006), pp. 39-42; and *see* also Holger Hestermeyer, *Human Rights and the WTO – The Case of Patents and Access to Medicines*, New York: Oxford University Press (2007), pp. 122-134.

[95] *See* Sarah Joseph, *Blame It to the WTO? A Human Rights Critique*, New York: Oxford University Press (2011), pp. 29-31.

mitment to the purpose and principles contained in the UN Charter and the UDHR.[96]

Second, the latest Universal Periodic Review[97] (UPR) process could shed some light on the argument of state practice. The UPR provides a method to evaluate human rights records of all UN Member States. Under the auspices of the Human Rights Council, the UPR is a state-driven process, the objective of which is to improve the human rights situation on the ground, to fulfill states' human rights obligations, and to give support for cooperation in the promotion and protection of human rights.[98] As explicitly described in the first paragraph, the process of review is based on the Charter of the United Nations, the UDHR, the ratified treaties, and the voluntary pledges.[99] By October 2011, the Human Rights Council has reviewed the records of all 193 UN Member States, including that of China. China has submitted its human rights records to the Council in 2009 and 2013. The Chinese government has reported several human rights developments and improvements in China regarding the rights contained in the UDHR and some civil and political rights.[100] The states' acts of reporting to the Council on their human rights conditions based on the UDHR as well as rec-

---

[96] United Nations, *Vienna Declaration and Programme of Action*, UN Doc. A/CONF. 157/23 (25 June 1993).

[97] UN Human Rights Council, *Institution-building of the United Nations Human Rights Council*, A/HRC/RES/5/1 (18 June 2007).

[98] Ibid., para. 4. The objectives of the review are:

(a) The improvement of the human rights situation on the ground;
(b) The fulfillment of the State's human rights obligations and commitments and assessment of positive developments and challenges faced by the State;
(c) The enhancement of the State's capacity and of technical assistance, in consultation with, and with the consent of, the State concerned;
(d) The sharing of best practice among States and other stakeholders;
(e) Support for cooperation in the promotion and protection of human rights;
(f) The encouragement of full cooperation and engagement with the Council, other human rights bodies and the Office of the United Nations High Commissioners for Human Rights.

[99] Ibid., para. 1.

[100] *See* UN Human Rights Council Working Group on the Universal Periodic Review, *National Report Submitted in Accordance with Paragraph 15 (A) of the Annex to Human Rights Council Resolution 5/1: China*, A/HRC/WG.6/4/CHN1 (10 November 2008), pp. 12-15 and UN Human Rights Council Working Group on the Universal Periodic Review, *National Report Submitted in Accordance with Paragraph 5 of the Annex to Human Rights Council Resolution 16/21: China*, A/HRC/WG.6/17/CHN/1 (5 August 2013), pp. 10-14.

ommending other states constitute state 'practice' within the meaning of customary international law.[101]

In sum, since "customary law as a source of law is based on the evolution of a behaviour to a habit that solidifies and raises expectations of that behaviour in others until, ultimately, *opinio juris* arises"[102], the UDHR is generally recognized and embraced by Nations States as a customary international law. Such a legal status is crucial not only because the UDHR has brought human rights within the corpus of positive international law, the inalienable rights and freedoms it intended to protect and promote need to be respected at all levels of human society. As Louis B. Sohn stressed:[103]

> "The Declaration, as an authoritative listing of human rights, has become a basic component of international customary law, binding on all states, not only members of the United Nations. Another revolutionary step thus has been taken in protecting human rights on a worldwide scale."

---

[101] *See* Sarah Joseph, *Blame It to the WTO? A Human Rights Critique*, New York: Oxford University Press (2011), pp. 29-31.

[102] Holger Hestermeyer, *Human Rights and the WTO – The Case of Patents and Access to Medicines*, New York: Oxford University Press (2007), p. 125.

[103] Louis B. Sohn, *The New International Law: Protection of the Rights of Individuals Rather Than States*, The American University Law Review, Vol.32, No.1 (1982), pp. 1-64 (p. 7).

II. Space of Human Rights Assessments under the Legal Framework of the WTO

The first section of Chapter 1 introduced the background analysis of both the WTO and international human rights. Section II will discuss the relationship of the two regimes. The first part is a short introduction providing the rationale for the connection between the WTO and human rights. The second part examines the human rights issues within the WTO legal context. Human rights-related trade measures can be categorized into restrictive measures and incentive measures, which are both conducted by states to protect or promote the human rights conditions either within their territories or in the targeted states. However, any trade restrictive measures can be deemed as protectionism and constitute barriers to trade within the meaning of the WTO. Therefore, the underlying issues are whether a WTO panel has the competence and jurisdiction to take human rights considerations into account in a dispute settlement process and whether a WTO Member State could derogate from its substantive obligations on the basis of human rights arguments.

A. Introduction

As discussed in section I, contemporary international systems of both the international trade and human rights regimes are aspired in their own way but based on the same set of historical backgrounds with mutually enforceable objectives. Although the history shows that trade liberalization partly goes hand in hand with the enhanced enjoyment and fulfillment of human rights, tensions between these two segments of the international legal systems cannot be overlooked. Since the late 1990s, the international human rights movements have been severely engaged in public debates concerning the impact of the economic legal system on the realization of human rights. It happened under the background of widespread concerns about the adverse effect of globalization. Most of the critics focused on how the international trade regime might constrain the policy choices of its Members to protect social justice and promote the enjoyment of human rights.[104]

---

[104] *See* in general Louis B. Sohn, *The New International Law: Protection of the Rights of Individuals Rather Than States*, The American University Law Review, Vol.32, No.1 (1982), pp. 1- 64; Thomas Cottier, *Trade and Human Rights – A Relationship to Discover*, Journal of International Economic Law, Vol.5, No.1 (2002), pp. 111-132; Gabrielle Marceau, *WTO Dispute Settlement and Human Rights*, European Journal of International Law, Vol.13 (2002), pp. 753-814; Frederick M Abbott, Christine Greining-

The WTO, which is the provider of a venue for the social construction of the international trade order and a critical forum for pursuing trade liberalization, attracted most of the attention from the debates. It is argued that many trade policies at the WTO aim at serving powerful producers' interests, and the efficiency to protect human rights or social justice at the international level is descending due to the ascendance of dominant international economic order.[105] Human rights advocates claimed that the elaboration of the WTO seemly drove toward the opposite direction of promoting and protecting human rights. For example, the panel and the Appellate Body's decisions on the SPS and the TBT have been criticized for unduly undermining Members' autonomy to vital social values within their territories.[106]

In addition, a strict interpretative approach adopted by both panels and the Appellate Body when considering the application of the general exception clauses of GATT Article XX and GATS Article XIV also has attracted critiques for not properly addressing human rights considerations within the WTO legal system. The purpose of the general exceptions is to provide a mechanism, by which, under specific conditions, Members are allowed to adopt and maintain measures that promote or protect significant social values and interest, even if those measures are inconsistent with the substantive obligations of the WTO covered agreements.[107] Whereas some of the exceptions might save human rights-related trade measures from WTO illegality, judging from the WTO ju-

---

Kaufmann, and Thomas Cottier (eds.), *International Trade and Human Rights: Foundations and Conceptual Issues*, University of Michigan: The World Trade Forum, Vol.5 (2006); and Thomas Cottier, Joost Pauwelyn, and Elisabeth Bürgi (eds.), *Human Rights and International Trade*, New York: Oxford University Press (2005).

[105] *See* Andrew T.F. Lang, Inter-regime Encounters. In: Sarah Joseph, David Kinley, and Jeff Waincymer (eds.), *The World Trade Organization and Human Rights – Interdisciplinary Perspectives*, Cheltenham: Edward Elgar Publishing (2009), pp. 163-180. Lang is of the opinion:

> The primary mechanism by which the human rights system achieves its objectives, the story goes, is losing its efficacy in the face of a newly powerful and newly dominant neoliberal international economic order. (p. 184)

[106] *See* Caroline E. Foster, Public Opinion and the Interpretation of the World Trade Organization's Agreement on Sanitary and Phytosanitary Measures. In: Sarah Joseph, David Kinley, and Jeff Waincymer (eds.), *The World Trade Organization and Human Rights – Interdisciplinary Perspectives*, Cheltenham: Edward Elgar Publishing (2009), pp. 285-312.

[107] *See* John H, Jackson, *The World Trading System: Law and Policy of International Economic Relations*, Cambridge, MIT Press (1989), p. 206.

risprudence, the judicial bodies usually interpret treaty exceptions strictly and narrowly.[108]

Consequently, after almost two decades since it was established in 1995, the WTO was criticized for operating in "splendid isolation" from other international institutions.[109] Human rights advocates argued that the WTO constrains its Members' autonomy to meet their human rights obligations and provide essential living standards to their citizens. WTO rules, however, should not be only seen as a set of constraining rules and the critics should not solely focus on how much sufficient policy space ought to be left for WTO Members to protect social values within their territories. As a rule-oriented system for international trade, the WTO shapes the domestic policy-making process to provide a desirable and predictable trading system for the global economy. At the most general level, improving the human conditions is a shared common purpose for both the trade and human rights regimes.

The Director-General of the WTO, Pascal Lamy, proclaimed that trade and human rights communities distrust each other, but "human rights and trade are mutually supportive. Human rights are essential to the good functioning of the multilateral trading system, and trade and WTO rules contribute to the realization of human rights".[110] The challenge before the international legal systems today is "how to influence the process of globalization in such a way that human poverty, exploitation and discrimination can be eliminated".[111] By achieving this end, it is crucial to stream human rights norms and values into the system of international financial and trade orders, for the WTO in particular. Although the WTO cannot perform as a human rights organization, it must take steps to recognize the human rights influence of its work to consolidate good governance in the WTO. The jurisdiction and competence of the WTO adjudi-

---

[108] *See* Christiane R. Conrad, *Processes and Production Methods (PPMs) in WTO Law: Interfacing Trade and Social Goals*, New York: Cambridge University Press (2011), pp. 147-149.

[109] Thomas Cottier, *Trade and Human Rights – A Relationship to Discover*, Journal of International Economic Law, Vol.5, No.1 (2002), pp. 111-132.

[110] *See* Pascal Lamy, *Towards Shared Responsibility and Greater Coherence: Human Rights, Trade and Macroeconomic Policy* (Speech at the Colloquium on Human Rights in the Global Economy, Co-organized by the International Council on Human Rights and Realizing Rights, Geneva) (13 January 2010). Available at http://www.wto.org/english/news_e/sppl_e/sppl146_e.htm. (accessed 18 October 2012)

[111] Robert Howse and Makau Mutua, *Protecting Human Rights in a Global Economy: Challenges for the World Trade Organization*, International Centre for Human Rights and Democratic Development (April 2000), p. 56.

cating bodies will be challenged when various interests at stake need to be balanced. Nonetheless, the mandate of the WTO is never limited to free trade, and a range of human rights considerations could have functional advantages for achieving consistency and enhancing the legitimacy of the international trading system.

B. The Legal Framework for the Human Rights Analysis under the Scope of the WTO

From the analysis aforementioned, it can be seen that at the international level, there is a need to reach the balance between the trade and human rights regimes. The section here, therefore, discusses the rationales of human rights-related trade measures and how each country implements them to protect and promote the human rights conditions of its citizens or the people in the target countries. These measures may come within the corpus of the WTO since they could be protectionism in nature or have adverse effects on international trade.

a. Rationales of Human Rights-related Trade Measures

Since 1945, the protection of human rights could be no longer be deemed as a domestic sovereign issue but a universal concern that requires international, multilateral, and regional cooperation. Although with evolving content and notions, the righteousness of human rights is so compelling that no country in the world is willing to oppose the ideas and values behind it explicitly. It is not to say there are no more human rights violations. States across the globe constantly abuse or invade primary individual's rights. People are deprived of their rights to food, to health, to medical treatment, to education, and even to life by the misbehaviour of their governments.

From the positive legal perspective, a number of the UN bodies are responsible for the enforcement machinery of human rights. The UN has the most considerable influence regarding the development of modern international human rights norms and standards. The UN Charter created several monitoring mechanisms in the UN system, including the Human Rights Council, the Universal Periodic Review, the Commission on Human Rights (replaced by the Human Rights Council Advisory Committee), the Special Procedures of the Human Rights Council and the Human Rights Council Complaint Procedure. The Human Rights Council, which was created by the UN General Assembly on the 15

March 2006 to replace the UN Commission on Human Rights[112], is the principal inter-governmental body within the UN system. The mandate of the Human Rights Council, in addition to promoting "universal respect for the protection of all human rights and fundamental freedoms for all"[113], includes authorizing the investigation of particular human rights situations, making recommendations to the General Assembly, and conducting the process of the Universal Periodic Review to monitor the human rights performance of all States.[114]

Another critical body within the UN system is the UN High Commissioner for Human Rights. The UN High Commissioner for Human Rights was established by the UN General Assembly on 20 December 1993 after the World Conference on Human rights in Vienna.[115] The Commissioner of Human Rights was founded almost five decades after the formation of the UN because the international community could not agree on the establishment of a single UN official with primary responsibility for the protection and promotion of human rights.[116] According to Resolution 48/141, which established the High Commissioner, the mandate of the commissioner includes promoting and protecting fundamental human rights, improving international cooperation, playing an active role in removing the obstacles to the full realization of all human rights by engaging in dialogues with all governments.[117]

---

[112] UN General Assembly, *Human Rights Council: Resolution adopted by the General Assembly on 15 March 2006*, A/RES/60/251 (3 April 2006).

[113] The General Assembly emphasized in Article 2 of the General Assembly Resolution that the Human Rights Council "shall be responsible for promoting universal respect for the protection of all human rights and fundamental freedoms for all, without distinction of any kind and in a fair and equal manner."

[114] Article 5(e) of the General Assembly Resolution confers the mandate of the Human Rights Council of undertaking a Universal Periodic Review process of all United Nations Member States.

[115] UN General Assembly, *High Commissioner for the Promotion and Protection of All Human Rights: Resolution adopted by the General Assembly*, A/RES/48/141 (20 December 1993).

[116] *See* Julia Kozma, The United Nations Human Rights System: The Genesis and Role of the Human Rights Council and the High Commissioner for Human Rights. In: Anja Mihr and Mark Gibney, *The SAGE Handbook of Human rights (Volume 2)*, Los Angles: SAGE Publications (2014), pp. 555-574.

[117] Article 4 of the Resolution 48/141 enumerates the general competence of the High Commissioner. The beginning of Article 4 asserts that the High Commissioner for Human Rights shall be the United Nations official with principal responsibility for United Nations human rights activities under the direction and authority of the Secretary-General.

Whereas the Human Rights bodies under the UN system in combination with the office of the High Commissioner for Human rights cover a wide variety of human rights concerns, their main tasks are mostly limited to monitoring and reporting human rights violations. In other words, the overall enforcement system of international human rights law is relatively weak and ineffective compared to the rule-oriented dispute settlement system under the DSU of the WTO. For example, while WTO adjudicating bodies' reports adopted by the DSB are automatically binding on all Member States, the opinions of the UN Human Rights bodies are non-binding and propositional in nature.

In principle, international standards of human rights could be enforced through internalizing the norms and rights into the domestic legal system.[118] However, it heavily depends on states themselves to implement the human rights obligations within their territories, either through the constitutional order or the national court system.[119] For countries unwilling to comply with the human rights obligations, the process of naming and shaming is often applied to condemn the violations. The reasoning for allocating the power to the states to decide the level of self-enforcement of human rights could be linked with some political realism; nevertheless, due to the lack of a strong remedy mechanism, states have gradually started to use trade measures to realize human rights protections.

b. Human Rights-related Trade Measures – Potential Violations of WTO Rules

Generally speaking, economic measures have been used by states to promote human rights compliance for a long time. Trade embargoes against countries where severe human right violations take place are not prohibited by customary international law and human rights law. Nevertheless, with the progress of trade liberalization and the establishment of the WTO, trade-related human rights measures are potentially in violation of international trade rules since the purports of the WTO are devoted to the trade compliance instead of trade sanctions. Any human rights countermeasures, which have the restrictive effect on interna-

[118] *See* Harold Hongju Koh, *How is International Human Rights Law Enforced?*, Indiana Law Journal, Vo. 74, Issue:4 (1 October 1999), pp. 1397-1417. (The author is of the view that international human rights are enforced through a transnational legal process of institutional interaction, interpretation of legal norms, and attempts to internalize those norms into domestic legal systems.)

[119] *See* Julia Kozma, The United Nations Human Rights System: The Genesis and Role of the Human Rights Council and the High Commissioner for Human Rights. In: Anja Mihr and Mark Gibney, *The SAGE Handbook of Human rights (Volume 2)*, Los Angles: SAGE Publications (2014), pp. 555-574.

tional trade, could constitute quantitative restrictions on the importation of goods and services or have a discriminatory impact on the Member States. Two types of measures are often implemented by countries to stress human rights concerns: trade restrictive and trade incentive measures.

i. Trade Restrictions

In recent years, states have progressively adopted trade measures to address human rights issues. Human rights trade-related restrictive measures arise either when a state attempts to impose economic sanctions on a target country to improve the human rights situation in the country or a state intends to restrict the import of a particular product due to concerns over human rights abuses associated with the product or concerns over the protection of human rights of its own populations.[120]

The embargo on Myanmar is one of the examples to promote human rights enjoyment through trade sanctions.[121] Myanmar was one of the wealthiest countries in Southeast Asia and was believed to be on a fast track to the development because of its significant natural resources.[122] However, in 1962 General Than Shwe overthrew the elected civilian government and replaced it with a repressive military government.[123] The military regime isolated Myanmar from the international community and formed a centrally planned economy. Despite strong economic growth in Southeast Asia, the UN declared Myanmar as a Least Developed Country in 1987.[124] In response, the United States adopted a series of acts to enforce Myanmar to reform the repressive government and to improve the human right violated situations. On January 15, 2003, the US House of Representatives passed the Burmese Freedom and Democracy Act of 2003 which bans the importation of any goods produced, manufactured, grown,

---

[120] *See* Gudrun Zagel, *The WTO and Trade-Related Human Rights Measures: Trade Sanctions vs. Trade Incentives*, Austrian Review of International and European Law, Vol.9 (2004), pp. 119-153.

[121] *See* Sarah Joseph, *Blame It to the WTO? A Human Rights Critique*, New York: Oxford University Press (2011), p. 92.

[122] *See* Robert H. Taylor, Pathways to the Present. In: Kyaw Yin Hlaing, Rober H. Taylor, and Tin Maung Maung Than (eds.), *Myanmar: Beyond Politics to Societal Imperatives 1* (2005), pp. 1-16.

[123] *See* Michael Ewing-Chow, *First Do No Harm: Myanmar Trade Sanctions and Human Rights*, Northwestern Journal of International Human Rights Vol.5, Issue:2 (Spring 2007), pp. 153-180.

[124] Ibid.

or assembled in Myanmar.[125] Unfortunately, according to the US report, the people of Myanmar have grown steadily poorer due to the sanctions. The US State Department estimated a loss of 60,000 jobs in the textile sector alone, and the per capita income in Myanmar fell from US$300 to US$225 between 2003 to 2004.[126]

The rationale for imposing trade sanctions is that economic sanctions are the most efficient legal measures available in general to punish a state for its abusive human rights behaviour.[127] Nevertheless, most trade sanctions aimed at the regime changes have done little to hurt those who wield power or have done little to gain the presumed desired effect of prompting a disgruntled population to force the regime to change its ways.[128] Trade sanctions usually instead often lead to the grave sufferings on the part of an innocent target population if the repressive government refuses to comply with the demands of the sanctioning states.[129]

The Economic and Social Council of the UN noted "while the impact of sanctions varies from one case to another, the Committee is aware that they almost always have a dramatic impact on the rights recognized in the Covenant. Thus, for example, they often cause significant disruption in the distribution of food, pharmaceuticals and sanitation supplies, jeopardize the quality of food and the availability of clean drinking water, severely interfere with the functioning of basic health and education systems, and undermine the right to work".[130] The Committee further proclaimed that the economic, social, and cultural rights must be fully taken into account when designing appropriate sanctions and the sanctioning country has the obligations to take economic or technical steps to

---

[125] Burmese Freedom and Democracy Act of 2003 (Burmese Freedom Act), Pub. L. No. 10-61, §§ 1-9, 117 Stat. 864 (2003) (codified as 50 USC § 1701 (2000)).

[126] US Department of State, *Report on US Trade Sanctions Against Burma*, Congressionally mandated Report submitted to Congress (28 April 2004). Available at https://2001-2009.state.gov/p/eap/rls/rpt/32106.htm. (accessed 03 November 2012)

[127] *See* James Harrison, *The Human Rights Impact of the World Trade Organization*, Oxford and Portland, Oregon: Hart Publishing (2007), pp. 98-99.

[128] *See* Carlos Manuel Vázquez, *Trade Sanctions and Human Rights – Past, Present and Future, Journal of International Economic Law*, Vol.6, Issue:4 (2003), pp. 797-839.

[129] *See* Gudrun Zagel, *The WTO and Trade-Related Human Rights Measures: Trade Sanctions vs. Trade Incentives*, Austrian Review of International and European Law, Vol.9 (2004), pp. 119-153.

[130] UN Economic and Social Council, *General Comment No.8 (1997) – The Relationship between Economic Sanctions and Respect for Economic, Social and Cultural Rights*, E/C.12/1997/8 (12 December 1997), para. 3.

respond to any 'disproportionate suffering vulnerable groups' within the target country.[131]

In addition to imposing trade sanctions on a target country, to comply with its own international human rights obligations, a WTO Member might restrict the import of a specific product, like toxic fibres or cigarettes, to protect and promote human rights of persons within its own country. The issue, therefore, is whether the adoption of the human rights-related restrictive measure, which aims at the protection of product safety or essential services such as water, health, or education to its own population, will violate a Member's obligations under the WTO. Likewise, more often than not, countries ban the importation of certain products because of human rights violations during the production process of the products, such as terrible working conditions and child labor. The so-called process and production methods (PPMs) have attracted considerable debate in the context of the WTO legal system because of its extra-territorial effect.[132] An extraterritorial measure is controversial since the rights concerned are the rights of people of exporting countries, rather than the people of the sanctioning Member. Under this circumstance, the mandate and jurisdiction of the WTO adjudicating bodies need to be considered to examine an extra-territorial issue.

ii. Trade Incentives

An alternative approach to promote and protect human rights is through trade incentives. As previously mentioned, human rights-related trade measures normally give rise to *prima facie* violations of various principles of WTO law, such as MFN, national treatment and zero quotas. WTO rules, however, leave some space for human rights conditionality. The Regional and Bilateral Trade Agreements (RTAs) and the General System of Preferences (GSP) are two prominent developments in the WTO for the promotion of human rights. The RTAs are regional or bilateral agreements between WTO Members for addi-

---

[131] Ibid., para. 11-14. (The Committee considers "the external entity has obligation to "take steps, individually and through international assistance and cooperation, especially economic and technical" in order to respond to any disproportionate suffering experienced by vulnerable groups within the targeted country.")

[132] *See* Thomas Cottier, *Trade and Human Rights – A Relationship to Discover*, Journal of International Economic Law, Vol.5, No.1 (2002), pp. 111-132 (112); and *see* also Carlos Manuel Vázquez, *Trade Sanctions and Human Rights – Past, Present and Future, Journal of International Economic Law*, Vol.6, Issue:4 (2003), pp. 797-839 (811-822).

tional trade concessions above and beyond WTO obligations.[133] The GSP is a unilateral programme implemented by developed countries to grant preferential tariff treatment to developing countries.[134]

In general, preferential treatment of one country over another is not in compliance with the most-favoured-nation treatment under Article I of the GATT which requires equal treatment to all like imported products unconditionally. Nonetheless, in order to raise the capability of developing countries to participate in international trade on the same footing, the GSP was introduced into the framework of the United Nations Conference on Trade and Development (UNCTAD) in the 1960's.[135] The legal basis of the GSP within the WTO is through the adoption of the 'Enabling Clause'[136] in 1979. The EU, the US and other industrialized nations have adopted various GSP measures in pursuing voluntary compliance with certain human rights standards from developing and least-developed countries.

The first paragraph of the Enabling Clauses explicitly asserts that "notwithstanding the provisions of Article I of the General Agreement, contracting parties may accord differential and more favourable treatment to developing countries, without according such treatment to other contracting parties." The measures covered by the Enabling Clauses are listed in paragraph 2. Paragraph 2 (a) of the Enabling Clauses states that preferential tariff treatment accorded by developed countries should be in accordance with the Generalized System of Preferences. The footnote 3 of the paragraph further defines the GSP as generalized, non-reciprocal, and non-discriminatory. In addition to preferential tariff treatment, the provision covers treatments concerning non-tariff measures (para. 2 (b)), economic mutual reduction or elimination of non-tariff measures (para. 2 (c)), and special treatment of the least developed countries (para. 2(d)).

While the underlying purpose of the Enabling Clause is to provide an equal standing for developing countries in the global trade, human rights-related conditionality has been criticized as an ineffective or even a harsh means of pro-

---

[133] *See* James Harrison, *The Human Rights Impact of the World Trade Organization*, Oxford and Portland, Oregon: Hart Publishing (2007), pp. 106-111.

[134] *See* Gudrun Zagel, *The WTO and Trade-Related Human Rights Measures: Trade Sanctions vs. Trade Incentives*, Austrian Review of International and European Law, Vol.9 (2004), pp. 119-153 (144-146).

[135] UNCTAD, *Expansion and Diversification of Exports of Manufacturers and Semi-manufacturers of Developing Countries*, Resolution 21 (ii) (1968).

[136] General Agreement on Trade and Tariff, *Differential and More Favourable Treatment Reciprocity and Fuller Participation of Developing Countries*, Doc. L/4903 (28 November 1979).

moting fundamental human rights and freedoms.[137] In contrast to its original good governance ideal, preferential treatments enacted by developed countries are often condemned as a disguised barrier to trade, and the measures practically allow further differentiation among developing countries. Nevertheless, compared to coercive trade sanctions, trade engagement policies in promoting human rights conditions could avoid some extraterritorial legal problems.

The *EC – Tariff Preferences*[138] case might provide some clarity to the application of trade preferences within the WTO legal system and help to assess under what conditions trade incentives could be rendered to promote the human rights conditions. *EC – Tariff Preferences* is the first WTO dispute where a developing country challenged a trade preference program from a developed country. In the case, India claimed that a number of special preferential treatment programs offered by the EU, which were intended to help developing countries combat illegal drug trafficking, constituted discriminatory treatment between different countries. The Appellate Body found the EC's special incentives on drugs arrangement to be inconsistent with Article I:1 of the GATT and cannot be justified under paragraph 2(a) of the Enabling Clause since the preference was only available to 12 beneficiaries without providing criteria or standards for the qualifications.[139]

First, both the panel and the Appellate Body confirmed that although it is not a legal obligation to undertake differential treatments for developing countries, a trade preference provided under the GSP system, which should be treated as a derogation measure from a positive obligation, must comply with certain legal conditions as set out in the relevant WTO rules, i.e., the Enabling Clause. The panel stated:

> "There is no legal obligation under GATT 1994 requiring a Member, e.g., to take an Article XX measure, or to take a national security measure, or to form a free-trade area or customs union with other Members. Members are free to choose whether to take these measures or to do nothing. If they decide to take such measures, they are authorized to do so by these provisions, subject to certain conditions. The fact that when Members choose to take

[137] *See* Ljiljana Biukovic, Is There Policy Space for Human Rights Linkages in China's Trade and Investment Network. In: Daniel Drache and Lesley A. Jacobs (eds.), *Linking Global Trade and Human rights*, New York: Cambridge University Press (February 2014), pp. 274-295 (292-293).

[138] Appellate Body Report, *European Communities – Conditions for the Granting of Tariff Preferences to Developing Countries* (cited as *EC – Tariff Preferences*), WT/DS246/AB/R (7 April 2004).

[139] Ibid., paras. 187-189.

> such measures, they are also required to comply with certain conditions prescribed in these exceptions' provisions ... *The existence of certain conditions relating to the application of an exception provision only signifies that the exception is "limited", not absolute, and that the authorization of derogation is tied to the fulfillment of certain conditions.*" (emphasis added)[140]

Further, the Appellate Body clarified that the term "non-discriminatory" in Footnote 3 to paragraph 2(a) of the Enabling Clause does not necessarily require 'identical' tariff preferences to 'all' developing countries. Read together with the term "generalized" in the sense that tariff preferences should remain generally applicable, the non-discriminatory requirement for the GSP system does not mean that all preference programs have to be identical, but the same treatments have to be accessible to all similarly-situated developing countries. The Appellate Body disagreed with the panel and stressed:

> "Paragraph 2(a), on its face, does not explicitly authorize or prohibit the granting of different preferences to different GSP beneficiaries. It is clear from the ordinary meanings of "non-discriminatory", however, that preference-granting countries must make available identical tariff preferences to all similar-situated beneficiaries."[141]

To support its definition of non-discriminatory, the Appellate Body referred to paragraph 3(c) of the Enabling Clause, which allows developed countries to "respond positively to the development, financial, and trade needs of developing countries".[142] The Appellate Body is of the opinion that the 'needs' of the developing countries should be determined on an objective standard recognized by the international community and not merely be based on the assertion of a preference-granting country. The Appellate Body identified:

---

[140] Panel Report, *European Communities – Conditions for the Granting of Tariff Preferences to Developing Countries* (cited as *EC – Tariff Preferences*), WT/DS246/R (1 December 2003), para. 7.37.

[141] Appellate Body Report, *European Communities – Conditions for the Granting of Tariff Preferences to Developing Countries* (cited as *EC – Tariff Preferences*), WT/DS246/AB/R (7 April 2004), para. 154.

[142] Para. 3(c) of the Enabling Clause regulates:

> 3. Any differential and more favourable treatment provided under this clause:
> c) shall in the case of such treatment accorded by developed contracting parties to developing countries to be designed and, if necessary, modified, to respond positively to the development, financial and trade needs of developing countries.

> "In our view, a "need" cannot be characterized as one of the specified "needs of developing countries" in the sense of paragraph 3(c) based merely on an assertion to that effect by, for instance, a preference-granting country or a beneficiary country. Rather, when a claim of inconsistency with paragraph 3(c) is made, the existence of a "development, financial [or] trade need" must be assessed according to an *objective* standard. Broad-based recognition of a particular need, set out in the WTO Agreement or in multilateral instruments adopted by international organizations, could serve as such a standard."[143]

In sum, in *EC – Tariff Preferences*, the Appellate Body recognized that the GSP system must comply with the conditions of the Enabling Clause and under the notion of 'non-discriminatory'. Preferential treatment could aim at those interests that developing countries have in common, as well as at those interests "shared by sub-categories of developing countries based on their particular needs".[144] The reference to the international objective standards to decide the 'needs' indicates that human rights conditionality in trade preference is permissible if the preference is granted on the basis of internationally recognized human rights, such as those rights enclosed in the UDHR, the ICCPR and the ICESCR.

It is also important to note that there must be a sufficient nexus between the preferential treatment and the 'needs' of the developing countries.[145] Put differently, tariff preferences should be able to 'effectively address' the particular development needs of developing countries. From a human rights perspective, the requirement suggests that in the context of a GSP scheme, any trade incentives intended to promote human rights conditions in target countries need to positively contribute to the human rights situation of the people in question.[146]

---

[143] Appellate Body Report, *European Communities – Conditions for the Granting of Tariff Preferences to Developing Countries* (cited as *EC – Tariff Preferences*), WT/DS246/AB/R (7 April 2004), para. 163.

[144] Ibid., para. 169.

[145] Ibid., para. 164. When considering the nexus between preferential treatment and the particular needs of the developing countries, the Appellate Body stated:

> …the expectation that developed countries will "respond positively" to the "needs of developing countries" suggests that a sufficient nexus should exist between, on the one hand, the preferential treatment provided under the respective measure authorized by paragraph 2, and on the other hand, the likelihood of alleviating the relevant "development, financial [or] trade need".

[146] *See* Gudrun Zagel, *The WTO and Trade-Related Human Rights Measures: Trade Sanctions vs. Trade Incentives*, Austrian Review of International and European Law, Vol.9 (2004), pp. 119-153. (148-151)

C. The Place for Human Rights Arguments under the WTO Dispute Settlement System

There is considerable disagreement among scholars, trade lawyers, and human rights advocates about the mechanisms by which to find the consistency between trade law and human rights law, especially when the forum considered is the WTO dispute settlement system. Some argued that violators of human rights are necessarily violators of WTO regulations[147], and others intend to use the human rights as defense to justify the violations of WTO market access rules. Thus, the threshold question is the extent to which the WTO can deal with all these concerns. In other words, are WTO Members allowed to raise human rights considerations in a dispute? Could a WTO panel have the competence to accept human rights allegations when no direct reference to human rights law can be found in the WTO agreements? If a panel agrees with the merit of the case, how could the panel and the Appellate Body respond to the human rights concerns within the trading system?[148]

WTO law is a specific system of international law specialized in dealing with trade controversies among its Member States. The WTO has its specific jurisdiction, the rules of applicable law, and the principles of interpretation. Under Article 1, 4, 7, and 11 of the DSU, a panel and the Appellate Body have limited domain to the covered agreements. Technically, WTO judiciary bodies can only interpret and apply rules under the covered agreement[149] and cannot add or diminish obligations of Members more than the agreements covered by the WTO. Therefore, it could be assumed that WTO adjudicating bodies cannot enforce or give direct effect to human rights provisions between WTO Members other than under the WTO provisions including the general exceptions.[150] Although a pan-

---

[147] *See* Robert Howse and Makau Mutua, *Protecting Human Rights in a Global Economy: Challenges for the World Trade Organization*, International Centre for Human Rights and Democratic Development (April 2000). In the Article Robert Howse and Makau Mutua wrote: It is absurd to expect a country that systematically violates basic human rights to faithfully execute and implement the processes that the WTO Agreement requires (p. 17).

[148] *See* James Harrison, *The Human Rights Impact of the World Trade Organization*, Oxford and Portland, Oregon: Hart Publishing (2007), pp. 187-224.

[149] The term "covered agreements" has been emphasized several times in the Articles of the DSU. It also appears in Article 2:1, Article 3:2 (Recommendations and rulings of the DSB cannot add or diminish the rights and obligations provided in the covered agreements), Article 4, Article 7, Article 11, etc.

[150] Article 7 of the DSU concerns the terms of reference of a WTO panel and stressed that the reference of the panel is:

el might have a defined jurisdiction, this does not constrain the panel's competence to take other international legal norms into account when interpreting or applying WTO rules in a dispute settlement process.[151]

a. Jurisdiction and the Applicable Law of the Adjudicative Branch of the WTO

There is no obligation in general international law to settle disputes and the jurisdiction of international tribunals is based on consents of the parties.[152] For example, the members of the UN are not subject to suits before the ICJ unless both of the parties agree to at least one type of contentious jurisdiction of the ICJ.[153] On the contrary, as noted above, due to the single-undertaking nature of the WTO, when a state becomes a member of the WTO, it automatically submits to the jurisdiction of the dispute settlement system. Since measures with relatively limited trade impact can still fall within the scope of the WTO, a panel's decision might have significant influence on the international legal order. Therefore, several issues pertaining to the relevance of international law for WTO law need to the distinguished. The jurisdiction of the WTO adjudicating bodies and the applicable law before them is examined first, followed by the analysis of how WTO law could be interpreted consistently with the principles of other international law.

i. The Limited Jurisdiction of WTO Panels and the Appellate Body

Pursuant to Article 1.1 of the DSU, the jurisdiction of a WTO panel is defined and limited to the violation of the WTO "covered agreements".[154] Article 7.1 of

---

> To examine, in the light of the relevant provisions in (name of the covered agreements(s) cited by the parties to the dispute), the matter referred to the DSB by (name of party) in document ... and to make such findings as will assist the DSB in making the recommendations or in giving the rulings provided for in that/those agreements(s).

[151] *See* Gabrielle Marceau, *WTO Dispute Settlement and Human Rights*, European Journal of International Law, Vol.13 (2002), pp. 753-814.

[152] *See* Ian Brownlie, *Principles of Public International Law*, Oxford University Press, 7th Edition (2008), pp. 701-725.

[153] *Statute of the International Court of Justice Article 36*, (Article 36:2: The states parties to the present Statute may at any time declare that they recognize as compulsory ipso facto and without special agreement, in relation to any other state accepting the same obligation).

[154] DSU Article 1:1:

> The rules and procedures of this Understanding shall apply to disputes brought pursuant to the consultation and dispute settlement provisions of the agreements listed in Appendix 1'. The

the DSU states that the standard terms of reference of WTO panels are '[to] examine, in the light of the relevant provisions in (name of the covered agreement(s) cited by the parties to the dispute), the matter referred to the DSB by (name of party) in document ... and to make such findings as will assist the DSB in making the recommendations or in giving the rulings provided for in that/those agreements(s)'.[155] Furthermore, Article 11 of the DSU instructs panels to 'make an objective assessment of the matter before it, including an objective assessment of the facts of the case and the applicability of and conformity with the relevant covered agreements'.[156] Finally, Article 3.2 of the DSU emphasizes "recommendations and rulings of the DSB cannot add to or diminish the rights and obligations provided in the covered agreements".

A WTO dispute settlement proceeding is therefore restricted to ruling on claims that are based on the WTO agreements. The WTO adjudicating bodies have the capability to interpret and apply WTO rules set out in the covered agreements, and the legal rights and obligations outside the WTO cannot be preserved by the dispute settlement system.[157] For example, an environmental or a human rights violation cannot be pursued as an independent claim before a WTO panel. Nevertheless, the limitation on the substantive jurisdiction of the WTO adjudicating bodies is not necessarily equal to the limitation on the applicable law available before panels and the Appellate Body.

ii. The WTO Applicable Law

The UN Convention on the Law of the Sea (UNCLOS) indicates that the International Tribunal for the Law of the Sea shall have "jurisdiction over any dispute concerning the interpretation or application of an international agreement related to the purpose of this Convention which is submitted to it in accordance with the agreement."[158] Article 293 of the UNCLOS, which concerns the appli-

---

covered agreements listed in Annex 1 to the DSU are Agreement Establishing the World Trade Organization, Multilateral Trade Agreements and Plurilateral Trade Agreements.

155 Article 7.1 of the DSU.

156 Article 11 of the DSU.

157 *See* Joost Pauwelyn, *Conflict of Norms in Public International: How WTO Law Relates to Other Rules of International Law*, Cambridge University Press (2003), pp. 440-486.

158 UN General Assembly, *Convention of the Law of the Sea* (10 December 1982). Article 288 of the UNCLOS stipulates:

> 2. A court or tribunal referred to in article 287 shall also have jurisdiction over any dispute concerning the interpretation or application of an international agreement related to the purposes of this Convention, which is submitted to it in accordance with the agreement.

cable law, provides: "A court or tribunal having jurisdiction under this section shall apply this Convention and other rules of international law not incompatible with this Convention."[159] Similar provisions are also reflected in Article 38 (1) of the ICJ Statute, which stipulates:

> "The Court, whose function is to decide in accordance with international law such disputes are submitted to it, shall apply (a) international conventions ... (b) international custom ... (c) the general principle of law ... (d) judicial decisions and the teachings of the most highly qualified publicists of the various nations, as subsidiary means for the determination of rules of law".[160]

One can presume that a court might have a limited jurisdiction on the one hand and unlimited sources of applicable law on the other. WTO law, unlike the UNCLOS or the Statute of the ICJ, does not include an explicit provision concerning the applicable law. Article 3.2 of the DSU requires that the existing WTO provisions are to be clarified 'in accordance with customary rules of interpretation of public international law'.[161] Consequently, the rules of interpretation laid down in the Vienna Convention, which have attained the status of the customary international law on treaty interpretation, are considered to be applicable.[162]

Article 31(1) of the Vienna Convention stipulates, "a treaty should be interpreted in good faith in accordance with the ordinary meaning to be given to the terms of the treaty in their context in the light of its object and purpose."[163] For example, in *US-Shrimp*, the Appellate Body stated:

---

[159] Ibid., Article 293 (Applicable Law).

[160] United Nations, *Statute of the International Court of Justice* (18 April 1946), Article 38.

[161] Article 3.2 of the DSU provides:

> The dispute settlement system of the WTO is a central element in providing security and predictability to the multilateral trading system. The Members recognize that it serves to preserve the rights and obligation of Members under the covered agreements, and to clarify the existing provisions of those agreements *in accordance with customary rules of interpretation of public international law*. Recommendations and rulings of the DSB cannot add to or diminish the rights and obligations provided in the covered agreements. (emphasis added)

[162] *See* Isabelle Van Damme, *Treaty Interpretation by the WTO Appellate Body*, The European Journal of International Law Vol.21, No.3 (2010), pp. 605-648.

[163] The United Nations, *Vienna Convention on the Law of Treaties*, United Nations, Treaty Series, Vol.1155 (23 May 1967), p. 331, Article 31.

> "In adopting its "threat to the multilateral trading system" analysis, the Panel fails to apply the ordinary meaning of the text: whether a justification can be presented for applying a measure in a manner which constitutes discrimination. Instead, the Panel expanded the ordinary meaning of the text to encompass a much broader and more subjective inquiry. As a result, the Panel would add an entirely new obligation under Article XX of the GATT 1944: namely that Members may not adopt measures that would result in certain effects on the trading system. Under the ordinary meaning of the text, there is sufficient justification for an environmental conservation measure if a conservation purpose justifies a difference in treatment between Members."[164]

Article 31 goes on by stating that the context for the purpose of interpretation shall include the preamble and annex and any subsequent practice in the application of the treaty which establishes the agreement of the parties regarding its interpretation shall be taken into account. Moreover, Article 31(3)(c) requires that when interpreting a treaty, together with the context, there shall be taken into account "any relevant rules of international law applicable in the relations between the parties". This provision provides that, in interpreting a treaty provision, all other international legal obligations that the parties have adhered to must be considered. Put differently, treaties should not be interpreted in a way that is inconsistent with other international legal obligations between the parties.[165]

In addition to the international law on treaty interpretation, other rules of general international law should also be the sources of law applicable to panels and the Appellate Body in dispute proceedings under the DSU.[166] As the panel in *Korea – Government Procurement* noted, the relationship of the WTO Agreement to customary international law is broader than international rules on interpretation. The panel stated that "customary international law applies generally to the economic relations between the WTO members. Such international law applies to the extent that the WTO treaty agreements do not "contract out"

[164] Appellate Body Report, *United States – Import Prohibition of Certain Shrimp and Shrimp Product* (cited as *US -- Shrimp*), WT/DS58/AB/R (12 October 1998), para. 13.

[165] *See* Christine Breining-Kaufmann, The Legal Matrix of Human Rights and Trade Law: State Obligation versus Private Rights and Obligations. In: Thomas Cottier, Joost Pauwelyn, and Elisabeth Bürgi (eds.), *Human Rights and International Trade*, New York: Oxford University Press (2005), pp. 95-136

[166] *See* Lorand Bartels, *Applicable Law in WTO Dispute Settlement Proceedings*, Journal of Trade Law, Vol.35, No.3 (2001), pp. 499-519.

from it".[167] In the footnote, the panel further emphasized the application of international law to the WTO:

> "We should also note that we can see no basis here for an *a contrario* implication that rules of international law other than rules of interpretation do not apply. The language of 3.2 in this regard applies to a specific problem that had arisen under the GATT to the effect that, among other things, reliance on negotiating history was being utilized in a manner arguably inconsistent with the requirements of the rules of treaty interpretation of customary international law." [168]

The rules of general international law consist of norms binding all members of the international community, and these rules are not applicable only to the extent that a treaty, the WTO Agreement, has contracted them out. Indeed, declining the application of general international law, including general principles of law such as good faith or the principle of proportionality, would seem to contradict the nature of the WTO Agreement as an international treaty.[169]

A more debatable issue is whether other international agreements, which are not referred in the WTO covered agreements, can also qualify as the applicable law before the WTO adjudicating bodies. The last sentence of Article 3.2 and Article 19.2 of the DSU explicitly state that restrictions on the application of other sources of law in any given case "in their findings and recommendations, the panel and Appellate Body cannot add or diminish the rights and obligations provided in the covered agreements".[170] Consequently, some commentators argue that WTO applicable law is constituted by the covered agreements and legal instruments adopted pursuant to the covered agreements. Joel Trachtman considered that "the mandate to WTO dispute resolution panels, to the Appellate Body, and to the Dispute Settlement Body is clear: apply (directly) only

[167] The Panel Report, *Korea – Measures Affecting Government Procurement* (cited as *Korea Government Procurement*), WT/DS163/R (adopted 1 May 2000), para. 7.96. The panel stated:

> Customary international law applies generally to the economic relations between the WTO Members. Such international law applies to the extent that the WTO treaty agreements do not "contract out" from it. To put it another way, to the extent there is no conflict or inconsistency, or an expression in a covered WTO agreement that implies differently, we are of the view that the customary rules of international law apply to the WTO treaties and to the process of treaty formation under the WTO.

[168] Ibid., para. 7.96, n. 753.

[169] *See* Isabelle Van Damme, *Treaty Interpretation by the WTO Appellate Body*, The European Journal of International Law Vol.21, No.3 (2010), pp. 605-648 (619).

[170] Article 19.2 of the DSU.

WTO law".[171] By referring to the DSU Article 3.2 and Article 19.2[172], Gabrielle Marceau suggested that "the application (or direct effect) of non-WTO provisions into the WTO legal system will always lead to an addition to or diminution of the covered agreements".[173] Marceau further argued that, however, a good faith interpretation will resolve most of the conflicts since it requires panels and the Appellate Body to consider various general principles of law and the relevant treaties when interpreting WTO provisions.[174]

The most prominent proponent of the alternative approach is Joost Pauwelyn. He claimed that the limitation on the substantive jurisdiction of WTO panels does not imply the same limitation on the applicable law available to the adjudicating bodies. A panel must take into account other rules of international law and "it is on the basis of this entire universe of legal norms applicable to the case at hand that the validity of a WTO claim must be assessed".[175] Pauwelyn suggested that panels should be able to apply rules of international law beyond the four corners of WTO rules, since, with reference to Article 11 of the DSU, failure to contemplate these other rules would preclude an "objective assessment of the applicability of the relevant covered agreements".[176] From his point of view, when a conflict arises, and if the relevant conflict rule demonstrates that the other rule overrides the WTO rule, the other rule must prevail.

While the applicability of international law to the WTO system as yet remains controversial, a number of the WTO disputes involving non-trade issues might shed some light.[177] In each of the cases, other international legal norms

---

[171] *See* Joel Trachtman, *The Domain of WTO Dispute Resolution*, Harvard International Law Journal, Vol.40 (1999), pp. 333-370. (Trachtman states that the explicit language in the DSU would be absurd if rights and obligations arising from other international law could be applied by the DSB and that with so much specific reference to the covered agreements as the law applicable to WTO dispute resolution, it would be odd if the members intended non-WTO law to be applicable.).

[172] DSU Article 19.2: In accordance with paragraph 2 of Article 3, in their findings and recommendations, the panel and Appellate Body Cannot add to or diminish the rights and obligations provided in the covered agreements.

[173] Gabrielle Marceau, *WTO Dispute Settlement and Human Rights*, European Journal of International Law Vol.13, No.4 (2002), pp. 753-814 (777).

[174] Ibid., p. 778.

[175] *See* Joost Pauwelyn, *Conflict of Norms in Public International: How WTO Law Relates to Other Rules of International Law*, Cambridge University Press (2003), pp. 117-118.

[176] Ibid., pp. 468-469.

[177] Eg. The Panel Report, *Thailand – Restrictions on Importation of and Internal Taxes on Cigarettes*, DS10/R-37S/200 (7 November 1990); The Panel Report, *Korea – Measures Affecting Imports of Fresh, Chilled and Frozen Beef*, WT/DS161-169/R, (10

and standards frequently played significant roles in the interpretation of WTO provisions and are applied in the course of legal reasoning. That is to say, on the one hand, in the event of a genuine conflict between the WTO Agreement and other sources of law, the WTO provisions shall not be overridden. On the other hand, as shown in the following section, a dynamic interpretative mechanism can create the potential of an interplay between the WTO law and other international law in a dispute settlement proceeding.

b. Consideration of Human Rights in WTO Law through Treaty Interpretation

As previously discussed, the defined domain of the WTO does not imply that the framework of the WTO is a sealed system, isolated from other general international law and human rights standards.[178] One should not confuse the jurisdiction of a tribunal with the law applicable in a given dispute. In the very first case, the Appellate Body explicitly stated that the WTO system cannot be construed in 'clinical isolation' of the widespread sources of public international law.[179] In several WTO cases, panels and the Appellate Body used rules of international law to interpret and clarify the meaning of the provisions of WTO law when public health[180] or environmental[181] concerns are at issue. In each of the cases, the non-trade rules have never been considered as a free-standing defense against claims of WTO violations but have been interpreted through relevant WTO provisions.[182]

January 2001); The Appellate Body Report, *European Communities – Measures Affecting the Importation of Certain Poultry Products*, WT/DS69/AB/R (23 July 1998).

[178] *See* Gabrielle Marceau, *WTO Dispute Settlement and Human Rights*, European Journal of International Law Vol.13, No.4 (2002), pp. 753-814 (779).

[179] Appellate Body Report, *United States – Standards for Reformulated and Conventional Gasoline* (cited as *US -- Gasoline*), WT/DS2/9 (20 May 1996), para. 16.

[180] The Panel Report, *Thailand – Restrictions on Importation of and Internal Taxes on Cigarettes* (cited as *Thailand -- Cigarettes*), DS10/R-37s/200, (7 November 1990); The Appellate Body Report, *EC – Measures Affecting Asbestos and Asbestos-containing Products* (cited as *EC – Asbestos*), WT/DS135/AB/R (12 March 2001).

[181] Appellate Body Report, *United States – Import Prohibition of Certain Shrimp and Shrimp Product* (cited as *US -- Shrimp*), WT/DS58/AB/R (12 October 1998).

[182] Appellate Body Report, *European Communities – Regime for the Importation, sale and distribution on bananas* (cited as *EC -- Bananas III*), WT/DS27/AB/R (25/September/1997). In *EC – Bananas III*, the panel and Appellate Body referred to the Lome' Convention 'only to the extent necessary to interpret the WTO provisions'. (para. 162). Panel Report, *Korea – Measures Affecting Imports of Fresh, Chilled and Frozen Beef* (cited as *Korea -- Beef*), WT/DS161/R WT/DS169/R (31 July 2000). In the case, the panel examined various bilateral agreements between Korea and the disputing

Therefore, to set the foundation of interpreting WTO provisions in the light of existing human rights law, the last section of Chapter 1 illustrates how a panel could refer to the international legal norms outside the WTO in the process of treaty interpretation. The first to be addressed is the non-discrimination provisions of the GATT and the GATS. The fundamental principle of non-discrimination rules of the WTO is that 'like' goods and services cannot be treated differently. What is the definition of like goods and services when referring to human rights-related trade measures? Can human rights be claimed by a Member as a defense to justify its WTO violation on the basis of the production or process methods (PPMs)? The second approach is how to apply or interpret human rights-related restrictive measures under the general exceptions clause of Article XX of the GATT and Article XIV of the GATS. The general exceptions clauses provide a mechanism for raising non-trade issues within the WTO and allow a Member State to deviate from its obligations to pursue legitimate aims or protect vital social values. Thus, the general exceptions by which human rights issues can be raised under the framework of the WTO[183] are potentially valuable.

i. 'Likeness' and Human Rights Trade Related-Measures in the Context of Non-discrimination Provisions under the WTO

Non-discrimination is a key concept in WTO law and policy. Two central non-discrimination principles of the WTO are the most-favoured-nation (MFN) and the national treatment obligation. The MFN obligation requires each WTO Member to adapt to every other Member State the most favourable treatment that is granted to any other country concerning the import and export of 'like' goods, services, and service suppliers.[184] For trade in goods, the uneven application of customs duties and other trade taxes are the most common form of discriminatory treatments that the MFN intends to avoid. For trade in services, the forms of applicable discriminatory measures tend to be much wider as a substantial amount of trade in services occurs inside a country rather than at the border. Therefore, Article II of the GATS is wide in the scope and applies to

---

parties for the sole purpose of interpreting an ambiguous WTO provision (paras. 539 et seq.)

[183] *See* in general Robert Howse and Makau Mutua, *Protecting Human Rights in a Global Economy: Challenges for the World Trade Organization*, International Centre for Human Rights and Democratic Development (April 2000).

[184] Article I of the GATT & Aricle II of the GATS.

"any measure covered by this Agreement", which includes regulations taken by the governments.[185]

The principle of non-discrimination in the form of national treatment deals with the competition between domestic and foreign goods, services, and service suppliers. National treatment obligation requires each WTO Member State to treat foreign goods, services and, service suppliers no less favourable than "like" domestic goods, services, and service suppliers once they cross the border. For trade in goods, national treatment tends to avoid protectionism in the application of internal taxes and regulatory measures. For trade in services, the focus of national treatment is on avoiding discriminatory internal regulations, such as subsidies or qualitative requirements. Consequently, the determination of whether a measure is discriminatory depends on, to some extent, how a panel interprets the terms of 'like goods' and 'like services'.[186] The broader the concept of 'like goods' and 'like services' is, the wider the scope of the non-discrimination provisions could be applied.

From the human rights standing, if the assessment of 'likeness' and 'less favourable treatment' is not confined in the economic framework, the differentiation made between the foreign and domestic products with regard to human rights protections might be justified on the basis of regulatory purposes. For example, do WTO non-discrimination provisions allow different treatment between imported and domestic chocolate because one is made by child labor or workers in slave-like situations? Do they allow the differentiation between two diamonds because one diamond is mined by a rebel group which committed serious human rights violations?

In *US – Tuna Dolphin I and II*,[187] a differentiation between tuna caught with dolphin-excluding devices and tuna caught without dolphin protection mechanisms was not recognized by the panel and the Appellate Body. Under the US Marine Mammal Protecting Act (MMPA), US fishermen must use certain fish-

[185] Article II of the GATS regulates the general obligations of Most-Favoured-Nation Treatment. Paragraph 1 of Article GATS Article II regulates:

> 1. With respect to any measure covered by this Agreement, each Member shall accord immediately and unconditionally to services and service suppliers of any other Member treatment no less favourable than that it accords to like services and service suppliers of any other country.

[186] Joost Pauwelyn, Comment: The unbearable lightness of likeness. In: Marion Panizzon, Nicole Pohl and Pierre Sauve (eds.), *GATS and the Regulation of International Trade in Services*, Cambridge: Cambridge University Press, pp. 358-369.

[187] Panel Report, *United States – Restrictions on Imports of Tuna* (cited as *US – Tuna I*), DS21/R (3 September 1991); and Panel Report, *United States – Restriction on Imports of Tuna* (cited as *US –Tuna II*), DS/29/R (16 June 1994).

ing techniques so as not to exceed an incidental taking of 10,000 dolphins per year. At the same time, for the imports of tuna to be allowed into the US market, the country of the origin must demonstrate that it has a regulatory regime in place regarding the taking of marine mammals that is comparable to that of the US vessels. Mexico challenged that the US import ban on tuna violated Article III:4 of the GATT as an internal regulation. For the purpose of GATT obligations, both panels decided that tuna caught in a dolphin-safe way could not be distinguished from other tuna. In *US – Tuna Dolphin I*, the panel stated:

> "5.10 The Panel noted that the United States had claimed that the direct import embargo on certain yellowfin tuna and certain yellowfin tuna products of Mexico constituted an enforcement at the time or point of importation of the requirements of the MMPA that yellowfin tuna in the ETP be harvested with fishing techniques designed to reduce the incidental taking of dolphins. The MMPA did not regulate tuna products as such, and in particular did not regulate the sale of tuna or tuna products….
> 5.11 The text of Article III:1 refers to the application to imported or domestic products of "law, regulation and requirements affecting the internal sale … of product" and "internal quantitative regulations requiring the mixture, processing or use of the product"; it sets forth the principle that such regulations on products not be applied so as to afford protection to domestic production. Article III:4 refers solely to law, regulations, and requirements affecting the internal sale, etc. of product. … Furthermore, the text of the Note Ad Article[188] III refers to a measure "which applies to an imported product and the like domestic product and is collected or enforced in the case of the imported products at the time or point of importation…"".[189]

The panel concluded that Article III and the Note Ad of GATT covers only the measures that are applied to the product as such. The US MMPA regulations could not be seen as being applied to tuna products as such since "they would not directly regulate the sale of the tuna and could not possibly affect tuna as a

[188] The Norte Ad Article III provides:

> Any internal tax or other internal charge, or any law, regulation or requirement of the kind referred to in Article III:1 which applies to an imported product and the like domestic product and is collected or enforced in the case of the imported product at the time or point of importation, is nevertheless to be regarded as an internal tax or other internal charges, or a law, regulation or requirement of the kind referred to in Article III:1, and is accordingly subject to the provisions of Article III.

[189] Panel Report, *United States – Restrictions on Imports of Tuna* (cited as *US – Tuna I*), DS21/R (3 September 1991), paras. 5.8-5.11.

product".[190] In other words, the panel is of the view that the taking of dolphins incidental to the taking of tuna could not possibly affect tuna as a product. Therefore, in compliance with Article III:4 of the GATT, the US has an obligation to accord treatment to Mexican tuna no less favourable than that accorded to the US tuna, regardless of whether the incidental taking of dolphins by Mexican vessels corresponds to that of the US vessels.

Also, based on the similar reasons, in *US – Shrimp*, measures distinguished between shrimp caught with a 'turtle excluder device' (TED) and shrimps caught without a TED were considered by the Appellate Body as measures differentiate between like shrimp products.[191] From the cases above, it might be seen that WTO jurisprudence suggested that when there is no physically evident difference in the final products, a WTO Member is obligated to treat foreign products no less favourable than domestic products regardless the method of which the product is processed or produced. Nevertheless, this strict interpretation of the 'likeness' was partly loosened later in the *EC – Asbestos* case.

In 1996, the French government enacted a decree banning the manufacture, sale, and importation of all variety of asbestos, as well as products containing asbestos (such as cement-based products containing asbestos to be used in construction). France justified the ban as a regulation to protect both workers and consumers against the risk of cancer. Canada is a major producer and exporter of chrysotile asbestos and challenged the French asbestos ban as a national treatment violation under Article: III of the GATT.

In order to examine the term 'likeness', the panel adopted an approach based on the Report of the Working Party on Border Tax Adjustment[192] and employed four general criteria in analyzing the meaning of 'likeness', including the properties, nature, and quality of the products; the end-use of the products; consumers' tastes and habits; and the tariff classification of the products.[193] The Panel

---

[190] Panel Report, *United States – Restrictions on Imports of Tuna* (cited as *US – Tuna I*), DS21/R (3 September 1991), para. 5.14.

[191] Panel Report, *United States – Import Prohibition of Certain Shrimp and Shrimp Product* (cited as *US -- Shrimp*), WT/DS58/R (15 May 1998); and Appellate Body Report, *United States – Import Prohibition of Certain Shrimp and Shrimp Product* (cited as *US -- Shrimp*), WT/DS58/AB/R (12 October 1998).

[192] General Agreement on Tariffs and Trade, *Report by the Working Party on Border Tax Adjustments*, L/3465 (20 November 1970), para. 18.

[193] 1970s, a GATT Working Party listed the basic factors which should be used when determining similar products. These criteria include "the product's end-users in a given market; consumers' tastes and habits, which change from country to country, and the product's properties, nature, and quality". In the 1980s, the panel on Japanese liquor taxes added another criterion, namely uniform classification in tariff nomenclatures.

found that chrysotile asbestos fibers and other fibers that can be substituted for asbestos fibers (in particular, polyvinyl alcohol fibers, cellulose and glass fibers, collectively referred to as PCG fibers) are 'like products'.[194] The panel concluded that by banning the importation of Canadian asbestos fibers while permitting the sale of French PCG fibers, France accorded less favourable treatment to imports as compared to like domestic products, and the measure at issue is in violation of Article III: 4.[195] On appeal, however, the Appellate Body reversed the panel's finding that the consideration of health effects could not be taken into account in the analysis of whether two products are "like" under Article III: 4 of the GATT.[196]

By finding that the panel was not erred in applying the Working Party Report, the Appellate Body further analyzed the case in three separate parts: elaborating the meaning of the term 'like products'; findings of error of law by the panel; and completing the analysis. First, when outlining the general approach to the interpretation of Article III: 4, the Appellate Body placed the emphasis on Article III: 1 of the GATT as a general-purpose provision which animates Article III as a whole and stated the purpose of the Article III is to provide "equality of competitive conditions for imported products in relation to domestic products".[197]

The Appellate Body concluded that "a determination of likeness under Article III: 4 is, fundamentally, a determination about the nature and extent of a competitive relationship between and among products".[198] The Appellate Body indicated that once a competitive relationship has been established with the degree and kind relevant to Article III: 4, the second element, namely "less fa-

---

[194] Panel Report, *European Communities – Measures Affecting Asbestos and Asbestos-containing Products* (cited as *EC – Asbestos*), WT/DS135/R (18 September 2000), paras. 8.147-8.150. When considering whether the 'health risk' criterion could be used to determine the 'like products', the panel stated:

> 8.149 We consider, moreover, that one of the EC's main arguments against the likeness between fibro-cement and chrysotile-cement products with respect to their properties, nature and quality and their end-use is based on the risk associated with the chrysotile which they contain. To the extent that in paragraph 8.132 we concluded that the "risk" criterion cannot be included among the criteria applicable to the determination of likeness under Article III:4.

[195] Ibid., paras. 8.151-8.158.

[196] Appellate Body Report, *European Communities – Measures Affecting Asbestos and Asbestos-Containing Products* (cited as *EC -- Asbestos*), WT/DS135/AB/R (5 April 2001).

[197] Appellate Body Report, *European Communities – Measures Affecting Asbestos and Asbestos-Containing Products* (cited as *EC -- Asbestos*), WT/DS135/AB/R (5 April 2001), para. 97-98.

[198] Ibid., para. 99.

vourable treatment" needs to be examined. As the Appellate Body noted, even if the two products are alike, it does not mean that a measure violates Article III: 4. Instead, a complaining Member must further prove that the measure at issue treats the group of like imported products less favourable than it accords to the group of like domestic products.[199] In other words, less favourable treatment represents the concept of anti-protectionism incorporated and a judgment of which implies a conclusion of protection.[200]

Second, the Appellate Body pointed out that the panel failed to weigh all of the evidence in making an overall determination of whether the products at issue could be characterized as 'like' products. According to the Appellate Body, the panel erred in entwining physical properties with the examination of end-uses and in concluding that health effects are irrelevant in analyzing the 'likeness' under Article III: 4. The Appellate Body disagreed with the panel that considering evidence relating to the health risks associated with a product would nullify the effect of general exception clause under Article XX(b) of the GATT.[201]

In addition, the panel also failed to consider all the evidence relating to consumer tastes and habits. The Appellate Body came closer to taking the judicial notice of human health as a fundamental concern when considering consumer tastes and habits. The Appellate Body considered that the test from the perspective of consumer tastes and habits is whether the products would be substitutable and in a competitive relationship in an idealized marketplace, in where consumers have full information, and where, at least through tort liability, negative externalities have already to some extent been internalized. The Appellate Body stated:

> "If the risks posed by a particular product are sufficiently great, the ultimate consumer may simply cease to buy that product. This would, undoubtedly, affect a manufacturer's decisions in the marketplace. Moreover,

---

[199] Ibid., para.100. The Appellate Body stated:

Thus, even if two products are "like", that does not mean that a measure is inconsistent with Article III:4. A complaining Member must still establish that the measure accords to the group of "like" *imported* products "less favourable treatment" than it accords to the group of "like" *domestic* products.

[200] Robert Howe and Elisabeth Tuerk, The WTO Impact on Internal Regulations – A Case Study of the Canada – EC Asbestos Dispute. In de Burca, G. and Scott, J. (ends), *the EU and the WTO: Legal and Constitutional Issues*, Oxford: Hart Publishing (2001), pp. 283-328.

[201] Appellate Body Report, *European Communities – Measures Affecting Asbestos and Asbestos-Containing Products* (cited as *EC -- Asbestos*), WT/DS135/AB/R (5 April 2001), paras. 111-118.

> in the case of products posing risks to human rights health, we think it likely that manufacturers' decisions will be influenced by other factors, such as the potential civil liability that might flow from marketing products posing a health risk to the ultimate consumer, or the additional cost associated with safety procedures required to use such products in a manufacturing process."[202]

Third, the Appellate Body completed the analysis of national treatment by applying the legal interpretation of Article III: 4 to correspond to the facts. The Appellate Body first considered the physical characteristics of Chrysotile fibres and PCG fibres and concluded that asbestos and substitutes are physically 'very different' because of the health significance of the disputed products at issue. Due to the very different physical characteristics, therefore, the Appellate Body suggested that Canada should bear a high burden to demonstrate that the products at issue are in a sufficiently close competitive relationship. The Appellate Body concluded that Canada presented *no* evidence on consumers' tastes and habit regarding chrysotile asbestos and PCG fibres.[203]

By reading the Appellate Body's opinion in *EC – Asbestos*, the decision that the chrysotile asbestos and PCG fibres are not 'like' products due to the 'very different physical characteristics and consumer perceptions' might open the door to incorporate human rights concerns within the WTO legal system through the notion of 'like products'.[204] The understanding of the Appellate Body was to apply the fundamental human health and interests at stake, not through examining the purpose of the regulation, but rather through analyzing the competitive relationship between the products at issue in the marketplace.[205] Although this decision still focused on physical attributes instead of on the protection of human life and health, it loosed the strict interpretations of 'like' products compared to the previous adjudicating bodies, which emphasized only the 'final product' itself when determining the 'likeness'.

It is interesting to mention that this approach did not satisfy one member of the Appellate Body division who suggested that the determination of "like products" should take into account issues beyond economic considerations. In a

---

[202] Ibid., para. 122.

[203] Ibid., paras. 136-139.

[204] *See* Adam McBeth, *International Economic Actors and Human Rights*, Oxford: Routledge (2010), p. 128.

[205] Robert Howe and Elisabeth Tuerk, The WTO Impact on Internal Regulations – A Case Study of the Canada – EC Asbestos Dispute. In de Burca, G. and Scott, J. (ends), *the EU and the WTO: Legal and Constitutional Issues*, Oxford: Hart Publishing (2001), pp. 283-328.

concurring opinion, the member stated that "the necessity or appropriateness of adopting a fundamentally economic interpretation of the likeness of products under Article III: 4 of the GATT 1994 does not appear to me to be free from substantial doubt".[206] This opinion might broaden the possibilities that products can be differentiated by reference to non-economic considerations; however, this could also be an open door for protectionist measures hidden by the environmental, social, human rights, or other conditions imposed on the importation of goods.

Additionally, the Appellate Body has made significant statements on the terms of less favourable treatment for future legal standings of human rights-related trade measures. According to the Appellate Body, although Article III:4 does not include the same separate condition in Article III: 1 which requires the measure is applied "so as to afford protection", showing a differential treatment between "like products" is not sufficient to establish a violation under Article III: 4. In *Korea – Beef*,[207] the Appellate Body held that countries' regulations might formally discriminate between imported and domestic products. Those regulations, however, must not modify the conditions of competition in the relevant market to the disadvantage of the imported products.[208] In *EC – Asbestos*, the Appellate Body explained that a mere finding of likeness between the two products does not oblige the defendant Member to treat them identically in regulations. The complaining Member must also demonstrate that the differences in regulations amount to 'less favourable' treatment as between domestic and imported like products, each taken as a group. The Appellate Body further addressed that the meaning of less favourable treatment must be informed by the general principle in Article III: 1, namely, anti–protectionism.[209]

This interpretation might provide a room for justifying a PPMs argument under the national treatment obligation. In other words, in situations where the regulatory distinction is based on the PPMs, even if the products are found to be alike, the regulatory differentiation may still survive if it does not constitute less

---

[206] Appellate Body Report, *European Communities – Measures Affecting Asbestos and Asbestos-Containing Products* (cited as *EC -- Asbestos*), WT/DS135/AB/R (5 April 2001), para. 154.

[207] Appellate Body Report, *Korea – Measures Affecting Imports of Fresh, Chilled and Frozen Beef* (cited as *Korea -- Beef*), WT/DS161/AB/R WT/DS169/AB/R (11 December 2000).

[208] Ibid., para. 144.

[209] Robert Howe and Elisabeth Tuerk, The WTO Impact on Internal Regulations – A Case Study of the Canada – EC Asbestos Dispute. In de Burca, G. and Scott, J. (ends), *the EU and the WTO: Legal and Constitutional Issues*, Oxford: Hart Publishing (2001), pp. 283-328.

favourable treatment of imported products than domestic products. That is to say, the finding of 'likeness' based on the economic framework is not necessarily decisive for the application of Article III:4 if the measure at issue is non-protectionist.

Later in *Dominican Republic – Cigarettes*,[210] the Appellate Body went one step further. In the case, the measure clearly had an adverse impact or effect on the group of imported cigarettes as opposed to the group of domestic cigarettes. On a per-cigarette basis, the bond of five million pesos to be paid by both importers and domestic producers of cigarettes imposed a higher burden on an imported cigarette than a domestic cigarette since importers sold fewer cigarettes in comparison with domestic producers. The Appellate Body stated that this disparate effect on imports was not enough to find a violation of Article III: 4 of the GATT 1994 if the detrimental effect is explained by factors unrelated to the 'foreign origin' of the product.[211]

The Appellate Body's interpretation of 'less favourable treatment' seems to indicate that a measure has a more detrimental effect on imports as opposed to like domestic products is not necessarily in violation of the national treatment obligation if the measure is intended to pursue a legitimate regulatory purpose. A non-protectionism approach might illustrate that the measure does not accord less favourable treatment to imports.[212] The complainant must demonstrate that the detrimental effects are related to the foreign origin of the products.

This approach may arguable reintroduce the 'aim and effect' test as being relevant under Article III:4. The 'aim and effect' test considers whether the regulatory distinction between foreign and domestic products is based on a non-protectionist regulatory purpose, such as for the protection of human rights. To ease the rigor of Article III:4 with regard to origin-neutral regulatory measures would provide a WTO Member an opportunity to pursue legitimate policy objectives. However, this test has been subsequently rejected by the WTO dispute settlement bodies in *Japan – Alcoholic Beverages*[213]. From the human rights

---

[210] Appellate Body Report, Dominican Republic – Measures Affecting the Importation and Internal Sale of Cigarettes (cited as *Dominican Republic -- Cigarettes*), WT/DS302/AB/R (25 April 2005).

[211] Ibid., para. 96.

[212] *See* Andrew Guzman, Joost Pauwelyn and Robert W. Hillman, *International Trade Law*, Aspen Publisher (2009), pp. 275ff.

[213] In *Japan – Alcoholic Beverages II*, both the panel and the Appellate Body rejected the application of 'aim and effect' test when considering a claim of GATT Article III:2 violation. The panel noted: "it would be a difficult exercise to determine which aim or aims should be determinative for applying the aim-and-effect test."

perspective, the 'aim and effect' test would seem to be preferable over a market criteria approach since it would allow a broader range of human rights measures to be accepted as non-discrimination within the meaning of Article III:4 of the GATT.

In sum, the non-discrimination provisions of the WTO agreements do have the potential to allow the differential treatment of products or services on the condition of human rights considerations. However, from all the case reviews illustrated above, one can see that the interpretation of 'like products' or 'less favourable treatment' from the WTO adjudicating bodies is complex and determined on a case-by-case basis. For example, in the more recent *EC – Seal Products* casae,[214] the Appellate Body went back to the strictly interpretative approach and ruled out the possibility of the regulatory distinction. The Appellate Body concluded that if the contested measure has a detrimental impact on the conditions of competition for "like" imported products, such detrimental impact will amount to treatment that is 'less favourable' within the meaning of Article III:4.[215] Due to the legal uncertainty, WTO Members often resort to the general exception clauses under Article XX of the GATT (or Article XIV of the GATS) to justify the breach of substantive obligations of the WTO agreements.

ii. Interpretation of the General Exceptions Clause with Human Rights Norms under GATT Article XX and GATS Article XIV

General exceptions clauses under the WTO provide mechanisms allowing the Member States to deviate from their GATT/GATS obligations to pursue non-trade but substantial state interests and objectives.[216] They recognized "the im-

(Panel Report, *Japan – Taxes on Alcoholic Beverages* (cited as *Japan – Alcoholic Beverage II*), WT/DS8/R & WT/DS10/R & WT/DS11/R (11/July/1996), para. 6.16.)

[214] Appellate Body Report, *European Communities – Measures Prohibiting the Importation and Marketing of Seal Products* (cited as *EC – Seal Products*), WT/DS 400/AB/R & WT/DS 401/AB/R (22 May 2014).

[215] Ibid., paras. 5.116-117. The Appellate Body stated:

> ..., the term "treatment no less favourable" in Article III:4 requires effective equality of opportunities for imported products to compete with like domestic products....If the outcome of this assessment is that the measure has a detrimental impact on the conditions of competition for like imported products, then such detrimental impact will amount to treatment that is "less favourable" within the meaning of Article III:4.

[216] There are three of the WTO agreements containing general exceptions clauses, including: Agreement on Government Procurement (AGP), Article XXIII. The Agreement on Trade-Related Aspects of Intellectual Property Rights also contains a general exception-type clause relating to the granting of patents. Article XX GATT and Article

portance of a sovereign nation being able to act to promote the purposes on the list of exceptions, even when such action otherwise conflicts with various obligations relating to international trade".[217] While none of the exceptions explicitly relate to human rights *per se*, some of the provisions might provide a legal standing for human rights considerations to be raised within the WTO. Three possible exceptions appear to have the potential to be used for a broader range of the human rights concerns. The exception clauses that might form the basis of the current analysis are the exception, allowing states to take measures for the protection of public morals or public orders; the exception allowing measures for protecting human, animal, or plant life or health; and the exception justifying measures for conserving exhaustible natural resources.

The general exceptions clauses, however, should not be interpreted as allowing governments the rights to take any domestic decisions which might affect the sovereignty of other Member States since the exceptions could then be invoked to nullify any WTO obligations at will.[218] Nor does it seem that the general exceptions clauses can be invoked to support any welfare-related domestic regulations since the clauses are exhaustible in the context of the permissible exceptions. Thus, it is necessary to undertake an assessment of the nature of the provisions and an assessment of how to interpret them to incorporate human rights norms and standards into the international economic system.

In order to keep up with the WTO principles, exceptions to treaty provisions are in general strictly interpreted by the WTO adjudicating bodies. The strict interpretation led to the critiques that the WTO fails to respect other crucial social values.[219] To qualify an exception, a measure must satisfy the two-tier (three elements) test: the specific exception and the chapeau. In *US – Gasoline*, the panel stated:

> "The Panel noted that as the party invoking an exception the United States bore the burden of proof in demonstrating that the inconsistent measures

---

XIV GATS will be emphasized here in the scope of this paper when referring to the human rights restrictive measures adopted by Member States.

[217] John H, Jackson, *The World Trading System: Law and Policy of International Economic Relations*, Cambridge, MIT Press (1997), p. 233.

[218] *See* C. McCrudden, *International Economic Law and the Pursuit of Human Rights: A Framework for Discussion of the Legality of 'Selective Purchasing' Laws under the WTO Government Procurement Agreement*, Journal of International Economic Law, Vol.2, Issue:1 (March 1999), pp. 3-48 (17).

[219] Gudrun Zagel, *The WTO and Trade-Related Human Rights Measures: Trade Sanctions vs. Trade Incentives*, Austrian Review of International and European Law, Vol.9 (2004), pp. 119-153.

> came within its scope. The Panel observed that the United States therefore had to establish the following elements:
> (1) that the *policy* in respect of the measures for which the provision was invoked fell within the range of policies designed to protect human, animal or plant life or health;
> (2) that the inconsistent measures for which the exception was being invoked were *necessary* to fulfill the policy objective; and
> (3) that the measures were to be applied in conformity with the requirements of the *introductory clause* of Article XX.
> In order to justify the application of Article XX(b), all the above elements had to be satisfied."[220]

To justify a human rights-related trade measure, therefore, three elements need to be satisfied. First, the contested measure must fall within the range of the policies designed to pursue the relevant end. Second, the measure must be necessary to achieve the designed goal. Finally, the measure must satisfy the chapeau of Article XX. Each of the elements will be illustrated to perceive how the WTO adjudicating bodies interpret the general exceptions criteria and the extent to which human rights can be used as a defense against the WTO illegality.

Specific Exceptions Under the General Exceptions Clause of the WTO

Both Article XX (a) of the GATT and Article XIV (a) of the GATS allow a WTO Member to exempt from its substantive obligations for protecting public morals. However, the concept of the public morals exception is relatively broad. Charnovitz argued that "the range of policies covered by Article XX(a) would seemingly, at least, include slavery, weapons, narcotics, liquor, pornography, religion, compulsory labor, and animal welfare".[221] Besides, there is little indication from the preparatory documents to the treaties to assist in clarifying the meaning of the term. Nevertheless, according to the Vienna Convention Article 31(1), a dictionary explanation will be the first choice to interpret the 'ordinary meaning' to the terms of the treaty. The Shorter Oxford English Dictionary defines 'public' as "of or pertaining to the people as a whole; belonging to, af-

[220] Panel Report, *United States – Standards for Reformulated and Conventional Gasoline* (cited as *US -- Gasoline*), WT/DS2/R (29 January 1996), para. 6.20

[221] *See* Steve Charnovitz, *The Moral Exception in Trade Policy*, Virginia Journal of International Law, Vol.38 (Summer 1998), p. 689-716 (709).

fecting, or concerning the community or nation".[222] It further describes 'morals' as "habits of life with regard to right and wrong conduct".[223] Webster's New International Dictionary gives 'moral' a definition as "conforming to a standard of what is good and right".[224] Still, expansive room has been left for the definition of the meaning of 'public morals'.

In *US – Gambling* the panel explained that the concept of public morals is generally a very flexible one and the content of which "can vary in time and space, depending upon a range of factors, including prevailing social, cultural, ethical, and religious values".[225] The panel further interpreted the term 'public morals' as denoting "standards of right and wrong conduct maintained by or on behalf of a community or nation"[226], and the notion of public order refers to "the preservation of the fundamental interests of a society, as reflected in public policy and law".[227] Although the panel stressed 'public morals' and 'public order' are two distinct concepts, it recognized that they protect largely similar values and thus some overlap might exist.[228]

From the definition given by the panel, one could argue that the norms and principles of contemporary human rights should be understood within the scope of 'standards of right and wrong conduct maintained by or on behalf of a community or nation'. It is necessary for panels and the Appellate Body to take a dynamic interpretation of the meaning of public morals to ensure the protection of international human rights when various interests are at stake. As Professor Howse argued:

> "In the modern world, the very idea of public morality has become inseparable from the concept of human personhood, dignity and capacity reflected in the fundamental rights. A conception of public morals or morality that excluded notions of fundamental rights would simply be contrary to the ordinary contemporary meaning of the concept."[229]

---

[222] The Shorter Oxford English Dictionary, Fifth Edition, Oxford University Press (2002).
[223] Ibid.
[224] Webster' New International Dictionary of the English Language (1946).
[225] Panel Report, *United States – Measures Affecting the Cross-Border Supply of Gambling and Betting Services* (cited as *US – Gambling*), WT/DS285/R (10 November 2004), para. 6.461.
[226] Ibid., para. 6.465.
[227] Ibid., para. 6.457.
[228] Ibid., para. 6.468.
[229] Robert Howse, *Back to the Court After Shrimp/Turtle? Almost but not Quite Yet: India's Short Lived Challenge to Labor and Environment Exceptions in the European's*

Furthermore, Article XX (b) of the GATT and Article XIV (b) of the GATS are the general exceptions clauses which permit the WTO Member States to adopt restrictive trade measures to protect human, animal, or plant life or health. Although none of the provisions directly indicate human rights protection, the WTO case law reveals the possibility to interpret the terms in the light of existing human rights obligations, especially with reference to the adequate standard of health (Article 12 ICESCR) and the right to life (Article 6 ICCPR). In *Thailand – Cigarettes*, the panel held that the ban on cigarette imports was not justified under Article XX (b) because there were other effective means of achieving such a policy objective.[230] However, the panel also stated that "smoking constituted a serious risk to human health and that consequently measures designed to reduce the consumption of cigarettes fell within the scope of Article XX (b). The Panel noted that this provision clearly allowed contracting parties to give priority to human health over trade liberalization; however, for a measure to be covered by Article XX (b) it had to be 'necessary'".[231]

Another example concerning Article XX (b) of the GATT is the *EC – Asbestos*[232] case. Canada claimed that France's asbestos ban violated Article III:4 of the GATT and the panel stated that although the ban constituted a violation, it was justified under Article XX (b) to protect human life and health. The Appellate Body further reinforced the panel's decision by stating that "we note that it is undisputed that WTO Members have the right to determine the level of protection of health that they consider appropriate in a given situation".[233] These cases give rise to the presumption that a WTO Member has broad discretion in taking measures to protect the life or health of their own people, as long as these measures are necessary to achieve the pursuing end.

Lastly, Article XX (g) of the GATT permits a Member State to adopt measures for the safeguard of exhaustible natural resources. Similarly, the provision is not directly designed for human rights protections. Rather, it concerns measures that protect environmental purposes. Nevertheless, the Article XX (g) cases are relevant to the extent that environmental measures can be necessary to

---

Union's Generalized System of Preferences, American University International Law Review, Vol.18, Issue:6 (2003), pp. 1333-1381 (1368).

[230] Panel Report, *Thailand – Restrictions on Importation of and Internal Taxes on Cigarettes* (cited as *Thailand -- Cigarettes*), DS10/R-37s/200, (7 November 1990), paras. 77-81

[231] Ibid., para. 73.

[232] Appellate Body Report, *European Communities – Measures Affecting Asbestos and Asbestos-Containing Products* (cited as *EC -- Asbestos*), WT/DS135/AB/R (5/April/2001).

[233] Ibid., para. 168.

protect human health as well as the rights to food and water.[234] In *US – Shrimp*, the panel and the Appellate Body adopted an evolutionary approach to treaty interpretation and referred to a number of non-WTO sources of international law to ascertain the meaning of terms under Article XX(g).[235] For example, the Appellate Body applied the Convention on International Trade in Endangered Species (CITES) as well as other multilateral environmental agreements as a means of interpreting the term 'exhaustible natural resources'.[236] Most of the treaties are not ratified by all WTO Member States. It could be indicated that the WTO Agreement should be interpreted in the light of other relevant and applicable rules of international law, including human rights law. In this context, it would be possible to interpret WTO provisions in a way that allows and encourages the WTO Members to respect all their obligations under international law.

Necessity Requirements

The public morals and health exceptions are permissible only if they are deemed to be necessary to achieve the respective purposes. In *Thailand – Cigarettes*, the panel set a restrictive test for the 'necessity' requirements and considered that a measure is justified as 'necessary' only when there are no available alternative measures that could be reasonably applied to achieve the desired end.[237] However, the panel and the Appellate Body in *Korea – Beef* modified the restrictive approach and adopted a weighing and balancing test, which is followed by the panels in numerous cases.

In *Korea – Beef*, the Appellate Body underscored that "the word necessary is not limited to which is indispensable or of absolute necessity or inevitable"[238]. The assessment of the necessity needs to take into account the relative im-

[234] UN Committee on Economic, *Social and Cultural Rights, General Comment No 14: The Right to the Highest Attainable Standard of Health (Article 12 of the Covenant)*, UN doc. E/C.12/2000/4 (11 August 2000), para. 15.

[235] Appellate Body Report, *United States – Import Prohibition of Certain Shrimp and Shrimp Product* (cited as *US -- Shrimp*), WT/DS58/AB/R (12 October 1998), paras. 129-130.

[236] Ibid., paras. 131-133.

[237] Panel Report, *Thailand – Restrictions on Importation of and Internal Taxes on Cigarettes* (cited as *Thailand -- Cigarettes*), DS10/R-37s/200, (7 November 1990), paras. 74-81.

[238] Appellate Body Report, *Korea – Measures Affecting Imports of Fresh, Chilled and Frozen Beef* (cited as *Korea -- Beef*), WT/DS161/AB/R & WT/DS169/AB/R (11 December 2000), para. 161.

portance of the common interests or values intended to be pursued by a Member State. The Appellate Body emphasized:

> "Measures which are indispensable or of absolute necessity or inevitable to secure compliance certainly fulfill the requirements of Article XX (d). But other measures, too, may fall within the ambit of this exception. As used in Article XX (d), the term necessary refers, in our view, to a range of degrees of necessity. At one end of this continuum lies "necessary" understood as "indispensable"; at the other end, is "necessary" taken to mean as "making a contribution to". We consider that a "necessary" measure is, in this continuum, located significantly closer to the pole of "indispensable" than to the opposite pole of simply "making a contribution to"."[239]

When determining whether a measure is necessary within the meaning of Article XX (d), the Appellate Body explained that the more vital or important the protected values are and the greater the contribution, the easier they would be deemed as necessary.[240] The Appellate Body concluded:

> "In sum, determination of whether a measure, which is not "dispensable", may nevertheless be "necessary" within the contemplation of Article XX (d), involves in every case a process of *weighing and balancing* a series of factors which prominently include the contribution made by the compliance measure to the enforcement of the law or regulation at issue, the importance of the common interests or values protected by that law or regulation, and the accompanying impact the law or regulation on imports or exports." (emphasis added)[241]

The necessity test is confirmed and refined in *EC – Asbestos*. In the case, the EC defended that the restrictive regulation is qualified as a permitted exception to the WTO violations under Article XX (b) of the GATT. The Appellate Body upheld the panel's findings and concluded that there was no "reasonably available alternative" to the prohibition of the French imports ban and, therefore, the French measure was necessary to protect human health within the meaning of Article XX (b). The Appellate Body established that the necessity does not relate to the goal of a measure, but rather the necessity of the means to that end. The Appellate Body also suggested that there might be different levels of scrutiny applicable to the analysis of whether a measure is necessary, which de-

[239] Ibid.
[240] Ibid., paras. 162-163.
[241] Ibid., para. 164.

pends on the importance of the objectives or interests it pursues. The Appellate Body asserted:

> "We indicated in *Korea – Beef* that one aspect of the "weighing and balancing process ... comprehended in the determination of whether a WTO-consistent alternative measure" is reasonably available is the extent to which the alternative measures "contribution to the realization of the end pursued." In addition, we observed, in that case, that "*the more vital or important the common interest or values" pursued, the easier it would be to accept as "necessary" measures designed to achieve those ends.* In this case, the objective pursued by the measure is the preservation of human life and health through the elimination, or reduction, of the well-known, and life-threating, health risks posed by asbestos fibres. *The value pursued is both vital and important to the highest degree.*" (emphasis added)[242]

In *US – Gambling*, the Appellate Body overturned the panel's decision and found that the US measures were necessary to protect public morals and public order within the meaning of Article XIV(a) of the GATS. The panel is of the opinion that the US should have negotiated with Antigua before banning the Internet gambling services. The Appellate Body disagreed with the panel and explained that a comparison between the challenged measure and possible alternatives must be conducted on the basis of the 'weighing and balancing' standard and should take into account the importance of the interests at issue. An alternative measure must not be merely theoretical in nature and should achieve the desired level of protection to the end pursued.[243] The Appellate Body concluded that "consultation was not an appropriate alternative for the Panel to consider because consultations are by definition a process, the results of which are uncertain and therefore not capable of comparison with the measures at issue in this case".[244] As no other alternative measures had been raised, the Appellate Body found that the measures were necessary to protect the US's chosen level of protection for public morality and public order.

In *Brazil – Tyres*, Brazil adopted a ban on the importation of retreaded tires. The European Communities complained that these Brazilian measures violated

---

242 Appellate Body Report, *European Communities – Measures Affecting Asbestos and Asbestos-Containing Products* (cited as *EC -- Asbestos*), WT/DS135/AB/R (5/April/2001), para. 172.

243 Appellate Body Report, *United States – Measures Affecting the Cross-Border Supply of Gambling and Betting Services* (cited as *US – Gambling*), WT/DS285/AB/R (7 April 2005), paras. 307-308.

244 Ibid., para. 317.

a number of GATT obligations, including Article I, Article III and Article XI. Brazil did not contest that its measures were not in violation of the GATT provisions. It argued instead that the measures were justified under Article XX (b) to protect human and animal life or health. The panel stated that "few interests are more vital and important than protecting human beings from health risks, and that protecting the environment is no less important".[245] The Appellate Body explained that to be characterized as necessary, the contribution of a measure to the achievement of the objective must be material, not merely marginal. Therefore, the contribution of the measure must "be weighed against its trade restrictive, taking into account the importance of the interests or the values underlying the objective pursued by it".[246] The Appellate Body concluded that the imports ban was necessary since the measures materially contributed to the realization of the important interests of human and animal life and health.

Lastly, in *China – Audiovisual Products,* the Appellate Body found the Chinese measures, which limit the right to import cultural goods to certain state-owned enterprises, are not necessary to protect public morals. According to the Appellate Body, the measures at issue are not necessary to protect public morals since China failed to establish a causal connection between the exclusive ownership of the state and the protection of public morals of the society and the existence of a less trade restrictive alternative. The Appellate Body agreed with the US that giving sole responsibility for conducting content review to the Chinese authority would constitute a genuine alternative.[247]

The Appellate Body's surprising decision has disappointed many who wished to use the WTO as a vector to promote fundamental human rights or reform domestic politics within China.[248] The *China – Audiovisual Products* case raised a fundamentally political issue concerning the content control that the Chinese government exerts with respect to information flows from foreign countries. By subscribing to the US view that central control of the content review system is an alternative WTO-consistent measure, the Appellate Body is

---

[245] Panel Report, *Brazil – Measures Affecting Imports of Retreaded Tyres* (cited as *Brazil – Tyres*), WT/DS332/R (12 June 2007), para. 7.108.

[246] Appellate Body Report, *Brazil – Measures Affecting Imports of Retreaded Tyres* (cited as *Brazil – Retreaded Tyres*), WT/DS332/AB/R (3 December 2007), para. 210.

[247] Panel Report, *China – Measures Affecting Trading Rights and Distribution Services for Certain Publications and Audiovisual Entertainment Products* (cited as *China – Audiovisual Products*), WT/DS363/R (12 August 2009), paras. 7.874 & 7.874.

[248] *See* Panagiotis Delimatsis, *Protecting Public Morals in a Digital Age: Revisiting the WTO Rulings on US – Gambling and China – Publications and Audiovisual Products*, Journal of International Economic Law, Vol. 14, No.2 (2011), pp. 257-293.

asking China to nationalize its decentralized censorship regime.[249] Such a proposition was criticized that it will result in backsliding towards less market access and a more constrained environment for freedom of information and expression.[250]

In sum, from the WTO jurisprudence, the word "necessary" within Article XX of the GATT and Article XIV of the GATS is not limited to that of the absolute necessity. A determination of whether a measure is necessary with respect to the objective pursued involves weighing and balancing all the distinct facts relating to the measure, which include the contribution of the measure; the importance of the common interests or values protected; and the impact of the measure on international trade. Once a preliminary conclusion has been reached that a measure is necessary to pursue legitimate public policy, a panel must further examine the measure with its possible alternatives. An alternative measure must be less trade restrictive than the measure at issue; the measure must preserve the responding member's right to achieve its desired level of protection; the measure must be reasonably available. Pursuant to Article 31 of the Vienna Convention, the WTO adjudicating bodies reiterated that treaty interpretation is ultimately a holistic exercise that should not be mechanically subdivided into rigid components.[251]

From a human rights perspective, WTO case law has signaled a great willingness of panels and the Appellate Body to concede the necessity of trade restrictive measures when public morals, public order, or public health issues are at stake. The adjudicating bodies adopted an evolutionary interpretative approach in the sense that the WTO Member States must be given some leeway to define and apply the policy objectives at the level of its own systems and values, and the concept policy objectives are flexible to the contemporary norms and

---

[249] *See* Mireille Cossy, *Determining "likeness" under the GATS: Squaring the Circle?*, World Trade Organization – Economic Research and Statistics Division, Staff Working Paper ERSD-2006-08, September 2006.

[250] *See* Panagiotis Delimatsis, The Puzzling Interaction of Trade and Public Morals in the Digital Era. In: Mira Burri & Thomas Cottier, *Trade Governance in the Digital Age World Trade Forum*, Cambridge University Press (2012), pp. 276-296.

[251] Appellate Body Report, *China – Measures Affecting Trading Rights and Distribution Services for Certain Publications and Audiovisual Entertainment Products* (cited as *China – Audiovisual Products*), WT/DS363/AB/R (21 December 2009), para. 348. The Appellate Body stated:

> Under Article 31 of the Vienna Convention, the "ordinary meaning" of treaty terms may be ascertained only in their context and in the light of the object and purpose of the treaty. In this respect, the Appellate Body has explained that interpretation pursuant to the customary rule codified in Article 31 of the Vienna Convention is ultimately a holistic exercise that should not be mechanically subdivided into rigid components.

standards.[252] Nevertheless, since the ultimate purpose of the exceptions clauses in Article XX of the GATT and Article XIV of the GATS is to strike a balance between trade liberalization and regulatory autonomy, a WTO Member should not be given full discretion to justify any restrictive measures under the name of public morals or public order.[253] Such an approach would undermine the object and purpose of the GATT and the GATS.

Chapeau

Lastly, if a human rights-related trade measure is provisionally justified under one of the specific exceptions in Article XX of the GATT and Article XIV of the GATS, the measure still needs to fulfill the requirements of the chapeau. The chapeau requires that the measure at issue must not be applied in a manner which would constitute a means of arbitrary or unjustifiable discrimination between countries where the same conditions prevail or constitute as a disguised restriction on international trade. The chapeau has been interpreted to prevent the abuse of the general exceptions by the WTO Member States.[254] In many cases, measures that have failed to pass the requirements of the chapeau have ultimately been found to be discriminatory in one way or another.[255] The chapeau of Article XX of the GATT reads:

> "Subject to the requirement that such measures are not applied in a manner which would constitute a means of arbitrary or unjustifiable discrimination between countries where the same conditions prevail, or a disguised restriction on international trade, nothing in this Agreement shall be construed to prevent the adoption or enforcement by any Member of measures..."[256]

---

[252] *See* Henrik Andersen, *Protection of Non-Trade Values in WTO Appellate Body Jurisprudence: Exceptions, Economic Arguments, and Eluding Questions*, Journal of International Economic Law, Vol. 18 (16 May 2015), pp. 383-405 (394-399).

[253] *See* Nicolas F. Diebold, *The Morals and Order Exceptions in WTO Law: Balancing the Toothless Tiger and the Undermining Mole*, Journal of Economic Law, Vol.11, No.1 (2007), pp. 43-74.

[254] Appellate Body Report, *United States – Standards for Reformulated and Conventional Gasoline* (cited as *US -- Gasoline*), WT/DS2/AB/R (29 April 1996), p. 22. The Appellate Body stated, "the purpose and object of the introductory clause of Article XX is generally the prevention of "abuse of the exceptions of Article XX"."

[255] *See* Sarah Joseph, *Blame It to the WTO? A Human Rights Critique*, New York: Oxford University Press (2011), pp. 115-117.

[256] Similar languages are contained in the chapeau of GATS Article XIV.

According to the WTO adjudicating bodies, the objective of the introductory clause of Article XX is to prevent the misuse of a Member's right to invoke the exceptions to derogate from its substantive obligations. In this way, the principle of proportionality is implicitly imposed into the particular interpretative approach of the language of the chapeau. As the Appellate Body stressed in *US – Shrimp*, the chapeau functions as weighing the balance between a Member's right to invoke the exceptions of Article XX on the one hand and the rights of other Members to be protected under the GATT.[257] Additionally, the undertaking to delineate the line between the interests is a delicate one and should be based on the specific circumstance of each case at issue. The Appellate Body stated:

> "The task of interpreting and applying chapeau is, hence, essentially the delicate one of locating and marking out a line of equilibrium between the right of a Member to invoke an exception under Article XX and the rights of the other Members under varying substantive provisions (e.g., Article XI) of the GATT 1994, so that neither the competing rights will cancel out the other and thereby distort and nullify or impair the balance of rights and obligations constructed by the Members themselves in that Agreement. The location of the line of equilibrium, as expressed in the chapeau, is not fixed and unchanging; the line moves as the kind and the shape of the measures at stake vary and as the facts making up specific cases differ."[258]

To determinate whether a measure constitutes 'arbitrary' or 'unjustifiable' discrimination between countries where the same conditions prevail, it is essential to consider the manner in which the measure is applied.[259] The Appellate Body in both *US – Gasoline* and *US –Shrimp* affirmed that the requirements set out in the chapeau do not apply to the measure itself or its specific content but

---

[257] Appellate Body Report, *United States – Import Prohibition of Certain Shrimp and Shrimp Product* (cited as *US -- Shrimp*), WT/DS58/AB/R (12 October 1998), para. 156. The Appellate Body stated:

> … a balance must be struck between the right of a Member to invoke an exception under Article XX and the duty of that same Member to respect the treaty rights of other Members. To permit one Member to abuse or misuse its right to invoke an exception would be effectively to allow that Member to degrade its own treaty obligations as well as to devalue the treaty rights of other Members.

[258] Ibid., para. 159.

[259] Appellate Body Report, *United States – Standards for Reformulated and Conventional Gasoline* (cited as *US -- Gasoline*), WT/DS2/AB/R (29 April 1996), p. 22. The Appellate Body expressed "the chapeau by its express terms address, not so much the questioned measure or its specific contents as such, but rather the manner in which that measure is applied."

to the manner in which the measure is applied.[260] Furthermore, in *EC – Seal Products*, the Appellate Body clarified that the manner in which a measures is applied should be discerned from the design, architecture, and the revealing structure of the measure. The process, therefore, involves a consideration of both the substantive and procedural requirements of the measure in question.[261]

Thus, the most significant factor in the assessment of the chapeau is the determination of whether "the discrimination can be reconciled with, or is rationally related to, the policy objective with respect to which the measure has been provisionally justified under one of the paragraphs of Article XX".[262] In other words, a measure would constitute arbitrary or unjustifiable discrimination if the cause of the discrimination bears no rational connection to the objective policy pursued under GATT Article XX.[263] The reasons given to the discrimination must be assessed in the light of the contribution of the discrimination to achieve the legitimate aim. The factor, however, is one element in a cumulative assessment of the chapeau. Other aspects should be taken into account to make an overall assessment. In *EC – Seal Products*, the Appellate Body explained:

> "… the relationship of the discrimination to the objective of a measure is one of the most important factors, but not the sole test, that is relevant to the assessment of arbitrary or unjustifiable discrimination. In other words, depending on the nature of the measure at issue and the circumstances of

---

[260] Appellate Body Report, *United States – Import Prohibition of Certain Shrimp and Shrimp Product* (cited as *US -- Shrimp*), WT/DS58/AB/R (12 October 1998), para. 115.

[261] Appellate Body Report, *European Communities – Measures Prohibiting the Importation and Marketing of Seal Products* (cited as *EC – Seal Products*), WT/DS 400/AB/R & WT/DS 401/AB/R (22 May 2014), para. 5.302.

[262] Ibid., para. 5.306 and 5.318.

[263] In the *Brazil – Retreated Tyres* case, the Appellate Body is of the opinion that "there is arbitrary or unjustifiable discrimination when a measure provisionally justified under a paragraph of Article XX is applied in a discriminatory manner between countries where the same conditions prevail, and when the reasons given for this discrimination bear no rational connection to the objective falling within the purview of a paragraph of Article XX, or would go against that objective. *The assessment of whether discrimination is arbitrary or unjustifiable should be made in the light of objective of measure.*" (emphasis added).
(Appellate Body Report, *Brazil – Measures Affecting Imports of Retreaded Tyres* (cited as *Brazil – Retreaded Tyres*), WT/DS332/AB/R (3 December 2007), para. 227.)

> the case at hand, *there could be additional factors that may also be relevant to that overall assessment.*" (emphasis added)[264]

This new interpretative approach in *EC – Seal Products* is applausive for human rights concerns since most trade restrictive measures aiming to promote or protect human rights conditions have no direct or least relationship between the sanctions and human rights policy objectives being advanced.[265] For example, while banning on the importation of the products produced by child labor might have a direct connection to the human rights protection under public morals exceptions, embargoing coal imports from a major coal exporting country to go against its repressive polity has no direct linkage between the measure at issue and human rights violations. The allowance for other factors to be taken into account within the meaning of 'arbitrary and unjustifiable discrimination' would render the defending party more space to justify the discriminatory effect of the measure at issue.

Moreover, any rigidly applied unilateral measures could also constitute arbitrary and unjustifiable discrimination. When a measure is applied without any reference to the differences in the conditions between countries or is applied in the light of ambiguous language, it may be deemed as 'arbitrary' or 'unjustifiable'. For the WTO adjudicating bodies, it is important for an importing Member, in the international trade relations, to inquire into the suitability of the measure at issue for the conditions prevailing in the other Member States and to pursue a cooperative arrangement[266] before implementing unilateral trade measures. In *US – Shrimp*, the Appellate Body accentuated:

> "164. It may be quite acceptable for a government, in adopting and implementing a domestic policy, to adopt a single standard applicable to all its citizens throughout that country. However, it is not acceptable, in international trade relations, for one WTO Member to use an economic embargo to require other Members to adopt essentially the same comprehensive regulatory program, to achieve a certain policy goal, as that in force within the

---

[264] Appellate Body Report, *European Communities – Measures Prohibiting the Importation and Marketing of Seal Products* (cited as *EC – Seal Products*), WT/DS 400/AB/R & WT/DS 401/AB/R (22 May 2014), para. 5.321.

[265] Sarah H. Cleveland, Human Rights Sanctions and the World Trade Organization. In: Francesco Francioni (ed.), *Environment, Human Rights and International Trade*, Oxford and Portland: Hart Publishing (2001), pp. 119-261.

[266] Appellate Body Report, *United States – Standards for Reformulated and Conventional Gasoline* (cited as *US -- Gasoline*), WT/DS2/AB/R (29 April 1996), pp. 24-25.

> Member's territory, without taking into consideration different conditions which may occur in the territories of those other Members.
> 165. We believe that discrimination results not only when countries in which the same conditions prevail are differently treated, but also when the application of the measure at issue does not allow for any inquiry into the appropriateness of the regulatory program for the conditions prevailing in those exporting countries."[267]

The Appellate Body further decided that by failing to conduct a "serious, across-the-board negotiation" with the other WTO Member States before enforcing the import prohibition, the US measure was found to be unjustifiable discrimination.[268] The Appellate Body concluded the US measure at issue was applied in a manner that constituted arbitrary discrimination since the application of the measure imposed a single, rigid, and inflexible requirement for its certification process and the exporting Members whose applications are rejected are not guaranteed basic fairness and due process.[269] The Appellate Body in *EC – Seal Products* is aware of the concerns in *US – Shrimp* and decided that the vague requirements of a measure in combination with a broad discretion of the recognized authorities to apply the requirements will not fulfill the elements in the context of the chapeau.[270]

It could be presumed that the requirements of the chapeau to the general exceptions clause are not easy to fulfill and the existing case law regarding envi-

---

[267] Appellate Body Report, *United States – Import Prohibition of Certain Shrimp and Shrimp Product* (cited as *US -- Shrimp*), WT/DS58/AB/R (12 October 1998), para. 164-165.

[268] Ibid., para. 166. The Appellate Body stated:

> Another aspect of the application of Section 609 that bears heavily in any appraisal of justifiable or unjustifiable discrimination is the failure of the United States to engage the appellees, as well as other Members exporting shrimp to the United States, in serious, across-the-board negotiations with the objective of concluding bilateral or multilateral agreements for the protection and conservation of sea turtles, before enforcing the import prohibition against the shrimp exports of those other Members.

[269] Ibid., paras. 180-181. (According to the Appellate Body, the certification process is applied in an arbitrary manner because the US measure failed to afford applicant countries notice and any formal opportunity to be heard. There is no procedure provided for review of, or appeal from, a denial of an application. Consequently, the Appellate Body concluded "the certification process followed by the United States thus appears to be singularly informal and casual, and to be conducted in a manner such that these processes could result in the negation of the rights of Members")

[270] Appellate Body Report, *European Communities – Measures Prohibiting the Importation and Marketing of Seal Products* (cited as *EC – Seal Products*), WT/DS 400/AB/R & WT/DS 401/AB/R (22 May 2014), para. 5.328.

ronmental matters and public health concerns shows that WTO panels and the Appellate Body have so far been quite restrictive in their interpretation of the chapeau. Nevertheless, the objective of the chapeau is to ensure the balance between a Member's right to regulate and the rights of other Members under the WTO Agreement.

According to the WTO adjudicating bodies, therefore, the chapeau of Article XX could be seen as an expression of the principle of good faith, which controls the exercises of the States' rights.[271] A strict interpretation of the chapeau does not necessarily render less space for non-trade values concerns. From the previous cases, the jurisprudence of the Appellate Body is moving toward the direction that the greater the significance of the pursued value is, the more likely it will prevail its burden on international trade. Such a proportionate effectiveness-balancing test should be able to apply in the context of the chapeau when different interests are at stake. Significantly, the Appellate Body recognized that the application of the chapeau should be conducted on a case-by-case basis, which provides some discretion for panels in the future case to develop proportionate principles for human rights concerns.

[271] Appellate Body Report, *United States – Import Prohibition of Certain Shrimp and Shrimp Product* (cited as *US -- Shrimp*), WT/DS58/AB/R (12 October 1998), para. 129.

III. Conclusion

To prepare the ground for the arguments in Chapters 3 and 4, the object of this chapter, then, is to analyze the relationship between the international trade and human rights regimes. The analysis is conducted from both historical and practical perspectives. In the process of global governance reform, the correlation between social and economic institutions is one of mutual dependence. However, with the widespread concerns of globalization and trade liberalization, many have argued that international trade systems, especially the WTO, constrain state policy choices to protect social justice and promote the enjoyment of human rights. In the field of contemporary international relations, therefore, it is crucial to discuss how to transform the economic legal system into a more effective instrument for protecting vital social values. The debate on trade and human rights, however, is enormously broad and involves various cultural, social, political and economic struggles both internal and external to each regime. The subject matter in the chapter, therefore, is mainly focused on the scope to consider whether the norms and standards of contemporary human rights law are efficiently protected and promoted under WTO law.

The historical material surveyed intends to look into the particular conception of the nature and purpose of trade and human rights. The birth of the post-war trade and human rights system was designed to maintain international stability, with complex compromises of traditional state-centric ideologies. Judging from the development of human rights, due to the gradual recognition of economic justice and the right to development, states' obligations have expanded to protecting and promoting economic, social, and, cultural rights alongside the liberty rights. Codification of the distributive rights in UN instruments provided a legal standing in which concerns about the social costs of global economic structures could take their place within the modern human rights movement.

The concerns of equitable economic growth, social welfare distribution, and the reduction of poverty are reflected in the criticism of the human rights impact of the WTO. Two observations from the material covered in this chapter might provide a picture of mutual compatibility between WTO law and human rights law. First, a closer look at the formation of international trading systems reveals that while free trade is the essential concept of the trade regime, it is never the only element of the foundations of trade liberalization. The morals of equality and sustainable development are enshrined in the preamble of the WTO Agreement. It is true that to a certain extent the WTO is oriented towards the pursuit of the removal of trade barriers. However, over the past two decades, the role of the WTO has not been static, but responsive to political and social developments over time. The assertion that mandate of the WTO is limited to trade issues overlooks the competence of the WTO to settle the social consequence of trade liberalization.

The second observation is that many of the principles and provisions of the WTO are negotiated in a broad or ambiguous fashion and the substantive content of WTO law, therefore, depends on how those provisions are interpreted and applied by panels and the Appellate Body in dispute settlement proceedings. In other words, with a limited domain but unlimited sources of applicable law, the WTO adjudicating bodies have the competence to interpret individual words and phrases of the WTO provisions in accordance with essential social values and fundamental human rights.

Evidence can be found in several cases when panels and the Appellate Body have dealt with the non-discrimination provisions and general exceptions clauses of the WTO Agreement. Most of the terms in those general principles, such as 'likeness', 'less favourable treatment', 'necessity', and 'public morals', are indeterminate but their interpretation could have been tied to significant social values. The Appellate Body emphasized that it is the nature and extent of a competitive relationship between the products in an idealized marketplace rather than the mere physical evidence in the 'final product' that determines the notion of 'like products'. This approach indicates that the non-discrimination provisions of the WTO rules have the potential to accept the differential treatment of the products in the light of human rights considerations.

Additionally, when interpreting the word 'necessary' within the meaning of the general exceptions clauses, the Appellate Body indirectly introduced the principle of proportionality into the WTO legal system and opened the door to weigh non-trade values in accordance with their degree of importance. The Appellate Body explained that the more vital the protected values are and the greater the contribution a measure has to the realization of the end pursued, the more probably it is that the measure would be considered as necessary. While there is no direct reference to the principle of proportionality in WTO law, its core concept of balancing competing interests and values is replicated in several WTO agreements and is applied in numerous cases by both panels and the Appellate Body. On the one hand, it is through this weighing and balancing process that the WTO adjudicating bodies have the competence to address non-trade values when various interests are at stake. On the other hand, incorporating general principles of law and customary international law into the WTO legal structure will enhance the legitimacy of the WTO as an international organization by clarifying imprecise provisions and improving the predictability of the international trading system.

Chapter 2. Internet Censorship and Human Rights Protection

Freedom of expression is the basis of human rights,
the source of humanity and the mother of truth.
To block freedom of speech is to trample on human rights,
to strangle humanity and to suppress truth
I have no enemies, my final statement
Liu Xiaoboo[1]

Since the emergence of the Internet in the 1960s, it has unprecedentedly become the most dominant instrument of the 21st century for people to access and disseminate information worldwide. Being more than just another information technology, the Internet has infiltrated into virtually every aspect of modern human life. Search engines, social networks, E-commerce, and other online platforms or applications have changed how people communicate and created new opportunities for self-expression, international trade, and political reform.[2] The role social and digital media have played in catalyzing and sustaining the Arab Spring highlighted the fact that the Internet, if properly supported, could not only foster innovation or economic growth but also contribute to the realization of essential human rights.

Unsurprisingly, the revolutionary effect of the Internet brings up a very fundamental question: should the Internet or Internet access be considered as a human right, which needs to be protected and promoted by the nation states? Vinton Cerf, one of the Internet pioneers, stated in The New York Times that "Internet access is not a human right." He argued, "technology is an enabler of rights, not a right itself. There is a high bar for something to be considered a human right. Loosely put, it must be among the things we as humans need in order to lead healthy, meaningful lives, like freedom from torture or freedom of conscience. It is a mistake to place any particular technology in this exalted category, since over time we will end up valuing the wrong things. For example, at one time if you didn't have a horse it was hard to make a living. But the important right in that case was the right to make a living, not the right to a horse.

---

[1] The phrase is written by Liu Xiaoboo, the 2010 Nobel Peace Prize laureate, on the eve of his imprisonment in China. The original quote is "表达自由，人权之基，人性之本，真理之母。封杀言论自由，践踏人权，窒息人性，压抑真理。"

[2] Reporters Without Borders, *Enemies of the Internet 2012*, Reporters Without Borders – For Freedom of Information (12 March 2012). Available at https://rsf.org/sites/default/files/rapport-internet2012_ang.pdf. (accessed 08 March 2014)

Today, if I were granted a right to have a horse, I'm not sure where I would put it".[3]

The immense value that the Internet has for individuals or global development makes this innovative information technology nothing to be compared to a horse to make a living. Like no other medium, the Internet enables individuals to seek, receive, and impart information and ideas of all kinds instantaneously and inexpensively on a global level. In the information age we are living in, the Internet is undoubtedly a major platform where individuals can carry out their right to freedom of expression, the right to assembly, and other fundamental human rights. States, therefore, should have positive obligations to guarantee the free flow of information on the Internet and ensure that the Internet is widely available, accessible, and affordable to all.[4]

In the past decade, many attempted to adjust essential human rights to the online worlds. The United Nation Special Rapporteur on the promotion and protection of the right to freedom of expression, Frank La Rue, released a series reports, which concerned the evolving legal restrictions on the freedom of expression on the Internet. He claimed that "the framework of international human rights law remains relevant today and equally applicable to new communication technologies such as the Internet".[5] Additionally, on the 29th June 2012, the United Nations passed a landmark resolution supporting freedom of expression on the Internet. It affirmed that "the same rights that people have offline must also be protected online, in particular, freedom of expression, which is applicable regardless of frontiers and through any media of one's choice, in accordance with article 19 of the Universal Declaration of Human Rights and the International Covenant on Civil and Political Rights".[6] All the efforts of the UN were intended to strengthen the legitimacy of Internet freedom.

---

[3] Vinton G. Cerf, *Internet Access is not a Human Right*, The NewYork Times (4 January 2012). Available at http://www.nytimes.com/2012/01/05/opinion/internet-access-is-not-a-human-right.html?_r=0. (accessed 15 March 2014)

[4] United Nation General Assemble, 66th session, *Promotion and protection of the right to freedom of opinion and expression*, U.N. Doc. A/66/290. (10 August 2011.)

[5] Frank La Rue, *Report on the Special Rapporteur on the Promotion and Protection of the Right to Freedom of Opinion and Expression*, UN General Assembly, A/HRC/17/27 (15 May 2011), para. 21. Available at http://www.ohchr.org/EN/Issues/FreedomOpinion/Pages/Annual.aspx. (accessed 03 April 2014)

[6] United Nations General Assembly, 20th session, *Promotion and protection of all human rights, civil, political, economic, social and cultural rights, including the right to development: The promotion, protection and enjoyment of human rights on the Internet*, U.N. Doc. A/HRC/20/L.13 (29 June 2012).

If the Internet is an important tool for developing and exercising human rights or if Internet freedom is a human right *per se*, what kind of legal frameworks can be applied to the unique characteristics of the Internet? The advent of the Internet has increased the possibilities for communication, enabled instant information sharing, and promoted democratic development. Nonetheless, the same innovations in technologies have concurrently increased states' abilities to monitor and control individuals' online activities. Thus, the critical issue Chapter 2 intends to analyze is how to interpret internationally recognized human rights law to protect and promote individuals' rights on the Internet from governmental intervention. Additionally, the sophisticated blocking or filtering mechanisms and mass data collection have raised new concerns for human rights violations. It is not to say information and communication technologies (ICTs) have changed the level of protection of human rights; however, these new technologies indeed signify that the traditional ways to fulfill fundamental human rights might be insufficient in the digital age.[7]

Against the background, section I of Chapter 2 delineates the connection between the Internet and the rights codified in contemporary human rights law. The discussion focuses on the freedom of expression and information and the right to privacy. Speech or information freedom is not only a fundamental human right but also an enabler of other rights and ensuring an individual's reasonable expectation of privacy on the Internet is primarily important since personal information is collected in an unprecedented way by both private and public entities. The value of the Internet will heavily depend on whether there is adequate privacy protection online. Section II of the Chapter examines whether new technologies have brought new threats to the human rights regime and how should governments, private actors, and individuals respond to these new threats.

[7] *See* Ada Bogliolo Piancastelli de Siqueira, *It's in the Way that You Use It: Revisiting Trade and Human Rights in the Case of Online Censorship*, Southwestern Journal of Int'l Law, Vol. 20 (2013), pp. 39-79.

I. The Internet and Fundamental Values of Human Rights

As stated in the UN resolution that the same right that people have offline should be protected online, the principles of freedom of expression and information and the right to privacy shall be applied to the online communicative forum to protect individuals' fundamental human rights from the unnecessary or disproportionate intervention of others. Noticeably, other human rights, such as the rights to freedom of association and assembly, the right to education, and the right to take part in cultural life, are also essential for human development in the digital age. Since freedom of expression and information and the right to privacy are both recognized as fundamental rights and as a means to achieve other important social values, the succeeding section mainly focuses on the discussion of the connection between these two rights and the Internet.

A. Freedom of Expression and Information in the Online World

The right to freedom of expression and information is a fundamental human right and a vital precondition for individual autonomy, self-expression, and self-fulfillment. This right is closely connected to the advancement of democratic practices or societal interests.[8] The United Nations Human Rights Committee has described freedom of expression as being of "paramount importance for any democratic society".[9] Sometimes the right to freedom of expression is described as an enablement of other human rights, such as the rights of assembly and association, the right to political participation, and culture rights.[10] Speech and information freedoms play a prominent role in protecting and promoting individuals' interests in the modern information world.

---

[8] *See* Rikke Frank Jørgensen, *Human Rights in the Global Information Society: The Right to Express Oneself and to Seek Information*, Massachusetts Institute of Technology (2006), pp. 53-71; and *see* also Tarlach Mcgonagle, The Development of Freedom of Expression and Information within the UN: Leaps and Bounds or Fits and Starts?. In: Tarlach McGonagle & Yvonne Donders, *The United Nations and Freedom of Expression and Information Critical Perspectives*, Cambridge University Press (June 2015), pp. 1-52.

[9] Human Rights Committee, *Tae Hoon Park v. Republic of Korea*, Communication No. 628/1995 (3 November 1998), para. 10.3.

[10] Ibid.

Despite the unique nature of the Internet which transcends national borders and eliminates barriers to the free flow of information,[11] the right to freedom of expression and information is not unconditionally guaranteed by technological innovation.[12] As ICTs evolved, so did the modalities by which governments used to censor and control the data traveling on the Internet. The purpose of this section, therefore, is to examine, first, whether the existing human rights law, internationally and regionally, could be interpreted to efficiently protect and promote freedom of expression and information on the Internet. Secondly, the limitations on the right will be discussed. Whereas the right to freedom of expression and information is not absolute but subject to specific limitations, any restrictions on the right have to comply with strict standards and correspond to the principles of necessity and proportionality.[13]

a. Freedom of Expression and Information on the Internet

The dynamic nature of the Internet-related technologies has raised the question of whether the current human rights legal instruments could apply to personal online behavior. Freedom of expression and information on the Internet can be diminished easily by the design of technologies or governmental policies. Internet censorship measures, such as online content monitoring or blocking, denial of services attacks, and self-censorship controls, are widely carried out by both democratic and authoritarian countries to restrict people's activities on the Internet. States have increasingly utilized communication data to support law enforcement or national security investigations. Some governments have implemented strict data retention regulations to enable ubiquitous online surveillance. Also, with the advent of the Internet, new private actors, for example, Internet service providers (ISPs), search engines, and social networks, also play significant roles in protecting fundamental human rights. Consequently, it is crucial to review the existing human rights regulations to examine whether they

[11] Center for Democracy & Technology, *"Regardless of Frontiers:" The International Right to Freedom of Expression in the Digital Age* (04 April 2011). Available at https://cdt.org/insight/regardless-of-frontiers-the-international-right-to-freedom-of-expression-in-the-digital-age/. (accessed 3 April 2014)

[12] *See* William Dutton, Anna Dopatka, Michael Hills, Ginette Law and Victoria Nash, *Freedom of Connection – Freedom of Expression: The Changing Legal and Regulatory Ecology Shaping the Internet*, Oxford Internet Institute, UNESCO (19 August 2011).

[13] *See* Rikke Frank Jørgenen, The Right to Express Oneself and to *See*k Information. In: Rikke Frank Jørgenen, *Human Rights in Global Information Society*, The MIT Press: Cambridge, Massachusetts, London, England (2006), pp. 53-71.

sufficiently address the threats and challenges brought by the Internet censorship mechanisms.[14]

At the international level, the right to freedom of expression and information is guaranteed by very similar terms in both Article 19 of the Universal Declaration of Human Rights (UDHR)[15] and Article 19 of the International Covenant on Civil and Political Rights (ICCPR)[16]. At the regional level, freedom of expression is promised by Article 10 of the European Convention on Human Rights (ECHR)[17], Article 11 of the Charter of Fundamental Rights of the European Union (EUCFR)[18], and Article 13 of the American Convention on Human Rights (ACHR)[19]. These guarantees are largely similar to those codified in Article 19 of the UDHR.

i. International Agreements on the Right to Freedom of Expression

Since the end of the Second World War, the right to freedom of expression has been enshrined in international human rights law to prevent unnecessary governmental intrusions. Regardless of the limitations, the international community has stated its commitments to the right to free expression and opinion in a series of fundamental agreements. As mentioned above, advances in ICTs have transformed the online environment into a dynamic ecosystem, which evidently has far-reaching consequences on how information and ideas are disseminated and processed. The following section, therefore, examines the current international agreements on the rights to freedom of expression and opinion and analyzes whether they are simultaneously applied to seeking, receiving and imparting information and opinions on the Internet.

---

[14] Frank La Rue, *Report of the Special Rapporteur on the Promotion and Protection of the Right to Freedom of Opinion and Expression*, UN General Assembly, A/HRC/23/40 (17 April 2013).

[15] United Nations General Assembly, *Universal Declaration on Human Rights*, 217A (III) (10 December 1948).

[16] UN General Assembly, *International Covenant on Civil and Political Rights*, United Nations, Treaty Series, Vol. 999 (16 December 1966), p. 171.

[17] Council of Europe, *European Convention for the Protection of Human Rights and Fundamental Freedoms*, as amended by Protocols Nos. 11 and 14, ETS 5 (November 1950).

[18] European Union, *Charter of Fundamental Rights of the European Union*, 2012/c 326/02 (26 October 2012).

[19] Organization of American States (OAS), *American Convention on Human Rights*, "Pact of San Jose", Costa Rica (22 November 1969).

The Universal Declaration of Human Rights (UDHR)

Article 19 of the UDHR is perhaps the best-known provision for free expression of any international instruments.[20] It sets out the right to freedom of expression as followed:

> Everyone has the right to freedom of opinion and expression; this right includes freedom to hold opinions without interference and to seek, receive and impart information and ideas through any media and regardless of frontiers.

The right, like any other democratic values, is not absolute but subject to limitations. The restrictions of the rights under the UDHR are stipulated in Article 29 and Article 30, which provide:

> Article 29
> 1. Everyone had duties to the community in which alone the free and full development of his personality is possible.
> 2. In the exercise of his rights and freedoms, everyone shall be subject only to such limitations as are determined by law solely for the purpose of securing due recognition and respect for the rights and freedoms of others and of meeting the just requirements of morality, public order and the general welfare in a democratic society.
> 3. These rights and freedoms may in no case be exercised contrary to the purposes and principles of the United Nations.
>
> Article 30
> Nothing in this Declaration may be interpreted as implying for any State, group or person any right to engage in any activity or to perform any act aimed at the destruction of any of the rights and freedoms set forth herein.

Although the UDHR is not a treaty *per se*, the influence of which on the international community should not be overlooked. The UDHR was adopted by the United Nations General Assembly as a resolution, which has no legal force on its own but creates moral obligations on nation states. As discussed in Chapter 1, despite the non-legally binding nature of the Declaration, "the majority of its provisions have come to acquire legally binding status through customary

[20] Center for Democracy & Technology, *"Regardless of Frontiers:" The International Right to Freedom of Expression in the Digital Age* (04 April 2011). Available at https://cdt.org/insight/regardless-of-frontiers-the-international-right-to-freedom-of-expression-in-the-digital-age/ (accessed 15 April 2014)

international law".[21] The legal standing of the UDHR as a customary international law means that the Declaration has significant impact on the development of all international, regional, and national human rights law.[22]

The broad and technology-neutral language of Article 19 of the UDHR makes the provision flexible enough to adapt to the technological changes. The term 'through any medium' indicates that Article 19 not only protects the substance of the information but also the means by which the information is delivered or imparted. For example, the right to seek for information might be interpreted to include searching for information on Internet through search engines, and the right to receive or impart information seems perfect to apply to the end-to-end social networks.[23] Therefore, the language of Article 19 is designed to incorporate the innovative modes of media in the future, including the Internet.[24]

Since the early stage of the advent of the Internet, the UN Special Rapporteur reports on the promotion and protection of the right to freedom of opinion and expression have specifically addressed the influence of new communication technologies to the individuals' enjoyment of freedom of expression. The Special Rapporteur emphasized that restrictions on the Internet without any legal basis, or on the basis of ambiguous terms described by laws, often create a chilling effect on the right to freedom of expression. States implementing such regulations violate their obligations under international human rights law. In the 1998 report to the Commission, the Special Rapporteur stressed:

> "The Special Rapporteur is of the opinion that the new technologies and, in particular, the Internet are inherently democratic, provide the public and

[21] *See* Tarlach Mcgonagle, The Development of Freedom of Expression and Information within the UN: Leaps and Bounds or Fits and Starts?. In: Tarlach McGonagle & Yvonne Donders, *The United Nations and Freedom of Expression and Information Critical Perspectives*, Cambridge University Press (June 2015), pp. 1-52.

[22] Virtually all human rights treaties adopted by UN bodies since 1948 elaborate principles set forth in the Universal Declaration. Regionally, both the American Convention and European Convention on Human Rights declare in the preamble that the principles to which they give effect are those set forth in the Declaration. Moreover, many countries have modeled clauses of their constitutions and statues on the UDHR.

[23] Center for Democracy & Technology, *"Regardless of Frontiers:" The International Right to Freedom of Expression in the Digital Age* (04 April 2011). Available at https://cdt.org/insight/regardless-of-frontiers-the-international-right-to-freedom-of-expression-in-the-digital-age/. (accessed 15 April 2014)

[24] Young Joon Lim and Sarah E. Sexton, *Internet as a Human Right: A Practical Legal Framework to Address the Unique Nature of the Medium and to Promote Development*, Wash J.L. Tech. & Arts, Vol.7 (2012), pp. 295-318.

individuals with access to information sources and enable all to participate actively in the communication process. The Special Rapporteur also believes that action by States to impose excessive regulations on the use of these technologies and, again, particularly the Internet, on the grounds that control, regulation and denial of access are necessary to preserve the moral fabric and cultural identity of societies is paternalistic. These regulations presume to protect people from themselves and, as such, they are inherently incompatible with the principles of the worth and dignity of each individual. These arguments deny the fundamental wisdom of individuals and societies and ignore the capacity and resilience of citizens, whether on a national, State, municipal, community or even neighborhood level, often to take self-correcting measures to re-establish equilibrium without excessive interference or regulation by the State."[25]

The International Covenant on Civil and Political Rights (ICCPR)

The ICCPR was entered into force on 23 March 1976 and has been ratified by 168 nations.[26] Article 19 of the ICCPR reiterates the key principles articulated in Article 19 of the UDHR and expands the scope of the responsibilities and restrictions of the right protected. Article 19 of the ICCPR comprises a statement of the right regarding freedom of expression and a list of the contexts in which the exercise of relevant rights in practice might be limited.[27]

Article 19 of the ICCPR reads:
1. Everyone shall have the right to hold opinions without interference.
2. Everyone shall have the right to freedom of expression; this right shall include freedom to seek, receive and impart information and ideas of all kinds, regardless of frontiers, either orally, in writing or in print, in the form of art, or through any other media of his choice.

---

[25] Special Rapporteur on the Promotion and Protection of the Right to Freedom of Opinion and Expression, *Question of the Human Rights of All Persons Subjected to Any Form of Detention or Imprisonment: Promotion and Protection of the Right to Freedom of Opinion and Expression*, Economic and Social Council, E/CN.4/1998/40 (28 January 1998).

[26] United Nations Human Rights, Office of the High Commissioner. Available at http://www.ohchr.org/en/professionalinterest/pages/ccpr.aspx. (accessed 20 April 2014)

[27] *See* Michael O'Flaherty, International Covenant on Civil and Political Rights: Interpreting Freedom of Expression and Information Standards for the Present and the Future. In: Tarlach McGonagle & Yvonne Donders, *The United Nations and Freedom of Expression and Information Critical Perspectives*, Cambridge University Press (June 2015), pp. 55-88.

> 3. The exercise of the rights provided in paragraph 2 of this article carries with it special duties and responsibilities. It may therefore be subject to certain restriction, but these shall only be such as are provided by law and are necessary:
>   a. For respect of the rights or reputations of others
>   b. For the protection of national security or public order (ordre public), or of public health or morals.

Paragraph 1 of Article 19 guarantees an individual's right to hold opinion without interference and paragraph 2 requires States parties to protect the right to freedom of expression, including the right to seek, receive, and impart information and ideas of all kinds regardless of frontiers. Paragraph 2 embraces the expression that may be regarded as deeply offensive; nevertheless, such offensive expression might be limited in accordance with the provision of paragraph 3 of Article 19 and Article 20.[28]

Like Article 19 of the UDHR, the rights under the ICCPR do not directly include the right to the Internet *per se*. Nevertheless, the Article explicitly protects a person's freedom of expression "through any other media of his choice". Article 19, therefore, is intended to include later developed technologies and should be able to apply to all forms of expression or information disseminated through the Internet.[29] The UN Special Rapporteur underscored that "Article 19 of the Universal Declaration of Human Rights and the Covenant was drafted with the foresight to include and to accommodate future technological developments through which individuals can exercise their right to freedom of expression. Hence the framework of international human rights law remains relevant today

---

[28] Human Rights Committee, *General Comment No. 34 Article 19: Freedoms of Opinion and Expression*, U.N. Doc. CCPR/C/GC/34 (12 September 2011). *See* Communication No. 136/1997, *Ross v. Canada*, adopted on 18 October 2000 (UN Human Rights Committee). The applicant, a former teacher, has been transferred to a non-teaching position because in his spare time he published books and pamphlets, and made public statements reflecting a discriminatory view against Jews. The UN Human Rights Committee held that the loss of a teaching position was a sufficient detriment to constitute a restriction on the author's right to freedom of expression since the decision was made provided by law, according to a legitimate aim and in compliance with the principle of necessity.

[29] *See* Molly Land, *Toward an International Law of the Internet*, Harvard International Law Journal, Vol. 54, No. 2 (Summer 2013), pp. 393-458.

and equally applicable to new communication technologies such as the Internet."[30]

In September 2011, the United Nations Human rights Committee adopted the General Comment No.34 to Article 19 of the ICCPR and suggested that freedom of opinion and expression are "indispensable conditions for the full development of the person."[31] The Comment stated that freedom of expression is necessary for government transparency and accountability, which are both essential elements for the promotion and protection of human rights.[32] The Comment also specifically emphasized that Article 19 protects all forms of expression and the means of their dissemination. Means of expression include all forms of audio-visual and electronic and Internet-based modes of expression.[33] It further stressed that States should take account of the extent to which developments in technologies have changed communication behaviors around the world and encouraged states to foster the independence of new media and to ensure access to individual thereto.[34]

With the advent of Web2.0[35], the Internet not only brings more information to the world but also facilitates the access to user-generated technology in ways

---

[30] Frank La Rue, *Report on the Special Rapporteur on the Promotion and Protection of the Right to Freedom of Opinion and Expression*, UN General Assembly, A/HRC/17/27 (15 May 2011), para. 21.

[31] Human Rights Committee, *General Comment No. 34 Article 19: Freedoms of Opinion and Expression*, U.N. Doc. CCPR/C/GC/34 (12 September 2011).

[32] Ibid., para. 3. The Comment articulated that freedom of expression is a necessary condition for the realization of the principles of transparency and accountability that are, in turn, essential for the promotion and protection of human rights.

[33] Ibid., para. 12. The Comment is of the view that paragraph 2 of the ICCPR protects all forms of expression and the means of their dissemination. The means of expression include not only books, newspapers, pamphlets, and banners, but also include all forms of audio-visual as well as electronic and Internet-based modes of expression.

[34] Ibid., para.15. The Comment emphasized states parties should take account of the extent to which developments in information and communication technologies, such as Internet and mobile based electronic information dissemination systems, have substantially changed communication practices around the world. There is now a global network for exchanging ideas and opinions that does not necessarily rely on the traditional mass media intermediaries. States parties should take all necessary steps to foster the independence of these new media and to ensure access of individuals thereto.

[35] The meaning of Web2.0 has evolved over time. However, the term is generally used to describe the second generation of the World Wide Web, where it moved from static HTML pages to more interactive and dynamic web platforms. Instead of putting emphasis on the one-way conversation, Web 2.0 focuses on the Internet users' abilities to

that empower individuals to participate in building democratic societies. Nevertheless, enhanced technological innovation is not equal to the greater freedom of expression.[36] In order to guarantee individuals' fundamental right of development and to promote the progress of society as a whole, the framework of international human rights law should remain applicable to the new communication technologies, including the Internet. In 2014, another resolution adopted by the UN Human Rights Council to promote and protect the enjoyment of human rights on the Internet affirmed the need for human rights to underpin Internet governance and recognized that government engagement must be in accordance with states' international human rights obligations. The resolution accentuated:

> "*Noting* that the exercise of human rights, in particular the right to freedom of expression, on the Internet is an issue of increasing interest and importance as the rapid pace of technological development enables individuals all over the world to use new information and communication technologies,
> *Calls upon* all States to address security concerns on the Internet in accordance with their international human rights obligations to ensure protection of freedom of expression, freedom of association, privacy and other human rights online, including through national democratic, transparent institutions, based on the rule of law, in a way that ensures freedom and security on the Internet so that it can continue to be a vibrant force that generates economic, social and cultural development." [37]

The right to freedom of expression under the ICCPR, like any other human rights, has its limitations. The ICCPR recognizes that the exercise of the right to freedom of expression carries with its special duties and responsibilities.[38] The constituent of the permissible limitations to the freedom of expression will be elaborated in the following section; notwithstanding, it is relevant to highlight here that any restrictions on the exercise of freedom of expression must be nar-

---

collaborate and share information online through social media, live-streaming videos, and blogging.

[36] United Nations Educational, *Scientific and Cultural Organization, Freedom of Connection Freedom of Expression – The Changing Legal and Regulatory Ecology Shaping the Internet*, Oxford Internet Institute (2011).

[37] United Nations General Assembly, Resolution adopted by the Human Rights Council, *26/13 The Promotion, Protection and Enjoyment of Human Rights on the Internet*, A/HRC/RES/26/13 (14 July 2014).

[38] Human Rights Committee, *General Comment No. 34 Article 19: Freedoms of Opinion and Expression*, U.N. Doc. CCPR/C/GC/34 (12 September 2011).

rowly defined and the relation between the right and restriction must not be reversed.[39]

The same standard should also be applied to freedom of expression on the Internet. The General Comment No.34 underscored that any limitations on the Internet-related information dissemination, either to the end-users or service providers, are only permissible to the extent that they are compatible with paragraph 3 of Article 19 of the ICCPR.[40] For example, the Comment stressed that counter-terrorism measures, implemented on the ground of national security, should not be excessively restrictive on access to information and the terms of which must be clearly defined "to ensure that they do not lead to unnecessary or disproportionate interference with freedom of expression".[41] The State party that evokes the restrictive measures has the burden to "demonstrate in specific fashion the precise nature of the threat to any of the enumerated grounds listed in paragraph 3 that has caused it to restrict freedom of expression".[42]

ii. Regional Agreements on the Right to Freedom of Expression

The right to freedom of expression is also guaranteed at the regional level. The regulations and case law from these regional human rights conventions highlight that freedom of expression is not only protected for the purpose of individual development but also for the integrity of the society as a whole. Notwithstanding most agreements are ratified before the advent of the Internet, all courts acknowledged the significant influence of the Internet on the realization of people's fundamental rights. Generally speaking, the application of freedom of expression in the online world is widely recognized in the regional human rights regime.

---

[39] UN Human Rights Committee (HRC), *CCPR General Comment No. 27: Article 12 (Freedom of Movement)*, CCPR/C/21/Rev.1/Add.9 (2 November 1999). In paragraph 13, the Committee States that:

> In adopting laws providing for restriction permitted by article12, paragraph 3, States should always be guided by the principle that the restriction must not impair the essence of the right (cf. article 5, paragraph 1); the relation between right and restriction, between norm and exception, must not be reserved. The law authorizing the application of restrictions should use precise criteria and may not confer unfettered discretion on those charged with their execution.

[40] Ibid., para. 43.

[41] Ibid., para .46. *See* Also Frank La Rue, *Report of the Special Rapporteur on the Promotion and Protection of the Right to Freedom of Opinion and Expression*, UN General Assembly, A/HRC/23/40 (17 April 2013), paras., 30-49.

[42] Ibid., para. 36.

The European Convention on Human Rights

The Council of Europe is composed of forty-seven Member States, and each of the members has ratified the European Convention for the Protection of Human Rights and Fundamental Freedoms (ECHR) of 1950. A key component of the ECHR system is the European Court of Human Rights (ECtHR), which has an independent application procedure allowing individuals to bring claims before the court when the protected right is violated by the specific State. The ECHR lays down the obligations that member states undertake to secure citizens' rights within their jurisdictions. From the history, the ECtHR has effectively interpreted the ECHR in a generally applicable way that provides guidelines for understanding the document in the modern context.[43]

The right to freedom of expression is guaranteed by Article 10 of the ECHR. Under the ECHR, freedom of expression is not only important in its own right but also a central part in litigations concerning other rights, such as the freedom of assembly, association, and demonstration.[44] The ECtHR has reiterated that "freedom of expression constitutes one of the essential foundations of a democratic society and one of the basic conditions for its progress and for each individual's self-fulfillment".[45] Article 10 of the ECHR provides:

> (1) Everyone has the right to freedom of expression. This right shall include freedom to hold opinions and to receive and impart information and ideas without interference by public authority and regardless of frontiers. This Article shall not prevent States from requiring licensing of broadcasting, television or cinema enterprises.
> (2) The exercise of these freedoms, since it carries with it duties and responsibilities, may be subject to such formalities, conditions, restrictions or penalties as are prescribed by law and are necessary in democratic society, in the interests of national security, territorial in-

[43] Russell L. Weaver, David F. Partlett and Mark D. Cole, Protecting Privacy in a Digital Age. In: Dieter Dörr and Russell L. Weaver, *The Right to Privacy in the Light of Media Convergence: Perspectives From Three Continent*, De Gruyter: Berlin (2012), pp. 1-30.

[44] *See* generally Flauss, Jean-Françosi, *The European Court of Human Rights and the Freedom of Expression*, Indiana Law Journal: Vol.84: Iss.3, Article 3 (2009); Monica Macovei, *A Guide to the Implementation of Article 10 of the European Convention on Human Rights,* Human Rights Hand Book, No.2, Second Edition, Council of Europe (2004); and Jochen Abr. Frowein, *Freedom of Expression under the European Convention on Human Rights,* in Monitor/inf 3, Council of Europe (1997).

[45] European Court of Human Rights, *Perna v. Italy*, Application No. 48898/99 (6 May 2003), para. 39.

> tegrity or public safety, for the prevention of disorder or crime, for the protection of health or morals, for the protection of the reputation or rights of others, for preventing the disclosure of information received in confidence, or for maintaining the authority and impartiality of the judiciary.

Three components of the right to freedom of expression are prescribed in paragraph 1 of Article 10, which includes freedom to hold opinions, freedom to impart information and ideas, and freedom to receive information and ideas. Any unnecessary restrictions on the right to freedom to hold opinions will be inconsistent with the nature of a democratic society.[46] Freedom to impart information and ideas should be considered complementary to freedom to receive information and ideas. Since individuals should enjoy the right to directly contact each other at will, States must not interfere between the imparter and receiver, unless under the circumstances prescribed by paragraph 2.[47]

According to the ECtHR, due to the central role of freedom to impart information in a democratic society, a speech affords a high level of protection when it involves matters of political or public concern,[48]and a State's margin of appreciation is more limited in the area of political discourse than in the area of moral concerns. Moreover, the right to disseminate information and ideas is not only limited to the information and ideas that are broadly accepted but also expanded to those unpleasant or potentially offensive expressions. In this respect, the ECtHR, in its landmark decision, *Handyside v. the United Kingdom*, stated:

> "The Court's supervisory functions oblige it to pay the utmost attention to the principles characterizing a "democratic society". Freedom of expression constitutes one of the essential foundations of such a society, one of the basic conditions for its progress and for the development of every man. Subject to paragraph 2 of Article 10 (art. 10-2), it is applicable not only to "information" or "ideas" that are favourably received or regarded as inof-

[46] Van Dijk and Van Hoof, *In Theory and Practice of the European Convention on Human Rights*, Report of the Committee of Ministers, Kluwer (1990), p. 413.

[47] Monica Macovei, *A Guide to the Implementation of Article 10 of the European Convention on Human Rights,* Human Rights Hand Book, No.2, Second Edition, Council of Europe (2004).

[48] European Court of Human Rights, *Hertel v. Switzerland*, ECHR 59/1997/843/1049 (25 August 1998). In the case, the Court stated:

> It is however necessary to reduce the extent of the margin of appreciation when what is at stake is not a given individual's purely "commercial" statements, but his participation in a debate affecting the general interest, for example, over public health in the instant case, it cannot be denied that such a debate existed. It concerned the effects of microwaves on human health.

> fensive or as a matter of indifference, but also to those that offend, shock or disturb the State or any sector of the population. Such are the demands of that pluralism, tolerance and broadmindedness without which there is no "democratic society"." [49]

In addition, freedom to receive information and ideas in Article 10 includes the right to gather and seek information through all possible lawful sources by using all possible methods.[50] In the *Leader v. Sweden* case, the ECtHR stated that the right to receive information under Article 10 "basically prohibited a Government from restricting a person from receiving information that others may wish or may be willing to impart to him".[51] In a more recent case, *Társaság a Szabadságjogokért v. Hungary,* the court delivered an important judgment in which it recognized the right to access official documents. The ECtHR made it clear that when public bodies hold information that is needed for public debate, the refusal to provide documents in the matter to those who are requesting access is a violation of the right to freedom of expression and information guaranteed under Article 10 of the ECHR.[52]

The Court further referred to the 'censorial power of an information monopoly' of public bodies, especially when the public authorities refuse to release information needed by the media or civil society organizations to perform their watchdog functions to contribute to the public debate.[53] The ECtHR underlined

---

[49] European Court of Human Rights, *Handyside v. the United Kingdom*, Application No. 5493/72, Series A no.24 (7 December 1976).

[50] Monica Macovei, *A Guide to the Implementation of Article 10 of the European Convention on Human Rights,* Human Rights Hand Book, No.2, Second Edition, Council of Europe (2004).

[51] European Court of Human Right, *Leander v. Sweden*, Application No. 9248/81, Series A no. 116 (23 March 1987).

[52] European Court of Human Rights, *Társaság a Szabadságjogokért v. Hungary*, Application No. 37374/05 (14 April 2009). "The Court considers that obstacles created in order to hinder access to information of public interest may discourage those working in the media or related fields from pursuing such matters. As a result, they may no longer be able to play their vital role as "public watchdogs" and their ability to provide accurate and reliable information may be adversely affected." (para. 38).

[53] Ibid., When considering the criteria of whether the measure is necessary in a democratic society, the Court stated that "it considers that the present case essentially concerns an interference – by virtue of the censorial power of an information monopoly – with the exercise of the functions of a social watchdog, like the press, rather than a denial of a general right of access to official documents.... Moreover, the State's obligations in matters of freedom of press include the elimination of barriers to the exercise of

that "the law cannot allow arbitrary restrictions which may become a form of indirect censorship should the authorities create obstacles to the gathering of information."[54] Moreover, Article 10 of the ECHR protects not only the substance of the information and ideas but also the methods in which they are expressed and received. In other words, any printed documents[55], radio broadcasts[56], paintings[57], films[58], or information imparted, disseminated, or received via the Internet are all guaranteed within the meaning of Article 10.

However, freedom of expression and information under the ECHR is also not unconditional. The second paragraph specifies that exercising the freedoms described in paragraph 1 carries its duties and responsibilities, and freedom of expression, under specific circumstances, can be curtailed in furtherance of a series of enumerated interests. Nevertheless, reading in correspondence with Article 17 of the ECHR, any restrictions, conditions, limitations on freedom of expression should never conflict with the substance of the right. Article 17 (Prohibition of abuse of rights) states:

---

press functions, where, in issues of public interest, such barriers exist solely because of an information monopoly held by the authorities." (para. 36).

[54] Ibid, para. 27.

[55] European Court of Human Rights, *Handyside v. the United Kingdom*, Application No. 5493/72, Series A no.24 (7 December 1976).

[56] European Court of Human Rights, *Groppera Radio AG and others v. Switzerland*, Application No. 10890/84, Series A no.173 (28 March 1990). In the case, the "Court does not consider it necessary to give on this occasion a precise definition of what is meant by "information" and "ideas". "Broadcasting" is mentioned in the Convention precisely in relation to freedom of expression. Like the Commission, the Court consider that both broadcasting of programmes over the air and cable retransmission of such programmes are covered by the right enshrined in the first two sentence of Article 10 § 1 (art. 10-1), without there being any need to make distinctions according to the content of the programmes. (para. 55)

[57] European Court of Human Rights, *Müller and Others v. Switzerland*, Application No. 10737/84, Series A no.133 (24 May 1988). Concerning whether an artistic work is included in the scope of Article 10, the Court stated that "[a]dmittedly, Article 10 (art.10) does not specify that freedom of artistic expression, in the issue here, comes within its ambit; but neither, on the other hand, does it distinguish between the various forms of expression. As those appearing before the Court all acknowledged, it includes freedom of artistic expression – notably within freedom to receive and impart information and ideas – which affords the opportunity to take part in the public exchange of cultural, political and social information and ideas of all kinds."

[58] European Court of Human Rights, *Otto-Preminger-Institut v. Austria*, Application No. 13470/87, Series A no.295-A (20 September 1994).

> Nothing in this Convention may be interpreted as implying for any State, group or person any right to engage in any activity or perform any act aimed at the destruction of any of the rights and freedoms set forth herein or at their limitation to a greater extent than is provided for in the Convention.

According to paragraph 2 of Article 10, any contracting States may intervene in the exercise of freedom of expression where three cumulative conditions are fulfilled. Any interference, e.g., formality, condition, restriction, or penalty, must (1) be prescribed by law; (2) have a legitimate aim under paragraph 2 of Article 10; and (3) be necessary in a democratic society. The ECtHR accentuated that any permissible limitation on the right to freedom of expression must be narrowly and strictly interpreted. For example, in the *Sunday Times v. United Kingdom* case, the ECtHR held:

> "Freedom of expression, as enshrined in Article 10 (art.10), is subject to a number of exceptions which, however, must be narrowly interpreted and the necessity for any restrictions must be convincingly established."[59]

First, the term "*prescribed by law*" refers to the quality of the law and requires that a law has to be public, accessible, predictable, and foreseeable. In *Association Ekin v. France*, the ECtHR pointed out that "the expression "prescribed by law", within the meaning of Article 10 § 2, requires firstly that the impugned measure should have some basis in domestic law; however, it also refers to the person concerned, who must moreover be able to foresee its consequences, and that it should be compatible with the rules of law".[60] Furthermore, the Court emphasized in several cases that in order to qualify as a 'law' within the meaning of Article 10, the law must be foreseeable and formulated with sufficient precision to enable an individual to regulate his conduct.[61]

---

[59] European Court of Human Rights, *Sunday Times v. United Kingdom (No.2)*, Application No. 13166/87 (26 November 1991).

[60] European Court of Human Rights, *Association Ekin v. France*, Application No. 39288/98 (17 July 2001).

[61] In *Sunday Times v. United Kingdom*, the Court stated:

> …a norm cannot not be regarded as a "law" unless it is formulated with sufficient precision to enable the citizen to regulate his conduct: he must be able – if need be with appropriate device – to foresee, to a degree that is reasonable in the circumstances, the consequences which a given action may entail. Those consequences need to be foreseeable with absolute certainty; experience shows this to be unattainable. Again, whilst certainty is highly desirable, it may bring in its train excessive rigidity and the law must be able to keep pace with changing circumstances. Accordingly, many laws are inevitably couched in terms which, to a greater or

Second, if a restrictive measure is 'prescribed by law', the measure must aim to pursue a legitimate objective. The list of the catalogue of possible restrictions on the freedom of expression under Article 10 of the ECHR is exhaustive. Contacting States cannot evoke any other reasons which are not encompassed in paragraph 2 as legitimate aims to justify the restrictive measures on the right to freedom of expression. The national courts must have the responsibility to identify the value protected by the domestic provision and recognize whether the value is one of those enumerated in paragraph 2.[62]

Lastly, the intervention in the exercise of freedom of expression is permissible only when it is necessary in a democratic society. The necessity test is a highly developed principle according to the decisions of the ECtHR. First, the Court has made it clear that for an interference to be necessary, it must reasonably serve a 'pressing social need'[63]. Second, the principle of proportionality must be applied in order to query whether the means are proportionate to the legitimate aim pursued.[64] Third, the Court must determine whether the "reasons given by the national authorities to justify the interference are relevant and sufficient".[65] While States have a certain margin of appreciation to determine whether such needs exist, this discretion is not unlimited as it goes hand in hand with the ECtHR's supervision.[66] The ECtHR has the ultimate authority to rule

---

> lesser extent, are vague and whose interpretation and application are questions of practice. (European Court of Human Right, *Sunday Times v. United Kingdom (No.1)*, Application No. 6538/74, para. 49 (26 April 1979))

[62] Monica Macovei, *A Guide to the Implementation of Article 10 of the European Convention on Human Rights*, Human Rights Hand Book, No.2, Second Edition, Council of Europe (2004).

[63] European Court of Human Rights, *Observer and Guardian v. the United Kingdom*, Application No. 13585/88 (26 November 1991). The Court stated:

> (c) The adjective "necessary", within the meaning of Article 10 para.2 (art.10-2), implies the existence of a "pressing social need". (para. 59).

[64] Ibid., para. 59-64.

[65] European Court of Human Rights, *Sunday Times v. United Kingdom (No.1)*, Application No. 6538/74 (26 April 1979). *See* also European Court of Human Rights, *Bladet Tromsø and Stensaas v. Norway*, Application No. 21980/93 (20 May 1999), para. 58.

[66] European Court of Human Rights, *Aleksey Ovchinnikov v. Russia*, Application No. 24061/04 (16 December 2010). As regards States' margin of appreciation, the Court held:

> In assessing whether such a "need" exists and what measures should be adopted to deal with it, the national authorities are left a certain margin of appreciation. This margin of appreciation is not, however, unlimited, but goes hand in hand with a European supervision by the Court, whose task it is to give a final ruling on whether a restriction is reconcilable with freedom of expression as protected by Article 10. (para. 46).

on whether the interference is reconcilable with the right to freedom of expression under Article 10 of the ECHR.

When considering the applicability of Article 10 of the ECHR to the Internet, it is important to bear in mind that in addition to the substance of information, Article 10 also applies to the various forms and means by which information is transmitted and received. As an innovative and powerful information medium, the Internet falls undoubtedly within the scope of Article 10. The ECtHR has recognized that "the Internet plays an important role in enhancing the public's access to news and facilitating the dissemination of information generally."[67]

Nevertheless, the Court has also noted that the principles of freedom of expression apply differently to different types of media and the extent of permissible restrictions depend on the nature of the medium.[68] Consequently, an analysis of the applicability of Article 10 to freedom of expression on the Internet needs to examine the unique characteristics of the Internet in comparison with traditional media.[69] For example, in *Stroll v. Switzerland*, the ECtHR believed that in the information age in which individuals are confronted with vast quantities of information, journalists' duties and responsibilities are reinforced for press publication on the Internet.[70]

In sum, while the ECtHR has interpreted Article 10 in a very flexible fashion to be compatible with the new prospects of freedom of expression in the digital age, it recognized a need for new balance between freedom of expression and other human rights on the Internet.[71] The Court also added more duties and re-

---

[67] European Court of Human Rights, *Times Newspapers Ltd (Nos.1 and 2) v. The United Kingdom*, Application No. 3002/03 and 23676/03 (10 March 2009), para. 27.

[68] European Court of Human Rights, *Jersild v. Denmark*, Application No. 15890/89, Series A no.298 (23 September 1994). When concerning the impact of the media, the Court explained:

> In considering the "duties and responsibilities" of a journalist, the potential impact of the medium concerned is an important factor and it is commonly acknowledged that the audiovisual media have often a much more immediate and powerful effect than the print media. ... The audiovisual media have means of conveying through images meanings which the print media are not able to impart. (para. 31).

[69] Center for Democracy & Technology, *"Regardless of Frontiers:" The International Right to Freedom of Expression in the Digital Age* (04 April 2011). Available at https://cdt.org/insight/regardless-of-frontiers-the-international-right-to-freedom-of-expression-in-the-digital-age/ (accessed 18 June 2014)

[70] European Court of Human Rights, *Stoll v. Switzerland*, Application No. 69698/01, para. 104 (10 December 2007).

[71] European Court of Human Rights, *Fredrik Neij and Peter Sunde Kolmisoppi v. Sweden*, Application No. 40397/12 (19 February 2013). In this case, the Court was asked to balance the interests between copyright owners and individuals' right to freedom of

sponsibilities of journalists with respect to the freedom of press online.[72] Therefore, it is unclear how the right to freedom of expression will be applied by the ECtHR in the near future. Given the risks brought by the Internet, this right is likely to be more limited than in the non-digital context; however, the ECtHR also emphasized more than once that the Internet is an important tool for individuals to exercise their freedom of expression and "any preliminary restriction to expression on the Internet is related to a heavy presumption of incompatibility with the Convention".[73]

The Charter of Fundamental Rights of the European Union (EUCFR)

The entry of the Lisbon Treaty into force in December 2009 not only changed the face of the European Union but also provided the full legal effect to the EUCFR.[74] Along with the Treaty on the EU and Treaty on the Functioning of the EU, the EUCFR is a legally binding document on all 28 Member States of the European Union. The Charter incorporates the whole range of civil, political, economic and social rights of European citizens. The Court of Justice of the European Union (ECJ), a judicial institution of the European Union, has its primary task to examine the legality of European Union measures and ensure the uniform interpretation and application of European Union law. According to Article 51 of the EUCFR, the jurisdiction of the ECJ is confined to the cases regarding EU law.[75]

The right to freedom of expression is enshrined in Article 11 of the EUCFR, which states in full:

---

expression. The Court stated that the Internet could, on the one hand, significantly enhance the exercise of certain human rights and fundamental freedoms while, on the other hand, it could adversely affect these and other such rights. The member States were recommended to elaborate a clear legal framework delineating the boundaries of the roles and responsibilities of all key stakeholders in the field of new information and communication technologies.

[72] European Court of Human Rights, *Stoll v. Switzerland*, Application No. 69698/01 (10 December 2007).

[73] European Court of Human Rights, *Yildirim V. Turkey*, Application No. 3111/10 (12 December 2012).

[74] European Union, *Charter of Fundamental Rights of the European Union*, 2012/c 326/02 (26 October 2012).

[75] Ibid., Article 51.

> 1. The provisions of this Charter are addressed to the institutions and bodies of the Union with due regard for the principle of subsidiarity and to the Member States only when they are implementing Union law. They shall therefore respect the rights, observe the principles and promote the application thereof in accordance with their respective powers.

> 1. Everyone has the right to freedom of expression. This right shall include freedom to hold opinions and to receive and impart information and ideas without interference by public authority and regardless of frontiers.
> 2. The freedom and pluralism of the media shall be respected.

While freedom of expression is guaranteed as a fundamental right under the EUCFR, the ECJ's decisions on human rights are sometimes controversial.[76] Reflecting the ECJ's understanding of itself as the judicial guardian of the single market based on the free movement of persons, goods, services, and capital,[77] it is not hard to infer that the ECJ is prone to subordinating fundamental human rights, including the right to freedom of expression, to economic interests. For example, in *Society for the Protection of the Unborn Child v. Grogan*, the ECJ found that the absolute ban on abortion information and on British medical facilities to carrying out terminations of pregnancies infringed the freedom to provide services and breached the right of the potential recipients of the service.[78] The same case was also brought in front of the ECtHR. On the contrary, the ECtHR founded that the measure in question is in violation of individuals' right to freedom of expression, guaranteed under Article 10 of the ECHR.[79] The ECJ's reasoning and methodology in the *Grogan* case has been criticized

---

[76] Maya Hertig Randall, *Human Rights Within a Multilayered Constitution: The Example of Freedom of Expression and the WTO*, Max Planck Yearbook of United Nations Law, Volume 26 (2012), p. 183-280.

[77] Treaty on the Functioning of the European Union (TFEU), which replaced the Treaty on European Union and the Treaty establishing the European Community after the enter into force of the Lisbon Treaty, guarantees the free movement of persons in Article 45, which states that "freedom of movement for workers shall be secured within the **Union**." Free movement of services is enshrined in Article 56 of the TEFU, which regulated that "within the framework of the provisions set out below, restrictions on freedom to provide service within the **Union** shall be prohibited in respect of nationals of Member States who are established in a **Member State** other than that of the person for whom the services are intended." Furthermore, in protection of free movement of capital, Article 63 of the TFEU stipulated "within the framework of the provisions set out in this chapter, all restrictions on the movement of capital between Member States and between Member States and third countries shall be prohibited."

[78] ECJ Case C-159/90, *The Society for the Protection of Unborn Children Ireland Ltd v. Stephen Grogan*, ECR I-4658 (1991).

[79] European Court of Human Rights, *Open Door Counseling Ltd and Dublin Well Women Centre Ltd and others v. Ireland*, Application No. 14234/88, Series A 264 A (29 October 1992).

that the court did not take fundamental rights seriously but used them as a means to foster economic interests.[80]

Nevertheless, the incorporation of the EUCFR into the EU legal system undoubtedly endows the fundamental rights protections with substantive legitimacy and may, therefore, "accelerate the departure from a predominantly economic focus of the European integration project".[81] For instance, in a later case, *Schmidberger*, the ECJ was asked to determine whether the domestic legislation at issue was compatible with the free movement of goods to the extent it permitted the temporary closure of a motorway for a demonstration intended to draw the public's attention to environmental issues.[82] The ECJ referred to the requirements of limitations on freedom of expression under Article 10 of the ECHR and stated explicitly that states enjoy a wide margin of appreciation to justify restrictions to free movement guarantees if such restrictions are proportionate in the light of the legitimate objective pursued, i.e., the protection of fundamental rights.[83]

Article 11 of the EUCFR corresponds to Article 10 of the ECHR, and the EUJ frequently cites ECtHR's judgments and treats them with deference. Pursuant to Article 52 (3) of the Charter[84], to the extent the rights contained in the EUCFR are accorded with the rights protected under the ECHR, the meaning and scope of those rights are the same as those guaranteed by the ECHR. The limitations on the rights should, therefore, not exceed those provided in Article 10 (2) of the ECHR. Consequently, freedom of expression has been recognized as a general principle of EU law by the ECJ, specifically as understood by Article 10 of the ECHR. Although Article 11 of the EUCFR does not define what constitutes 'expression', it should expand to a range of forms beyond just speech. The concept that freedom of expression covers not only the substance of

---

[80] *See* Diarmuid Rossa Phelan, *Right to Life of the Unborn v Promotion of Trade in Services: The European Court of Justice and the Normative Shaping of the European Union*, The Modern Law Review, Vol.55, No.5 (September 1992), pp. 670-689.

[81] *See* Maya Hertig Randall, *Human Rights Within a Multilayered Constitution: The Example of Freedom of Expression and the WTO*, Max Planck Yearbook of United Nations Law, Volume 26 (2012), p. 183-280.

[82] ECJ Case C-112/00 *Eugen Schmidberger, Internationale Transporte und Planzüge v. Republic Österreich,* [2003] ECJ I-5659, para. 80.

[83] Ibid, paras. 82-93.

[84] Article 52 (3) of the EU Charter of the Fundamental Rights:

> 3. In so far as this Charter contains rights which correspond to the rights guaranteed by the Convention for the Protection of Human Rights and Fundamental Freedoms, the meaning and scope of those rights shall be the same as those laid down by the said Convention. This provision shall not prevent Union law from providing more extensive protection.

the ideas and information but also the form in which they are conveyed is also recognized by the ECJ.[85]

The terms used in Article 11 are broad and have been interpreted dynamically by the ECJ when considering the changes in communication and information technologies.[86] The Luxemburg Court dealt with a few cases concerning the right to freedom of expression on the Internet and copyright protection. Under Article 17 (2) of the EUCFR, the intellectual property right is protected as a fundamental right.[87] In *Sabam v. Netlog*, the ICJ was asked to rule on the issue of whether the legislative authorities were entitled, pursuant to EU law, to impose on ISPs the obligations to adopt a filtering system for detecting possible copyright infringements.[88] After considering the EUCFR and the E-Commerce Directive, which governs the responsibility of ISPs, the ECJ stated:

> "..., in adopting the injunction requiring the hosting service provider to install the contested filtering system, the national court concerned would not be respecting the requirement that a fair balance be struck between the right to intellectual property, on the one hand, and the freedom to conduct business, the right to protection of personal data and the freedom to receive or impart information, on the other."[89]

By clarifying that the right to intellectual property is not an absolute right, the court found that the requirement to adopt a filtering system is disproportionate since, first, it would compel the ISPs to install a complicated, costly, and per-

---

[85] ECJ Case C-316/09, *MSD Sharp v. Dohme*, GmbH [2011] ECJ I-3295. The Court stated:

> The referring court explains that publications on the Internet also fall within the scope of Title VIII of Directive 2001/83 when they are intended to promote sales and that it matters little whether they are presentations promoting the medicinal product concerned or other information relating to it. (para. 17).

[86] *See* Steve Peer, Tamara Hervey, Jeff Kenner, and Angela Ward, *The EU Charter of Fundamental Rights – A Commentary*, Hart Publishing: United Kingdom (2014), pp. 311-340.

[87] Article 17 of the EU Charter of Fundamental Rights (Right to property):

> Everyone has the right to own, use, dispose of and bequeath his or her lawfully acquired possessions. No one may be deprived of his or her possessions, except in the public interest and in the cases and under the conditions provided by law, subject to fair compensation being paid in good time for their loss. The use of property may be regulated by law in so far as is necessary for the general interest.
>
> Intellectual property shall be protected.

[88] ECJ Case C-360/10, *Belgische Vereniging van Auteurs, Componisten en Uitgevers CVBA (SABAM) v. Netlog NV* (16 February 2012).

[89] Ibid., para. 51.

manent computer system at its own expense. The requirement would result in the restriction of the right to carry out economic activities, which is protected under Article 16 of the EUCFR[90]. Second, the Court considered the filtering system constituted a violation of Article 8 and Article 11 of the EU Charter and infringed individuals' right to privacy and right to freedom of expression.

The case can be seen as a crucial step taken by the ECJ to protect fundamental rights on the Internet. Nevertheless, the decision seems to downgrade the role entrusted to freedom of expression as a vital element for promoting individuals' self-fulfillment and autonomy, since freedom of expression and the right to privacy were considered secondarily after the freedom to economic activity. Some criticized that "the judges of Luxembourg have not demonstrated a full emancipation from the original economic dimension of the EU in granting protection to fundamental rights".[91] The legal standing of the application of the right to freedom of expression on the Internet may remain unclear under EU law.

Meanwhile, the Guidelines on Freedom of Expression Online and Offline adopted by the EU Council in May 2014 might shed some light on possible future developments.[92] The document is intended to identify and clarify a range of principles with regard to freedom of expression, communication, and freedom of press. The Guidelines emphasize that freedom of expression should be interpreted broadly while the exceptions should be interpreted narrowly and subject to the tests of legality, necessity, and proportionality.

In particular, the Guidelines identify that all human rights that exist offline must also be protected online, especially the right to freedom of opinion and expression and the right to privacy.[93] Additionally, the document also under-

---

[90] Article 16 of the EU Charter of the Fundamental Rights guaranteed the freedom to conduct a business: The freedom to conduct a business in accordance with Community law and national laws and practices is recognized.

[91] *See* Oreste Pollicino, European Judicial Dialogue and the Protection of Fundamental Rights in the New Digital Environment: An Attempt at Emancipation and Reconciliation: The Case of Freedom of Speech. In: Morano-Foadi Sonia and Vickers Lucy (eds.), *Fundamental Rights in the EU: A Matter for Two Courts,* Hart Publishing: United Kingdom (March 2015), pp. 93-114.

[92] Council of The European Union, *EU Human Rights Guidelines on Freedom of Expression Online and Offline, Foreign Affairs Council Meeting*, Brussels (12 May 2014).

[93] Ibid., By recognizing the open nature of the Internet and its impact on individuals' fundamental right, the Guidelines stress,

> 6. … All human rights that exist offline must also be protected online, in particular the right to freedom of opinion and expression and the right to privacy, which also includes the protection of personal data.
>
> 35. The global and open nature of the Internet is providing citizens with new opportunities for exchanging information and opinions. The obligations of States under international human

scores that restrictions on the exercise of freedom of expression may not put in jeopardy the right itself and any limitations that prevent the flow of information offline or online must be in conformity with the permissible limitations as set out in international human rights law.[94] By adopting the Guidelines, the EU subjected its principles of freedom of expression to internationally recognized standards and committed itself to promote an unhindered, uncensored, and non-discriminatory access to information and communication technologies for all.

The American Convention on Human Rights

The inter-American human rights system can be traced back to April 1948, when the American Declaration of the Rights and Duties of Man was adopted. The American Declaration was the first international human rights instrument since the document was adopted a few months before the adoption of the Universal Declaration. The IACHR was created in 1959 and acted as a principal and autonomous organ of the Organization of American States (OAS), whose mission is to promote and protect human rights in the American hemisphere.[95] Together with the Inter-American Court of Human Rights, the IACHR is one of the institutions within the inter-American system for the protection and observance of fundamental human rights.

The American Convention on Human Rights (American Convention) was adopted in 1969 and entered into force in 1978.[96] The Convention is ratified by 25 countries. The scope of the right to freedom of expression under the American Convention, in comparison with the ECHR and ICCPR, was designed to be more generous in its protection of the right. For the purpose of the following

rights law, in particular the right to freedom of expression, the right to privacy and the protection of personal data, extend to the online sphere in the same way as they apply offline.

[94] Ibid., the Guidelines highlight, "any restriction that prevents the flow of information offline or online must be in line with permissible limitations as set out in international human rights law." (para. 16).

[95] *See* David J. Padilla, *The Inter-American Commission on Human Rights of the Organization of American States: A Case Study*, American University International Law Review, Vol.9, Issue:1 (1993), pp. 95-115.

[96] A complete overview of free expression law and practice in the Inter-American system could be found in the Annual Report of the Inter-American Commission on Human Rights, *Reports of the Special Rapporteur for Freedom of Expression*, OEA/Ser.L/V/II (30 December 2009).

analysis, it is necessary to place the full text of Article 13 of the American Convention:[97]

> Freedom of Thought and Expression
> 1. Everyone has the right to freedom of thought and expression. This right includes freedom to seek, receive, and impart information and ideas of all kinds, regardless of frontiers, either orally, in writing, in print, in the form of art, or through any other medium of one's choice.
> 2. The exercise of the right provided for in the foregoing paragraph shall not be subjected to prior censorship but shall be subject to subsequent imposition of liability, which shall be expressly established by law to the extent necessary to ensure:
> a. Respect for the rights or reputations of others; or
> b. The protection of national security, public order, or public health or morals.
> 3. The right of expression may not be restricted by indirect methods or means, such as the abuse of government or private controls over newsprint, radio broadcasting frequencies, or equipment used in the dissemination of information, or by any other means tending to impede the communication circulation of ideas and opinions.
> 4. Notwithstanding the provisions of paragraph 2 above, public entertainments may be subject by law to prior censorship for the sole purpose of regulating access to them for the moral protection of childhood and adolescence.
> 5. Any propaganda for war and any advocacy of national, racial, or religious hatred that constitutes incitements to lawless violence or to any other similar action against any person or group of persons on any grounds including those of race, color, religion, language, or national origin shall be considered as offenses punishable by law.

According to case law, the Inter-American Commission and the Inter-American Court underlined that the importance of freedom of expression within the sphere of human rights originates in its structural relationship to the democratic society.[98] In the Annual Report of the office of the Special Rapporteur for freedom of expression, the Rapporteur emphasized that "the link between freedom of expression and democracy is so important that, according to the Inter-

[97] Organization of American States, *American Convention on Human Rights "Pact of San Jose, Costa Rica"*, B-32 (22 November 1969).
[98] I/A Court H.R., *Compulsory Membership in an Association Prescribed by Law for the Practice of Journalism (Arts. 13 and 29 American Convention on Human Rights)*, Advisory Opinion OC-5/85, Series A No. 5. (13 November 1985), para. 70.

American Commission, the very purpose of Article 13 of the American Convention is to strengthen the operation of deliberation and a pluralistic democratic system through the protection and promotion of the free circulation of information, ideas and expressions of all kinds".[99]

The inter-American human rights system is relatively broad when compared with the European systems. First, the language, "either orally, in print, in the form of art or through any other medium of one's choice", used in Article 13.1 shows that the provision is in line with Article 19 of the ICCPR. Therefore, the Convention was designed to encompass technological developments, which were not foreseen at the time of the drafting,[100] and any types of Internet-related networks should provide the same level of protection to freedom of expression within the meaning of Article 13 of the American Convention.[101]

Second, Article 13.2 of the American Convention explicitly states that the exercise of the right to freedom of expression "shall not subject to prior censorship". In the Declaration of Principles of Freedom of Expression, which constitutes a basic document for interpreting Article 13 of the American Convention, the Inter-American Commission emphasized the vital influence of prior censorship and stated that "prior censorship, direct or indirect interference in or pressure exerted upon any expression, opinion, or information transmitted through any means of oral, written, artistic, virtual or, electronic communication must be prohibited by law".[102] According to the Commission, prior censorship produces an extreme and radical suspension of freedom of expression as it prevents the free circulation of information, ideas, opinions, or news in advance. Nevertheless, pursuant to Article 13.4, prior censorship is allowed in the case of public entertainments, but only in order to regulate the access for the moral protection of children and adolescents.

Lastly, Article 13.3 of the American Convention further prohibits the indirect restrictions on freedom of expression. Both governments and private actors

---

[99] The Inter-American system could be found in the Annual Report of the Inter-American Commission on Human Rights, *Reports of the Special Rapporteur for Freedom of Expression*, OEA/Ser.L/V/II, Chapter III (30 December 2009), para. 8.

[100] Center for Democracy & Technology, *"Regardless of Frontiers:" The International Right to Freedom of Expression in the Digital Age* (04 April 2011). Available at https://cdt.org/insight/regardless-of-frontiers-the-international-right-to-freedom-of-expression-in-the-digital-age/. (accessed 22 June 2014)

[101] Office of the Special Rapporteur for Freedom of Expression of the Inter-American Commission on Human Rights, *Freedom of Expression and the Internet*, OEA/Ser.L/V/II (2013).

[102] Inter-American Commission on Human Rights (IACHR), *American Declaration of the Rights and Duties of Man*, 2 May 1948. Principle 5.

should not indirectly abuse their power to control or restrict the right to expression over 'newsprint, radio broadcasting frequencies, or equipment used in the dissemination of information'. Read together with Article 1 of the American Convention; Article 13.3 imposes not only negative obligations on States to not to adopt restrictive measures of indirect characters, which interfere with the rights of the individuals, but also positive obligations to ensure the interference does not come from private control.[103] Additionally, according to the Inter-American Court of Human Rights, indirect methods listed in Article 13.3 are not exclusive and the term 'any other means' should include indirect means derived from the new communication and information technologies.

To sum up, the rights protected in Article 13 of the American Convention apply to traditional media as well as to the Internet. The report of the OAS Office of the Special Rapporteur for Freedom of Expression explicitly asserted that Article 13 applies fully to communications, ideas, and information distributed through the Internet.[104] The report also acknowledged that steps should be taken to progressively guarantee access to the Internet for all persons to ensure the effective and universal enjoyment of the right to freedom of expression.[105] When considering the legislative limitations on the free flow of information on the Internet, the Special Rapporteur suggested that due to the unique characteristics of the Internet, the evaluation of each restrictive measure must be conducted in a systemic digital perspective.[106] Ultimately, the impact of a restriction on the Internet's capacity to guarantee and promote freedom of expression needs be weighed against the benefits it would have in protecting other interests.

---

[103] Compulsory Membership in an Association Prescribed by Law for the Practice of Journalism (Art.13 and 29 of the American Convention on Human Rights), *Advisory Opinion OC-5/58*, Inter-Am.Ct.H.R. (Ser.A) N0.5 (1985), para. 48.

[104] Office of the Special Rapporteur for Freedom of Expression of the Inter-American Commission on Human Rights, *Freedom of Expression and the Internet*, OEA/Ser.L/V/II (2013).

[105] Ibid., pp. 15-23.

[106] The report suggested that when applied to measures that could compromise the Internet, the requirements should be evaluated from a systematic digital perspective, which includes: (1) legal enshrinement; (2) seeking a crucial goal; (3) necessity, suitability and proportionality of the measure for achieving the aim sought; (4) judicial guarantees; and (5) satisfaction of due process, including user notifications.

b. Permissible Limitations to Freedom of Opinion and Expression on the Internet

As illustrated in the previous section, the right to freedom of expression is a fundamental human right of the greatest importance. At the same time, like most values in the modern democratic society, it is universally recognized that the right is not without conditions. Despite the different grounds and contexts, almost every international or regional human rights system has developed some criteria of limitations on freedom of expression. The discussion in this section focuses on the methodology for analyzing restrictions on the freedom of expression and how to apply the standards in the digital environment. Evaluation of the specific areas of restrictions, such as defamation, public morals, or national security, will not be included.

International human rights law has developed a general three-part test for assessing restrictions on freedom of expression. The test is elaborated in numerous international human rights treaties and examined by various international human rights courts. According Article 19 & 29 of the UDHR, Article 19(3) of the ICCPR, Article 10(2) of the ECHR, and Article 13 (2) of the American Convention, an interference in an individual's right to freedom of expression must be prescribed by law, to pursue a legitimate aim, and to be necessary in a democratic society. The three-part test has to be cumulative. As stated in the decision of UN Human Rights Committee in *Mukong v. Cameroon*:

> "Under article 19, everyone shall have the right to freedom of expression. Any restriction of the freedom of expression pursuant to paragraph 3 of article 19 must cumulatively meet the following conditions: it must be provided for by law, it must address one of the aims enumerated in paragraph 3(a) and (b) of article 19 and must be necessary to achieve the legitimate purpose." [107]

Additionally, although a state might enjoy a certain margin of appreciation in assessing the need for and extent of the interference of freedom of expression, this discretion may not jeopardize the right itself. The derogation must be compatible with the provisions of the treaties relied upon, and "the relation between right and restriction, between norm and exception, must not be reversed."[108] As stipulated in Article 5 paragraph 1 of the ICCPR, "nothing in the present Cove-

[107] UN Human Rights Committee (HRC), *Mukong v, Cameroon*, Communication No. 458/1991(21 July 1994), para. 9.7.
[108] UN Human Rights Committee (HRC), *CCPR General Comment No. 27: Article 12 (Freedom of Movement)*, CCPR/C/21/Rev.1/Add.9 (2 November 1999).

nant may be interpreted as implying for any State, group or person any right to engage in any activity or perform any act aimed at the destruction of any of the rights and freedoms recognized herein or at their limitation to a greater extent than is provided for in the present Covenant." The similar language is also underlined in Article 17 of the ECHR.[109]

The first criterion of the three-part test is that any restrictions must be prescribed by law. First, elected representatives, working through parliament, should have the power to impose restrictive measures on a right or a freedom.[110] Nevertheless, the term 'law' should not only refer to the statutory law but also to the unwritten law, i.e., the common law. In the *Sunday Times v. United Kingdom* case, the ECtHR emphasized that declining the common law as a type of law within the scope of Article 19(3) will strike at the very roots of States' legal system.[111] Secondly, the law must be adequately accessible to the public. The citizen must be able to have the knowledge of what is adequate in the circumstances of the legal rules applicable to the given case.[112] Third, the law must be formulated with sufficient precision to enable the citizens to foresee the consequences which a given action may entail. Vague and wide provisions are susceptible to broad interpretation by the authorities and those subject to the law. As a result, the imprecise laws will exert a chilling effect on freedom of expres-

[109] Article 17 of the ECHR:

> Nothing in this Convention may be interpreted as implying for any State, group or person any right to engage in any activity or perform any act aimed at the destruction of any of the rights and freedoms set forth herein or at their limitation to a greater extent than is provided for in the Convention.

[110] *See* UN Human Rights Committee, *General Comment No. 34, Article 19: Freedoms of Opinion and Expression*, U.N. Doc. CCPR/C/GC/34 (12 September 2011); UN Human Rights Committee (HRC), *CCPR General Comment No. 27: Article 12 (Freedom of Movement)*, CCPR/C/21/Rev.1/Add.9 (2 November 1999); and Christoph Grabenwarter, *European Convention on Human Rights Commentary*, C.H. Beck oHG, Hart, Nomos, Heibing Lichtenhahn Verlag, München (2014), pp. 262-291.

[111] European Court of Human Right, *Sunday Times v. United Kingdom (No.1)*, Application No. 6538/74 (26 April 1979). When considering the interference "prescribed by law", the Court stated:

> 47. ... It would clearly be contrary to the intention of the drafters of the Convention to hold that a restriction imposed by virtue of the common law is not "prescribed by law" on the sole ground that it is not enunciated in legislation: this would deprive a common-law State which is Party to the Convention of the protection of Article 10(2)(art.10-2) and strike at the very roots of that State's legal system.

[112] Ibid., para. 49.

sion. The scope of the foreseeability, however, varies depending on the content of the text at issue.[113]

The second criterion requires that any restrictions must serve one of the legitimate purposes expressly enumerated in the text. Variation exists among the different Conventions when concerning the legitimate purposes for which freedom of expression may be restricted. Article 29 of the UDHR permits restrictions only to secure due recognition and respect for the rights and freedoms of others and to meet the just requirements of morality, public order, and the general welfare. Article 19 (3) of the ICCPR allows the restrictions to protect the rights or reputations of others, national security, ordre public, public health, and public morals. Article 13 of the American Convention follows the language of the ICCPR except that it adopts the term 'public order' instead of 'ordre public' to narrow the scope of the application. Lastly, the permissible limitations listed in Article 10 (2) of the ECHR are broader than other international human rights treaties. The legitimate objectives include the interests of national security, territorial integrity or public safety, the prevention of disorder or crime, the protection of the reputation or rights of others, the prevention of the disclosure of information received in confidence, and the maintenance of the authority and impartiality of the judiciary.

Third, any restrictions on freedom of expression must be necessary to pursue the legitimate aim. Necessity is a complicated concept but represents as a high threshold for States seeking to justify a restriction on fundamental human rights. As cited in several cases by the ECtHR:

> "Freedom of expression, as enshrined in Article 10, is subject to a number of exceptions, which, however, must be narrowly interpreted and the necessity for any restrictions must be convincingly established."[114]

---

[113] European Court of Human Rights, *Chauvy and Others v. France*, Application No. 64915/01 (29 June 2004). To analyze the foreseeable law, the Court held:

> 44. The scope of the notion of foreseeability depends to a considerable degree on the content of the text in issue, the field it is designed to cover, and the number and status of those to whom it is addressed. … A law may still satisfy the requirement of foreseeability even if the person concerned has to take appropriate legal advice to assess, to a degree that is reasonable in the circumstances, the consequences which a given action may entail.

[114] European Court of Human Rights, Observer and Guardian v. the United Kingdom, Application No. 13585/88, para. 59 (26 November 1991). European Court of Human Rights, *Sunday Times v. United Kingdom (No.2)*, Application No. 13166/87(26 November 1991), para. 50.

The international courts often first assess whether there is a pressing or substantial social need when considering the necessity test. While States might have a certain margin of appreciation in deciding whether such a need exists, the degree of the latitude a State might enjoyed needs to be balanced with the underlying right. It is the court that is empowered to have the final ruling on whether a restriction is reconcilable with freedom of expression.[115]

In addition, a limitation on the right must not be overbroad and must conform to the principle of proportionality. That is to say; an interfered measure has to be carefully designed so as to be the least restrictive to the right at issue. The Inter-American Court of Human Rights has recognized that if there are various options to achieving the legitimate purpose, that with least restricts the right protected must be selected.[116] Likewise, the measure must be proportionate to the interest to be protected. In other words, the benefit in terms of protecting the interests must be greater than the harm caused to the freedom of expression. Finally, States have the burden to demonstrate the precise nature of the threat and the necessity of the specific action taken. As suggested by the General Comment No.34 to Article 19 of the ICCPR:

> "The Committee recalls that the scope of this freedom is not to be assessed by reference to a "margin of appreciation" and in order for the Committee to carry out this function, a State party, in any given case, must demonstrate in specific fashion the precise nature of the threat to any of the enumerated grounds listed in paragraph 3 that has caused it to restrict freedom of expression."[117]

B. The Right to Privacy in the Online World

The right to privacy is not a recent concern accompanying the advent of the Internet but an ancient right. Being distinct from the public sphere, the refer-

---

[115] *See* UN Human Rights Committee, *General Comment No. 34, Article 19: Freedoms of Opinion and Expression*, U.N. Doc. CCPR/C/GC/34 (12 September 2011); Christoph Grabenwarter, *European Convention on Human Rights Commentary*, C.H. Beck oHG, Hart, Nomos, Heibing Lichtenhahn Verlag, München (2014); and European Court of Human Rights, *Sunday Times v. United Kingdom (No.2)*, Application No. 13166/87 (26 November 1991), para. 50.

[116] I/A Court H.R., *Compulsory Membership in an Association Prescribed by Law for the Practice of Journalism (Arts. 13 and 29 American Convention on Human Rights)*, Advisory Opinion OC-5/85, Series A No. 5 (13 November 1985), para. 46.

[117] UN Human Rights Committee, *General Comment No. 34, Article 19: Freedoms of Opinion and Expression*, U.N. Doc. CCPR/C/GC/34 (12 September 2011), para. 36.

ences to the private life of the personal domain have been rooted in the times of ancient Greece. Some protection of privacy existed in England as back as the 14th century.[118] Privacy reemerged as a key issue of modern times in the late 1800s when Samuel Warren and Louis Brandeis published their famous article in 1980, "*The Right to Privacy*". In the seminar paper, Warren and Brandeis defined privacy as the "right to be let alone" and asserted that the protection of the private realm is the foundation of individual freedom and is designed to protect the integrity of a person.[119]

Privacy is deeply rooted in the essential needs of a human being.[120] The concept of privacy is fundamentally about autonomy, knowledge, self-determination, power, and human dignity and integrity. The right to privacy represents the rights of individuals to control what is known about themselves and what other people know about them. The right to privacy provides individuals the power to reject intervention in their private life from both the governments and private sectors. Furthermore, the right to privacy reinforces other fundamental human rights such as the freedom of expression and information, and freedom of association.[121]

Despite being as a widely accepted right, there is no simple definition of the right to privacy that is universally understood in the same way. The notion of privacy is developed and shaped by social trends and available technologies. Since there is no widespread norm for what comprises socially appreciated behaviour, the definition of the right to privacy is different from culture to culture and country to country.[122] Whereas the securing of the right to privacy depends largely on the circumstances of individual cases, the core value of the privacy

---

[118] Electronic Privacy Information Center, *Privacy and Human Rights 2006: An International Survey of Privacy Laws and Developments*, Electronic Privacy Information Center and Privacy International, Washington, DC (2007), p. 5.

[119] Samuel Warren and Louis Brandeis, *The Right to Privacy*, Harvard Law Review 193, Vol.4, No.5 (15 December1980), pp. 193-220.

[120] *See* Toby Mendel, Andrew Puddephatt, Ben Wagner, Dixie Hawtin and Natalia Torres, *Global Survey on Internet Privacy and Freedom of Expression*, United Nations Educational, Scientific and Cultural Organization (2012), pp. 9-12.

[121] Ibid. (The right to privacy underpins many human rights, the right to freedom of association, freedom of belief and freedom of expression being particularly significant examples. If privacy is protected, then the integrity of the individual is assured, and this is the foundation of other rights and freedoms designed to protect the dignity of the person.)

[122] *See* James Waldo, Herbert S.Lin, and Lynette I. Millett (eds.), *Engaging Privacy and Information Technology in a Digital Age*, Washington, DC: The National Academic Press (2007), pp. 21-27.

for human dignity and integrity is internationally recognized and protected under international human rights law.

In modern human rights, privacy is enshrined in several international human rights conventions and treaties, including Article 12 of the UDHR, Article 17 of the ICCPR, and Article 8 of the ECHR. However, accompanied by the expanding application of new technologies, concerns about privacy incursion have been augmented in the past two decades. In the digital era, while new communication technologies enhance an individual's ability to seek, receive, and impart information and ideas, the same technologies have also enriched the capacity of the governments and private enterprises to collect and analyze personal information in an unprecedented way. The purpose of this section, therefore, is to address the importance of the right to privacy in the digital age and examine the legitimacy of the interference of the right with internationally recognized norms and standards of human rights law.

a. Privacy as a Fundamental Human Rights

Privacy in the modern world is protected by two forms of law. First are the constitutional and international rules and regulations in which privacy is protected as an individual right to identify a person. The second form of privacy law is related to the personal information handled by both the government and private sectors.[123] In the context of personal information, Alan Westin defined the right to privacy as "the claim of individuals, groups, or institutions to determine for themselves when, how, and to what extent information about them is communicated with others."[124] Thus, a positive obligation to protect privacy includes the protection of personal information, which is particularly relevant to privacy on the Internet.

A direct and explicit protection of privacy can be found in the international human rights law. Article 12 of the UDHR stipulates:

> No one shall be subjected to arbitrary interference with his privacy, family, home or correspondence, nor to attacks upon his honour and reputation. Everyone has the right to the protection of the law against such interference or attacks.

---

[123] *See* Gus Hosein, Privacy as Freedom. In: In: Rikke Frank Jørgenen, *Human Rights in Global Information Society*, The MIT Press: Cambridge, Massachusetts, London, England (2006), pp. 121-147.
[124] Alan F. Westin, *Privacy and Freedom*, Atheneum Press: New York (1967).

Under the UDHR, privacy is a foundation of human dignity. While the UDHR is not legally binding, and a country's reputation is the only incentive for complying with the Declaration, as a universal statement of values, the principle of a person's right to privacy against arbitrary interference embedded in the UDHR is strong and clear. States have the obligations to ensure that the regulations are enacted on the basis of good governance and guarantee that individuals' privacy should not be subject to arbitrary or unlawful interference.[125]

The right to privacy is also legally protected under Article 17 of the ICCPR, which regulates:

> 1. No one shall be subjected to arbitrary or unlawful interference with his privacy, family, home or correspondence, nor to unlawful attacks on his honour and reputation.
> 2. Everyone has the right to the protection of the law against such interference or attacks.

Under Article 17, states have both the negative and positive obligations to not arbitrarily interfere in the private life of individuals and to implement laws to prevent the interference of personal privacy. The UN Human Rights Committee clarified in a General Comment on Article 17 that the right to privacy encompasses the right to protection against all interferences and attacks whether they derive from the governments or natural or legal person.[126]

Article 8 of the ECHR regulates the right to privacy in rather different terms in comparison with the UDHR and ICCPR. Article 8 reads as:

> 1. Everyone has the right to respect for his private and family life, his home and his correspondence.
> 2. There shall be no interference by a public authority with the exercise of this right except such as is in accordance with law and is necessary in a democratic society in the interests of national security, public safety or the economic well-being of the country, for the prevention of disorder or crime, for the protection of health or morals, or for the protection of the rights and freedoms of others.

---

[125] *See* UNESCO, *Keynotes to Foster Inclusive Knowledge Societies: Access to Information and Knowledge, Freedom of Expression, Privacy, and Ethics on a Global Internet*, United Nations Education, Scientific and Cultural Organization (2015), pp. 55-66.

[126] UN Human Rights Committee (HRC), *CCPR General Comment No. 16: Article 17 (Right to Privacy), The Right to Respect of Privacy, Family, Home and Correspondence, and Protection of Honour and Reputation* (8 April 1988), para.1.

Under the structure of Article 8, the right to privacy is formulated into two parts. First, Article 8 paragraph 1 sets out the precise privacy rights, which are guaranteed to an individual by the State: the right to respect for private life, family life, home, and correspondence. The second part refers to the paragraph 2, which makes it clear that the right to privacy is not absolute but subject to limitations; however, interference in personal privacy is allowed only when it is in accordance with the law and necessary in a democratic society in pursuit of a legitimate aim.

The two divisions of Article 8 imply a two-stage test for the examination of the possible privacy intrusion from the public authority.[127] The first stage concerns the applicability of Article 8 and considers whether the individual's right has been interfered with. If Article 8 is found to be applicable, the Court needs to further examine whether the interference of the right to privacy can be justified with reference to the requirements of paragraph 2.

No further explanation is given to the meaning of the term 'private life' and the ECtHR has refrained from proposing a general definition of privacy. However, the Court has a rich history of reviewing member states' regulations that failed to protect individuals' right to privacy. For example, in *Niemietz v. Germany*, when considering the definition of 'private life', the ECtHR held that "the Court does not consider it possible or necessary to attempt an exhaustive definition of the notion of private life."[128] In *Von Hannover v. Germany*, the Court alleged that the concept of private life extends to "aspects relating to personal identities, such as a person's name, or a person's picture"[129] and includes "a person's physical and psychological integrity."[130] Furthermore, the ECtHR

---

[127] Ursula Kikelly, *The right to respect for private and family life – A guide to the implementation of Article 8 of the European Convention on Human Rights*, Council of Europe, Strasburg Cedex (2001).

[128] European Court of Human Rights, Niemietz v. Germany, Application No. 13710/88 (16 December 1992) para. 29. The Court stated:

> The Court does not consider it possible or necessary to attempt an exhaustive definition of the notion of "private life". However, it would be too restrictive to limit the notion to an "inner circle" in which the individual may live his own personal life as he chooses and to exclude therefrom entirely the outside world not encompassed within that circle. Respect for private life must also comprise to a certain degree the right to establish and develop relationships with other human beings.

[129] European Court of Human Rights, Von *Hannover v. Germany*, Application No. 59320/00 (24 June 2004), para. 50.

[130] Ibid., the Court stated

> Furthermore, private life, in the Court's view, includes a person's physical and psychological integrity; the guarantee afforded by Article 8 of the Convention is primarily intended to ensure the development, without outside interference, of the personality of each individual in his relations with other human beings.

defined that the right to privacy extends to an individual's intention to ensure the development, without outside interference, to the personality of each individual in his relations with other human beings.[131] Therefore, 'private life' should include the right to develop relationships with other persons.

With respect to information privacy, the obligation to protect privacy and personal information in the digital age often refers to the concept of data protection.[132] On the Internet, protection of privacy can be conceptualized as protection of personal data, which is collected, stored, used, and articulated online.[133] The first modern data protection law was enacted in the German state of Hesse in 1970[134]. It was followed by the national law of Sweden in 1973[135], Germany in 1977[136]. The movement subsequently led to the Directive 95/46/EC of the European Parliament and of the Council of 24 October 1995 on the protection of individuals with regard to the right to personal information. The Directive 95/46/EU, all known as Data Protection Directive (DPD), concerns the processing of personal data and the free movement of the collected information. Article 1(1) of the DPD defines data protection as protection of the "fundamental rights and freedoms of natural persons, and in particular their right to privacy, with respect to the processing of personal data".[137] Accordingly, the substance of the data protection law regulates one or all stages in the processing of personal information, which is normally defined as information relating to an identified or identifiable person.[138]

---

[131] Ibid.

[132] Gus Hosein, *Human Rights in the Global Information Society: Privacy as Freedom*, Massachusetts Institute of Technology, pp. 121-147, (2006).

[133] UNESCO, *Keynotes to Foster Inclusive Knowledge Societies: Access to Information and Knowledge, Freedom of Expression, Privacy, and Ethics on a Global Internet*, United Nations Education, Scientific and Cultural Organization (2015), pp. 55-66.

[134] Datenschutzgesetz (Data Protection Act) (Oct. 7, 1970) HESSISCHES GESETZ- UND VERORDNUNGSBLATT I.

[135] Sweden, *Data Protection Act*, No. 289 (1973).

[136] Gesetz zum Missbrauch personenbezogener Daten bei der Datenverarbeitung (Act Concerning the Abuse of Data in Data Processing) (Jan. 27, 1977), BGBL I p. 201.

[137] European Union, *Directive 95/46/EC of the European Parliament and of the Council on the Protection of Individuals with Regard to the Processing of Personal Data and on the Free Movement of Such Data* (24 October 1995), Article 1(1).

[138] Ibid., Article 2 (a):

> (a) "personal data" shall mean any information relating to an identified or identifiable nature person ("data subject"); an identifiable person is one who can be identified, directly or indirectly, in particular by reference to an identification number or to one or more factors specific to his physical, physiological, metal, economic, cultural, or social identity.

Information privacy law is designed to protect individuals against the misuse of their information by both the governments and private entities. This right has been increasingly challenged because of the ongoing innovated information technologies. More debates relating to data protection and the Internet will be fully discussed in Section II when considering the new threats to privacy in the digital age. However, it is important to bear in mind that many of the intellectual revolutions in privacy were influenced by technology. Warren and Brandeis described that the advent of photography and sensationalist journalism led to information "what is whispered in the closet shall be proclaimed from the house-tops".[139] The advent of the Internet brought Warren and Brandeis' concern into a globally interacted level. Therefore, data protection law and modern privacy law should arise in response to new information and communication technologies.

b. Permissible Limitations to Individual's Right to Privacy

The right to privacy is not absolute. Like freedom of expression, the right must be interpreted and weighed alongside other socially essential values and goals. Under international human rights law, both Article 12 of the UDHR and Article 17 of the ICCPR stipulate that no one should be subjected to arbitrary or unlawful interference with his or her privacy, family, home or correspondence. In other words, interference with an individual's right to privacy is only permissible if the intrusion is neither arbitrary nor unlawful.

The General Comment No.16 adopted by the Human Rights Committee explained that according to Article 17 of the ICCPR, any interference with the right to privacy could only take place by law, and the law must comply with the provisions, aims, and objectives of the ICCPR.[140] The Comment further defines the term 'arbitrary interference' as following:

> "The expression "arbitrary interference" is also relevant to the protection of the right provided for in article 17. In the Committee's view, the expression "arbitrary interference" can also extend to interference provided for under the law. The introduction of the concept of arbitrariness is intended to guarantee that even interference provided by law should be in accordance

[139] Samuel Warren and Louis Brandeis, *The Right to Privacy*, Harvard Law Review 193, Vol.4, No.5 (15 December1980), pp. 193-220.

[140] UN Human Rights Committee (HRC), *CCPR General Comment No. 16: Article 17 (Right to Privacy), The Right to Respect of Privacy, Family, Home and Correspondence, and Protection of Honour and Reputation* (8 April 1988), para. 3.

> with the provisions, aims and objectives of the Covenant and should be, in any event, reasonable in the particular circumstances."[141]

The General Comment did not explain the meaning of the phrase "reasonable in the particular circumstances"; nevertheless, the interpretation of the term can be found in several communications of the UN Human Rights Committee. For example, in *Toonan v. Australia*, the Committee interpreted that the requirement of reasonableness indicates "any interference with privacy must be proportional to the end sought and be necessary in the circumstances of any given case".[142] In *M.G v. Germany*, the Committee considered the circumstance in the case is unreasonable since "the interference with the author's privacy and her honour and reputation was disproportionate to the end sought and therefore 'arbitrary'".[143]

Accordingly, limitations to the right to privacy reflected in Article 17 of the ICCPR must be provided for by law and necessary for pursuing a legitimate aim. The measure adopted by either the governments or private entities should be the least intrusive option available and comply with the principle of proportionality.[144] Finally, the burden of proof lies on the authorities to demonstrate that the limitation is proportionally connected to a legitimate aim. In sum, any interference to the right to privacy must comply with the overarching principles of legality, necessity, and proportionality, and the interference must be performed in good faith.

Article 8 of the ECHR formulates a fairly thorough methodology for analyzing limitations to the right to privacy.[145] In order to comply with Article 8, any interference must be securitized by the criteria listed in paragraph 2. A Court must examine whether the interference is in accordance with the law, whether it pursues a legitimate aim, and whether it is necessary in a democratic society.

First of all, the ECtHR explained that the term 'in accordance with law' means there must be a law that regulates the conditions for an intrusion. In

---

[141] Ibid., para. 4.

[142] UN Human Rights Committee, *Toonan v. Australia*, Communication No. 488/1992, U.N. Doc. CCPR/C/50/D/488/1992 (1994), para. 8.3

[143] UN Human Rights Committee, *M.G. v. Germany*, Communication No. 1482/2006, U.N. Doc. A/63/40, Vol.II (23 July 2008), paras. 10.1 and 10.2.

[144] Human Rights Council, *The Right to Privacy in the Digital Age: Report of the Office of the United Nations High Commissioner for Human Rights*, UN General Assembly, A/HRC/27/37 (30 June 2014), paras. 21-27.

[145] *See* Toby Mendel, Andrew Puddephatt, Ben Wagner, Dixie Hawtin and Natalia Torres, *Global Survey on Internet Privacy and Freedom of Expression*, United Nations Educational, Scientific and Cultural Organization (2012).

Malone v. United Kingdom, for example, the practice of 'metering' phone calls conducted by the Post Office was examined. The process of metering involves the use of a device, a meter check, to register the numbers dialed on a particular telephone and the time and duration of each call. The Court explained that by its very nature, metering might be distinguished from the interception of communications; however, under the circumstance when there is no law that requires the Post Office to pass the records over to the police, releasing the information to the police without the consent of an individual or in the absence of a subpoena constitutes an interference with personal privacy protected under Article 8 of the ECHR.[146]

Furthermore, in order to satisfy the legal requirement of Article 8, the quality of the law in question must be such that it is foreseeable to the persons concerned. In *Andersson v. Sweden*, the ECtHR stated:

> "The Court recalls that the expression "in accordance with the law", within the meaning of Article 8 para. 2(art.8-2), requires firstly that the impugned measures should have a basis in domestic law. It also refers to the quality of the law in question, requiring that it be accessible to the persons concerned and formulated with sufficient precision to enable them – if need be, with appropriate advice – to foresee, to a degree that is reasonable in the circumstances, the consequences which a given action may entail."[147]

Once interference is found to be in accordance with law, the Court will proceed to question whether it pursues a legitimate aim under Article 8 paragraph 2. Paragraph 2 contains a list of legitimate objectives. In general, the ECtHR pays little effort in determining the concept of a legitimate aim.[148] In *Leander v. Sweden*, for example, the Court made reference in one short paragraph that "the aim of the Swedish personal control system is clearly a legitimate one for the pur-

---

[146] European Court of Human rights, *Malone v. United Kingdom*, Application No. 8691/79 (2 August 1984), paras. 56 & 83-86. When considering the applicability of Article 8 of ECHR, the Court stated:

> The records of metering contain information, in particular the numbers dialed, which is an integral element in the communications made by telephone. Consequently, release of that information to the police without the consent of the subscriber also amounts, in the opinion of the Court, to an interference with the right guaranteed by Article 8(art.8).

[147] European Court of Human rights, *Margareta and Roger Andersson v. Sweden*, Application No. 12963/87 (25 February 1992), para. 75.

[148] Ursula Kikelly, *The right to respect for private and family life – A guide to the implementation of Article 8 of the European Convention on Human Rights*, Council of Europe, Strasburg Cedex (2001).

poses of Article 8 (art.8), namely the protection of national security".[149] At large, the Court will accept that States act properly to pursue the legitimate aim, even where the 'aim' is the issue in a dispute.

Lastly, interference of the right to privacy must be necessary in a democratic society. 'Necessary in a democratic society' indicates that there must be a pressing social need and that the interference must be proportionate to the legitimate aim pursued. The Court elaborated in *Olsson v. Sweden* that "the notion of necessity implies that the interference corresponds to a pressing social need and, in particular, that it is proportionate to the legitimate aim pursued; in determining whether an interference is "necessary in a democratic society"".[150] Nevertheless, application of the principle of proportionality is a complicated process and must be conducted on a case-by-case basis. For example, in *S & Marper v. The United Kingdom*[151] and *Dudgeon v. The United Kingdom*[152], the ECtHR is of the opinion that interference to the right protected under Article 8 is more likely to be unnecessary when individuals have a higher expectation of privacy under the specific circumstance.

[149] European Court of Human Right, *Leander v. Sweden*, Application No. 9248/81, Series A no. 116 (23 March 1987), para. 49.

[150] European Court of Human Rights, *Olsson v. Sweden*, Application No. 10465/83 (March 1998), paras. 27-29.

[151] European Court of Human rights, *S & Marper v. The United Kingdom*, Application No. 30562/04 (04 December 2008), paras. 119-125. The Court found:

> "the blanket and indiscriminate nature of the powers of retention of the fingerprints, cellular samples and DNA profiles of persons suspected but not convicted of offences, as applied in the case of the present applicants, fails to strike a fair balance between the competing public and private interests and that the respondent State has overstepped any acceptable margin of appreciation in this regard. Accordingly, the retention at issue constitutes a disproportionate interference with the applicants' right to respect for private life and cannot be regarded as necessary in a democratic society."

[152] European Court of Human Rights, *Dudgeon v. The United Kingdom*, Application No. 7525/76 (22 October 1981), para. 52. The Court stated:

> However, not only the nature of the aim of the restriction but also the nature of the activities involved will affect the scope of the margin of appreciation. The present case concerns a most intimate aspect of private life. Accordingly, there must exist particularly serious reasons before interferences on the part of the public authorities can be legitimate for the purpose of paragraph 2 of Article 8(art. 8-2).

II. New Technologies, New Threats?

Innovations in communication and information technologies have completely revolutionized modern civilization; nevertheless, developments in technology have often led to concerns about the impact of those advances on individuals' fundamental rights.[153] Freedom of information and expression is critical for ensuring the accountability and transparency of good governance in a society, and the right to privacy is essential for personal dignity and self-determination. The diverse threats to both rights online have emerged during the past decade from the ongoing revelations of Internet censorship and mass surveillance conducted by both the governmental and private entities.

Although censorship is an old phenomenon for political, cultural, and security reasons, concerns about the policies and practices governing the Internet that undermine the values people cherish as fundamental are growing.[154] Since the right to privacy could be seen as an enabler of other fundamental human rights, including freedom of expression, the first part of Section II focuses on examining whether new ICTs bring new threats to an individual's right to a reasonable expectation of privacy. The second part provides an overall analysis of how the new threats urge governments, both nationally and internationally, to establish legal systems to protect the right to privacy on the Internet in accordance their international human rights obligations.

A. New Threats to the Right to Privacy

As described in Section I, in the digital age, information privacy, as an essential element of the right to privacy, is defined as the ability of an individual to have some measures of control over his or her own information in order to pursue self-interests without interference from those who are in possession of the personal data. The protection of information privacy also includes the assurance of fair information practices. Fair information practices require either the govern-

---

[153] *See* UNESCO, *Keynotes to Foster Inclusive Knowledge Societies: Access to Information and Knowledge, Freedom of Expression, Privacy, and Ethics on a Global Internet*, United Nations Education, Scientific and Cultural Organization (2015); *see* also Russell L. Weaver, David F. Partlett and Mark D. Cole, Protecting Privacy in a Digital Age. In: Dieter Dörr and Russell L. Weaver, *The Right to Privacy in the Light of Media Convergence: Perspectives From Three Continent*, De Gruyter: Berlin (2012), pp. 1-30.
[154] Ibid.

ments or private entities to provide adequate privacy protections for the collection or usage of personal information.[155]

The technological developments in the past two decades have progressively challenged the right to privacy and information privacy. Since privacy has long been shaped by available technologies, concerns about personal information control are unsurprisingly part of the debate to the impact of communication technologies. The old expression "knowledge is power" demonstrates the significance of possessing related information in order to participate in political, social, and economic activities. If the power is concentrated in the hands of those who have sufficient knowledge, in the information age we are living in today, the one who controls information controls power.[156] The power could be allocated to the states by mass collecting citizens' personal information, and the power could be assembled to the private enterprises by storing, analyzing, and disseminating consumers' data. This power, however, is also crucial for individuals' autonomy, self-determination, dignity, and integrity in the modern democratic society. Consequently, there is an urgent need to find a balance between personal privacy and other social interests in the contemporary society.

a. Personal Data Collection

This first concern regarding information privacy in the digital age is personal data collection. Advanced technologies have been equipped to access and collect types of information that would have been difficult, if not impossible, to assemble in the past. For example, decades ago, the impact of data collection was not a significant issue since the relevant information was inaccessible for practical reasons. Different pieces of personal data were stored in separate entities which made it very difficult to formulate a pattern of an individual's behavior.[157] New technologies, however, make the impossible possible. Sometimes it only takes a one-click effort to collect all the information contained within the aggregated database. Each mobile phone and any device attached to the Internet has a unique IP address that makes every connection traceable.

---

[155] *See* James Waldo, Herbert S.Lin, and Lynette I. Millett (eds), *Engaging Privacy and Information Technology in a Digital Age*, Washington, DC: The National Academic Press (2007), pp. 19-54.

[156] *See* Lorna Stefanick, *Controlling Knowledge: Freedom of Information and Privacy Protection in a Networked World*, Edmonton: Athabasca University Press (2011), pp. 13-15.

[157] *See* Toby Mendel, Andrew Puddephatt, Ben Wagner, Dixie Hawtin and Natalia Torres, *Global Survey on Internet Privacy and Freedom of Expression*, United Nations Educational, Scientific and Cultural Organization (2012), pp. 22-47

A perceptible IP address affects a person's physical identity in many ways. For example, by placing cookies in personal web browsers, the websites would be able to collect a vast amount of information relating to the person' online activities[158], and a person's identification can be easily deduced through cross-examining his/her online behaviors from the stored databases. IP address tracking is one of the numerous methods used to collect personal information. The Global Position System (GPS), which can detect the exact location of a person, is implemented as a default function in almost every smartphone and other electronic devices. Closed-Circuit Television (CCTV) cameras have been widely deployed by the governments for data acquisition[159]. The tremendous amount of collected personal data in combination with efficient electronic storage result in substantive privacy concerns.

b. Economical and Efficient Electronic Storage (Big Data)

The technology of electronic information storage is another potential threat to the right to privacy. Increased computing capability for storing electronic information means that information, once collected, can be cheaply and persistently stored, consolidated, and analyzed. Over the past decades, memory size has increased by a factor of 100 or more, which allows faster computing on more massive data sets than before.[160] Additionally, while the price of long-term storage has been decreasing rapidly, the capability to assess a large amount of information has been increasing. Traditionally, data filtered was limited to a certain amount or discarded after a specific limited time to minimize the cost of storage. Considerable effort was expended in ensuring that the collected data

---

[158] *See* Peter Carey, *Data Protection: A Practical Guide to UK and EU Law*, Oxford University Press: United Kingdom (2015), pp. 281-282. (While a cookie serves many function, it is in essence a small text file created by a website that is stored in a user's computer either temporarily or permanently to memorize the user's information and preference. A cookie, therefore, is most often used for saving settings, such as username or password, on the user's system, and for sending those settings back to the server that originally created it.)

[159] Closed Circuit Television (CCVT) is a system where the circuit in which the video is transmitted is closed and all the involved elements, including the camera, display monitors, and recording devices, are connected with each other. CCTV is primarily for surveillance and security purpose.

[160] Waldo, Herbert S. Lin and Lynette I. Millett, *Engaging Privacy and Information Technology in a Digital Age*, Washington, DC: The National Academic Press (2007), pp. 88-121.

were compressed and reduced. With the increased capacity of data storage, compression or reduction of information is no longer needed.

The concern regarding personal information protection is exacerbated when databases are combined with each other. The ability to access the information gathered and stored on the computing machinery[161] has made great strides in the past 10 years. Information systems have moved from isolated programmes into a globally interconnected network. Once data are collected and aggregated, a sophisticated analysis of the data for future needs could be efficiently processed. What is more troubling is that the new technologies allow data to be analyzed for purposes other than those for which the information was originally gathered.[162] Data mining, for example, is an automatic or semi-automatic procedure to process a significant quantity of information in order to extract previously unknown connections among data elements or to discover patterns from independent materials.[163] Although data mining might be conducted for social or political science researches, it often processes the data in a way that a user does not have the chance to consent to the use if his or her information. The consequence is that people will lose the control over their personal data since they do not have the acknowledgment of how, when, where and for what purpose the data are collected, stored, analyzed, and disseminated.[164]

c. The Internet Intermediaries

The role of the Internet intermediaries in the information age represents another risk to the right to privacy. The increasing power of intermediaries to control personal data has given rise to a number of concerns about whether current reg-

[161] Cloud computing is one of the technologies, which allows users to store information on the Internet instead of physical computers. Individuals or corporations can effectively rent computing capacity from remote service providers. From a privacy perspective, users have already lost control over their personal information once they transmitted the data across the Internet, and laws covering cloud computing data are not well defined.

[162] *See* Christina Gagnier, Regulating the Man Behind the Curtain. In: Future of the Privacy Forum, *Big Data and Privacy: Making Ends Meet*, Stanford Law School the Center of Internet and Society (2013), pp. 35-38.

[163] *See* Fayyad, U., Grinstein, G and Wierse, A, *Information Visualization in Data Mining and Knowledge Discovery*, San Francisco: Morgen Kaufman Publisher (2002). *See* also Usama Fayyad, *The Digital Physics of Data Mining*, Communications of ACM, Vol.44, Issue: 3 (March 2001).

[164] *See* James Waldo, Herbert S. Lin, and Lynette I. Millett (eds), *Thinking About Privacy: Chapter 1 of "Engaging Privacy and Information Technology in Digital Age"*, Journal of Privacy and Confidentiality, Vol.2, No.1 (2010), pp. 19-50.

ulations are sufficient enough to protect an individual's privacy against interference from the private entities. As Tim Wu described in *The Master Switch*, "The rise of the networking did not eliminate intermediaries, but rather changed who they are."[165] The role of Internet intermediaries goes far beyond the role of traditional physical companies. ISPs, search engines, or website operators obtain and handle an abundance of user information, and all the databases gathered are at the discretion of these private companies to decide to either safeguard or demolish the rights and freedoms of their users on the Internet.

ISPs play an essential part as intermediaries on the Internet. ISPs are largely operated by private entities to provide services for online activities. Many ISPs conduct data mining, including gathering information and analyzing users' interests or preference, in order to sell the information to interested companies or individuals. Most people do not realize or could not recognize that ISPs are collecting information about their online activities. More importantly, ISPs are frequently coerced into voluntarily policing user activities.[166] Both the democratic and authoritarian governments frequently request ISPs to monitor, filter, or report consumers' online behaviors. The collected information is used either to identify criminal activities or to eliminate dissentient opinions. The situation is more complicated in the context that the intermediary role is played by state-own service providers since they are less independent from the government and the monitoring processes are normally non-transparent.

Search engines represent a good example of how ISPs can have adverse impact on people's right to privacy. Search engines provide Internet users the access to a vast amount of information in an organized system and in a relatively short time. Companies, such as Google, Bing, Yahoo!, and Baidu, implement sophisticated algorithms to link the location of the information with the requesting computer within a second.[167] All an Internet user needs to do is to type in a few keywords that might be associated with the information. This new technology comes along with new privacy concerns. Like many Internet services, search engines are provided as free services with business models based on

---

[165] Tim Wu, *The Master Switch: The Rise and Fall of Information Empires*, New York: Random House (2010).

[166] *See* Toby Mendel, Andrew Puddephatt, Ben Wagner, Dixie Hawtin and Natalia Torres, *Global Survey on Internet Privacy and Freedom of Expression*, United Nations Educational, Scientific and Cultural Organization (2012).

[167] Sergey Brin and Lawrence Page, *The Anatomy of a Large-Scale Hypertextual Web Search Engine*, Seventh International World-Wide Web Conference (WWW 1998) (1998).

advertising.[168] However, in exchange for the free usage, users voluntarily provide their personal data to search engine companies. As Lu Xun, one of the leading figures of modern Chinese literature, once said, "of course, money cannot buy freedom, but freedom can be sold for money".[169] While Internet users are willing to take advantage of the 'free services' such as free search engines, email accounts, or picture sharing applications, they simultaneously trade their personal information to those companies. Consequently, in the past few years, protests against personal privacy invasion conducted by the huge ISP companies are spread out worldwide.

Most Internet-related companies are consumer-oriented businesses, which rely profoundly on consumers' trust to survive. In order to respond to gradually expanding public concerns, in late 2008, Yahoo!, Google, and Microsoft helped launch the Global Network Initiative (GNI)[170], a multi-stakeholder initiative. Through the GNI, companies work with human rights groups, academic experts, and socially responsible investors to promote the implementation of baseline standards to protect freedom of expression and the right to privacy on the Internet.[171] The main purpose of the GNI is not only to guarantee the credibility and accountability of its members' behaviors but also to "respect and work to protect the privacy rights of users when confronted with government demands, laws, or regulations that compromise privacy in a manner inconsistent with internationally recognized laws and standards".[172] The influence of the GNI to reinforce public trust is becoming promising since more and more gigantic mainstream Internet companies such as Facebook, LinkedIn, and Procera Net-

[168] Take Google as an example. Sixty billion dollars was the annual revenue of the world's largest search engine. 96% of Google's revenue is from advertising. Google has a very popular auction-based advertising program called "Google AdWords" which is sponsored by advertisers who pay Google every time a user clicks on any of those ads.
[169] Lu Xun, *The True Story of Ah Q* (1923). Lu Xun's original works were mostly satirical criticisms of Confucianism and feudalism. He was highly acclaimed by the Chinese communist government.
[170] Global Network Initiative. Available at http://globalnetworkinitiative.org. Because of the complicated jurisdictional issues and culture diversity, the main task for the GNI is to minimize harm while maximizing the good that the new information technologies bring to people around the world. (accessed 28 July 2014)
[171] Rebecca Mackinnon, *Consent of the Networked – The Worldwide Struggle for Internet Freedom*, New York: Basic Books (2012), pp. 169-186.
[172] Global Network Initiative, *GNI Principles on Freedom of Expression and Privacy* (2008). Available at http://globalnetworkinitiative.org/sites/default/files/GNI-Principles-on-Freedom-of-Expression-and-Privacy.pdf. (accessed 28 July 2014)

works are participating in this global initiative to protect and promote people's fundamental human rights on the Internet.[173]

d. Mass Surveillance Mechanisms

The last but indeed not the least risk to modern privacy rights are the various surveillance mechanisms adopted by the governments, either in democratic or authoritarian countries. In addition to the GPS and CCTV systems mentioned above, the deep packet inspection (DPI) technology is pervasively used as a generic Internet control method by the States. The DPI has the capacity to look into specific content traveling through the Internet as a packet.[174] Initially, the DPI was used by the ISPs for bandwidth management to block spam at the network level and to protect the ISPs from certain malware attacks[175].

Nevertheless, the DPI technology is widely reported as being used by the governments to monitor and censor their citizens' online activities. For example, during a public protest in the Islamic Republic of Iran, many of the activists were arrested, investigated, and sentenced because of the sophisticated Internet interception technologies provided by Nokia Siemens[176]; the great firewall shield built by the Chinese government to utilize the DPI to monitor or intercept Internet traffic if sensitive content had been detected by the system[177]; in the aftermath of September 11 terrorist attacks, the administration of President George W. Bush authorized the National Security Agency to monitor communications to and from the US. New surveillance technologies in accompaniment

[173] *See* The Global Network Initiative, *2014 Annual Report Protecting and Advancing Freedom of Expression and Privacy in Information and Communication Technologies*, GNI (2014).

[174] Toby Mendel, Andrew Puddephatt, Ben Wagner, Dixie Hawtin and Natalia Torres, *Global Survey on Internet Privacy and Freedom of Expression*, United Nations Educational, Scientific and Cultural Organization (2012), pp. 42-43.

[175] Ben Wagner, *Deep Packet Inspection and Internet Censorship: International Convergence on an 'Integrated Technology of Control'*, Global Voices Advocacy Defending Free Speech Online (2009).

[176] Bahrain Center for Human Rights, *Bloomberg: Torture in Bahrain Becomes Routine with Help From Nokia Siemens* (25 August 2011). Available at http://www.bahrainrights.org/en/node/4549. (accessed 02 August 2014)

[177] *See* Richard Clayton, Steven J. Murdoch, and Robert N. M. Watson, Ignoring the Great Firewall of China. In: Danezis G., Golle P. (eds), *Privacy Enhancing Technologies*, Lecture Notes in Computer Science, Vol.4258, Berlin, Heidelberg: Springer (2006).

with new Internet censorship policies entail governments with the possibility to access any online information without a clear articulation of suspicion.[178]

It is undeniable that concerns about national security and criminal activities in the digital age are substantial; however, any Internet censorship measures, which might jeopardize individuals' fundamental rights need to be enacted in the light of internationally recognized human rights law. In response to the on-going threat to the right to privacy on the Internet, numerous national, regional, and international governments and organizations have endeavored to ameliorate the current privacy rules to cater to the new needs of the present stage and into the future. The following section will discuss how the existing legal systems react to rapidly innovated technologies when the right to privacy is on the edge in the modern information age.

B. Privacy Protection in the Digital Age – Information Privacy and Data Protection

The central issue of privacy protection on the Internet is the relationship between the right to privacy and data protection. Privacy and data protection might not be identical concepts; however, the underlining principle of data protection can be directly derived from the right to privacy. For instance, both Article 8 of the ECHR and Article 8 and 52 of the EUCFR guarantee the protection of personal data and specify that limits on the right must be accordance with the law and subject to the principles of proportionality and necessity.[179] Article 29 Data Protection Working Party Opinion emphasized that "the protection of personal data evolved from the right to private life as provided for in Art. 8 of the ECHR of 1950".[180] Therefore, there is a clear link between the right to a private and family life and the right to data protection.

---

[178] Gus Hosein, Privacy as Freedom. In: In: Rikke Frank Jørgenen, *Human Rights in Global Information Society*, The MIT Press: Cambridge, Massachusetts, London, England (2006), pp. 121-147.

[179] Gehan Gunasekara, *Paddling in Unison or Just Paddling? International Trends in Reforming Information Privacy Law*, International Journal of Law and Technology, Vol.22, No.2 (2014), pp. 141-177.

[180] Article 29 Data Protection Working Party, *Opinion 01/2014 on the application of necessity and proportionality concepts and data protection within the law enforcement sector*, WP 211(27 February 2014), para. 2. It states:

> An examination of past, present and future data protection legislation reveals that the protection of personal data *evolved from the right to private life as provided for in Art.8 of the ECHR of 1950*. With the increase of new technologies and surveillance possibilities both in the public and in the private sector, it became apparent that there needed to be further protection for individuals from third parties (particularly the State) in addition to defensive rights

Data protection has emerged recently because of concerns that digital personal information might be abused by the governments or private entities. However, due to the lack of internationally unified data protection standards in the information age, comparing existing legal frameworks is critical to revealing potential future developments in the data protection policy area. From the following section, one can observe that on a very general level, the data protection rules usually put emphasis on the conditions for collecting, storing, and using personal information, on the individuals' right to control the information, and on the oversight system to ensure the possible protection and remedies.[181] From a comparative perspective, European regulations are quite advanced in ensuring the high level of data protection. In the United States and Asia, the emphasis is more focused on self-regulatory approaches.

a. The United Nations

In 1990 the United Nations General Assembly adopted the Resolution 45/95 Guidelines for the Regulation of Computerized Personal Data Files in the form of a non-binding guidance document.[182] The Guidelines set out ten principles for data protection. The primary focus of the principles is not limited to national rules but also to the activities of inter-governmental organizations. The principles apply to both the publicly and privately held computerized files that contain personal information on individuals. The Guidelines also provide the limitations on transfer of data, but only to the extent that the protection of privacy demands. Furthermore, the exceptions from the principles are also recognized by the Guidelines.[183] Paragraph 6 of the Guidelines explicitly stated, "Departure from principles 1 to 4 may be authorized only if they are necessary to protect national security, public order, public health or morality, as well as, inter alia, the rights

recognized under Art. 8 of the ECHR by ensuring that the individual *had the right to control his/her own personal data*. (emphasize added).

(Article 29 Data Protection Working Party was set up under Article 29 of the Directive 95/46/EC. It is an independent European advisory body on data protection and privacy.)

[181] *See* Toby Mendel, Andrew Puddephatt, Ben Wagner, Dixie Hawtin and Natalia Torres, *Global Survey on Internet Privacy and Freedom of Expression*, United Nations Educational, Scientific and Cultural Organization (2012).

[182] UN General Assembly, *Guidelines for the Regulation of Computerized Personal Data Files*, A/RES/45/95 (34 December 1990).

[183] 10 principles listed in the UN Guidelines 45/95 include:

1. Principle of lawfulness and fairness; 2. Principle of accuracy; 3. Principle of the purpose-specification; 4. Principle of interested-person access; 5. Principle of non-discrimination; 6. Power to make exception; 7. Principle of security; 8. Supervision and sanctions; 9. Transborder data flows; and 10. Field of application.

and freedoms of others, especially persons being persecuted (humanitarian clause) provided that such departures are expressly specified in a law or equivalent regulation promulgated in accordance with the internal legal system, which expressly states their limited and sets forth appropriate safeguards".[184]

b. The Organization for Economic Co-Operation and Development (OECD)

The OECD, a thirty-nation forum that promotes economic growth and development, enacted one of the earliest data protection regulations which interfaces with various jurisdictional legal frameworks.[185] The OECD developed a set of principles known as the Guidelines on the Protection of Privacy and Transborder Flows of Personal Data (OECD Guidelines) in 1980.[186] Part Two of the OECD Guidelines contains eight basic principles of national applications. The principles require specific indications from the governments and organizations about why the information is collected and with whom the information is shared. Additionally, the collected personal data should be retained securely, maintained accurately, and not be used or shared without specified reasons. Individuals should have the right to access their information and request corrections when necessary. Principles of good faith, transparency, and fairness are enshrined in the OECD Guidelines.[187] Despite the non-binding nature, the principles have significant influence on subsequent national, regional, and international developments in protecting information privacy. Evidence can be seen in the European Unions' Privacy Directive, the US–EU 'Safe Harbor' regime, and the Asia-Pacific Economic Cooperation Privacy Framework.

---

[184] Ibid., para. 6.

[185] The OECD was organized by 18 European countries plus the United States and Canada to create an organization dedicated to economic development in 1960. It has 35 Member countries today. The mission of the OECD is to promote policies that will improve the economic and social well-being of people around the world. For more information, *see* http://www.oecd.org/about/. (accessed 15 August 2014)

[186] The Organization for Economic Co-operation Development (OECD), *Recommendation of the Council Concerning Guidelines Governing the Protection of Privacy and Transborder Flows of Personal Data* (23 September 1980) (The Guidelines were update in 2013).

[187] *See* Wafa Tim, *Global Internet Privacy Rights - A Pragmatic Approach,* University of San Francisco Intellectual Property Law Bulletin, Vol. 13 (31 May 2009), pp. 131-159.

c. The Asia-Pacific Economic Cooperation

In 2005, 21 countries of the Asia-Pacific Economic Cooperation (APEC) agreed on the first comprehensive global data privacy legal framework in Asia, the APEC Privacy Framework.[188] The preamble of the Framework clarifies that the adoption of the Framework is to reflect the need to maintain consumer trust and confidence in privacy to prevent economies from gaining all of the benefits of electronic commerce.[189] The central part of the APEC Privacy Framework is a set of nine principles, which are roughly similar to the UN Guidelines and the OECD Guidelines, and they mainly apply to personal information processed by personal information controllers. Both the terms of 'personal information' and 'controller' are broadly defined in paragraph 9 and 10, respectively. The former is defined as information about an identified or identifiable individual and the latter is described as a person or organization who controls the collection, holding, processing, or use of personal information.[190] The Framework specifically incorporates a certain degree of flexibility of the application on the basis of each member's economic, social, political, and cultural backgrounds, as well as the needs to protect national security, public safety, and public policy.[191]

Even with a principle-oriented legal structure, the APEC Privacy Framework has little practical impact on ensuring privacy protection because of some fundamental shortcomings. The Framework is not binding on member states, and its flexible and self-regulated interpretative system provides a carte blanche for both private and governmental information collectors to conduct on behalf of their own interests. Besides, the Framework requires no oversight mechanisms. The vague and ambiguous voluntary implementation procedure might be the result of the diverse culture and political backdrop of the evolved contracting states. Many APEC members are not fully developed in their domestic structures, and some Asiatic national governments contain a strong authoritarian streak. Consequently, any specific or compulsory obligations might lead to strong objections within the forum among member states.[192]

---

[188] Asia-Pacific Economic Cooperation, *APEC Privacy Framework*, APEC Secretariat, Singapore (2005). Available at https://www.apec.org/Groups/Committee-on-Trade-and-Investment/~/media/Files/Groups/ECSG/05_ecsg_privacyframewk.ashx. (accessed 18 August 2014)

[189] Ibid.

[190] Ibid. paras. 9-10.

[191] Ibid. paras. 12-13.

[192] Wafa Tim, *Global Internet Privacy Rights - A Pragmatic Approach,* University of San Francisco Intellectual Property Law Bulletin, Vol. 13 (31 May 2009), pp. 131-159.

d. European Perspectives

The protection of private life and individual information received intensive deliberation in Europe long before the advent of modern communication technologies. As described previously, both the ECHR and EUCFR provide a high level of protection to the right to privacy. However, when considering data protection on the multilateral level within Europe, it is imperative to clarify the difference between the protections provided by the Council of Europe and the European Union. While the legal frameworks of the Council of Europe are constituted by the relevant Conventions, which are signed and ratified by the Member States, the regulations formulated by the European Union are mandatory for the Member States.

i. The Council of Europe and the ECHR

Whereas Article 8 of the ECHR does not explicitly guarantee the right to personal information and data protection, the ECtHR has recognized that various aspects of data protection right are derived from the right to respect for private and family life, home, and correspondence. For example, in a number of cases, the ECtHR held that the collection of private information engages concerns for private life. In *Murray v. the United Kingdom*, the applicants contended that the recording and the collection of personal information relating to themselves upon arrest by government agents are in violation of Article 8 of the ECHR. Despite the fact that the issues complained of were justified under the paragraph 2 of Article 8, the Court stated, “it was not contested that the impugned measures interfered with the applicants’ exercise of their right to respect for their private life and family life and their home”.[193] In *Von Hannover v. Germany*, the Monegasque princess claimed that the Courts of Germany had insufficiently protected her rights against the publication of photos of her personal life although these activities took place in public places. The ECtHR reiterated that “a zone of interaction of a person with others, even in a public context … fall within the scope of “private life”.[194] The Court further recognized that “increased vigilance in protecting private life is necessary to contend with new communication technologies, which make it possible to store and reproduce personal data”.[195] Ac-

---

[193] European Court of Human Rights, *Murray v. The United Kingdom*, Application No. 14310/88 (28 October 1994), para. 66-68.

[194] European Court of Human Rights, Von *Hannover v. Germany*, Application No. 59320/00 (24 June 2004), para. 50.

[195] Ibid., para. 70.

cordingly, personal information should be protected within the meaning of Article 8 of the ECHR.

The ECtHR also conceded the right of individuals to access information relating to themselves held by public authorities. In *Leander v. Sweden*, the applicant was dismissed from a museum job with the Swedish Naval Base because of national security concerns. However, the applicant was refused access to the information relating to his personal files, which were the reason provided for the employment termination.[196] When considering the interference to private life, the Court stated:

> "It is uncontested that the secret police-register contained information relating Mr. Leander's private life.
> Both the storing and the release of such information, which were coupled with a refusal to allow Mr. Leander an opportunity to refute it, amounted to an interference with his right to respect for private life as guaranteed by Article 8-1(art.8-1)." [197]

In addition, the protection of personal data was recognized as a separate right in the Convention 108 of the Council of Europe, which accepted the critical impact of the automated processing of personal data on the right to privacy.[198] The Convention 108 came in to force on 1 October 1985 and was open for ratification by non-member states of the Council of Europe, including non-European countries. The reference to the right to privacy in Article 1 shows that the right to data protection interrelates with the right to the privacy.[199] The Convention applies to all data processing carried out by both private and public entities and protects individuals against the abuses of collected personal information. The principles laid down in the Convention include the fair and lawful collection of personal information, legitimate purpose for storage, and reasonable period for data retention.[200] The Convention also constituted an important

---

[196] European Court of Human Right, *Leander v. Sweden*, Application No. 9248/81, Series A no. 116 (23 March 1987), paras. 9-16.

[197] Ibid. para. 48.

[198] Council of Europe, *Convention for the Protection of Individuals with regard to Automatic Processing of Personal Data*, EST 108, Strasbourg (28 January 1981).

[199] Ibid., Article 1:

> The purpose of this Convention is to secure in the territory of each Party for every individual, whatever his nationality or residence, respect for his rights and fundamental freedoms, and in particular his right to privacy, with regard to automatic processing of personal data relating him ("data protection").

[200] European Union Agency for Fundamental Rights, *Handbook on European data protection law*, Luxemburg: Publication Office of the European Union (2014), pp. 11-31.

source of inspiration for one of the most prominent legal instruments regulating data protection – *Data Protection Directive 95/46* of the European Union.

ii. The European Union and the EUCFR

The European Union system represents a strong data protection regime and has had a significant global influence on the privacy protection. Under the EUCFR, the right to the protection of personal data has been elevated to the status of a fundamental right within the EU legal order, alongside the right to privacy. Article 8 of the Charter provides:

> 1. Everyone has the right to the protection of personal data concerning him or her.
> 2. Such data must be processed fairly for specified purposes and on the basis of the consent of the person concerned or some other legal basis laid down by law. Everyone has the right of access to data which has been collected concerning him or her, and the right to have it ratified.
> 3. Compliance with these rules shall be subject to control by an independent authority.

In addition, Article 52 of the Charter sets out the scope of the limitations to the rights articulated in Article 8. Article 52 (1) requires that:

> Any limitation on the exercise of the rights and freedoms recognized by this Charter must be provided by law and respect the essence of those rights and freedoms. Subject to the principle of proportionality, limitations may be made only if they are necessary and genuinely meet objectives of general interest recognised by the Union or the need to protect the rights and freedoms of others.

On the basis of Article 8, the data processing should be fair, for a specific purpose, and based on a consent. Subjects of the data should have the right to access and rectify their data, and oversight shall be carried out by an independent body. Limitations on the rights must be provided by law and must be subject to the principle of proportionality and necessity. Pursuant to Article 52 (3) of the Charter, in so far as the Charter contains rights which correspond to rights guaranteed by the ECHR, the meaning and scope of those rights shall be the same as those laid down by the ECHR. It can be inferred that the substance of Article 8 of the ECHR is applicable as a part of the general principles of EU law when considering personal information cases, and Article 7 and 8 of the Charter should be jointly read together[201]. Evidence can be found in the recent jurisprudence of the ECJ.[202]

In addition to the CHREU, the principle EU legal instrument on data protection is the Directive 95/46/EU, or the DPD. Since many Member States has already implemented national data protection law by the time the Directive was adopted, the aim of which was to harmonize data protection law at the national level and to ensure a unified high standard of protection to personal information.[203] As the ECJ noted, the Directive is intended to ensure that the level of protection of the rights and freedoms of individuals with regard to the processing of personal data is equivalent in all Member States.[204] The ECJ has authority to determine whether a Member State has fulfilled its obligations under the DPD and to make a preliminary decision when considering the validity of the Directive.[205]

The basic approach to the Directive is the extensive application of the rules and the narrow interpretation of the limitations. Personal data in Article 2 is defined as information relating to an identified or identifiable natural person.[206] Processing is described as an operation on personal data, either automatically or manually, including collection, storage, recording, and so on.[207] A controller is

[201] Some scholars argued that data protection should be recognized as a self-standing fundamental right and any possible interference has to be determined on the basis of the data protection principles without any recourse to the right to privacy. *See* Maria Tzanou, *Data Protection as a Fundamental Right Next to Privacy? 'Reconstructing' a not so New Right*, International Data Privacy Law, Vol.3, No.2 (2013), pp. 88-100; and *see* also Julie E Cohen, *Examined Lives: Information Privacy and the Subject as Object*, Stanford Law Review, Vol. 52 (2000), pp. 1371-1483.

[202] *See* ECJ case C-291/12, *Schwarz v. Stadt Bochum* (17 October 2013); *see* also ECI Joint Cases C-92/09 and C-93/09, *Volker und Markus Sheck GbR and Hartmut Eifert v. Land Hesen* (9 September 2010), para. 52

[203] European Union Agency for Fundamental Rights, *Handbook on European data protection law*, Publication Office of the European Union, Luxemburg (2014), pp. 11-31.

[204] ECJ joint cases C-468/10 and C-469/10, *Asociación Nacional de Establecimientos Financieros de Crédito and Federación de Comercio Electrónico y Marketing Directo v. Administración del Estado* (24 November 2011), para. 28.

[205] European Union Agency for Fundamental Rights, *Handbook on European data protection law*, Publication Office of the European Union, Luxemburg (2014), pp. 11-31.

[206] Data Protective Directive 95/46/EC Article 2(a):

> 'personal data' shall mean any information relating to an identified or identifiable natural person ('data subject'); an identifiable person is one who can be identified, directly or indirectly, in particular by reference to an identification number or to one or more factors specific to his physical, physiological, mental, economic, cultural or social identity;

[207] Data Protective Directive 95/46/EC Article 2 (b):

stated as someone, natural or legal person, who "alone or jointly with others determines the purposes and means of the processing of personal data".[208] In accordance with the relevant definitions, any individual who stores information relating to other people, such as email address, in any digital device is a controller. Nevertheless, Article 3 provides that the Directive shall not apply to the processing of personal data for the purposes outside the scope of Community law or the processing conducted by a natural person in the course of a purely personal or household activity.[209] Household processing has been seen as a freedom of a private individual.

The consent of the subject is the basis for legitimate data processing under the DPD. Article 2 (h) regulates that a consent "shall mean any freely given specific and informed indication of his wishes by which the data subject signifies his agreement to personal data relating to him being processed".[210] The consent can be given explicitly or non-explicitly. The implicit consent could be concluded from the circumstances; nevertheless, the consent must be given in an unambiguous way.[211] Thus, in determining whether the data subject consented to the data processing of personal information, there should be no reasonable doubt on his or her intention.

Article 6 of the Directive sets the principles of data protection and acts as a starting point for the subsequent articles. Personal data are required to be:

(a) processed fairly and lawfully;
(b) collected for specified, explicit and legitimate purpose and not further processed in a way incompatible with those purposes. Further processing of data for historical, statistical or scientific purposes shall not be considered as incompatible provided that Member States provide appropriate safeguards;
(c) adequate, relevant and not excessive in relation to the purposes for which they are collected and/or further processed;

'processing of personal data' ('processing') shall mean any operation or set of operations which is performed upon personal data, whether or not automatic means, such as collection, recording, organization, storage, adaptation, or alteration, retrieval, consultation, use, disclosure by transmission, dissemination or otherwise making available, alignment or combination, blocking, erasure or destruction;

208 Data Protective Directive 95/46/EC Article 2 (d).

209 Data Protective Directive 95/46/EC Article 3 (2).

210 Data Protective Directive 95/46/EC Article 2 (h).

211 Data Protective Directive 95/46/EC Article 7:
(a) the data subject has unambiguously given his consent
Data Protective Directive Article 26:
(a) the data subject has given his consent unambiguously to the proposed transfer;

(d) accurate and, where necessary, kept up to date; every reasonable step must be taken to ensure that data which are inaccurate or incomplete, having regard to the purposes for which they were collected or for which they are further processed, are erased or rectified;
(e) kept in a form which permits identification of data subjects for no longer than necessary for the purposes for which the data were collected or for which they are further processed. Member States shall lay down appropriate safeguards for personal data stored for longer periods for historical, statistical or scientific use.

Article 7 and 8 of the DPD stand as rules on the lawful processing of personal information. Chapter II of the Directive provides that, in addition to the exceptions permitted under Article 13, all processing of personal data must comply, first, with the principles relating to data quality set out in Article 6 of the directive and, second, with one of the criteria listed in Article 7.[212] According to Article 7, personal data may be processed only if the data subject has unambiguously given his consent. The data processing is legitimate if the processing is necessary to comply with a legal obligation to which the controller is subject to protect the vital interests of the data subject, to perform of a task carried in the protect public interest or in the exercise official authority, and to defend the legitimate interests of the controller or the third party/parties. Nevertheless, such interests should not override the interest of the fundamental rights and freedoms of the data subject.[213] The ECJ held that "Article 7 of the Directive 95/46/EU set out an exhaustive and restrictive list of cases in which the processing of personal data can be regarded as being lawful".[214]

Article 8 contains a detailed description for lawful processing of sensitive information. Sensitive personal data includes information revealing racial or ethnic origin, political opinions, religious or philosophical beliefs, trade-union

---

[212] ECJ cases C-542/06, *Heinz Huber v. Bundesrepublik Deutschland* (16 December 2008), para. 48; ECJ Joined cases C-468/10 and C-469/10, *Asociación Nacional de Establecimientos Financieros de Crédito and Federación de Comercio Electrónico y Marketing Directo v. Administración del Estado*, (24 November 2011), para. 26.
[213] Data Protective Directive 95/46/EC Article 7 (a)-(f).
[214] ECJ case Joined cases C-468/10 and C-469/10, *Asociación Nacional de Establecimientos Financieros de Crédito and Federación de Comercio Electrónico y Marketing Directo v. Administración del Estado* (24 November 2011), para. 30 & 32. The Court emphasized:

> It follows that Member States cannot add new principles relating to the lawfulness of the processing of personal data to Article 7 of the Directive 95/46 or impose additional requirements that have the effect of amending the scope of one of the six principles provided for in Article 7.

membership, and the information concerning health and sex life. The list is exhaustive under Article 8 (2), and Article 8 (3) provides enumerated exemptions to the Article 8 (1) prohibitions. These exemptions include explicit consent of data subject, vital interest of the data subject, and legitimate interests of others and public interest.[215]

Moreover, Article 10 and 11 define the rules of transparency of data processing. The principle of fair processing requires the transparency of the data processing. Under Article 10 and 11, individuals must be informed of the identity of the controller, the purpose of the data processing, and any further information to guarantee the fair processing in respect to the data subject. Further information includes the recipients of the data, as well as the existence of the right to access and the right to rectify the data. [216] Under the general exemptions, paragraph 2 of Article 11 provides that "paragraph 1 shall not apply where, in particular for processing for statistical purposes or for the purposes of historical or scientific research, the provision of such information proves impossible or would involve a disproportionate effort or if recording or disclosure is expressly laid down by law".[217]

Exemptions and restrictions of the obligations and rights provided for in Article 6 (1), 10, 11 (1), 12 and 21 (see below) are allowed under Article 13 of the Directive 95/46/EU. Exceptions are permissible where they are necessary to safeguard national and public security, to prevent criminal offense, to protect an important economic or financial interest of a Member State, to conduct monitoring with the exercise of official authority, or to defend the rights and freedoms of the data subject or others.[218]

Under Article 16 and 17, the rules on secure processing require the controllers and the processors to implement appropriate technical and organizational measures to prevent any unauthorized interference or disclosure with data processing operations.[219] Confidentiality and security are mandatory requirements for data processing.[220] Article 18, 19, and 21 refer to the rules on transparency of data processing, especially the rules on notification and publication. National law should request controllers to notify the competent supervisory authority of their processing operations for further publication in the future. The publication

---

215 Data Protective Directive 95/46/EC Article 8 (1) – (3).

216 Data Protective Directive 95/46/EC Article 10 (a) – (c).

217 Data Protective Directive 95/46/EC Article 11 (2).

218 Data Protective Directive 95/46/EC Article 13 (1).

219 European Union Agency for Fundamental Rights, *Handbook on European data protection law*, Publication Office of the European Union, Luxemburg (2014), pp. 79-101.

220 Data Protective Directive 95/46/EC Article 16 and 17 (1) – (4).

of notifications by the supervisory authority must be in the form of a special register. Article 18 (2) stipulates that an exemption from the notification or publication is allowed under the circumstance where the rights and freedoms of the data subject are unlikely to be adversely affected by the processing operations.[221]

The Directive also provides the rules for both the free flow of data between the Member States and the requirements for the transfer of personal data to third countries outside the EU. For example, Article 25 (1) regulates, "the transfer to a third country of personal data which are undergoing processing or are intended for processing after transfer may take place only if, ..., the third country in question ensures an adequate level of protection".[222] Derogations of the transborder data principles are recognized in Article 26.

The European Commission is responsible for releasing formal adequacy decisions and deciding whether a third country has an adequate level of privacy protection. In the case of the United States, the Department of Commerce has developed the International Safe Harbour Privacy Principles Certification Program which allows the US companies to apply voluntarily for the certifications.[223] Because of the different approaches to privacy between the EU and the US, the US regulations for privacy and data protection are not qualified as adequate within the meaning of Article 25 of the Directive 95/46/EU. The principles listed in the certification are along the same lines as the European data protection rules and private companies can apply certifications if they comply with the Safe Harbour Privacy Principles.[224]

Article 28, 29, and 30 provide two types of institutional structures. First, each Member State must establish a complete, independent supervisory or oversight body, which shall, in particular, be endowed with investigative power, active power of intervention, and the power to engage in legal proceedings and to hear complaints.[225] Second, there is a so-called Article 29 Working Party on the Protection of Individuals with regard to the Proceeding of Personal Data. The Arti-

[221] Data Protective Directive 95/46/EC Article 18, 19, and 20.

[222] Data Protective Directive 95/46/EC Article 25 and 26.

[223] Rolf H. Weber, *Transborder data transfer: concepts, regulatory approaches and new legislative initiatives*, International Data Privacy Law, Vol.3, Issue: 2 (May 2013), pp. 117-130.

[224] United States Department of Commerce, *Issuance of Safe Harbor Principles and Transmission of European Commission*, 65 Fed Reg. 45666 (2000). A Safe Harbour agreement also exists between the United States and Switzerland. Seven Safe Harbor Principles include: (1) Notice, (2) Choice, (3) Onward Transfer, (4) Security, (5) Data Integrity, (6) Access, and (7) Enforcement.

[225] Data Protective Directive 95/46/EC Article 28.

cle 29 Working Party is composed of the representatives of the supervisory authority or authorities designed by each Member State whose principal function is advisory in nature.[226]

Serving as a reference model for good governance, the Directive is one of the most protective legal documents on data protection. Nevertheless, it has been criticized that, in terms of long-term plans, the Directive is not sufficient for privacy protection toward a globally networked society. The arguments include that it is out-of-date, it is excessively bureaucratic and burdensome, and some of the rules are unrealistic against a backdrop of high-volume and rapid data flows.[227] Consequently, in order to address the genuine risks of the fundamental rights of individuals in the digital era and to provide consistent and effective implementation methods on privacy protection, it is widely accepted that the Directive needs to be updated.

Legislation has always lagged behind technological advances and it is a challenge for the authorities to formulate policies to adapt to the ever-changing environment. In order to build a strong and coherent legal framework for data protection in the EU, on 25 January 2012, the European Commission released its final Proposal for Privacy Regulation[228]. Whereas the DPD is self-implementing,[229] the Regulation is self-executing and has a direct legal force on each Member State. The change in legal status is mainly to prevent data protection rules from being implemented in a fragmented manner throughout the EU.

In line with the "Better Regulation" policy, the Proposal of Privacy Regulation intends to improve "the internal market dimension of data protection", to make "the exercise of data protection rights by individuals more effective", and

---

[226] Data Protective Directive 95/46/EC Article 29 & 30.

[227] Neil Robinson, Hans Graux, Maarten Botterman, Lorenzo Valeri, *Review of EU Data Protection Directiev: Summary*, Information Commissioner's Office (May 2009).

[228] European Commission, *Proposal for a Regulation of the European Parliament and of the Council on the protection of individuals with regard to the processing of personal data on the free movement of such data (General Data Protection Regulation)*, 25.1.2012, COM (2012) 11 final, 2012/2011 (COD) (25 January 2012).
(On 27 April 2016, the General Data Protection Regulation (GDPR) was adopted as a regulation by European Parliament and the Council of European Union. The GDPR will take effect from 25 May 2018 and will replace the Data Protection Directive 95/46/EC. As a regulation, GDPR will directly bind all the state members without further self-implementation.)

[229] Under the EU laws, Directives only oblige Member States to bring their law into conformity with their provisions.

to create "a comprehensive and coherent framework covering all areas of Union competence".[230]

The draft proposes a number of new changes. The most significant alteration is the extended jurisdiction of the Regulation as it applies to all companies processing the personal information of data subjects residing in the EU and to the processing of personal information by controllers or processors in the EU, even if the processing action takes place outside the EU. Additionally, the Regulation will establish a new body, the European Data Protection Board, to replace the Article 29 Working Party. The European Data Protection Board, with expanded power, consists of the heads of the supervisory authority of each Member State and of the European Data Protection Supervisor.[231]

Several innovative developments are introduced by the Proposal. The first is the right to be forgotten, also known as Data Erasure. Under Article 17, a data subject has the right to request a data controller to erase his or her personal information and cease further dissemination of the data, especially when the data "no longer necessary in relation to the purposes for which the data are collected or otherwise processed" or "when the storage period consented to has expired".[232] The exception to the right to be forgotten is allowed only to the extent that processing is necessary for exercising the right to freedom of expression and information, for compliance with a legal obligations, for reasons of public interests, for archiving purposes in scientific or historical research[233] and for the establishment, exercise, or defence of legal claims.[234] Article 17 also enables a data subject to request a data controller who has made his or her personal data

[230] European Commission, *Proposal for a Regulation of the European Parliament and of the Council on the protection of individuals with regard to the processing of personal data on the free movement of such data (General Data Protection Regulation)*, 25.1.2012, COM (2012) 11 final, 2012/2011 (COD) (25 January 2012), p. 4.

[231] GDPR Article 64.

[232] Ibid., Article 17 – *Right to be forgotten and to erasure*:

> The data subject shall have the right to obtain from the controller the erasure of personal data relating to them and the abstention from further dissemination of such data, especially in relation to personal data which was made available by the data subject while he or she was a child, where one of the following grounds applies:
>
> The data is no longer necessary in relation to the purposes for which they were collected or otherwise processed;
>
> The data subject withdraws consent on which the processing is based according to point (a) of Article 6(1), or when the storage period consented to has expired, and where there is no other legal ground for the processing of the data;

[233] GDPR Article 17 (3)(c).

[234] GDPR Article 17 (4)(d).

public to inform the data processors that the data subject wishes them to erase all links to or copies of the personal information.[235]

Despite its groundbreaking design, the 'right to be forgotten' principle is controversial. One the one hand, the right to be forgotten seems to be a useful tool for compelling controllers to erase personal data which is no longer necessary. On the other hand, as more information is disseminated across the Internet, the rule of Data Erasure has been criticized for putting controllers or processors in a burdensome predicament and, therefore, suppressing technological innovation.[236] For example, to hold search engines or social networks liable for erasing unflattering information on data subjects might lead to chilling effects for service providers and result in high-level self-censorship atmosphere on the Internet.[237] Furthermore, the proposed exceptions to the right to be forgotten might be inadequate to address the need for data retention in the light of revolutionary new technologies which make new use of personal information feasible.[238]

The changes to the rules on trans-border data flows have also attracted much attention. Article 40 under Chapter V of the GDPR alters the presumption stated in the Directive 95/46/EU that personal data may not be transferred when absenting an adequate level of protection in the recipient country.[239] According to Chapter V, regarding the transfer of personal data to third countries or international organizations, the Commission is empowered to make adequacy decisions with respect to the level of personal data protection conferred by the juris-

---

235 GDPR Article 17 (2):

> Where the controller referred to in paragraph 1 has made the personal data public, it shall take all reasonable steps, including technical measures, in relation to data for the publication of which the controller is responsible, to inform third parties which care for processing such data, that a data subject requests them to erase any links to, or copy or replication of that personal data. Where the controller has authorized a third-party publication of personal data, the controller shall be considered responsible for that publication.

236 *See* Gehan Gunasekara, *Paddling in Unison or Just Paddling? International Trends in Reforming Information Privacy Law*, International Journal of Law and Technology, Vol.22, No.2 (2014), pp. 141-177 and *see* also Paul De Hert, A Human Rights Perspective on Privacy and Data Protection Impact Assessments. In: D Wright and P De Hert, *Privacy Impact Assessment*, Dordrecht Heidelberg London New York: Springer (2012), pp. 33-59.

237 *See* Luke Danagher, *An Assessment of the Draft Data Protection Regulation: Does it Effectively Protect Data?*, European Journal of Law and Technology, Vol. 3, No.3 (2012).

238 *See* Paul De Hert, A Human Rights Perspective on Privacy and Data Protection Impact Assessments. In: D Wright and P De Hert, *Privacy Impact Assessment*, Dordrecht Heidelberg London New York: Springer (2012), pp. 33-59.

239 Data Protective Directive 95/46/EC Article 25 and 26.

dictions to which the controller intends to send the information.[240] To access the adequacy of the level of protection, the Commission shall take into account the rule of law, the existence and effective functioning independent supervisory authorities, and the international commitments of the third country. In the absence of the adequacy decision, personal data might be transferred outside the EU if the controller or processor has provided appropriate safeguards.[241] The legal impact of the regulations may raise extra-territoriality concerns.

The newly proposed regulations make some valuable improvements to the current situation on data transfer, but also raise many questions. Under Article 45, adequacy decisions may no longer be subject to any authorization, which will, in turn, reduce the administrative burden for data controllers. However, the logistics of how adequacy decisions are issued is not mentioned at all. The possible solution might be that the EU Commission should rely on the Convention 108 by facilitating the approval of adequacy decisions for countries that have ratified this Convention.[242] Another concern is the lack of liability rules. Under the current liability rules, the Article 29 Working Party requires that the binding corporate rules (BCRs) contain a duty for the EU headquarters of the company, or a delegated subsidiary in the EU, to hold liability for the violation.[243] On the contrary, the proposed regulations do not require such liability but refer to the acceptance of liability by a controller or processor established in the territory of a Member State.[244] This approach might eventually give companies more flexibility in structuring their liability scheme.[245]

---

[240] GDPR Article 45:

> 1. A transfer of personal data to a third country or an international organization may take place where the Commission has decided that the third country, a territory or one or more specified sectors within that third country, or the international organization in question ensures an adequate level of protection. Such a transfer shall not require and specific authorization.

[241] GDPR Article 46.

[242] Christopher Kuner, *The European Commission's Proposed Data Protection Regulation: A Copernican Revolution in European Data Protection Law*, Bloomberg BNA Privacy and Security Law Report, 11 PVLR 06 (02 June 2012), pp. 1-15.

[243] Article 29 Working Party, *Working Document setting up a table with the elements and principles to be found in Binding Corporate Rules*, WP 153 (24 June 2008), para. 4.

[244] General Data Protection Regulation Article 43 (2)(f)

[245]*See* Christopher Kuner, *The European Commission's Proposed Data Protection Regulation: A Copernican Revolution in European Data Protection Law*, Bloomberg BNA Privacy and Security Law Report, 11 PVLR 06 (02 June 2012). pp. 1-15; and *see* also Muge Fazioglu, *Forget Me Not, The Clash of the Right to the Forgotten and Freedom of Expression on the Internet*, International Data Privacy Law, Vol.3, No.3 (2013), pp. 149-157.

e. The United States of America

Since most of the transnational Internet companies are based in the United States, the US's privacy protection policy has an imperative international influence.[246] The existing US legal systems for privacy or data protection, however, have been criticized for not responding effectively to the new challenges posed by innovative technologies. There are two central privacy systems of the current US paradigm – constitutional perspectives and tort protections which are examined respectively below.

Although there is no direct guarantee of privacy in the United States Constitution, the right can be derived from a number of constitutional provisions. The most significant principle of privacy protection comes from the Fourth Amendment of the Bill of Rights, which protects individuals against unreasonable searches and seizures from the government.[247] In the landmark decision of *Katz v. United States*, the court stated that individuals have to show both actual expectation (subjective) and reasonable expectation (objective), which is recognized by the society, of privacy.[248] In *Katz*, the court is of the opinion that the listening device attached outside of the phone booth by the federal government is an intrusion on a person's expectation of privacy. The court noted:

> "What a person knowingly exposes to the public, even in his own home or office, is not a subject of the Fourth Amendment protection. But what he seeks to preserve as private, even in the area accessible to the public, may be constitutionally protected."[249]

While the *Katz* test provided a certain degree of protection to individuals' right to privacy, the test itself, along with the lines of the Fourth Amendment, has not evolved in a way that offered a sufficient response to the challenges brought by advanced ICTs. For example, when considering the voluntary transfer of information to a third party, the courts' decisions raise various questions

---

[246] *See* Toby Mendel, Andrew Puddephatt, Ben Wagner, Dixie Hawtin and Natalia Torres, *Global Survey on Internet Privacy and Freedom of Expression*, United Nations Educational, Scientific and Cultural Organization (2012).

[247] United States Constitution Amendment IV:

> The right of the people to be secure in their persons, houses, papers, and effects, against unreasonable searches and seizures, shall not be violated, and no warrants shall issue, but upon probable cause, supported by oath or affirmation, and particularly describing the place to be searched, and the persons or things to be seized.

[248] United States Supreme Court, *Katz v. United States*, 369 F.2d 130, 134 (9th Cir. 1966), rev'd, 389 US 347 (18 December 1967), p. 361(Harlan concurring).

[249] Ibid., p. 351.

with regard to the meaning of reasonable expectation of privacy in a digital society. In both *Smith v. Maryland*[250] and *United States v. Miller*[251], the court held that a individual does not hold an expectation of privacy in information turned over to a third party. In the digital world we live in, sending e-mails through the Internet means sharing information with Internet service providers, searching a website means providing personal preference to search engines, and storing files on cloud computing means handing personal data to cloud servers. The right to privacy will be severely compromised if the information flowing through the Internet is deemed as information voluntarily conveyed to a third party. However, the courts' precedents have not been overruled and the meaning of expectation needs to be further defined and interpreted.[252]

The concept of the tort invasion of privacy can be traced back to the seminal article, *The Right to Privacy*, written by Samuel Warren and Louis Brandeis. The authors suggested that property law is not a sufficient basis to protect the right to keep one's "thoughts, sentiments, and emotions private". Instead, it is "the more general right of an individual to be let alone."[253] In addition, William L. Prosser's 1960 article, *Privacy*, presents another major step in the develop-

[250] United States Supreme Court, *Smith v. Maryland*, 442 US 735 (20 June 1979).
(In the case, the telephone company, at police request, installed at its central offices a pen register to record the numbers dialed from the telephone at the petitioner's home. The Supreme Court ruled that the petitioner in all probability entertained no actual expectation of privacy in the phone numbers he dialed, and even if he did, this expectation was not 'legitimate'. The court further stated that when the petitioner voluntarily conveyed numerical information to the phone company and exposed that information to its equipment in the normal course of business, he assumed the risk that the company would reveal the information to the police.)

[251] United States Supreme Court, *United States v. Miller*, 425 US 435 (21 April 1976).
(In the case, the respondent contended that the subpoena duces tecum pursuant to which the material has been produced by the banks were defective and that the records relating to his accounts at two banks had thus been illegally seized in violation of the Fourth Amendment. The court held that there is no legitimate expectation to privacy in the contents of the original checks and deposit slips. The Fourth Amendment does not prohibit the obtaining of information revealed to a third party and conveyed by him to Government authorities.)

[252] *See* Russell L. Weaver, *The Fourth Amendment, Privacy and Advancing Technology*, Mississippi Law Journal, Vol.80, No.3 (2011), pp. 1131-1227 (1187-1195).

[253] Samuel Warren and Louis Brandeis, *The Right to Privacy*, Harvard Law Review 193, Vol.4, No.5 (15 December1980), pp. 193-220.

ment of the right to privacy in tort law.[254] In the article, Prosser outlined four separate and distinct causes of action for the tort invasion of privacy:

> "1. Intrusion upon the plaintiff's private facts about the plaintiff;
> 2. Public disclosure of embarrassing private facts about the plaintiff
> 3. Publicity which places the plaintiff in a false light in the public eye.
> 4. Appropriation, for the defendant's advantage, of the plaintiff's name or likeness."[255]

The four elements were later incorporated into the Restatement (Second) of Torts.[256] While the constitutional right of privacy protects citizens from the governmental interference, the right to privacy under the tort law protects individuals from the acts of private individuals or businesses. As the court in *Katz v. United States* explained that the Fourth Amendment "protects individual privacy against certain kinds of governmental intrusion", but "a person's general right to privacy – his right to be let alone by other people – is, …, left largely to the law of the individual States".[257]

In addition to the constitution and tort law systems, a large number of federal statutory schemes in the US are ratified to cope with various sectors and areas of privacy concerns. For example, the Omnibus Crime Control and Safe Street Act of 1968 provides a right of action for anyone whose communication has been intercepted without consent[258], and the Right to Financial Privacy Act of 1978 protects the privacy and confidentiality of financial records.[259] Furthermore, the Electronic Communication Privacy Act (ECPA) of 1986 was designed to protect private electronic communication from unauthorized govern-

---

[254] *See* Eli A Meltz, *No Harm, No Foul? "Attempted" Invasion of Privacy and the Tort of Intrusion Upon Seclusion*, Fordham Law Review, Vol. 83, Issue: 6 (2015), pp. 3431-3470.

[255] William L. Prosser, *Privacy*, California Law Review, Vol. 48, Issue:3 (1960), pp. 383-423.

[256] Restatement (Second) of Torts, § 652B-E (1977).

[257] United States Supreme Court, *Katz v. United States*, 369 F.2d 130, 134 (9th Cir. 1966), rev'd, 389 US 347 (18 December 1967), pp. 350-351.

[258] 18 USC. § 2520 (a):

> any person whose wire, oral, or electronic communication is intercepted, disclosed, or intentionally used in violation of this chapter may in a civil action recover from the person or entity, other than the United States, which engaged in that violation such relief as may be appropriate.

[259] 12 USC. §§2401-3422.

ment access.[260] The ECPA is composed of three separated Acts: the Wiretap Act, Stored Communication Act and Pen Register Act. Nevertheless, the PATRIOT Act of 2001 has enormously reduced the function of the ECPA by expanding the power of security and law enforcement to intercept private information or communication if the national security concern is at issue.[261]

Lastly, the report released by Obama Administration needs further attention. The report, Consumer Data Privacy in a Networked World: A framework for Protecting Privacy and Promoting Innovation in the Global Digital Economy[262], sets out a proposed policy framework for US consumer privacy protection. The proposed framework consists of four essential elements: the Consumer Privacy Bill of Rights (CPBR); a multi-stakeholder process to establish voluntarily enforceable codes of conduct; an enforcement system, primarily performed by the Federal Trade Commission (FTC); and a commitment to increase international interoperability between the United States and the privacy framework of other countries. The goal of the White House report is to establish a secure privacy protection system in order to promote the innovation in new information technologies, to adapt privacy principles to the dynamic environment of the commercial Internet, and ultimately to provide consistent protection for consumers both nationally and internationally.[263] However, the CPBR is not designed to alter existing privacy regulations outside the purely commercial and consumer-oriented context.[264] In other words, existing laws and policies governing the federal government will remain unaffected.

The White House's privacy policy is based on the CPBR which proposed seven principles for fair information practice, which include Individual Control, Transparency, Respect for Context, Security, Access and Accuracy, Focused Collection, and Accountability.[265] The CPBR reflects the efforts to clarify data protection on a global scale and ensure the flexibility of its application, which is critical to innovation in the commercial world on the Internet. For example,

---

[260] Electronic Communications Privacy Act of 1986, 18 USC §2510-22. Wiretap Act, 18 USC. §2515. Stored Communication Act, 18 USC. §§2701-12. Pen Register Act, 18 USC. §3121.

[261] Uniting and Strengthening America by Providing Appropriate Tools Required to Intercept and Obstruct Terrorism Act of 2001 (USA PATRIOT ACT), Pub. L. No.107-56.

[262] The White House, *Consumer Data Privacy in a Networked World: A Framework for Protecting Privacy and Promoting Innovative in the Global Digital Economy*, Washington (February 2012).

[263] Ibid.

[264] Ibid, pp. 36-37.

[265] Ibid.

when considering the processing of personal data, the CPBR provides separate standards for consumer-facing companies and third parties,[266] and the principle of Respect for Context requires companies to provide heightened "Transparency and Individual Choice", which is prominent and easily actionable by consumers at the time of data collection, if they will use or disclose personal data for other purpose other than the one that consumers originally consent to.[267]

Although this approach can be observed as an innovative method to adapting to the constantly evolving technologies since the purposes to use and disclose personal data may change over time in ways not foreseeable at the time of the collection, it can also argue that this flexible manner provides a vague and inadequate protection to consumers' right to privacy.[268] Most importantly, the effect of the CPBR for protecting people's right to privacy on the Internet is questionable since the Bill is not designed to alter existing privacy regulations outside the purely commercial and consumer-oriented context.[269] In other words, existing laws and policies governing the federal government will remain unaffected.

---

[266] Ibid., p. 13.
[267] Ibid., p. 16.
[268] *See* Gehan Gunasekara, *Paddling in Unison or Just Paddling? International Trends in Reforming Information Privacy Law*, International Journal of Law and Technology, Vol.22, No.2 (2014), pp. 141-177.
[269] The White House, *Consumer Data Privacy in a Networked World: A Framework for Protecting Privacy and Promoting Innovative in the Global Digital Economy*, Washington (February 2012), pp. 36-37.

III. Conclusion

Innovation in ICTs has reshaped the ways in which people access, receive, and disseminate information. On the one hand, with the advent of Web 2.0, the Internet enhances the communicative power of individuals and brings more information to an increasing number of people around the world. On the other hand, Internet policies and regulations have been gradually implemented to restrict and control the free flow of information. It was only recently that human rights advocates have begun to realize that the protection of fundamental human rights on the Internet is pivotal to the development, dignity, and integrity of individuals. In 2012, a UN resolution proclaimed that, "the same rights that people have offline must also be protected online." However, due to the unique characteristics of the Internet, the interpretation and application of existing human rights laws to online activities depends on the various economic, political, and cultural backgrounds of each country. Therefore, by examining the protection of freedom of expression and information and the right to privacy by national, regional, and international layers of governance, Chapter 2 has explored the interface between the Internet and human rights in the context of international human rights law.

Freedom of expression and information is essential for each individual's self-fulfillment and is guaranteed in the UDHR, ICCPR, ECHR, EUCFR, and American Convention on Human Rights. Using different descriptions, all the human rights agreements protect people's freedom to seek, receive, and impart information and ideas of all kinds through any medium regardless of frontiers. Two observations can be drawn from the broad language that defines freedom of expression. First, the right to expression is not limited to disseminating broadly accepted information or ideas but includes unpleasant and dissident opinions. Second, freedom of expression protects not only the substance of information but also the means by which information is expressed and received. From the research covered in the chapter, regional and international human rights courts have recognized that the means of expression include the dissemination of information via the Internet. Freedom of expression is not guaranteed by technological innovation but needs to be explicitly and systematically protected through adequate policies and practice.

The right to privacy is essential to personal autonomy and self-determination. Regardless of the conceptual difficulty of defining privacy, a person's right to privacy in the digital age should be protected substantively and procedurally against arbitrary or unlawful interference with his or her private life. Data protection provides individuals with the right to control and manage personally identifiable information that is collected, stored, and disseminated by governments or private entities. The ultimate objective of data protection is to ensure that the processing of personal data is carried out in a fair and transparent manner. Although it is unclear whether all the interests that modern data protection laws aim to safeguard, such as data security and data quality, are within the range of traditionally defined concepts of privacy, under the premise of pursuing the principle of legality and proportionality for the processing of personal information, the essence of data protection principles conforms to the meaning of the right to privacy guaranteed by international human rights law.

The final conclusion of Chapter 2 is that freedom of expression and information and the right to privacy are applicable to individuals' activities on the Internet, and states must ensure that any Internet censorship measures implemented on the basis of national security, public morals, or public order comply with their obligations under international human rights law. Put differently, any restriction to or interference with an individual's fundamental rights on the Internet must be prescribed by law, pursue a legitimate aim, and be in conformity with the principle of necessity. Policy and law on the Internet without any legal basis or on the basis of broad and ambiguous terms will create a chilling effect on the right to freedom of expression and lead to arbitrary interference with personal privacy and private life. How to balance fundamental human rights and other social interests in the contemporary information society in all layers of governance has far-reaching implications for human development. However, the balance should be guided by the principle that "the relation between right and restriction, between norm and exception, must not be reversed".[270]

[270] UN Human Rights Committee (HRC), *CCPR General Comment No. 27: Article 12 (Freedom of Movement)*, CCPR/C/21/Rev.1/Add.9 (2 November 1999).

Chapter 3. Restrictions on Internet-related Commercial Activities and the WTO

As described in Chapter 2, Internet censorship measures adopted by the governments might severely undermine individuals' fundamental human rights online if they are not formulated in conformity with the norms and standards of international human rights law. Chapter 3 assesses whether WTO rules are relevant or flexible enough to accommodate international trade conducted through the Internet. While the technological advances enhanced international trade in all aspects, national regulatory responses, from the areas of telecommunication and audiovisual services to the regimes of copyrights and cultural policy, have challenged the roles of international economic institutions in the digital age. Consequently, if WTO law could be interpreted and applied in an evolutionary and resilient manner to adapt to the changes brought about by new information and communication technologies, it may bring about some legal consistency and certainty to the increasing digital trade.

Section I provides an overview of the relationship between digital trade and the WTO. The first part of the section discusses the role of the GATT in regulating information technology (IT) products. Despite most digital trade debates put emphasis on trade in services, the regulations on trade in goods are still relevant with respect to digitally delivered products since the line between goods and services of an electronically delivered product is far from settled. Additionally, the Information Technology Agreement (ITA), ratified by 81 WTO Members, represents more than 97% of the overall trade in IT products and provides a gradual and anticipated elimination of all tariffs and equivalent import charges on IT products. The second part examines the applicability of GATS rules to digital trade. Because almost all commercial activities on the Internet involve some online data processing or computer-based services, the GATS will inevitably occupy a prominent role in the assessment of Internet-related measures.

Section II and Section III provide the case reviews of recent disputes brought in front the WTO judiciary bodies: *US – Gambling* and *China – Audiovisual Products*. Both of the cases considered Internet-related measures. While the WTO was negotiated before the widely use of the internet, the WTO jurisprudence sheds some light on how to link WTO rules with technologies that did not exist at the time the GATT/GATS were drafted. As the WTO dispute settlement mechanism, described as the "jewel in the crown" of the WTO legal structure, is unique in the modern international judiciary system,[1] the case study intends to examine whether panels and the Appellate Body have the competence to interpret WTO rules to the Internet-related measures which might have adverse impact on international trade.

Some might argue that such an approach goes beyond the ordinary meanings of the WTO and the intentions of the negotiators. Nevertheless, an international organization like the WTO with 160 plus Members States needs to develop in line with the contemporary concepts and doctrines. As John H. Jackson point out, perhaps the most significant lesson one can learn from the GATT/WTO story is:

> "Human institutions inevitably evolve and change, and concepts which ignore that, such as concepts which try to cling to "original intent of the draftspersons," or some inclination to disparage or deny the validity of some of these evolutions and changes, could be damaging to the broader purposes of institutions. Governments (or society) which consent to become members of institutions must do so with the realization that institutional structures will not be frozen in time, and that such consent will certainly bring some surprises to the constituencies concerned."[2]

---

[1] *See* Thomas Bernauer, Manfred Elsig and Joost Pauwelyn, The World Trade Organization's Dispute Settlement Mechanism – Analysis and Problem's. In: Martin Daunton, Amrita Narlikar & Robert M. Stern (eds), *The Oxford Handbook of the World Trade Organization*, Oxford University Press (2012), pp. 487-506.

[2] John H. Jackson, *Sovereignty, the WTO, and Changing Fundamentals of International Law*, New York: Cambridge University Press (2006), p. 82.

I. Digital Trade and the World Trade Organization

The global expansion of the Internet has not only advanced the way people seek, receive, and impart information but has also led to a tremendous increase in the electronic delivery of digital products and services.[3] In 1998, delegates at the Second WTO Ministerial Conference recognized that the Internet provided unprecedented opportunities for global electronic commerce and realized the importance of establishing a comprehensive work programme to examine all trade-related issues in the digital age.[4] After the Conference, on the 25 May 1998, the Ministers adopted the Declaration on Global Electronic Commerce, which called on Members to "continue their current practice of not imposing customs duties on electronic transmissions".[5] Furthermore, in September 1998, the General Council of the WTO established a Work Programme on Electronic Commerce. The Work Programme defines the term electronic commerce (E-commerce) as "the production, distribution, marketing, sale or delivery of goods and services by electronic means".[6] In undertaking the work, the General Council requested the Council for Trade in Services, the Council for Trade in Goods, the Council for TRIPS, and the Committee on Trade and Development to examine and report E-commerce issues in their relevant legal framework.[7]

The discussion of E-commerce within the WTO remains ongoing. For example, in 2009, on the Geneva Ministerial Conference, WTO Members decided to renew the Work Programme and maintain current practice of not imposing customs duties on electronic transmission until 2011.[8] On the 2011 Geneva Ministerial Conference, WTO Members emphasized the development dimension in the Work Programme, particularly Internet connectivity and the assessment of all information and telecommunications technologies, with specific considerations to the developing and least-developed countries.[9] On the Bali Ministerial

---

[3] *See* Mira Burri & Thomas Cottier, Introduction: Digital technologies and international trade regulation (2012). In: Mira Burri and Thomas Cottier (eds.), *Trade Governance in the Digital Age – World Trade Forum*, Cambridge University Press, pp. 1-14.

[4] WTO, Ministerial Declaration on Global E-Commerce, WT/MIN(98)/DEC/2, 20 May 1998.

[5] Ibid.

[6] WTO, Working Programme on Electronic Commerce, WT/L/274, 30 September 1998.

[7] Ibid.

[8] WTO, Report of the 17 November 2009 meeting of the General Council, Work Programme on Electronic Commerce, Dedicated Discussions under the auspices of the General Council, WT/GC/W/613, 9 November 2009.

[9] WTO Ministerial Conference, Work Programme on Electronic Commerce, Decision of 17 December 2011, WT/L/843, 19 December 2011.

Conference in 2013, WTO Members reiterated that continuing E-commerce negotiations must adhere to the basic principles of the WTO, including non-discrimination, predictability, and transparency. Members agreed to extend non-duty practice on electronic transmission until 2015.[10]

Although WTO Members and the Secretariat have successfully described the critical and urgent issues of E-commerce within the WTO, the process of converting thought into action is relatively slow.[11] While digital trade has grown substantially in the past decade, there have been no substantive results from the Ministerial Conference or the Dedicated Discussions on E-Commerce. WTO Members even failed to reach a consensus on simple issues, such as establishing a permanent duty-free moratorium on digital trade.[12] Nevertheless, the recent court practices of the WTO adjudicating bodies have shown some promising signs of connecting WTO law with Internet-related trade measures.

Before examining the application of WTO law to digital trade, it is vital to address the issue of classifying the content of the electronic transmission. In other words, whether the delivery of electronic products should be qualified as trade in goods or as trade in services.[13] Due to the innovative ICT technologies, products can be stored, used, and distributed in intangible digital forms. Whereas WTO Members agreed that the majority of electronically transmitted products are services,[14] there is still a lack of clarity with regard to the classification of specific products.[15] It is uncontested that the products purchased on the Internet and delivered physically involve the movement of goods, and the online services that do not include storing and downloading activities from consumers

[10] WTO Ministerial Conference, Work Programme on Electronic Commerce, Decision of 7 December 2013, WT/MIN(13), WT/L/907, 11 December 2013.

[11] *See* Sacha Wunsch-Vincent, Trade Rules of the Digital Age (2008). In: Marion Panizzon, Nicole Pohl and Pierre Sauve (eds.), *GATS and the Regulation of International Trade in Services*, Cambridge: Cambridge University Press.

[12] *See* Sacha Wunsch-Vincent, Toward Coherent Rules for Digital Trade (2012). In: Mira Burri and Thomas Cottier, *Trade Governance in the Digital Age*, Cambridge: Cambridge University Press.

[13] Rolf H. Weber, *Digital Trade in WTO-Law – Taking Stock and Looking Ahead*, Asian Journal of WTO & Int'l Health Law and Policy (AJWH), Vol. 5:1 (2010).

[14] WTO General Council, Dedicated Discussion on Electronic Commerce Under the Auspices of the Central Council on 15 June 2001, Summary by the Secretariat of the Issues Raised, WT/GC/W436, 6 July 2001.

[15] Ibid. The Dedicated Discussion highlighted that:

> A number of delegations agreed that a majority of electronically transmitted products were indeed services. However, there was still a lack of clarity with regard to the classification under GATT and GATS of certain products which can be delivered both in electronic form and on a physical carrier.

are categorized as services.[16] The situation is less clear and more controversial when the end-product is delivered electronically. The question arises, for example, whether online newspapers should be examined under the GATT as commodities or should be considered under the less restrictive obligations of the GATS as services.

The difficulty in classifying digitally delivered products stems from two definitional issues. First, the meaning of 'goods' and 'services' is unclear.[17] No definition of the term 'goods' can be found in any GATT provisions, and the phrase 'services' is vaguely defined as any service in any sector except services supplied in the exercise of governmental authorities.[18] These unclear definitions result in the ambiguous boundary between the GATT and the GATS. Second, neither the classification system of the GATT (Harmonized System)[19] nor of the GATS (Service Sectoral Classification List, W/120)[20] provides an explicit guideline to the meaning of 'digital products'.[21] On the one hand, since both the Harmonized System and ITA do not cover the content of the product, but the carrier media[22], no classification mechanism is available to the digital delivery

---

[16] Tim Wu, *The World Trade Law of Censorship and Internet Filtering*, Chicago Journal of Int'l Law, Vol.7, Issue 1 (2006).

[17] *See* Sacha Wunsch-Vincent, *The WTO, the Internet and Trade in Digital-Products: EU-US Perspectives*, North America: Hart Publishing (2006), pp. 48-62. *See* also Rolf H. Weber, *Digital Trade in WTO-Law – Taking Stock and Looking Ahead*, Asian Journal of WTO & Int'l Health Law and Policy (AJWH), Vol. 5:1 (2010), and Rolf H. Weber, *Digital Trade and E-Commerce: Challenges and Opportunities of the Asia-Pacific Regionalism*, Asian Journal of WTO & Int'l Health Law and Policy (AJWH), Vol. 10:32 (2015).

[18] GATS, Article I, ¶ 3(b).

[19] The Harmonized Commodity Description and Coding System, also known as the Harmonized System of tariff nomenclature is an internationally standardized system of names and numbers to classify trade products. It came into effect in 1988 and had since been developed and maintained by the World Customs Organization.

[20] There is no obligation on WTO Members to use any particular classification system in undertaking commitments. Nevertheless, an informal document produced for the services negotiation during the Uruguay Round, the Services Sectoral Classification List (W/120), was used and continues to be used as the principal guiding classification system.

[21] *See* U.N. Info. & Comm. Tech. Task Force, WTO, E-Commerce and Information Technologies: From the Uruguay Round Through the Doha *Development Agenda: A Report of the UN ICT Task Force,* (2005) (prepared by Sasha Wunsch-Vincent), pp. 145-149.

[22] The ITA obligation asks the Member States to eliminate duties on covered information technology products and aims at eliminating non-tariff barriers to trade on IT-

if no physical attributes are attached to the product. On the other hand, as most of the Internet-related services did not exist at the time when the Council for Trade in Services adopted the W/120, it is problematic to apply the new services to the current classification system under the GATS.

As illustrated in the following sections, the classification of electronically delivered products has a significant influence on future development in digital trade since the level of trade liberalization under the GATT and GATS is very different. Under the GATT, all products are subject to most-favoured-nation, national treatment, and market access obligations. Unlike the GATT, due to the complexity of trade in services and the purpose of progressive trade liberalization, the GATS consists of a set of general and specific obligations. The specific obligations of a Member apply only to the extent that the Member undertakes the commitments on the services at the issue in its GATS Schedule. The 'positive list' approach of the GATS allows a Member to decide the scope of its market access and national treatment obligations. Therefore, under the GATS, "liberalization only takes place to the extent of specific acceptance of assumed obligations".[23]

A. The GATT and Digital Trade

The role of the GATT to trade in ICT products is critical in two respects. The first is that the rules and obligations under the GATT are applicable to digitally delivered products if the products are considered as 'goods' within the meaning of the GATT. Secondly, the development of an effective global information and communication system depends on the capability and opportunity to connect the required equipment, such as computers, telephones, decoders, modems, and basic infrastructures.[24] Liberalization on the ICT products will have a profound impact on access to the Internet and the prosperity of digital trade. Since the GATT does not directly address digital products, the ITA, therefore, provides a unique regime for trade in ICT products and secures zero duties on digitally delivered goods.

---

products. The Agreement is plurilateral in nature and was concluded at the Singapore Ministerial Conference in December 1996.

[23] *See* Rolf H. Weber, *Digital Trade in WTO-Law – Taking Stock and Looking Ahead*, Asian Journal of WTO & Int'l Health Law and Policy (AJWH), Vol. 5:1 (2010).

[24] *See* David Luff, Convergence: A buzzword to remain? (2012), In: Mira Burri and Thomas Cottier, *Trade Governance in the Digital Age*, Cambridge: Cambridge University Press, pp. 65-90. *See* also Mira Burri, The International Economic Law Framework for Digital Age, ZeitSchrift für Schweiyerisches Recht 135 (2015), pp. 10-72.

a. The General Agreement on Tariffs and Trade (GATT)

The starting point for understanding the obligations of the GATT is through Article II: Schedules of Concession. Under Article II, Members are obligated to not impose a higher tariff on particular products than the ones they have committed to in the tariff schedule.[25] Many of the remaining GATT provisions are designed in large part to reinforce the basic tariff obligations. Furthermore, Member States have to implement tariff measures in a non-discriminatory manner. The most prominent non-discrimination principles under the GATT are most-favoured nation (MFN) of Article I and national treatment obligation of Article III.

The MFN principle is specified in the very first article of the GATT. Article I:1 stipulates:

> With respect to customs duties and charges of any kind imposed on or in connection with importation or exportation or imposed on the international transfer of payments for imports or exports, and with respect to the method of levying such duties and charges, and with respect to all rules and formalities in connection with importation, and with respect to all matters referred to in paragraph 2 and 4 of Article III, any advantage, favour, privilege or immunity granted by any contracting party to any product originating in or destined for any other country *shall be accorded immediately and unconditionally to like product originating in or destined for the territories of all other contracting parties*. (emphasis added)

The central purpose of the MFN obligation is to ensure that all WTO Members have the equal opportunity to export to or import from other WTO Members. Whenever a Member negotiates and grants trade concessions to another Member, such concessions must be automatically extended to all other States. Furthermore, even outside of trade negotiations, whenever a WTO Member enacts certain trade-restrictive rules or tariff quotas, the Member cannot, according to the MFN obligation, discriminate between products from one WTO

[25] *See* generally also John H. Jackson, William J. Davey, Alan O. Sykes, Jr., *Legal Problems of International Economic Relations: Cases, Materials and Text (Fourth Edition)*, West Group (2002), pp. 208-245.

Member and like products from any other Member.[26] Therefore, Article I:1 of the GATT covers both border measures and internal measures.

The principle of non-discrimination is also reflected in national treatment obligation. Article III:1 of the GATT sets out the general principle of national treatment which requires that WTO Members should not afford protection of domestic products through internal measures. In other words, once a product passes the border into a domestic market, the treatment of the product should be the same to the like domestic products and subject to the identical regulatory regime. Article III:1 reads as follow:

> The contracting parties recognize that internal taxes and other internal charges, and law, regulations and requirements affecting the internal sale, offering for sale, purchase, transportation, distribution or use of products, and internal quantitative regulations requiring the mixture, processing or use of products in specified amounts or proportions, should not be applied to imported or domestic products so as to afford protection to domestic production.

The panel in *EC – Seal Products* recognized that the intent of Article III is to "provide equal conditions of competition once goods have been cleared through customs".[27] That is to say, the fundamental purpose of the national treatment obligations under the GATT is to avoid protectionism through regulating the scope of internal taxes and regulatory measures.[28] Paragraph 2 of Article III requires national treatment with respect to internal taxation, and paragraph 4 of regulates that imports receive treatment "no less favorable" than that accorded to like domestic products concerning regulatory burdens.

---

[26] Note that there are crucial and wide-ranging exceptions to the MFN principle, in particular, GATT Article XXIV permitting certain preferential trade agreements (PTAs) or regional trade agreements (RTAs). Another exception is the so-called Enabling Clause, which allows developed countries to extend tariff preferences to developing countries exclusively.

[27] Panel Report, *Italian Discrimination Against Imported Agricultural Machinery*, 7th Supp. BISD 60, 23 October 1958, para. 13.
(Appellate Body Report, *European Communities – Measures Prohibiting the Importation and Marketing of Seal Products*, WT/DS 400/AB/R & WT/DS 401/AB/R (22 May 2014).)

[28] Appellate Body Report, *Japan – Taxes on Alcoholic Beverages* (cited as *Japan – Alcoholic Beverages II*), WT/DS8/AB/R; WT/DS10/AB/R WT; DS11/AB/R (4 October 1996), p. 16.

The non-discrimination principle in both Article I and Article III of the GATT covers both *de jure* as well as *de facto* discriminations. Put differently, while a measure treats two like products differently on the basis of the origins explicitly violate non-discrimination obligations, an origin-neutral measure might also have a detrimental effect on foreign products in practice. In *Canada – Auto*, the Appellate Body stated:

> "Neither the words "*de jure*" not "*de facto*" appear in Article I:1. Nevertheless, we observe that Article I:1 does not cover only "in law", or *de jure*, discrimination. As several GATT panel reports confirmed, Article I:1 covers also "in fact," or *de facto*, discrimination."[29]

Under Article III of the GATT a *de facto* discrimination exists when a measure treats domestic and foreign products in an identical manner but adversely affects the imported products, or when a measure treats two different but competitive products in the same way but has a detrimental effect on the imports.[30] The function of the national treatment obligation would be considerably diminished if its application is restricted only to *de jure* discriminatory measures.

The key component of non-discrimination principle is the concept of 'likeness'. Since the GATT does not provide a clear definition for 'like products', the WTO adjudicating bodies have recognized that the scope of the term 'likeness' may vary depending on the context in which it is used. The Appellate Body's decision in *Japan – Alcoholic Beverages II*, which is regularly cited by the subsequent panels, held:

> "... The concept of "likeness" is a relative one that evokes the image of an accordion. The accordion of "likeness" stretches and squeezes in different places as different provisions of the *WTO Agreement* are applied. The width of the accordion on any one of those places must be determined by the particular provision in which the term "like" is encountered as well as

[29] Appellate Body Report, *Canada-Certain Measures Affecting the Automotive Industry* (cited as *Canada -- Autos*), WT/DS139/AB/R; WT/DS142/AB/R (31 May 2000), para. 78.

[30] *See* Federico Ortino, WTO Jurisprudence on De Jure and De Facto Discrimination. In: Federico Ortino and Ernst-Ulrich Pertersmann, *The WTO Dispute Settlement Sysetem 1995-2003*, Kluwer Law International (2004), pp. 217-262.

> by the context and the circumstances that prevail in any given case to which that provision may apply."[31]

On a case-by-case basis, the determination of whether two products are 'like products' is, essentially, a determination about the nature and extent of the competitive relationship between and among the disputed products in a particular market. The Report of the Working Party on Border Tax Adjustments outlined four general criteria in analyzing "likeness": (i) the properties, nature, and quality of the products; (ii) the end-use of the products; (iii) consumers' tastes and habits in respect of the products; and the tariff classification of the products.[32] Nevertheless, these criteria are merely tools to assist in the task of examining the relevant evidence. "They are neither a treaty-mandated nor a closed list of criteria that will determine the legal characterization of product".[33]

Although most of the debates on digital trade focused on trade in services, the regulations on trade in digitally delivered goods still maintain relevancy. Since the issue concerning how to draw the line between goods and services in the digital age is far from settled, the concept of 'likeness' among foreign and domestic digital products will remain critical in determining the substantive scope of the non-discrimination obligations under the GATT.

b. The Information Technology Agreement (ITA)

Since IT products have become more and more important in the world economy and the GATT does not address digital products directly, during the Singapore WTO Ministerial Conference in December 1996, the ITA was adopted by 14 signatories, which represented 19 WTO Members and separate customs territories.[34] As stated in the Declaration on Trade in Information Technology Products, the proclaimed objectives of the ITA are to achieve maximum freedom of world trade in information technology products, to encourage the continued technological development of the information technology industry on a world-

---

[31] Appellate Body Report, *Japan – Taxes on Alcoholic Beverages* (cited as *Japan – Alcoholic Beverages II*), WT/DS8/AB/R; WT/DS10/AB/R WT; DS11/AB/R (4 October 1996), p. 21.

[32] General Agreement on Tariffs and Trade, Report by the Working Party on Border Tax Adjustments, L/3465 (20 November 1970), para. 18.

[33] Appellate Body Report, *European Communities – Measures Affecting Asbestos and Asbestos-Containing Products*, WT/DS135/AB/R (5/April/2001), para. 102.

[34] WTO, Ministerial Conference, Ministerial Declaration on Trade in Information Technology Products, WT/MIN (96)/16 (13/December/1996).

wide basis, and to enhance market access opportunities for information technology products.[35] The Agreement, therefore, provides for the gradual and anticipated elimination of all tariffs and equivalent import charges on IT products.[36]

The attached documents Annex A and B contain the product coverage of the ITA. Annex A lists four to six digital codes of the included products pursuant to the Harmonized System used by the GATT. Annex B covers a positive list of specific products and each country is left to classify the list with the appropriate Harmonized System categories. The list includes various high technology products such as computers, flat panel displays, computer network equipment, telecommunication apparatus, data-storage media, and software.[37] Due to the mandatory binding effect of the list, the ITA Member States must not declare any exceptions to the covered products. However, developing country Members may require longer transition periods for domestic implementation.

The ITA is plurilateral in nature and only binds the Members that have signed it. Nevertheless, the ITA is constructed on the basis of the MNF principle. Consequently, all WTO Members (not limited to the signatory states) benefit from the market access commitments of the ITA participants.[38] In spite of the free-riding concerns, the ITA covers more than 97% of the overall trade in IT products.[39]

Subscribed by 29 Members initially, following the recent accession of the Republic of Seychelles, the ITA now covers 81 WTO Members (including China, the biggest producer of IT products). Since the ITA has been criticized for not being able to efficiently accommodate technological change, in July 2015, 18 years after the entry into force of the original agreement, 53 states agreed to the expansion of ITA coverage.[40] According to the new WTO agreement, import tariffs on 201 high-tech products will be eliminated. It is estimated that the annual trade will be $1.3 trillion, accounting for approximately 10% of the

---

[35] Ibid.

[36] *See* David Luff, Convergence: A buzzword to remain? (2012), In: Mira Burri and Thomas Cottier, *Trade Governance in the Digital Age*, Cambridge: Cambridge University Press, pp. 65-90.

[37] WTO, *15 Years of the Information Technology Agreement: Trade, Innovation and Global Production Networks*, Geneva: World Trade Organization (2012).

[38] *See* Rolf H. Weber, *Digital Trade in WTO-Law – Taking Stock and Looking Ahead*, Asian Journal of WTO & Int'l Health Law and Policy (AJWH), Vol. 5:1 (2010).

[39] WTO, *15 Years of the Information Technology Agreement: Trade, Innovation and Global Production Networks*, Geneva: World Trade Organization (2012).

[40] WTO, *Briefing note: The Expansion of Trade in Information Technology Products (ITA Expansion)* (16 December 2015).

overall volume of trade in goods.[41] Products covered by the re-negotiated ITA include new generation multi-component integrated circuits (MOCs), touch screens, GPS navigation equipment, portable interactive electronic education devices, video games consoles, and medical equipment.[42] The far-reaching consequence of the zero-tariff policy on the newly included products will significantly boost trade in IT products and reduce prices for consumers globally.

B. The GATS and Digital Trade

Since digital trade is often associated with transactions that do not encompass tangible goods, and almost all commercial activities on the Internet involve some online data-processing or computer-related services, the GATS inevitably occupies a prominent role in assessing whether WTO rules remain relevant in the digital age. The GATS, one of the pillars of the WTO Agreement, is part of the WTO's single undertaking. The objective of the GATS is to establish a set of multilateral rules governing international trade in services by breaking down national barriers and protecting equal competitive opportunities for foreign services and service providers.[43] As proclaimed in the preamble of the GATS, Members are:

> "Wishing to establish a multilateral framework of principles and rules for trade in services with a view to the expansion of such trade under conditions of transparency and progressive liberalization as a means of promoting the economic growth of all trading partners and the development of developing countries;"

Trade in services is complex since it is affected by a variety of domestic regulations instead of by border measures due to the intangible nature of ser-

---

[41] Ibid.

[42] WTO General Council, Declaration on the Expansion of Trade in Information Technology Product, WT/L/956 (28 July 2015).

[43] *See* generally John H. Jackson, William J. Davey, Alan O. Sykes, Jr., *Legal Problems of International Economic Relations: Cases, Materials and Text (Fourth Edition)*, West Group (2002), Markus Krajewski, *National Regulation and Trade Liberalization in Services – The Legal Impact of the General Agreement on Trade in Services (GATS) on National Regulatory Autonomy*, Kluwer Law International (2003), Nicolas F. Diebold, *Non-Discrimination in International Trade in Service – Likeness in WTO/GATS*, Cambridge University Press (2010), and Kern Alexander and Mads Andenas, *The World Trade Organization and Trade in Services*, Leiden; Boston: Matinus Nijhoff (2008).

vices.[44] The internal domestic regulatory issues include qualifications and licensing requirements in professional services, safety standards in transportation service, and universal assessment requirements in health and education services. Additionally, being aware of the possible tension between trade liberalization in services and national regulatory autonomy, the GATS explicitly recognizes, "the right of Members to regulate, and to introduce new regulations, on the supply of services within their territories in order to meet national policy objective."[45] Thus, on the one hand, the GATS aims at progressive liberalization on services. On the other hand, it upholds the right of a Member to regulate in order to pursue national policy objectives.

Article I specifies the broad scope application of the GATS. Under Article I, the GATS applies to measures by Members affecting trade in service.[46] Measures by Members include not only measures taken by central, regional, and local governments and authorities, but also measures adopted by non-governmental agencies in the exercise of government authorizations.[47] However, an explicit definition of the phrase "affecting trade in services" is nowhere to be found under the GATS. In *Canada – Automotive Industry*, the Appellate Body applied two criteria to examine the meaning of the term and stated:

> "With these treaty provisions in mind, we believe that at least two key legal issues must be examined to determine whether a measure is one "affecting trade in services": first, whether there is "trade in services" in the sense of Article I:2; and second, whether the measure in issue "affects" such trade in services within the meaning of Article I:1."[48]

---

[44] Aaditya Mattoo and Pierre Sauvé, Domestic Regulation and Trade in Services: Key Issues. In: Aaditya Mattoo and Pierre Sauvé, *Domestic Regulation and Service Trade Liberalization*, World Bank and Oxford University Press (2003), pp. 1-7.

[45] *See* General Agreement on Trade in Services Preamble.

[46] GATS Article I:3(b): "services include any service in any sector except services supplied in the exercise of governmental authority." The term 'exercise of governmental authority' is further explained in Article I: 3(c): "a service supplied in the exercise of governmental authority means any service which is supplied neither on a commercial basis, nor in competition with one or more service suppliers."

[47] GATS Article I:3(a). Furthermore, the term 'measures' defined in Article XXVIII (a) of GATS, which regulates:

> (a) "measure" means any measure by a Member, whether in the form of a law, regulation, rule, procedure, decision, administrative action, or any other form;

[48] Appellate Body Report, *Canada – Certain Measures Affecting the Automotive Industry* (cited as *Canada – Autos*), WT/DS139/AB/R and WT/DS142/AB/R (1 May 2000), para. 155.

Correspondingly, first, the 'trade in services' could refer to the four modes of supply listed in Article I:2 (a)-(d) of the GATS, which include cross-border supply, consumption abroad, consumer presence, and presence of nature persons.[49] Second, as explained by the Appellate Body, the word 'affecting' indicates a broad scope of application.[50] Therefore, even if a measure is not intended to regulate trade in services, the measure might still be subject to the GATS if it has an impact on trade in services.

Moreover, in contrast to the mandatory classification system of the GATT, the classification system of the GATS, the W/120, is not compulsory. The market access and national treatment obligations under the GATS are subject only to the specific commitments undertaken by Members. The commitments apply to the sectors or subsectors inscribed in a Member's service Schedule. The classification system of the GATS, annotated with relevant numbers of the United Nations Central Product Classification (CPC) system, is a relatively comprehensive document which consists of 11 service sectors plus an extra category for "other services not included elsewhere". The 11 sectors are further subdivided into some 160 sub-sectors.

Because of the complicated structure and the complex application of the W/120, the Council for Trade in Services adopted the Scheduling Guidelines in 2001 to assist WTO Members in preparing their service schedules on specific commitments.[51] Article XX:1 of the GATS stipulates that a Member's service Schedule shall differentiate three types of commitments: market access, national treatment, and other commitments.[52] Furthermore, by using the W/120 and CPC,

---

[49] Article I:2 stipulates:

(a) Cross-border supply (mode 1): from the territory of one Member into the territory of any other Member;

(b) Consumption abroad (mode 2): in the territory of one Member to the service consumer of any other Member;

(c) Commercial presence (mode 3): by a service supplier of one Member, through commercial presence in the territory of any other Member;

(d) Presence of natural persons (mode 4): by a service supplier of one Member, through presence of natural persons of a Member in the territory of any other Member.

[50] Appellate Body Report, *European Communities – Regime for the Importation, sale and distribution on bananas* (cited as *EC -- Bananas III*), WT/DS27/AB/R (25/September/1997), para. 220.

[51] WTO Council of Trade in Services, Guidelines for the Scheduling of Specific Commitments under the General Agreement on Trade in Services, S/L/92 (28/March/2001), para. 1.
(The Council recognized that "a common format for schedules as well as standardization of the terms used in schedules are necessary to ensure comparable and unambiguous commitments".)

[52] GATS Article XX: Schedules of Specific Commitments regulates that:

the Scheduling Guidelines suggest that WTO Members should arrange their specific commitments based on the sectors and sub-sectors approaches and on the modes of supply.[53] A sample of Schedule of Commitment is provided by the WTO Secretariat.

GATS Training Module:

Sector or sub/sector	*Limitations on market access*	*Limitations on national treat-ment*	*Additional commitments*
I. Horizontal Commitments			
All Sectors Included in This Schedule	4) Unbound, other than for (a) … (b) …	3) Authorization is required for acquisition of land foreigners.	
II. Sector-Specific Commitments			
4. Distribution Services C. Retailing services (CPC 631,632)	1) Unbound (except for mail order: none) 2) None. 3) … 4) …	1) Unbound (except for mail order: none). 2) None. 3) … 4) …	

Source: WTO Secretariat, GATS Training Module, Chapter 2: Main Building Blocks: Agreement, Annexes, and Schedules. Available at https://www.wto.org/english/tratop_e/serv_e/cbt_course_e/c2s6p2_e.htm. (accessed 11 August 2011)

---

1. Each Member shall set an in a schedule the specific commitments it undertakes under Part III of this Agreement. With respect to sectors where such commitments are undertaken, each Schedule shall specify:
   a) terms, limitations and conditions on market access;
   b) conditions and qualifications on national treatment;
   c) undertakings relating to additional commitments;

[53] *See* WTO Council of Trade in Services, Guidelines for the Scheduling of Specific Commitments under the General Agreement on Trade in Services, S/L/92 (28/March/2001), para. 36-49.

According to the Guidelines, a Schedule should be based on the four modes of supply. A Schedule is separated into a horizontal commitment which applies to trade in services in all scheduled services sectors unless otherwise specified, and a sector-specific commitment that applies to trade in services in a particular sector. Furthermore, if a Member undertakes the full commitments of either market access or national treatment obligations, the Member should mark in the appropriate column: None. In the case where the Member remains free in a given sector or in the mode of supply to impose limitations on market access or national treatment, the word 'unbound' should be marked in the appropriate column. In the situation when a Member commits only under a particular circumstance, the Member should specify that the measures maintained are inconsistent with market access or national treatment obligation.[54]

The positive list approach of the GATS scheduling system has a significant impact on digital trade in services. By the time the GATS was concluded in 1995, the Internet and Internet-related services did not attract too much attention from the WTO negotiators. Nevertheless, over the past decade, due to the rapid development of ICTs, almost all kinds of services are convertible into digital forms.[55] Consequently, the issue of whether digital services are covered by the current classification system under the GATS is arising among scholars, trade negotiators, and even the adjudicating bodies.[56] As illustrated above, since most of the GATS obligations only take effect when a commitment is undertaken by a WTO Member in a specific sector or subsector of its GATS Schedule, the scope and definition of the committed services are crucially important in clarifying a Member's obligations under the WTO.

In addition to the scheduling system, the GATS consists of a set of general rules (Part II of the GATS: Article II to XV) and a sector of specific commitments (Part III of the GATS: Article XVI to XVIII). While the general provisions, with some exceptions, apply to measures affecting all services, the specific commitments only apply to measures that a WTO Member undertakes regarding market access or national treatment obligations in a specific service sector in the Schedule. The most relevant general obligations relating to digital trade are the most-favoured-nation treatment of Article II, the transparency rules

[54] *See* WTO Council of Trade in Services, Guidelines for the Scheduling of Specific Commitments under the General Agreement on Trade in Services, S/L/92 (28/March/2001), para. 36-49.

[55] *See* Lee Tuthill and Martin Roy, GATS Classification Issues for Information and Communication Technology Services (2012), In: Mira Burri and Thomas Cottier, *Trade Governance in the Digital Age*, Cambridge: Cambridge University Press, pp. 157-178.

[56] *See* Rolf H. Weber, *Digital Trade in WTO-Law – Taking Stock and Looking Ahead*, Asian Journal of WTO & Int'l Health Law and Policy (AJWH), Vol. 5:1 (2010).

of Article III, the domestic regulations of Article VI and the general exceptions of Article XIV. The market access obligation of Article XVI and the national treatment requirement of Article XVII are illustrated in the specific commitments analysis.

a. The General Obligations

Article II through Article XV of the GATS provide for general obligations and disciplines applicable to all WTO Members. The most-favoured-nation treatment, transparency obligation, domestic regulations, and general exceptions are the most relevant GATS provisions with regard to the Internet-related trade measures

i. Most-Favoured-Nation (Article II of the GATS)

Article II:1 of the GATS stipulates:

> With respect to any measure covered by this Agreement, each Member shall accord immediately and unconditionally to services and service suppliers of any other Member treatment no less favourable than that it accords to like services and service suppliers of any other country.

Under the MFN obligation, WTO Members shall not treat services or service suppliers of one member less favourable than services or service suppliers of other members. Three criteria need to be fulfilled for a measure to be inconsistent with Article II:1: (1) the measure at issue is the measure covered by the GATS; (2) the services or service suppliers concerned are like services or service suppliers; and (3) a less favourable treatment exists among services or service suppliers of other Members.[57]

According to the definition of Article I, a measure is covered by the GATS if it is a measure by a Member affecting trade in services. As mentioned before, the term "affecting" has been broadly interpreted by the WTO panels. Therefore, the MFN obligation apply to both measures directly governing the supply of services and those governing other objects but indirectly affecting trade in ser-

[57] *See* Federico Ortino, The Principles of Non-Discrimination and Its Exceptions in GATS: Selected Legal Issues. In: Kern Alexander and Mads Andenas, *The World Trade Organization and Trade in Services*, Leiden; Boston: Matinus Nijhoff (2008), pp. 173-204.

vices.[58] In order to examine whether a measure is consistent with Article II:1, a panel needs to analyze all the relevant facts to determine how the measure affects the services or service suppliers concerned. In *Canada – Automobile Industry*, the Appellate Body explained:

> "As we stated earlier in respect of whether the measure at issue "affect trade in services", the Panel failed to demonstrate how the import duty exemption granted to certain manufacturers, but not to other manufacturers, affects the supply of wholesale trade services and the suppliers of wholesale trade services of motor vehicles. …, the Panel has neither assessed the relevant facts … nor has it interpreted Article II of the GATS and applied that interpretation to the facts it found."[59]

As to the meaning of the term "likeness", Article II should be read together with national treatment under Article XVII of the GATS. The concept of 'like services' and 'like service suppliers' are not defined in the GATS, and a few early cases only defined that to the extent the service suppliers provide like services, they are like service suppliers.[60] Nevertheless, in a recent case, the Appellate Body interpreted the concepts of 'like services' and 'like service suppliers' under Article XVII, which might provide some reference to the similar concepts in Article II:1. In *China – Electronic Payment*, the panel found that the key issue of the likeness analysis is the 'competitive relationship of the services being compared'.[61]

In the case, when considering the less favourable treatment under Article II:1 of the GATS, the Appellate Body rejected the panel's comparison of the 'treatment no less favourable' standard between Article II and Article XVII. However, the Appellate Body confirmed the panel's comparative analysis between Article I of the GATT and Article II of the GATS[62] and concluded that less

[58] Ibid.

[59] Appellate Body Report, *Canada – Certain Measures Affecting the Automotive Industry* (cited as *Canada – Automatic Industry*), WT/DS139/AB/R and WT/DS142/AB/R (19/June/2000), para. 181.

[60] Panel Report, *EC – Banana III*, para. 7.322 and Panel Report, *Canada – Automatic Industry*, para. 10.248. The panel in *Canada – Automatic Industry* reiterated that "we agree that to the extent that the service suppliers concerned supply the same services, they should be considered 'like' for the purpose of this case."

[61] Panel Report, *China – Certain Measures Affecting Electronic Payment Services* (cited as *China – Electronic Payment*), WT/DS413/R (16/July/2012), para. 7.702.

[62] Appellate Body Report, *European Communities – Regime for the Importation, sale and distribution on bananas* (cited as *EC -- Bananas III*), WT/DS27/AB/R (25/September/1997), para. 231-232.

favourable treatment under Article II of the GATS should cover both *de jure* and *de facto* discrimination or it would be too convenient for Members to circumvent the basic purpose of the Article. The Appellate Body held:

> "... there is more than one way of writing a *de facto* non-discrimination provision. Article XVII of the GATS is merely one of many provisions in the *WTO Agreement* that requires the obligation of providing "treatment less favourable". The possibility that the two Articles may not have exactly the same meaning does not imply that the intention of the drafters of the GATS was that a *de jure*, or formal, standard should apply in Article II of the GATS. ... the ordinary meaning of this provision does not exclude *de facto* discrimination. Moreover, if Article II was not applicable to *de facto* discrimination, it would not be difficult – and, indeed, it would be a good deal easier in the case of trade in services, than in the case of trade in goods – to devise discriminatory measures aimed at circumventing the basic purpose of this Article."[63]

ii. Transparency (Article III of the GATS)

Together with non-discrimination and market access, transparency is one of the fundamental principles of WTO law.[64] Regulatory transparency plays a pivotal role in preventing unnecessary barriers to trade for both goods and services since the openness in the decision-making processes creates greater compliance, less burdensome regulations, predictable conditions of market access, and ultimately the accountability and legitimacy of regulatory authorities.[65] Furthermore, the transparency requirement in domestic regulations is foremost important to the domain of trade in services since most barriers to trade in services arise from miscellaneous domestic laws, regulations, and practices. The lack of

---

[63] Ibid, para. 233.

[64] WTO Background Note by the Secretariat, *The Fundamental WTO Principles of National Treatment, Most-Favoured-Nation Treatment and Transparency*, WTO Working Group on the Interaction between Trade and Competition Policy, WT/WGTCP/W/114 (14/April/1999).

[65] For the concepts of transparency and domestic regulations *see* general OECD, Working Party of the Trade Committee, Strengthening Regulatory Transparency: Insights for the GATS from the Regulatory Reform Country Reviews, TD/TC/WP (99) 43/FINAL (12/April/2000); Keiya Iida and Julia Nielson, Transparency in Domestic Regulation: Practices and Possibilities. In: Aaditya Mattoo and Pierre Sauvé, *Domestic Regulation and Service Trade Liberalization*, World Bank and Oxford University Press (2003), pp. 7-27; and Rüdiger Wolfrum, Peter Tobias Stoll and Clemens Feinäugle (eds), *WTO -- Trade in Services*, Netherlands: Koninklijke Brill NV (2008).

transparency will increase the complexity and uncertainty of supplying services. Being more than a tool for trade liberalization, "transparency in such regulatory processes is not a static or preliminary element, but a dynamic and ongoing process that goes to the heart of fair and rational policymaking and regulation."[66]

In general, two types of transparency obligations can be attributed to WTO law.[67] The first is the obligation on publications and notifications regarding domestic measures, and the second is the obligation on the administration and application of the measures which could affect national regulations with different intensities. The transparency requirements under the GATS cover both categories. Article III contains the publication and notification requirements, and Article VI, with some subsections that are limited to services where specific commitments are undertaken, concerns the administration and application of domestic regulations.

Article III of the GATS regulates the general obligation regarding transparency of measures affecting trade in services. Under Article III: 1 and 2, WTO Members are obliged to promptly publish or otherwise make publish publicly available, through websites, for example, all relevant measures of general application which pertain to or affect trade in services. Article III:3 concerns Members' obligations to promptly notify the Council for Trade in Services, on the annual basis, of all new, or any changes to existing laws, regulations, or administrative guidelines that significantly affect trade in services. The scope of Article III:3 is narrower than that of Article III:1 and applies only to measures covered by specific commitments.

Article III:4 requires that WTO Members shall respond promptly to any request by another Member for specific information of any of its measures within the meaning of Article III:1. Members shall set up inquiry points to provide specific information upon request with respect to measures subject to the notification requirement in Article III:3. Nevertheless, only governments, not individual service suppliers or NGOs, are allowed to access information through enquiry points. Also, under Article III:5, "any Member may notify to the Council for Trade in Services any measures, taken by any other Member, which it considers affects the operation of this Agreement".

---

66 OECD, Working Party of the Trade Committee, Strengthening Regulatory Transparency: Insights for the GATS from the Regulatory Reform Country Reviews, TD/TC/WP (99) 43/FINAL (12/April/2000), para. 5.

67 Transparency obligations can also be found in GATT Article X, Article 7 and Article 8 of the Agreement on Sanitary and Phytosanitary Measures (SPS), and Article 2 and Article 5 of the Agreement on Technical Barrier to Trade (TBT).

iii. Domestic Regulation (Article VI of the GATS)

Transparency obligations are also incorporated in Article VI of the GATS. Given the significant impact of regulatory barriers to trade in services, Article VI directly addresses domestic regulations, which have a profound influence on the liberalization of services under the scope of the GATS.[68] In the words of Mattoo and Sauvé, "coupled with Article XVI on market access and Article XVII on national treatment, Article VI can indeed be seen as the third complementary dimension of a three-pronged approach to effectiveness access to service markets." [69] While market access addresses both discriminatory and non-discriminatory quantitative restrictive measures and national treatment prohibits *de jure* and *de facto* discriminatory treatment, domestic regulations in the context of Article VI recognize non-quantitative measures that are not inherently discriminatory but seriously impede trade in services.

Article VI is divided into two parts: due process procedure and substantive application. Due process obligations are incorporated in Article VI: 1-3 and 6, which are closely related to the transparency provisions of Article III of the GATS. Substantive obligations are regulated in Article VI:4 and 5. Article VI:1 applies to specific commitments and requires WTO Members to ensure that, "all measures of general application affecting trade in services are administered in a reasonable, objective and impartial manner".[70] The primary objective of Article VI:1 is to prevent trade in services from being hindered by the arbitrary application and administration of domestic regulations. Different from Article III:1, the scope of the provision is explicitly limited to sectors where specific commitments are undertaken, and Article VI:1 should only apply to the administration of the measures, not to their specific content.[71]

---

[68] *See* Jan Wouters and Dominic Coppens, GATS and Domestic Regulation: Balancing the Right to Regulation and Trade Liberalization. In: Kern Alexander and Mads Andenas, *The World Trade Organization and Trade in Services*, Leiden; Boston: Matinus Nijhoff (2008), pp. 207-262.

[69] Aaditya Mattoo and Pierre Sauvé, Domestic Regulation and Trade in Services: Key Issues. In: Aaditya Mattoo and Pierre Sauvé, *Domestic Regulation and Service Trade Liberalization*, World Bank and Oxford University Press (2003), p. 3.

[70] GATS Article VI:1 reads as follows:

> In sectors where specific commitments are undertaken, each Member shall ensure that all measures of general application affecting trade in services are administered in a reasonable, objective and impartial manner.

[71] The panel in the *US – Gambling* confirmed Article VI:1 as a procedural requirement. The Panel stated that "the Panel is of the view that Article VI:1 does not apply to measures of general application themselves but rather, to the administration of these measures.". (Panel Report, *United States – Measures Affecting the Cross-Border Supply*

Article VI:2 requires the maintenance or establishment of judicial, arbitral, or administrative tribunals or procedures to review administrative decisions affecting trade in services and provide appropriate remedies if justified. Article VI:2 provides a general obligation and is not limited to specific commitments. In addition, the provision contains an individual right to request the review of an administrative decision. Nevertheless, the obligation is mitigated by the fact that no particular institutional structure of the review system is required. Besides, pursuant to Article VI:2 (b), a Member may deviate from the requirements of Article VI:2(a) if instituting reviewing tribunals or procedures are inconsistent with the Member's constitutional structure or the nature of its legal system. In essence, the obligations in the context of Article VI:2 correspond with the fundamental principles of the rule of law and due process.

When authorization is needed for the supply of a service, Article VI:3 obliges administrative authorities of WTO Members to notify the service suppliers of the status of the application within a reasonable period of time after submitting the applications.[72] The obligations contained in Article VI:3 apply only to the services of which specific commitments are undertaken. The panel in *US – Gambling* indicated that "Article VI:3 imposes transparency and due process obligations with respect to the processing of applications for authorization to supply in a sector where specific commitments have been undertaken".[73] Furthermore, Article VI:6 requires that "in sectors where specific commitments regarding professional services are undertaken, each Member shall provide for adequate procedures to verify the competence of professionals of any other Member".[74] Since the term 'adequate procedures' is not further defined, it needs to be interpreted on a factual basis.[75] Although the requirements of Article VI: 1-3 and 6 are procedural in nature, the general principles of due process and good governance flow into the GATS system through these provisions.[76]

---

of Gambling and Betting Services (cited as *US – Gambling*), WT/DS285/R (10 November 2004), para. 6.423).

72 Panel Report, *United States – Measures Affecting the Cross-Border Supply of Gambling and Betting Services* (cited as *US – Gambling*), WT/DS285/R (10 November 2004).

73 Ibid., para. 6.432.

74 Article VI:6 of the GATS.

75 *See* Rüdiger Wolfrum, Peter Tobias Stoll and Clemens Feinäugle (eds), *WTO -- Trade in Services*, Netherlands: Koninklijke Brill NV (2008), pp. 165-196.

76 *See* Panagiotis Delimatsis, *Due Process And 'Good' Regulation Embedded in the GATS – Disciplining Regulatory Behaviour in Services Through Article VI of the GATS*, Journal of International Economic Law 10 (1) (2007), pp. 13-50.

The substantive obligations of Article VI, which potentially have a broad impact on Members' regulatory autonomy, are stipulated in Article VI: 4 and 5 of the GATS. Article VI:4 contains a mandate for the negotiation of future disciples for domestic regulations and Article VI:5 provides the provisional application when the criteria of paragraph 4 are pending entry into force. Article VI:4 is designed to develop necessary disciplines to ensure that domestic measures relating to the quality of services do not constitute unnecessary barriers to trade. The GATT, especially the rules under the TBT and SPS, has perceived that the non-discriminatory national regulations still have potential restrictive effects on international trade, even if these regulations do not explicitly restrict access to the market.[77] Based on the same logic, Article VI:4 requires the Council for Trade in Services to formulate disciplines to ensure that the domestic requirements on the quality of services are no more burdensome than necessary to achieve the purposes. Article VI: 4 reads as follows:

> With a view to ensuring that measures relating to qualification requirements and procedures, technical standards and licensing requirements do not constitute unnecessary barriers to trade in services, the Council for Trade in Services shall, through appropriate bodies it may establish, develop any necessary disciplines. Such disciplines shall aim to ensure that such requirements are, *inter alia*:
> (a) based on objective and transparent criteria, such as competence and the ability to supply the service;
> (b) not more burdensome than necessary to ensure the quality of service;
> (c) in the case of licensing procedures, not in themselves a restriction on the supply of service.

Pending the entry into force of the disciplines under Article VI:4, Article VI:5 requires:

> (a) In sectors which a Member has undertaken specific commitments, pending the entry into force of disciplines developed in these sectors pursuant to paragraph 4, the Member shall not apply licensing and qualifica-

[77] For example, TBT Article 2.2 requires "members shall ensure that technical regulations are not prepared, adopted or applied with a view to or with the effect of creating unnecessary obstacles to international trade. For this purpose, technical regulations shall not be more trade-restrictive than necessary to fulfill a legitimate objective." SPS Article 2.2 also regulates, "members shall ensure that any sanitary or phytosanitary measure is applied only to the extent necessary to protect human, animal or plant life or health, is based on scientific principles and is not maintained with sufficient scientific evidence."

tion requirements and technical standards that nullify or impair such specific commitments in a manner which:

(i) does not comply with the criteria outlined in subparagraphs 4(a), (b) or (c); and

(ii) could not be reasonably have been expected of that Member at the time the specific commitments in those sectors were made.

(b) In determining whether a Member is in conformity with the obligation under paragraph 5(a), account shall be taken of international standards of relevant international organizations[78] applied by that Member.

As mentioned previously, while the GATS is intended to promote progressive liberalization for trade in services, it also respects a Member's regulatory autonomy with regard to vital social interests. For example, an environmental protection measure might have an adverse impact on the entry of foreign services and service providers into the domestic market and constitute barriers to trade in services. Thus, Article VI:4 contains a mandate for the Council for Trade in Services to develop disciplines to ensure that measures relating to licensing requirements and procedures, qualification requirements and procedures, and technical standards do not constitute unnecessary barriers to trade in services.

On this basis, on 1 March 1995, the Council for Trade in Services created the Working Party on Professional Services (WPPS). The WPPS developed Disciplines on Domestic Regulation in the Accountancy Sector (S/L/64)[79], which was adopted by the Council in December 1998. On 26 April 1999, the WPPS was replaced by the Working Party on Domestic Regulation (WPDR), which was established by the Decision on Domestic Regulation from Council for Trade in Services.[80] Although the WPDR received a broader mandate than the WPPS and conducted a series of negotiations[81], the Accountancy Disciplines is so far the only regulation that has been established under Article VI:4 of the GATS.

---

[78] The term "relevant international organizations" refers to international bodies whose membership is open to the relevant bodies of at least all Members of the WTO. (Footnote 3 to GATS Article VI:5).

[79] WTO Council for Trade in Services, Disciplines on Domestic Regulation in the Accountancy Sector, S/L/64 (17 December 1998).

[80] WTO Trade in Service, Decision on Domestic Regulation – adopted by the Council for Trade in Services on 26 April 1999, S/L/70 (28 April 1999).

[81] The Council for Trade in Services entrusts the WPDR to "develop any necessary disciplines to ensure that measures relating to licensing requirements and procedures, technical standards and qualification requirements and procedures do not constitute unnecessary barriers to trade in services." (WTO Trade in Service, Decision on Domestic Regulations – adopted by the Council for Trade in Services on 26 April 1999, S/L/70 (28 April 1999).)

The first paragraph of the Accountancy Disciplines narrows the reach to measures with specific commitments in the accountancy sectors and excludes measures that fall within the scope of Article XVI (market access) and Article XVII (national treatment). Furthermore, the Disciplines contain a necessity test which regulates that WTO Members shall ensure that licensing requirements and procedures, qualification requirements and procedures, and technical standards are not more trade restrictive than necessary to fulfill a legitimate objective. Legitimate objectives are, *inter alia*, the protection of consumers, the quality of service, professional competence, and the integrity of the profession.[82]

The first critical concern of the applicability of future disciplines under Article VI:4 is whether these disciplines should apply to all service sectors or only to sectors where specific commitments are undertaken. Contrary to other provisions in Article VI, paragraph 4 does not explicitly address the limitation to specific committed service sectors. The debates in the WPDR focused on the horizontal (general) disciplines and some Members suggested that the absence of such limitation was intentional.[83] Nevertheless, this does not preclude the future negotiation on sectoral disciplines.[84] If the underlying rationale of Article VI:4 is to ensure regulatory measures affecting trade in services will not undermine the value of the market access, imposing obligations under Article VI:4 to a Member who makes no specific commitments in the relevant service sectors would contradict the purpose of the Article.[85] Accountancy Disciplines has also adopted the same approach. While the negotiations in the WPDR are still in

[82] WTO Council for Trade in Services, *Disciplines on Domestic Regulation in the Accountancy Sector*, S/L/64 (17 December 1998), paras. 1 and 2.

[83] WTO Council for Trade in Services, Article VI:4 of the GATS: Disciplines on Domestic Regulation Applicable to All Services – Note by the Secretariat, S/C/W/96 (1 March 1999), para. 15.

[84] *See* WTO Trade in Service Division, Disciplines on Domestic Regulation Pursuant to GATS Article VI:4 – Background and Current State of Play, June 2011.

[85] *See* Aaditya Mattoo and Pierre Sauvé, Domestic Regulation and Trade in Services: Key Issues. In: Aaditya Mattoo and Pierre Sauvé, *Domestic Regulation and Service Trade Liberalization*, World Bank and Oxford University Press (2003), pp. 1-7; *see* also Jan Wouters and Dominic Coppens, GATS and Domestic Regulation: Balancing the Right to Regulation and Trade Liberalization. In: Kern Alexander and Mads Andenas, *The World Trade Organization and Trade in Services*, Leiden; Boston: Matinus Nijhoff (2008), pp. 207-262 and Markus Krajewski, *National Regulation and Trade Liberalization in Services – The Legal Impact of the General Agreement on Trade in Services (GATS) on National Regulatory Autonomy*, Kluwer Law International (2003), pp. 129-138.

progress, most WTO Members seem to reach a consensus favoring sectoral disciplines.[86]

The second debatable issue of Article VI:4 is the measures covered in the provision. The emerging consensus in the WPDR seems limited to the five types of measures listed in Article VI:4.[87] The Report by the Chairman of the Council for Trade in Services to the Trade Negotiation Committee defined that the measures covered in Article VI:4 should only include measures relating to licensing requirement, licensing procedures, qualification requirements, qualification procedures and technical standards.[88]

The third and the most controversial legal issue of Article VI:4 is whether the provision is mutually exclusive with Article XVI and XVII of the GATS and whether it is limited to non-discriminatory measures. No direct answer can be found from the text of the provision. A detailed examination of the relations among market access, national treatment and domestic regulations is discussed in Chapter 4 when analyzing the *US – Gambling* case. In essence, although a measure could fall within the ambit of all rules, an overlapping approach between Article XVI & XVII and Article VI:4 seems not to be preferable. For example, the Accountancy Disciplines explicitly exclude the measures falling within the scope of Article XVI or XVII[89] and the Secretariat of the WPDR reiterated in several reports that "Article VI:4 was not designed to handle measures scheduled under Article XVI and XVII".[90] The arguments are based on the legal certainty and the rationale of the disciplines within the structure of the GATS.

---

[86] For example, both WPDR Chairman Reports in 2007 and 2011 emphasized "disciplines apply to measures by Members relating to licensing requirement and procedures, qualification requirements and procedure, and technical standards affecting trade in services in sectors where specific commitments are undertaken." (S/WPDR/W45 (14 April 2011), p.16.)

[87] The same approach is adopted by the Accountancy Disciplines. The concept that the measures regulated in Article VI:4 should be limited to the five types of measures has been emphasized in several WPDR Chairman's texts. (The latest one is Chairman's Text 2009).

[88] WTO Council for Trade in Services Special Session, Negotiation on Trade in Services, TN/S/36 (21 April 2011), pp. 22-26.

[89] WTO Council for Trade in Services, Note by the Secretariat, Article VI:4 of the GATS: Disciplines on Domestic Regulation Applicable to All Services, S/C/W/96 (1 March 1999), para. 13-14.

[90] WTO WPDR, Note by the Secretariat, Report on the Meeting Held on 2 October 2001, S/WPDR/M/13 (21 November 2001), para. 9.

Lastly, Article VI:4 (b) requires future disciplines to be "no more burdensome than necessary to ensure the quality of the service". The wording of this provision seems to imply that the term 'necessary' will play an essential role in assessing the elements of restrictive domestic regulations under Article VI:4.[91] The Accountancy Disciplines require that domestic regulations within the context of Article VI:4 "are not more trade restrictive than necessary to fulfill a legitimate objective". The legitimate objectives listed in the Disciplines are non-exhaustive. In the work of the WPDR, in spite of some disagreements, most WTO Members agree with the same open-ended approach under Article VI:4.[92]

Nevertheless, the specific content of the necessity within the meaning of Article VI:4 attracted intense debate in the WPDR. Firstly, it is unanimous among WTO Members and WTO jurisprudence that the purpose of the necessity test is not to examine the necessity of domestic policy objectives but to consider the necessity of the measure taken to achieve the intended policy objectives.[93] Member States typically have a margin of appreciation in determining the level of protection with respect to the policy objectives pursued. For example, when considering the context of the SPS Agreement, the Appellate Body stated that the determination of the appropriate level of protection is "a prerogative of the Member concerned and not of a Panel or of the Appellate Body".[94]

According to WTO case law, for a measure to be necessary, it needs not to be indispensable in relation to the policy objective.[95] In every case, a process of weighing and balancing a series of factors needs to be applied. If a preliminary necessity of the measure can be established after examining the importance of the interests at stake, the extent of the contribution of the measure to the objective, and the restrictive impact on international trade, the result must be con-

[91] *See* Margareta Djordjevic, *Domestic Regulation and Free Trade in Services – A Balancing Act*, Legal Issues of Economic Integration 29(3) (2002), pp. 305-322.

[92] WTO WPDR, Note by Secretariat, Report on the Meeting Held on 3 July, S/WPDR/M/12 (16 August 2001), Annex Informal Summary of the checklist of issues for WPDR, para. 6.

[93] For example, in *US – Gasoline*, the Appellate Body has stressed, "WTO Members have a large measure of autonomy to determine their own policies on the environment (including its relationship with trade), their environmental objectives and the environmental legislation they enact and implement." (Appellate Body Report, *United States – Standards for Reformulated and Conventional Gasoline* (cited as *US -- Gasoline*), WT/DS2/9 (20 May 1996), p. 30.)

[94] Appellate Body Report, *Australia – Measures Affecting Importation of Salmon* (cited as *Australia -- Salmon*), WT/DS18/AB/R (20 October 1998), para. 199.

[95] Appellate Body Report, *Korea – Measures Affecting Imports of Fresh, Chilled and Frozen Beef* (cited as *Korea -- Beef*), WT/DS161/AB/R & WT/DS169/AB/R (11 December 2000), para. 161.

firmed by comparing the measure with its reasonable alternatives.[96] The possible alternatives must be less trade restrictive and reasonably available to achieve the same level of protection.

In the work of the WPDR, WTO Members emphasized the importance of the concept of "reasonable availability" for the necessity test in future disciplines under the scope of Article VI:4. The proposal submitted by Australia suggested that, modeled on SPS Article 5(6) and footnote 3 thereto, "a measure is not more trade-restrictive than required unless there is another measure, reasonably available taking into account technical and economic feasibility, that achieves a legitimate policy objective and is significantly less restrictive to trade".[97] The European Community suggested that the necessity test should be applied equivalently to the concept of proportionality. In the EC's view, "a measure should be not more trade restrictive/not more burdensome than necessary if it is not disproportionate to the objective pursued".[98] Nevertheless, whether the principle of proportionality advocated by the EC includes proportionality *stricto sensu*, which requires an overall weighing and balancing of the costs and benefits of the measure[99], is highly controversial.

Pending the entry into force of the disciplines pursuant to Article VI:4, Article VI:5 provides the requirements laid down in Article VI:4 (a) – (c) for services to which a Member has undertaken specific commitments. Furthermore, according to Article VI:5 (a) (ii), the licensing and qualification requirements and technical standards must not nullify or impair specific commitments in a manner which could not have been reasonably expected at the time the specific commitments were made. A non-violation concept of nullification and impairment indicates that the scope of Article VI:5 will depend on the extent of legit-

---

[96] Appellate Body Report, *Brazil – Measures Affecting Imports of Retreaded Tyres* (cited as *Brazil – Retreaded Tyres*), WT/DS332/AB/R (3 December 2007), para. 178.

[97] WTO WPDR, *Communication from Australia -- Necessity and Transparency*, S/WPDR/W/8 (15 September 2000), paras. 3-6.

[98] WTO WPDR, *Communication from the European Communities and their Member States -- Domestic Regulation: Necessity and Transparency*, S/WPDR/W/14 (1 May 2001), paras. 17 & 22.

[99] The three steps test is normally applied by the ECJ to determine the principle of proportionality. First, the measure adopted must be suitable to achieve its objective. Second, the measure must be necessary. Last is known as *stricto sensu*, which requires the benefit of the measure must not be disproportionate to the interests or rights that the measure confines.

imate expectations of Member States.[100] Article VI:5, in addition, excludes all measures which existed at the time of scheduling.[101] In other words, Article VI:5 only applies to new regulations that could not have been reasonably expected at the time a Member had undertaken specific commitments. Article VI:5 has been commented on as a standstill obligation.[102]

Finally, Article VI:5 (b) requires that when determining whether a Member's measure is consistent with the requirements under Article VI:5(a), "account shall be taken of international standards of relevant international organizations applied by that Member". Contrary to the SPS and TBT[103], which provide the presumption of compliance, VI:5 (b) does not provide such a presumption in favor of international standards. The WTO Secretariat encouraged a strong presumption of "necessary" in favor of requirements based on international standards.[104] Nevertheless, taking into account the different political, economic, and cultural backgrounds of the vast amount of WTO Members and the disadvantages of developing countries participating in the construction of international standards, whether a strong presumption of compliance with international standards should be adopted by Article VI:5 (b) is still debatable.

---

[100] Markus Krajewski, *National Regulation and Trade Liberalization in Services – The Legal Impact of the General Agreement on Trade in Services (GATS) on National Regulatory Autonomy*, Kluwer Law International (2003), pp. 151-153.

[101] WTO Council for Trade in Services, Note by the Secretariat, *Article VI:4 of the GATS: Disciplines on Domestic Regulation Applicable to All Services*, S/C/W/96 (1 March 1999), para. 11.

[102] Joel P. Trachtman, Negotiation on Domestic Regulation and Trade in Services (GATS Article VI): A Legal Analysis of Selected Current Issues. In Ernst-Ulrich Petersmann and James Harrison (eds.), *Reforming the World Trading System: Legitimacy, Efficiency, and Democratic Governance*, Oxford: Oxford University Press (2005), p. 213.

[103] TBT Article 2.5 regulates:

> "… Whether a technical regulation is prepared, adopted or applied for one of the legitimate objectives explicitly mentioned in paragraph 2, and is in accordance with relevant international standards, it shall be rebuttably presumed not to create an unnecessary obstacle to international trade."

SPS Article 3.2 regulates:

> "Sanitary or Phytosanitary measures which conform to international standards, guidelines or recommendations shall be deemed to be necessary to protect human, animal or plant life or health, and presumed to be consistent with the relevant provisions of this Agreement and of GATT 1994."

[104] WTO Council for Trade in Services, Note by the Secretariat, Article VI:4 of the GATS: Disciplines on Domestic Regulation Applicable to All Services, S/C/W/96 (1 March 1999), paras. 35-42.

iv. The General Exceptions Clause (Article XIV of the GATS)

Article XIV of the GATS provides a mechanism allowing Members of the WTO to deviate, under certain conditions, from their trade obligations in order to pursue legitimate non-economic objectives. The general exception provisions enumerate an exhaustive list of objectives, which includes, *inter alia*, public morals, public order, safety, public health, and environmental protection. The ultimate purpose of the general exceptions under the GATS is to find an adequate equilibrium between progressive liberalization of trade and the regulatory autonomy of Members to pursue important national values of the society.[105] While it may be argued that a closed list of legitimate public interests will infringe on a Member's sovereign right to regulate, the WTO adjudicating bodies have adopted an evolutionary approach for interpretation and construed the listed objectives in a rather expansive manner.[106]

US – Gambling is the first, but definitely not the last, WTO dispute featuring the public morals clause under Article XIV(a) of the GATS. The general requirements for determining whether a WTO-inconsistent measure can be justified under the exception provisions will be illustrated in the next section, which provides a critical review of the *US – Gambling* case. It is worth noting here that due to the innovation in ICTs, the general exceptions clause is likely to play a vital role in the future WTO disputes. The new types of services, the advent of electronically delivered products, and the borderless nature of the Internet have triggered regulatory responses at all levels of governance that have an excessive influence on the existing regimes for telecommunications, audiovisual services, intellectual property, and cultural products.[107] In the absence of a global legal reaction to the digital revolution, new national and regional regulations are increasingly designed to protect local values or to maintain traditional sovereign power. More than often, such regulations have the negative impact on international trade and result in protectionism.

The merit of the general exceptions clause is to strike a balance between the right of a Member to legitimately deviate from its substantive WTO obligations

[105] *See* Panagiotis Delimatsis, *Protecting Public Morals in a Digital Age: Revisiting the WTO Rulings on US – Gambling and China – Publications and Audiovisual Products*, Journal of International Economic Law, Vol. 14, No.2 (2011), pp. 257-293.

[106] *See* Cottier, Delimatsis & Diebold, Article XIV GATS General Exceptions (2008). In: Rüdiger Wolfrum, Peter Tobias Stoll and Clemens Feinäugle (eds), *WTO -- Trade in Services*, Netherlands: Koninklijke Brill NV, pp. 287-328.

[107] *See* Mira Burri & Thomas Cottier, Introduction: Digital technologies and international trade regulation (2012). In: Mira Burri and Thomas Cottier (eds.), *Trade Governance in the Digital Age – World Trade Forum*, Cambridge University Press, pp. 1-14.

and the duty of that Member to respect the treaty rights of other Members.[108] Whereas an expansive application of the general exceptions might risk undermining the WTO's substantial progress toward trade liberalization, a constricted approach might jeopardize the regulatory autonomy of a Member with regard to the protection of its societal values.[109] Consequently, further clarification is needed for some doctrinal issues regarding Article XIV of the GATS in terms of digital trade.

b. Specific Commitments

Part III of the GATS reflects a bottom-up approach to the liberalization of trade in services. The purpose of drafting the specific commitments in Part III was to "capture all types of trade barriers to trade in services and establish a mechanism for scheduling specific commitments on them".[110] Market access obligation in Article XVI limits the use of certain quantitative restrictions on the committed services, and national treatment obligation in Article XVII prohibits discriminatory treatment between foreign and domestic services or service suppliers. Additionally, Article XVIII of the GATS allows Members to negotiate commitments with respect to other types of restrictions that do not fall within the scope of Article XVI and Article XVII.[111] By realizing that there may be other types of restrictions on trade in services which would not be captured by the disciplines of market access and national treatment, Article XVIII aims to provide a legal framework for Members to negotiate and schedule specific commitments for measures outside the scope of Article XVI and Article XVII.[112]

---

[108] Appellate Body Report, *United States – Import Prohibition of Certain Shrimp and Shrimp Product* (cited as *US -- Shrimp*), WT/DS58/AB/R (12 October 1998), para. 156.

[109] *See* Nicolas F. Diebold, *The Morals and Order Exceptions in WTO Law: Balancing the Toothless Tiger and the Undermining Mole*, Journal of Economic Law, Vol.11, No.1 (2007), pp. 43-74; and *see* also Jeremy C. Marwell, *Trade and Morality: The WTO Public Morals Exception After Gambling*, New York University Law Review, Vol.81, pp. 802-842.

[110] WTO Committee on Specific Commitments, Note by the Secretariat, Additional Commitments under Article XVIII of the GATS, S/CSC/W34 (16 July 2002), para. 3.

[111] GATS Article XVIII states as follows:

> Members may negotiate commitments with respect to measures affecting trade in services not subject to scheduling under Article XVI or XVII, including those regarding qualifications, standards or licensing matters. Such commitments shall be inscribed in a Member's Schedule.

[112] WTO Committee on Specific Commitments, Note by the Secretariat, Additional Commitments under Article XVIII of the GATS, S/CSC/W34 (16 July 2002), paras. 3-5.

i. Market Access (Article XVI of the GATS)

The general principle of market access in the context of the GATS is stipulated in paragraph 1 of Article XVI:1 which requires WTO Member treat all services and service suppliers of any other Member no less favourable than that provided for under the terms, limitations, and conditions agreed and specified in its Schedule. Article XVI:2 further explains what kind of measures are considered as restrictive measure within the meaning of Article XVI. The measures listed in paragraph 2 are exhaustive, and most of them are quantitative in nature. For the analysis of Internet-related trade measures, Article XVI:2(a) and (c) are the most relevant provisions since they regulate the limitations on the number of services or service suppliers. Article XVI:2 stipulates:

> 2. In sectors where market-access commitments are undertaken, the measures which a Member shall not maintain or adopt either on the basis of a regional subdivision or on the basis of its entire territory, unless otherwise specified in its Schedule, are defined as:
> (a) limitations on the number of service suppliers whether in the form of numerical quotas, monopolies, exclusive service providers or the requirements of an economic needs test;
> (c) limitations on the total number of service operations or on the total quantity of service output expressed in terms of designated numerical units in the form of quotas or the requirement of an economic needs test;

The scope of the market access obligation of a WTO Member is defined by reference to the specific commitments of the Member in particular services sectors and modes of supply.[113] Put differently, a Member is allowed to maintain or adopt a market access restrictive measure if it has not undertaken the market access commitments with regard to the relevant service sectors. Therefore, in a dispute involving market access violations, a panel needs to examine the Schedule of the challenged Member and the actual treatment of the measure at issue.[114]

---

[113] *See* Stefan Zlepting, The GATS and Internet-Based Services: Between Market Access and Domestic Regulation. In Kern Alexander and Mads Andenas, *The World Trade Organization and Trade in Services*, Leiden; Boston: Matinus Nijhoff (2008), pp. 381-410.

[114] Panel Report, *United States – Measures Affecting the Cross-Border Supply of Gambling and Betting Services* (cited as *US – Gambling*), WT/DS285/R (10 November 2004), paras. 6.263-6.267.

Article XVI covers both discriminatory and non-discriminatory market access barriers since the Article aims at measures which restrict trade in services through the application of quantitative limitations. Furthermore, the 2001 Scheduling Guidelines emphasizes that "all measures falling under any of the categories listed in Article XVI:2 must be scheduled, whether or not such measures are discriminatory according to the national treatment standard of Article XVII".[115] It should also be noted that contrary to qualitative restrictions, the quantitative restrictions listed in Article XVI:2 (a)-(d) should be considered as 'maximum limitations', which set minimum market access commitments for foreign services and service suppliers. The fundamental difference between a qualitative and quantitative restriction is that while the former is usually intended to serve a legitimate objective, the latter is normally presumed to be protectionist.[116]

ii. National Treatment Obligation (Article XVII of the GATS)

Unlike the national treatment obligation under Article III of the GATT, which is considered as a general obligation that applies to all WTO Member States, Article XVII of the GATS applies only to measures affecting trade in services to which, and to the extent, that a WTO Member has made an explicit commitment to the specific service sector. Article XVII requires a Member to treat service and service suppliers of another Member no less favourable than its own like services and service suppliers. Paragraph 1 of Article XVII regulates:

> In the sectors inscribed in its Schedule, and subject to any conditions and qualifications set out therein, each Member shall accord to services and service suppliers of any other Member, in respect of all measures affecting the supply of services, treatment no less favourable than that it accords to its own like services and service suppliers.

Paragraph 2 and 3 further define the meaning of 'less favourable treatment':

> 2. A Member may meet the requirement of paragraph 1 by according to services and service suppliers of another Member, either formally identical

[115] WTO Council of Trade in Services, Guidelines for the Scheduling of Specific Commitments Under the General Agreement on Trade in Services, S/L/92 (28/March/2001), para.8.

[116] *See* Joost Pauwelyn, *Rien ne Ve Plus? Distinguish Domestic Regulation from Market Access in GATT and GATS*, World Trade Review 4:2 (2006), pp. 131-170.

> treatment or formally different treatment to that it accords to its own like services and service suppliers.
> 3. Formally identical or formally different treatment shall be considered to be less favourable if it modifies the conditions of competition in favour of services or service suppliers of the Member compared to like services or service suppliers of any other Member.

Article XVII of the GATS aims to guarantee equal competitive opportunities for like services and service providers of other Members.[117] According to the wording of the article and the opinions from the WTO adjudicating bodies, four elements need to be examined to determine whether a measure is consistent with the national treatment obligation: (1) whether a Member has undertaken a national treatment commitment in a relevant service sector and/or mode of supply; (2) whether the measure at issue affects the supply of services; (3) whether the domestic and foreign services and service suppliers are like services or like service suppliers; and (4) whether the measure accords no less favourable treatment to both domestic and foreign services and service suppliers.[118]

Like market access commitments, a Member's commitments to national treatment also constitute an integral part of the WTO agreements and should be interpreted in accordance with customary international rules on treaty interpretation. This approach has a significant influence on digital trade in services in several perspectives. First, in determining whether a term in a Member's Schedule encompasses distribution by electronic means, panels and the Appellate Body recognized that the meaning of the terms should not be decided by the intent of the Member at the time the Schedule was negotiated, but in accordance with the ordinary meaning to be given to the terms of the Schedule in their context and in the light of its object and purpose.[119] The Appellate Body has adopted an evolutionary approach to treaty interpretation and stated that if a term used in a Member's GATS Schedule is sufficiently generic, the application of the term may change over time.[120] This methodology could expand the scope of

[117] Panel Report, *China – Certain Measures Affecting Electronic Payment Services* (cited as *China – Electronic Payment*), WT/DS413/R (16/July/2012), para. 7.700.
[118] Appellate Body Report, *China – Measures Affecting Trading Rights and Distribution Services for Certain Publications and Audiovisual Entertainment Products* (cited as *China – Audiovisual Products*), WT/DS363/AB/R (21 December 2009), para. 7.944.
[119] Article 31 (1) of the VCLT regulates:

> A treaty shall be interpreted in good faith in accordance with the ordinary meaning to be given to the terms of the treaty in their context and in the light of its object and purpose.

[120] Appellate Body Report, *China – Measures Affecting Trading Rights and Distribution Services for Certain Publications and Audiovisual Entertainment Products* (cited as *China – Audiovisual Products*), WT/DS363/AB/R (21 December 2009), para. 396.

a Member's Schedule to the emerged new services brought about by the new technologies.

Second, the interpretation of the terms 'like services' and 'like service suppliers' also influences the application of national treatment obligations in Internet-related trade in services. One of the critical unsolved issues regarding national treatment in digital trade is whether a service provided through electronic delivery should be considered 'like' other services supplied through traditional methods. The WTO Secretariat emphasized in an explanatory note that likeness in the national treatment should not depend on the means by which the product is delivered.[121] Furthermore, in the Work Programme on Electronic Commerce, many WTO Members agreed that the term 'likeness' should not be decided by whether a service is delivered electronically.[122] However, the uncertainty of the issue persists.

Nevertheless, as later illustrated in the *US – Gambling* case review, the panel and the Appellate Body observed that the determination of 'likeness' under Article XVII of the GATS must be made on a case-by-case basis by taking into account the evidence as a whole. In the recent *China – Electronic Payment* case, in order to decide the concept of 'like services' under Article XVII, the panel examined the ordinary meaning of terms 'like' and 'like services'. According to the panel, "services could qualify as 'like' if they are essentially or generally the same".[123] The panel further considered the context of the phrase 'like services' by referring to Article XVII:3 of the GATS. Article XVII:3 regulates that a measure is considered a less favourable treatment if it 'modifies the conditions of competition' to the detriment of foreign services. In accordance with the principle of treaty interpretation under Article 31 and 32 of the Vienna Convention, the panel decided that 'like' domestic and foreign services must be services that are in a competitive relationship.[124] The panel emphasized that "only if the foreign and domestic services in question are in such a relationship can a

---

[121] When considering the likeness in GATS Article XVII, the Secretariat emphasized that: "likeness in the national treatment context also depends in principle on attributes of the product or supplier per se rather than on the means by which the product is delivered."
(WTO Council for Trade in Services, Note by the Secretariat, The Work Programme on Electronic Commerce, S/C/W/68 (16 November 1998), para. 33.)

[122] WTO Trade in Service, Work Programme on Electronic Commerce -- Progress Report to the General Council, Work Programme on Electronic Commerce, S/L/74 (27 July 1999), para. 8.

[123] Panel Report, *China – Certain Measures Affecting Electronic Payment Services* (cited as *China – Electronic Payment*), WT/DS413/R (16/July/2012), para. 7.699.

[124] Ibid, para. 7.700.

measure of a Member modify the conditions of competition in favour of one or other of these services".[125] Consequently, services provided in electronic methods and in traditional means should be considered as 'like services' if they are in a competitive relationship in a given market.

[125] Ibid.

II. GATS Application – The *US -- Gambling* Case

Innovation in ICTs has led to the increasing delivery of cross-border electronic services. Nevertheless, from the structural overview provided above, one can perceive that there is no explicit legal framework for digital trade in the context of WTO law. Whereas WTO Members initiated a comprehensive Work Programme on E-Commerce in 1998, no tangible conclusion on any of the critical issues relating to digital trade has since been reached. In addition, because of the political and cultural diversity of the Internet, it's hard to coordinate different interests and policy objectives among WTO Members.[126]

Nevertheless, the panel and the Appellate Body's opinions in *US – Gambling*, shed some light on several controversial issues regarding trade in services on the Internet. Section II provides a thorough analysis of the case and intends to examine whether or to what extent the GATS is applicable to the cross-border electronically delivered services. The analysis starts with a brief description of the case. Section B considers the scope of a Member's specific commitments under its GATS Schedule. The application of market access and national treatment obligations to Internet-based services are considered respectively in Section C and D. Last but not least, Section E provides a detailed discussion on the general exceptions clause under Article XIV (a) of the GATS.

A. The Background and Summary of the Case: United States – Gambling

In March 2003, Antigua and Barbuda (hereafter "Antigua") initiated a WTO dispute to challenge a series of US measures that affect the cross-border supply of online gambling and betting services of foreign service providers.[127] Before the panel, Antigua claimed that the restrictions imposed by the US federal and

---

[126] For example, the different directions adopted by the US and the EU in negotiating the trade treatment of digitally delivered content products are due to different rationales. The goals to preserve a free trade environment for E-commerce and to protect freedom of speech are parameters that influence the US's negotiation approach. The EU, on the other hand, focuses more on preserving cultural diversity in the digital age. Consequently, how to support the content industry, which is deemed as the main vector of cultural values, is the core rationale for the EU's negotiating process. (*See* Sacha Wunsch-Vincent, *The WTO, the Internet and Trade in Digital-Products: EU-US Perspectives*, North America: Hart Publishing (2006), pp.103-164).

[127] Panel Report, *United States – Measures Affecting the Cross-Border Supply of Gambling and Betting Services* (cited as *US – Gambling*), WT/DS285/R (10 November 2004).

state laws resulted in a "total prohibition" on the cross-border supply of gambling services from Antigua.[128] Antigua further contended that since the US made full mode 1 commitments on market access and national treatment in its GATS Schedule, the "total prohibition" on the services in question was inconsistent with Article XVI:1, XVI:2, XVII:1, XVII:2, XVII:3, VI:1, VI:3 and XI:1 of the GATS.[129]

The US replied that restrictions on the remote supply of gambling services are due to the regulatory concerns of the government. The US argued that the explosive growth in the remote supply of gambling over the past decade might have or has had the potential for the involvement of organized crimes in Internet gambling, such as money laundering or fraud schemes.[130] For the US, protection of the young and possible health risks of addiction are moral objectives that need to be defended.[131] In addition, the US asserted that it has never made specific commitments for measures affecting gambling services, which is categorized under sub-sector 10.D of the W/120 and listed "964" as the corresponding CPC number.[132] The US further argued that the restrictions on a certain remote supply of gambling services are expressed as limitations on the character of the activity supplied rather than in a numerical form prohibited within the ambit of Article XVI:2.[133] Finally, the US claimed that the general exceptions clause under Article XIV of the GATS would justify the deviation from its commitments because of the overriding public moral considerations.[134]

The issues before the panel, therefore, are whether the US has made the specific commitments in its GATS Schedule to liberalize trade in gambling services, whether the US prohibitions on Internet gambling amount to an impermissible market access restriction under Article XVI, and whether the US measures fall within the scope of Article XIV (a) to protect public morals or maintain public order.

After evaluating Antigua's claims with respect to the federal and state regulations of the US, the panel concluded that the US GATS Schedule includes specific commitments on gambling and betting services under sub-sector 10.D and,

---

128 Ibid., para. 6.561.

129 Ibid., para. 2.1.

130 Ibid., paras. 3.17 and 6.559.

131 Ibid., para. 3.18

132 A detailed discussion of specific commitments US made on its GATS Schedule can be found in the following section B.

133 Panel Report, *United States – Measures Affecting the Cross-Border Supply of Gambling and Betting Services* (cited as *US – Gambling*), WT/DS285/R (10 November 2004), paras. 3.124-3.141.

134 Ibid., paras. 269-283.

therefore, its measures are in violation of Article XVI:1 and Article XVI:2 of the GATS. The panel further decided that the measures at issue cannot be justified under Article XIV(a) since they are not necessary within the meaning of the provision and they are inconsistent with the requirements of the chapeau of Article XIV of the GATS.[135]

In January 2005, the US appealed the panel's rulings to the Appellate Body. In April 2005, the Appellate Body issued a report that upheld most of the panel's findings. The Appellate Body supported the panel's conclusion that subsector 10.D of the US's GATS Schedule includes specific commitments on gambling and betting services. When reviewing the panel's decisions on market access violations, the Appellate Body concluded that a prohibition on the remote supply of a service constitutes a "limitation on the number of service suppliers" within the meaning of Article XVI:2(a) and a "limitation on the total number of service operations or on the total quantity of service output" within the meaning of Article XVI:2(c). The Appellate Body also agreed that the health and risk concerns fall within the scope of public morals and/or public order under Article XIV(a). Nevertheless, the Appellate Body disagreed with the panel's decision that the US measures are not 'necessary' to pursue legitimate objectives. In contradiction of the panel, the Appellate Body found that only the Interstate Horseracing Act is inconsistent with the requirements of the chapeau of Article XIV.[136]

The DSB adopted the Appellate Body report. A WTO Arbitrator was appointed by the Director-General to decide the 'reasonable period of time' for the US to implement the rulings of the DSB.[137] After the deadline of April 2006 and after the US failed to amend the measure in question, Antigua, in June 2007, requested permission to retaliate, pursuant to Article 22.2[138] of the DSU, against the US by suspending the related obligations of Antigua under the GATS and the Agreement on Trade-Related Aspects of Intellectual Property Rights (TRIPS). The WTO Arbitrator determined that Antigua may request authoriza-

[135] Appellate Body Report, *United States – Measures Affecting the Cross-Border Supply of Gambling and Betting Services* (cited as *US – Gambling*), WT/DS285/AB/R (7 April 2005), paras. 5 & 6.

[136] Ibid, paras. 373 & 374.

[137] *United States – Measures Affecting the Cross-Border Supply of Gambling and Betting Services*, Arbitration under Article 21.3(c) of the Understanding on Rules and Procedures Governing the Settlement Disputes, WT/DS285/13 (19 August 2005).

[138] The DUS Article 22.2 stipulates:

> … If no satisfactory compensation has been agreed within 20 days after the date of expiry of the reasonable period of time, any party having invoked the dispute settlement procedures may request authorization from the DSB to suspend the application to the Member concerned of concessions or other obligations under the covered agreements.

tion from the DSB to suspend its obligations under the TRIPS toward the US at a figure of US$21 million annually.[139]

Before analyzing the case, it is important to emphasize that in *US – Gambling*, the panel and the Appellate Body clarified the applicability of the GATS rules to the cross-border supply of Internet-related services.[140] As mentioned earlier, it was unclear before *US – Gambling* whether the GATS obligations adopted in 1994 are applicable to services supplied by technologies that were not yet foreseeable by WTO Members at the time of the negotiations. Although the panel and the Appellate Body did not explicitly address the issue in the case, they also did not hesitate to apply the GATS framework to the measures concerning trade in services on the Internet. The panel confirmed that electronically delivered services should be categorized as mode 1, the cross-border supply of services, within the meaning of Article I:2 of the GATS.[141]

The Appellate Body upheld the panel's findings that the specific commitments in the US Schedule extend to the cross-border electronic supply of gambling and betting services.[142] The adjudicating bodies' opinions have ascertained that measures related to the supply of services through electronic means of delivery, especially through the Internet, fall within the scope of GATS obli-

---

[139] *United States – Measures Affecting the Cross-Border Supply of Gambling and Betting Services*, Recourse to Arbitration by the United States under Article 22.6 of the DSU, Decision by the Arbitrator, WT/DS285/ARB (21 December 2007), para. 3.189.

[140] *See* Rolf H. Weber, *Digital Trade in WTO-Law – Taking Stock and Looking Ahead*, Asian Journal of WTO & Int'l Health Law and Policy (AJWH), Vol. 5:1 (2010); Stefan Zlepting, The GATS and Internet-Based Services: Between Market Access and Domestic Regulation. In Kern Alexander and Mads Andenas, *The World Trade Organization and Trade in Services*, Leiden; Boston: Matinus Nijhoff (2008), pp. 381-410; Sacha Wunsch-Vincent, *The Internet, cross-border trade in services, and the GATS: lessons from US – Gambling*, World Trade Review, 5:3 (2006), pp. 319-355; and Markus Krajewski, *Playing by the Rules of the Game? Specific Commitments after US – Gambling and Betting and Current GATS Negotiations*, Legal Issues of Economic Integration, 32(4) (2005), pp. 417-447.

[141] Panel Report, *United States – Measures Affecting the Cross-Border Supply of Gambling and Betting Services* (cited as *US – Gambling*), WT/DS285/R (10 November 2004). The panel stated:

> "… mode 1 under the GATS encompasses all possible means of supplying services from the territory of one WTO Member into the territory of another WTO Member. Therefore, a market access commitment for mode 1 implies the right for other Members' suppliers to supply a service through all means of delivery, whether by mail, telephone, the Internet, etc., unless otherwise specified in a Member's Schedule." (para. 6.258)

[142] Appellate Body Report, *United States – Measures Affecting the Cross-Border Supply of Gambling and Betting Services* (cited as *US – Gambling*), WT/DS285/AB/R (7 April 2005), paras. 213 & 265.

gations. While the case provided a legal certainty on the technological neutrality of the GATS, the negotiators should pay more attention to new mode 1 commitments. In the view that an Internet-based service is now considered as a means of delivery included in mode 1 cross-border supply and the possibility of unforeseeable new services in the future, a WTO Member might liberalize some services it did not intend to at the time of negotiations. As illustrated in the following sections, it is the common intention of the parties rather than the intent of an individual Member that will be considered when a panel interprets the specific commitments in the Member's GATS Schedule.[143]

B. The Interpretation of Specific Commitments in the US GATS Schedule

In *US – Gambling*, Antigua claimed that the US GATS Schedule includes specific commitments on gambling and betting services. Antigua further asserted that since the US undertook the full market access and national treatment commitments, the measures at issue are in violation of the obligations under the GATS. The US vigorously denied that it had made any commitments concerning gambling and betting services. The US asserted, by omitting "sporting" services from the scope of subsector 10.D, it intended to exclude gambling and betting services from the framework of its Schedule.[144]

Despite with different interpretation methods, both the panel and the Appellate Body came to the same conclusion that the US has undertaken specific commitments on gambling and betting services in its Schedule. This conclusion has a profound influence on how to treat Internet-based services in WTO law. Many services, which only appeared after the advent of the Internet, are not listed in the GATS services classification system or the corresponding CPC codes. To ascertain the meaning of a concession in a Schedule, the Appellate Body recalled that as WTO Members' schedules form an integral of the GATS, they represent a "common agreement among all Members".[145] In other words,

---

[143] The Appellate Body in *US – Gambling* case stated:

> … the task of ascertaining the meaning of a concession in a Schedule, like the task of interpreting any other treaty text, involves identifying the *common intention* of Members, and is to be achieved by following the customary rules of interpretation of public international law, codified in Article 31 and 32 of the Vienna Convention. (Ibid., para. 159.)

[144] Panel Report, *United States – Measures Affecting the Cross-Border Supply of Gambling and Betting Services* (cited as *US – Gambling*), WT/DS285/R (10 November 2004), para. 3.51.

[145] Appellate Body Report, *United States – Measures Affecting the Cross-Border Supply of Gambling and Betting Services* (cited as *US – Gambling*), WT/DS285/AB/R (7 April 2005), para. 159.

the scope of a specific commitment undertaken by a Member should be interpreted according to the common intention of the parties during the multilateral negotiating process, instead of to an individual negotiator's assumption or intention.[146]

The issue relating to the US Schedule is whether the specific commitment made by the US on 'other recreational services' under sub-sector 10.D of the W/120 covers online gambling and betting services. There is no further instruction concerning the meaning of 'other recreational services' in the W/120 list. Nevertheless, gambling and betting services are categorized as a sub-class (CPC 96492) of CPC 9649. Controversially, the words 'gambling and betting services' do not appear in the US Schedule, and the US did not adopt the provisional CPC to enter its GATS commitments. The relevant section of the US Schedule is shown in Table 1, and the corresponding CPC code is provided in Table 2. In order to determine the scope of the US commitments, both the panel and the Appellate Body began the analysis with examining the 'ordinary meaning' of the terms 'Other Recreational Services' and 'Sporting Services'.

Sector or sub-sector	Limitations on Market Access	Limitations on National Treatment
10. RECREATIONAL, CULTURAL, & SPORTING SERVICES		
D. OTHER RECREATIONAL SERVICES (excepting sporting)	1) None 2) None 3) The number of concessions available for commercial operations in federal, state and local facilities is limited 4) Unbound, except as indicated in the horizontal section	1) None 2) None 3) None 4) None

Table 1. Excerpt from the United States Schedule of specific commitments[147]

[146] Markus Krajewski, *Playing by the Rules of the Game? Specific Commitments after US – Gambling and Betting and Current GATS Negotiations*, Legal Issues of Economic Integration, 32(4) (2005), pp. 417-447.

[147] General Agreement on Trade in Services, The United States of America, Schedule of Specific Commitments, GATS/SC/90 (15 April 1994).

W/120	10-D. Recreational, cultural and sporting services (other than audiovisual services)/ Sporting and other recreational services
UNCPC	964 Sporting and other recreational services
UNCPC sub-class	9641 Sport services 96411 Sports event promotion services 96412 Sports event organization services 96413 Sports facility operation services 96419 Other sporting services
	9649 Other recreation services 96491 Recreation park and beach services 96492 Gambling and betting services 96499 Other recreational services n.e.c.

Table 2. U.N. provisional Central Product Classification List

a. Ordinary Meaning – Dictionary Definition

Following the footsteps of *EC – Computer Equipment*[148], the panel in *US – Gambling* is of the view that the primary purpose of treaty interpretation is to identify the common intention of the parties, and the "Vienna Convention rules have been developed to help in assessing in objective terms what was or what could have been the common intention of the parties to a treaty".[149] Article 31(1) of the VCLT requires a treaty to be interpreted in good faith in accordance with the ordinary meaning to be given to the terms of the treaty in their context and in the light of its object and purpose.

Since the US claimed that gambling and betting services should be considered as sporting services, which is excluded in sub-sector 10.D of its Schedule,

---

[148] When considering the nature of tariff commitment of the GATT, the Appellate Body in *EC – Computer Equipment* asserted:

> Tariff negotiations are a process of reciprocal demands and concession, of "give and take". It is only normal that importing Members define their offers (and their ensuing obligations) in terms which suit their needs. On the other hand, exporting Members have to ensure that their corresponding rights are described in such a manner in the Schedules of importing Members that their export interests, as agreed in the negotiations, are guaranteed. … Indeed, the fact that Members' Schedules are an integral part of the GATT 1994 indicates that, while each Schedule represents that tariff commitments made by *one* Member, they represent a common agreement among *all* Members.

(Appellate Body Report, *European Communities – Customs Classification of Certain Computer Equipment* (cited as *EC – Computer Equipment*), WT/DS62/AB/R WT/DS67/AB/R WT/DS68/AB/R (5 June 1998), para. 109.)

[149] Panel Report, *United States – Measures Affecting the Cross-Border Supply of Gambling and Betting Services* (cited as *US – Gambling*), WT/DS285/R (10 November 2004), para. 6.53.

the panel began the analysis with the dictionary definition of the term 'sporting' to determine its ordinary meaning. After examining the definition of the term 'sporting' in a large number of dictionaries and the meaning of the term in French and Spanish, the panel found that the ordinary meaning of "sporting" does not include gambling.[150] The panel further considered the dictionary definition of the terms "recreational services" and "entertainment services", and observed that the dictionary meaning of the terms does not allow it to reach a definitive conclusion.[151] The panel concluded that "dictionary definitions do not necessarily provide a final answer and leave many interpretive questions open".[152] The panel, therefore, turned to consider the context in which the relevant terms from sector 10.D of the US's Schedule are situated.

The Appellate Body also noticed the range of possible meanings of the word 'sporting' could include the meaning suggested by both the US and Antigua and considered that "dictionaries, alone, are not necessarily capable of resolving complex questions of interpretation, as they typically aim to catalogue *all* meanings of words – be those meanings common or rare, universal or specialized."[153] The Appellate Body's opinion reflected the views of previous WTO cases that using the dictionary definition to decide the ordinary meaning of a term is just the first step in the process and a substantive interpretation should rely on other contextual and teleological methods.[154]

b. The Context and Supplementary Means of Interpretation

According to Article 31 and Article 32 of the Vienna Convention, the content of resorting to interpretative methods is comprehensive, including the context, the objective and purpose of the treaty, and supplementary means of interpretation. The Appellate Body in *EC – Chicken* clarified that "interpretation pursuant to

---

[150] Ibid., paras. 6.54-6.61.

[151] Ibid., paras. 6.62-6.67.

[152] Ibid., para. 6.67.

[153] Appellate Body Report, *United States – Measures Affecting the Cross-Border Supply of Gambling and Betting Services* (cited as *US – Gambling*), WT/DS285/AB/R (7 April 2005), para. 164.

[154] Appellate Body Report, *Canada – Measures affecting the export of Civilian Aircraft* (cited as *Canada -- Aircraft*), WT/DS70/AB/R (2 August 1999), para. 153.
Later in *EC – Asbestos* case, when considering the ordinary meaning of "like products" in GATT Article III:4, the Appellate Body reiterated "dictionary meanings leave many interpretive questions open." (Appellate Body Report, *European Communities – Measures Affecting Asbestos and Asbestos-Containing Products* (cited as *EC -- Asbestos*), WT/DS135/AB/R (5/April/2001).)

the customary rules codified in Article 31 of the Vienna Convention is ultimately a holistic exercise that should not be mechanically subdivided into rigid components."[155]

Considering the context in which the relevant terms from sector 10 of the US Schedule are situated, both the panel and the Appellate Body relied principally on two documents: the 1993 Scheduling Guidelines and the W/120 list. Both of them had been prepared and circulated by the GATT Secretariat at the request of parties to the Uruguay Round negotiations in order to explain how commitments should be set out in WTO Members' GATS Schedules.[156] Although the documents are not legally binding, and WTO Members are not obligated to adopt the W/120 list, they still have a profound interpretative value in clarifying the correct and accurate meaning of a Member's specific commitments in its Schedule.

The W/120 list contains a nomenclature of service sectors and sub-sectors based on the UN Central Product Classification. As shown in Table 2 above, the services at issue, gambling and betting services, are categorized under sub-sector 10.D of the W/120 Sporting and other recreational services. CPC 964, which is corresponding to sub-sector 10.D, is divided into two sub-classes: 9641 'Sporting services' and 9649 'Other recreational services'. Whereas the US argued that gambling services should be classified under Sporting services, which are excluded in its GATS Schedule, under the CPC classification system, gambling and betting services fall within the scope of CPC 9649 'Other recreational services'. The issue, therefore, is whether the W/120 and CPC could be applied to the US Schedule when the service classification system of the US is based on neither of the documents.

The 1993 Scheduling Guidelines was circulated by the GATT Secretariat and called for the general use of the W/120 list. In the absence of other specific sector classifications or detailed descriptions of the service sectors, the Guidelines suggested:

> "The legal nature of a schedule as well as the need to evaluate commitments, require the greatest possible degree of clarity in the description of each sector or sub-sector scheduled. In general, the classification of sectors and sub-sectors should be based on the Secretariat's revised Services Sec-

---

[155] Appellate Body Report, *European Communities – Customs Classification of Frozen Boneless Chicken Cuts* (cited as *EC -- Chicken*), WT/DS269/AB/R WT/DS286/AB/R (12 September 2005), para. 176.

[156] Scheduling of Initial Commitments on Trade in Services: Explanatory Note (1993 Scheduling Guidelines), MTN.GNS/W/164 (3 September 1993), para. 1.

> toral Classification List. Each sector contained in the Secretariat list is identified by the corresponding Central Product Classification (CPC) number. Where it is necessary to refine further a sectoral classification, this should be done on the basis of the CPC or other internationally recognized classification (e.g., Financial Service Annex)."[157]

The panel considered that both the 1993 Scheduling Guidelines and W/120 should be deemed as part of the context within the meaning of Article 31:2(a) and (b) of the Vienna Convention. That is to say, although the two documents are not legally binding *per se*, they could be considered as agreements made between all Members or as instruments made by one or more Members but accepted by all Members. Thus, the panel proceeded to use the 1993 Scheduling Guidelines and W/120 to determine the ordinary meaning of the terms in the US Schedule. The panel found that "where the US Schedule follows W/120 without any clear departure and in the absence of any specific definition, the United States has created an expectation that its commitments must be interpreted in the light of W/120 and the corresponding CPC number."[158] Accordingly, since the respective CPC classification corresponds to 'other recreational services', which include 'gambling and betting services'[159], the panel concluded that the US Schedule "is to be understood to include a specific commitment on gambling and betting services under sub-sector 10-D".[160] Although the Appellate Body believed that the 1993 Scheduling Guidelines and W/120 should be considered as a supplementary means of interpretation within the meaning of Article 32 of the Vienna Convention, the Appellate Body reached the same conclusion.[161]

The decisions have two meaningful implications. First, it is the 'common intention of the Members' that counts in order to ascertain the meaning and the scope of a commitment in a Member's Schedule. Both the panel and the Appellate body agreed that Members' GATS Schedules are an integral part of the

---

[157] 1993 Scheduling Guidelines, para. 16.

[158] Panel Report, *United States – Measures Affecting the Cross-Border Supply of Gambling and Betting Services* (cited as *US – Gambling*), WT/DS285/R (10 November 2004), para. 6.93.

[159] *See* Table 1 and Table 2 above.

[160] Panel Report, *United States – Measures Affecting the Cross-Border Supply of Gambling and Betting Services* (cited as *US – Gambling*), WT/DS285/R (10 November 2004), para. 6.93.

[161] Appellate Body Report, *United States – Measures Affecting the Cross-Border Supply of Gambling and Betting Services* (cited as *US – Gambling*), WT/DS285/AB/R (7 April 2005), para. 204.

GATS, and the process of identifying the original meaning of a Member's concession involves identifying the common intention of all Members. The notion that the purpose of interpretation is to identify the common intention of the parties is generally accepted by WTO jurisprudence.[162] As the panel pointed out:

> "We note in this regard that the United States may well have inadvertently undertaken specific commitments on gambling and betting services. However, it is not for the Panel to second-guess the intentions of the United States at the time the commitment was scheduled. Rather, our role is to interpret and apply the GATS in light of the facts and evidence before us."[163]

Secondly, for any future disputes, unless a WTO Member has clearly indicated in its Schedule that the commitments are not intended to be in accordance with the W/120 and corresponding CPC classification, panels and the Appellate Body will presumably follow the structure and language of the W/120 and CPC nomenclature to interpret a Member's GATS Schedule.164 Although the Appellate Body's decision that the 1993 Scheduling Guidelines and W/120 constitute supplementary means under Article 32 of the Vienna Convention rather than 'context' within meaning of Article 31(2) is controversial165, it is certain

---

[162] Appellate Body Report, *European Communities – Customs Classification of Certain Computer Equipment* (cited as *EC – Computer Equipment*), WT/DS62/AB/R WT/DS67/AB/R WT/DS68/AB/R (5 June 1998), para. 93.

[163] Panel Report, *United States – Measures Affecting the Cross-Border Supply of Gambling and Betting Services* (cited as *US – Gambling*), WT/DS285/R (10 November 2004), para 7.3.

[164] *See* Markus Krajewski, *Playing by the Rules of the Game? Specific Commitments after US – Gambling and Betting and Current GATS Negotiations*, Legal Issues of Economic Integration, 32(4) (2005), pp. 427-429. *See* also Eric H. Leroux, From Periodicals to Gambling: A review of systemic issues addressed by WTO adjudicatory bodies under the GATS (2008). In: Marion Panizzon, Nicole Pohl, and Pierre Sauvé, *GATS and the Regulation of International Trade in Services*, Cambridge University Press, pp. 236-275.

[165] For example, F. Ortino criticized that the Appellate Body's interpretative process has proceeded in a too-formalistic and mechanical way, and it undermined the hermeneutic value of the contextual and teleological dimensions of treaty interpretation. The author also emphasized that "a holistic approach to treaty interpretation would require reaching a conclusion on the ordinary meaning of the term at issue only upon an examination of all the relevant terms, rather than examining each element in turn until the meaning of the term at issue is revealed (as the Appellate Body seemed to indicate in *Gambling*)." (Federico Ortino, *Treaty Interpretation and the WTO Appellate Body Report in US – Gambling: A Critique*, Journal of International Economic Law 9(1) (January 2006), pp. 117-148 (131).)

that the WTO adjudicating bodies will recourse to both the documents as interpretative methods to define the ordinary meanings of the terms in WTO Members' GATS Schedules.

C. GATS Article XVI Market Access

After finding that the US has undertaken a full commitment on market access to the cross-border supply of gambling and betting services, the panel and the Appellate Body continued to examine whether the US measures violate the provisions under Article XVI of the GATS. Antigua argued that the three federal laws, the Wire Act, Travel Act and Illegal Gambling Business Act constituted a complete ban on cross-border supply and violated Article XVI:1, Article XVI:2(a), and Article XVI:2(c). The US claimed that a commitment on market access only prohibits the use of quantitative measures listed in Article XVI:2., and the restrictions on remote gambling services are expressed as limitations on the character of the activity supplied, not as quantitative limitations.

Because of the intangible nature of services, barriers to trade in services mostly originate from domestic measures within the border of Member States.[166] Therefore, except for Article XVI:2(f), which directly stipulates at imported services by prohibiting limitations on foreign capital, other measures listed in Article XVI:2 are the typical quantitative market access restrictions in the domestic regulatory framework which treat services and service suppliers of other Members less favourable than the conditions and limitations specified in a Member's Schedule.[167] Article XVI targets quantitative measures since they are considered to be the most damaging policies for market access and are typically deemed as protectionist.

Furthermore, the reference to "no less favourable treatment" requires a comparison between the standards of treatment described in a Member's Schedule and the actual treatment of foreign services or service suppliers. Therefore, the treatment of domestic services or service suppliers is not a concern under Article XVI. To a certain extent, the non-discriminatory design of the market access obligations of trade in services limits the regulatory autonomy of WTO Mem-

[166] *See* Stefan Zlepting, The GATS and Internet-Based Services: Between Market Access and Domestic Regulation. In Kern Alexander and Mads Andenas, The World Trade Organization and Trade in Services, Leiden; Boston: Matinus Nijhoff (2008), pp. 391-396.

[167] *See* Markus Krajewskli, *Playing by the Rules of the Game? Specific Commitments after US – Gambling and Betting and Current GATS Negotiations*, Legal Issues of Economic Integration, 32(4) (2005), pp. 417-447.

bers.[168] This limitation on a Member's right to regulate has led to intense discussions among scholars about the Appellate Body's decisions on market access in the case.

US – Gambling is the first case where the WTO adjudicating bodies had the chance to interpret the scope and application of market access obligations under the GATS. However, many critics argued that the decisions of both the panel and the Appellate Body blurred the distinction between market access and domestic regulations. More importantly, the criticism emphasized that the rulings will unduly constrain WTO Members' discretion to regulate trade in services and seriously threaten the domestic regulatory autonomy.[169] Despite the disapproval, due to the complexity of trade in services, the precise lines between market access, national treatment, and domestic regulations are inherently unclear.[170] Therefore, the task of the WTO adjudicating bodies in *US – Gambling* to interpret market access obligations is not easy, and the panel and the Appellate Body were not wrong in deciding that a total prohibition on the cross-border supply of services in respect of which a full market access commitment has been undertaken is not compatible with the obligations under Article XVI:2(a) and (c) of the GATS.

---

[168] See Markus Krajewski, *National Regulation and Trade Liberalization in Services – The Legal Impact of the General Agreement on Trade in Services (GATS) on National Regulatory Autonomy*, Kluwer Law International (2003), pp. 82-84. *See* also Panagiotis Delimatsis, *Don't Gamble with GATS – The Interaction between Article VI, XVI, XVII, and XVIII GATS in the Light of the US – Gambling Case*, Journal of World Trade 40 (6) (2006), pp. 1059-1080.

[169] *See* Joost Pauwelyn, *Rien ne Ve Plus? Distinguish Domestic Regulation from Market Access in GATT and GATS*, World Trade Review 4:2 (2006), pp. 131-170; Federico Ortino, *Treaty Interpretation and the WTO Appellate Body Report in US – Gambling: A Critique*, Journal of International Economic Law 9(1) (January 2006), pp. 117-148; Markus Krajewski, *Playing by the Rules of the Game? Specific Commitments after US – Gambling and Betting and Current GATS Negotiations*, Legal Issues of Economic Integration, 32(4) (2005), pp. 417-447; and Joel P. Trachtman, Negotiation on Domestic Regulation and Trade in Services (GATS Article VI): A Legal Analysis of Selected Current Issues. In Ernst-Ulrich Petersmann and James Harrison, *Reforming the World Trading System: Legitimacy, Efficiency, and Democratic Governance*, Oxford: Oxford University Press (2005).

[170] *See* Nancy J. King and Kishani Kalupahana, *Choosing Between Liberalization and Regulatory Autonomy under GATS: Implications of US – Gambling for Trade in Cross-Border Services*, Vand. J.Transnat'l L. 1189, V. 40 (November 2007), pp. 1192-1298.

a. Whether the Six Types of Restrictions on Market Access Obligations are Exhaustive

The second paragraph of Article XVI lists six types of limitations on the market access that are prohibited unless they are scheduled in Members' GATS commitments. Before examining whether the US measures violate its market access commitment, the panel and to a lesser extent the Appellate Body first clarified that the limitations enumerated under Article XVI:2 were considered to be exhaustive. By considering the ordinary meaning and the context of Article XVI, as well as the object and purpose of the GATS and by referring to the 1993 Scheduling Guidelines, the panel concluded that Article XVI:2 complements Article XVI:1 in that it exhaustively defined the measures that are prohibited by the Article.[171] In sum, the six types of imitations in Article XVI:2, which cannot be maintained or adopted unless otherwise being scheduled in a WTO Member's commitments, exhaust the categories of market access restrictions prohibited by the provision.

The panel and the Appellate Body further tackled the issue of whether the elaborations in each of six types of measures are illustrative or exhaustive limitations. For example, Article XVI:2(a) stipulates that a Member shall not maintain or adopt "limitations on the number of service suppliers whether in the form of numerical quotas, monopolies, exclusive service providers or the requirements of an economic needs test". Antigua argued that by using the word 'whether', the limitation methods were intended to be illustrative rather than exhaustive. Nevertheless, the panel disagreed with Antigua and considered the list as exhaustive. The panel held:

> "With respect to Article XVI:2(a), we note that there is no word or term at the conclusion of that subparagraph that could be construed as creating an illustrative list, such as "any other form" or "any other measure". In these circumstances, we consider that the word "whether" identifies an exhaustive list of limitations that are covered by Article XVI:2(a), namely, "limitations in the form of numerical quotas, monopolies, exclusive service suppliers or requirements of an economic needs test".[172]

[171] Panel Report, *United States – Measures Affecting the Cross-Border Supply of Gambling and Betting Services* (cited as *US – Gambling*), WT/DS285/R (10 November 2004), paras. 6.298 & 6.318.

[172] Panel Report, *United States – Measures Affecting the Cross-Border Supply of Gambling and Betting Services* (cited as *US – Gambling*), WT/DS285/R (10 November 2004), para. 6.325.

Hence, the types of limitations listed in Article XVI:2 are exhaustive as well as the list of prohibited measures in each of the limitations in Article XVI:2. That is to say, under Article XVI:2(a), in respect to a full market access commitment, limitations on the number of service suppliers are only prohibited if they take the form of numerical quotas, monopolies, exclusive service suppliers, or the requirements of an economic needs test. Likewise, limitations on the total number of service operations or on the total quantity of service output under Article XVI:2(c) are prohibited if they are articulated in terms of designated numerical unites in the form of quotas or the requirement of an economic needs test.

b. Quantitative Violations within the Meaning of GATS Article XVI:2(a) and (c)

One of the most controversial issues in *US – Gambling* is whether a measure, which constitutes a total prohibition on a mode of supply, is a quantitative restriction prohibited under Article XVI:2(a) and (c), though the limitation is not expressed with reference to numerical units. Antigua alleged that the US measures are in violation of Article XVI:2(a) since they constituted a total prohibition on cross-border supply of gambling and betting services and, therefore, limited the number of service suppliers. Antigua further argued that the complete ban on the cross-border supply also qualified as a limitation on the total number of service operations, which is inconsistent with Article XVI:2(c).

The US contended that Article XVI does not enshrine a general rule that prohibits restrictive measures on market access in whole or in part. Instead, only the measures that fall within the specific categories listed in Article XVI:2 are impermissible. The US claimed that since the laws at issue prescribed a prohibition on the character of certain services and not on the number of service suppliers or service operations, they are not in violation of Article XVI:2. Both the panel and the Appellate Body disagreed with the US and concluded that the total prohibition on a mode of supply amounts to a zero quota of the services or service suppliers and constitutes a quantitative limitation within the meaning of Article XVI:2(a) and Article XVI:2(c).

The WTO adjudicating bodies concluded that the US measures, which prohibited the supply of gambling and betting services through the Internet in respect of which a full market access commitment has been undertaken, amount to a zero quota on the services and service suppliers. The Appellate Body first recognized that the market access obligations should not be applied to measures which simply have effects on numerical quotas.[173] However, the Appellate Body also acknowledged that the words of Article XVI:2 should not be interpreted "as prescribing a rigid mechanical formula"[174] and the limitations covered in the Article cannot "take a single form, nor be constrained in a formulaic manner".[175] These are the basic standards the Appellate Body followed throughout its analysis to decide whether a total prohibition on the supply of a service is equivalent to a zero quota and whether a zero quota is a quantitative limitation within the scope of Article XVI:2(a) and (c).

When considering whether a total prohibition on the cross-border supply of service amounts to a zero quota, as it limits to zero the number of services or service suppliers in respect of which a full market access commitment has been undertaken, the panel asserted and endorsed by the Appellate Body that:

> "It is true that the wording of Article XVI:2(a) covers numerical quotas other than zero. That is because the subparagraph is designed, in part, to indicate the limitations, short of total prohibition, that Members may specify in their schedules, on the number of service suppliers. The fact that the terminology embraces lesser limitations, in the form of quotas greater than zero, cannot warrant the conclusion that it does not embrace a greater limitation amount to zero. Paragraph (a) does not foresee a "zero quota" because paragraph (a) was not drafted to cover situations where a Member wants to maintain full limitations. If a Member wants to maintain a full prohibition, it is assumed that such a Member would not have scheduled such a sector or sub-sector and, therefore, would not need to schedule any limitation or measures pursuant to Article XVI:2."[176]

Also, when considering whether a zero quota limitation can be seen as a quantitative limitation within the meaning of Article XVI:2(a), the Appellate Body clarified that when determining the compatibility of a measure with Article XVI:2, the form of the measure is not decisive, but rather the quantitative

---

[173] Appellate Body Report, *United States – Measures Affecting the Cross-Border Supply of Gambling and Betting Services* (cited as *US – Gambling*), WT/DS285/AB/R (7 April 2005), para. 232.

[174] Ibid., para. 231.

[175] Ibid., para. 247.

[176] Panel Report, *United States – Measures Affecting the Cross-Border Supply of Gambling and Betting Services* (cited as *US – Gambling*), WT/DS285/R (10 November 2004), para. 6.331. Appellate Body Report, *United States – Measures Affecting the Cross-Border Supply of Gambling and Betting Services* (cited as *US – Gambling*), WT/DS285/AB/R (7 April 2005), para. 234.

nature of the measure involved.[177] The Appellate Body asserted that "it is clear that the thrust of sub-paragraph (a) is not on the *form* of limitations, but on their numerical, or quantitative nature."[178] Therefore, limitations in the form of "numerical quotas" within Article XVI:2(a) should be interpreted as limitations with numerical characteristics. Accordingly, a total prohibition on the supply of the services qualifies as a measure with quantitative effects and falls within the scope Article XVI:2(a). The Appellate Body stated:

> "Thus, a "numerical quota" within Article XVI:2(a) appears to mean a quantitative limit on the number of service suppliers. The fact that the word "numerical" encompasses things which "have the characteristics of a number" suggests that limitations "in the form of a numerical quota" would encompass limitations which, even if not in themselves a number have the characteristics of a number. Because zero is quantitative in nature, it can, in our view, be deemed to have the "characteristics of" a number – that is, to be "numerical"."[179]

The Appellate Body further looked into the 1993 Scheduling Guidelines and confirmed that any measure equivalent to a zero quota falls under Article XVI:2(a). The Appellate Body referred to paragraph 6 of the 1993 Scheduling Guidelines, which provides examples of the types of limitations that fall within the scope of sub-paragraph (a) of Article XVI:2. The 1993 Scheduling Guidelines provide that a nationality requirement for service suppliers is equal to a zero quota and must therefore by scheduled as an exception from a WTO Member's market access obligations. The Appellate Body relied on the Scheduling Guidelines and concluded that measures equivalent to a zero quota are within the meaning of Article XVI:2(a).[180]

Lastly, the panel and the Appellate Body concluded that in respect of a full market access commitment, if one, several, or all means of delivery cannot be used to supply a cross-border service, such prohibition constitutes a limitation on the number of service suppliers in the form of numerical quotas under Article XVI:2(a). The panel stated:

---

[177] *See* Panagiotis Delimatsis, *International Trade in Services and Domestic Regulations – Necessity, Transparency, and Regulatory Diversity,* Oxford University Press (2007), pp. 131-140.

[178] Appellate Body Report, *United States – Measures Affecting the Cross-Border Supply of Gambling and Betting Services* (cited as *US – Gambling*), WT/DS285/AB/R (7 April 2005), para. 232.

[179] Ibid., para. 227.

[180] Ibid., paras. 236-237.

> "The Panel is of the view that *such a prohibition is a "limitation on the number of service suppliers in the form of numerical quotas" within the meaning of Article XVI:2(a) because it totally prevents the use by service suppliers of one, several or all means of delivery that are included in mode 1.*" (emphasis added).[181]

Based on similar reasoning, the Appellate Body reached the same conclusion with respect to Article XVI:2(c). The Appellate Body stressed that although it is not necessary or appropriate for them to draw the line between quantitative and qualitative measures, it is enough, in this case, to decide the measures at issue amount to a zero quota on service operations or the total quantity of service output.[182] Therefore, the US measures at issue are in violation of market access obligations under both Article XVI:2 (a) and (c).

D. GATS Article XVII National Treatment

The national treatment standard of the GATS is not a general obligation but only applies to the service sectors in which specific commitments are undertaken and is subject to any conditions and qualifications set out in a Member's service Schedule. The positive or bottom-up approach of Members' scheduling commitments with the negative or top-down methodology of limitations on national treatment reflects the fundamental purpose of progressive liberalization of the GATS.[183] In addition, Article XVII of the GATS extends the obligations to both *de jure* and *de facto* discriminations. That is to say, formally identical treatment might as well be inconsistent with national treatment obligation if it

[181] Panel Report, *United States – Measures Affecting the Cross-Border Supply of Gambling and Betting Services* (cited as *US – Gambling*), WT/DS285/R (10 November 2004), para. 6.338. Appellate Body Report, *United States – Measures Affecting the Cross-Border Supply of Gambling and Betting Services* (cited as *US – Gambling*), WT/DS285/AB/R (7 April 2005), para. 239.

[182] Appellate Body Report, *United States – Measures Affecting the Cross-Border Supply of Gambling and Betting Services* (cited as *US – Gambling*), WT/DS285/AB/R (7 April 2005), paras. 243-252.

[183] *See* Working Group on the Relationship Between Trade and Investment, *Note by the Secretariat: Non-Discrimination Most-Favoured-Nation Treatment and National Treatment*, WT/WGTI/W118 (4 June 2002), para 8., Wei Wang, *On the Relationship Between Market Access and National Treatment Under the GATS*, The International Lawyer Vol. 46, No.4 (Winter 2012), pp.1045-1065, and Nicolas F. Diebold, *Non-Discrimination in International Trade in Service – Likeness in WTO/GATS*, Cambridge University Press (2010), pp. 103-126.

modifies the conditions of competition in favour of like domestic services or service suppliers, and formally different treatment might not necessarily be in violation of Article XVII if it does not alter such conditions.

As mentioned in Section I, the interpretation of the indeterminate terms in Article XVII will have a profound impact on the Internet-related trade in services. The Internet does not only transform traditional services into electronically delivered services, new services, such as e-mails, search engines, and social media, are becoming indispensable on a daily basis. The concepts of 'like services' and 'like service suppliers' will play a critical role in defining WTO Members' national treatment obligations for digital trade. However, the WTO adjudicating bodies have either avoided or only marginally touched upon this issue. *US – Gambling* is the first case in which the panel had the opportunity to clarify the meaning of national treatment obligations under the GATS in the context of the electronically delivered services. Nevertheless, while the panel has applied a strict technological neutrality test, it still left important problems untouched, such as whether a service supplied electronically, i.e., through the Internet, should be considered 'like' services supplied through traditional means.

In *US – Gambling*, the panel was asked to examine the 'likeness' between electronically delivered services and non-electronically delivered services under Article XVII. Nevertheless, having found a violation of Article XVI, out of judicial economy, neither the panel nor the Appellate Body ruled on the issues claimed by both parties.[184] In the absence of jurisprudence, it is unclear how a panel will apply the national treatment obligations to services delivered through electronic means or new online services. Thus, the following section provides some interpretative methods for Internet-related services within the context of Article XVII of the GATS.

a. 'Like' Services and Service Suppliers Analysis

The concepts of like services and service suppliers under the GATS is complicated and not without controversy. As Mireille Cossy pointed out, "there is perhaps only one point on which everyone agrees: the application of the national treatment obligation and the determination of likeness gives rise to a wider range of questions – and uncertainties – under the GATS than under the

[184] Panel Report, *United States – Measures Affecting the Cross-Border Supply of Gambling and Betting Services* (cited as *US – Gambling*), WT/DS285/R (10 November 2004), para. 6.426.

GATT."[185] Also, the advent of electronically delivered services makes the already tangled concept of 'likeness' more elusive. In general, when considering electronic delivery of services, the main issue regarding the scope of 'likeness' under Article XVII of the GATS is whether the method of delivery affects the nature of the specific GATS commitments.[186] Factors considered in the subsequent analysis include the principle of technological neutrality and the concept of likeness between electronic and non-electronic delivery of services.

i. Technological Neutrality

As mentioned previously, the Interim Report issued by the Council for Trade in Services addressed the common understanding among the Members that the GATS should apply to all services regardless of the means by which they are delivered. The Report further noted that "*technological neutrality* of the Agreement would also mean that electronic supply of services is permitted by specific commitments unless the schedule states otherwise".[187] In sum, all the GATS provisions, either relating to the general obligations or specific commitments, are applicable to the supply of services through electronic means since no area of the WTO rules differentiates one service from another on the basis of the means by which the service is delivered.[188] This approach corresponds to WTO case law and is supported by the Council for Trade in Services.

The technological neutrality methodology was also adopted by the panel in *US – Gambling*. As part of the analysis of Article XVI, the panel applied the principle of technological neutrality when determining whether a commitment for mode 1 supply of services, i.e., cross-border supply of services, includes the delivery of services through electronic means, the panel stated:

---

185 Mireille Cossy, *Determining "likeness" under the GATS: Squaring the circle?*, World Trade Organization – Economic Research and Statistics Division, Staff Working Paper ERSD-2006-08, September 2006.

186 Sacha Wunsch-Vincent, *The Internet, cross-border trade in services, and the GATS: lessons from US – Gambling*, World Trade Review, 5:3 (2006), p. 329.

187 WTO Council for Trade in Services, Work Programme on E-Commerce – Interim Report to the General Council, S/C/8 (31/March/1999), para. 4 (emphasis added).

188 WTO Council for Trade in Services, Note by the Secretariat, The Work Programme on Electronic Commerce, S/C/W/68 (16 November 1998), para. 3, the Note addressed:

> ... The Agreement makes no distinction between the different technological means by which a service may be delivered – whether in person, by mail, by telephone or across the Internet. The supply of services through electronic means is therefore covered by the Agreement in the same way as all other means of delivery.

> "Article I:2(a) of the GATS defines "mode 1", otherwise referred to as "cross-border", as the supply of a service "from the territory of one Member into the territory of any other Member". The definition does not contain any indications as to the means that can be used to supply services cross-border. This indicates, in our view, that the GATS does not limit the various technologically possible means of delivery under mode 1."[189]

The panel is of the opinion that "a market access commitment for mode 1 implies the right for other Members' suppliers to supply a service through all means of delivery, whether by mail, telephone, Internet, etc., unless otherwise specified in a Member's Schedule".[190] Therefore, "where a full market access commitment has been made for mode 1, a prohibition on one, several or all means of delivery included in this mode 1 would be a limitation on market access for the mode."[191] According to the panel, any limitations on the means of delivery would nullify the benefits of other Members under a full mode 1 commitment.

Applying the technological neutrality principle eliminates legal uncertainties of the applicability of GATS rules to electronically delivered services.[192] Meanwhile, this technology-neutral interpretation makes it difficult for a Member who undertakes a full market access commitment for cross-border services but wishes to simultaneously maintain restrictions on the services supplied through the Internet.[193] Despite the confirmation of technological neutrality within the context the GATS, it is unfortunate that both the panel and the Appellate Body decided not to rule on the relevant questions regarding national treatment obligations. Nevertheless, on the basis of WTO jurisprudence, the same principle should be applied when interpreting a Member's commitments under Article XVII and when clarifying the meaning of the terms of the article.

---

[189] Panel Report, *United States – Measures Affecting the Cross-Border Supply of Gambling and Betting Services* (cited as *US – Gambling*), WT/DS285/R (10 November 2004), para. 6.281.

[190] Ibid., para. 6.285.

[191] Ibid.

[192] Sacha Wunsch-Vincent, *The WTO, the Internet and Trade in Digital-Products: EU-US Perspectives*, North America: Hart Publishing (2006), pp. 174-175.

[193] *See* Nancy J. King and Kishani Kalupahana, *Choosing Between Liberalization and Regulatory Autonomy under GATS: Implications of US – Gambling for Trade in Cross-Border Services*, Vand. J.Transnat'l L. 1189, V. 40 (November 2007), pp. 1192-1298.

ii. The Likeness between Electronically Supplied Services versus Non-Electronically Supplied Services

In the Work Programme on E-commerce, the WTO Secretariat recognized that the concept of 'likeness' is the central issue when applying GATS non-discrimination obligations to measures restricting the electronic supply of services.[194] In an explanatory note, the Secretariat stated that "likeness in the national treatment context also depends in principle on attributes of the product or suppliers *per se* rather than on the means by which the product is delivered."[195] Put differently, according to the principle of technology neutrality, the scope of 'likeness' should not depend on whether a service is provided electronically or otherwise. Nevertheless, the explanatory notes are not legally binding, and further considerations on the issue of likeness are required.

The panel and the Appellate Body in *US – Gambling* missed the opportunity to interpret the concept of 'likeness' for Internet-related services under Article XVII. In the case, both the complainant and respondent raised the issue relating to the likeness between electronically and non-electronically delivered services. Antigua argued that services and service suppliers of Antigua are like those of the US, and in the context of mode 1 commitment to national treatment, the means of delivery, either through the cross-border supply or onsite supply, is irrelevant.[196] Antigua further claimed that services supplied through different modes of supply are 'like services'.[197]

In reply, the US underlined that Antigua failed in its burden to provide evidence to demonstrate that Antiguan services and service suppliers are "like" the US domestic services and service suppliers for the purpose of Article XVII. According to the US, the services supplied electronically and non-electronically are not like services because of differential characteristics of services and ser-

---

[194] WTO Trade in Service, Work Programme on Electronic Commerce -- Progress Report to the General Council, Work Programme on Electronic Commerce, S/L/74 (27 July 1999), paras. 8 and 18.

[195] WTO Council for Trade in Services, Note by the Secretariat, The Work Programme on Electronic Commerce, S/C/W/68 (16 November 1998), para. 10. When considering 'likeness' under GATS Article II, the Note stated:

> In principle, likeness depends on attributes of the product or supplier *per se* rather than on the means by which the product is delivered. If two like services were treated differently because they were delivered in different ways, then such treatment could be challenged as being inconsistent with the MFN obligations.

[196] Panel Report, *United States – Measures Affecting the Cross-Border Supply of Gambling and Betting Services* (cited as *US – Gambling*), WT/DS285/R (10 November 2004), para. 3.148.

[197] Ibid., para. 3.150.

vice suppliers, differential risks, differential consumer tastes, and differential end-uses.[198] In addition, the US contested that a difference based on regulatory distinction needs to be taken into account when assessing the term 'likeness'.[199]

The arguments put forward by both Antigua and the US on the criteria for determining the likeness of services and service suppliers represented the depth of the complexity of the issue involved. While most WTO Members agreed that the concepts of 'like services' and 'like service suppliers' should be determined by the adjudicating bodies on a case-by-case basis, both the panel and the Appellate Body in *US – Gambling* seemed to try to avoid a head-on crash on this issue due to the difficulty of comprehending the concept of likeness in services.[200] Nevertheless, given the increasing trend to extend scheduled national treatment commitments and the rapid growth of electronically delivered services, how to establish a clear reference for determining likeness between electronic and non-electronic services is of the utmost importance for the WTO adjudicating bodies and GATS negotiators in the future.

The opinions of the panel in the recent *China – Electronic Payment* case did not directly address the above-mentioned issue but its analysis of like services and service suppliers may shed some light. In the case, the panel first emphasized that the criteria applied in determining 'like products' under GATT Article III should not directly transpose to the determination of likeness in the context of GATS Article XVII because of the important dissimilarities between the two areas of trade.[201] The panel further defined that services could qualify as 'like' if they are essentially or generally the same. By examining the context of GATS Article XVII, the panel deduced that like services are services that are in a competitive relationship with each other.[202] Finally, in the light of the complexity of trade in services, the panel is of the opinion that determination of 'like services' and 'like service suppliers' should be made on a case-by-case basis. In sum, according to the panel, if the foreign and domestic services in question in a particular case are essentially or generally the same in competitive terms, those services should be 'like services' in the meaning of Article XVII of the GATS.[203]

---

[198] Ibid., para. 3.188-3.196.
[199] Ibid., para. 3.188.
[200] Mireille Cossy, *Determining "likeness" under the GATS: Squaring the circle?*, World Trade Organization – Economic Research and Statistics Division, Staff Working Paper ERSD-2006-08, September 2006, pp. 2-6.
[201] Panel Report, *China – Certain Measures Affecting Electronic Payment Services* (cited as *China – Electronic Payment*), WT/DS413/R (16/July/2012), para. 7.698.
[202] Ibid., paras. 7.600-7-701.
[203] Ibid., para. 7.702.

Therefore, the determination of likeness is the determination about the nature and extent of a competitive relationship between the foreign and domestic services and service suppliers in the given market, and such a decision should be based on the evidence as a whole. In other words, different means of supply does not, by itself, make the services unlike. The adequate standard for comparison is based on the likeness between foreign and domestic services and service suppliers, and the evaluation will involve a series of issues that are closely related to the suppliers of services.[204] The extension of likeness to service suppliers under the GATS reflects that it is difficult to separate the services from the service suppliers in reality since service providers are "part of the continuing nature of the service".[205] The characteristics or the quality of the service suppliers are crucial in determining likeness between different methods of supply because the services supplied through different means are usually identical services. The panel in *China – Electronic Payment* emphasized that a separate inquiry into the meaning of 'like service suppliers' is essential and the mere fact that the services in the specific circumstance are the same services is not sufficient to presume the service suppliers are automatically the same.[206]

With reference to the Report of the Working Party on *Border Tax Adjustments*, the Appellate Body in *EC – Asbestos* established four criteria for determining likeness under Article III of the GATT, including: the property, nature and quality of the product, the end-use of the products in a given market, consumer tastes and habits, and the tariff classification of the product.[207] Although these parameters should not directly apply to the determination of likeness under GATS Article XVII due to the inherent difference between goods and services, consumer tastes and end-use of the products are relatively significant in the services context.[208] According to the Appellate Body in *EC – Asbestos*, the

---

[204] *See* Mireille Cossy, *Determining "likeness" under the GATS: Squaring the circle?*, World Trade Organization – Economic Research and Statistics Division, Staff Working Paper ERSD-2006-08, September 2006.

[205] Nicolaïdis K. & Trachtman J.P., From Policed Regulation to Managed Recognition in GATS (2000). In: P. Sauvé and R.M. Stern (ed.), *GATS 2000 – New Directions in Services Trade Liberalization*, p. 253.

[206] Panel Report, *China – Certain Measures Affecting Electronic Payment Services* (cited as *China – Electronic Payment*), WT/DS413/R (16/July/2012), para. 7.705.

[207] Appellate Body Report, *European Communities – Measures Affecting Asbestos and Asbestos-Containing Products* (cited as *EC -- Asbestos*), WT/DS135/AB/R (5/April/2001), para. 101.

[208] *See* Mireille Cossy, *Determining "likeness" under the GATS: Squaring the circle?*, World Trade Organization – Economic Research and Statistics Division, Staff Working Paper ERSD-2006-08, September 2006, pp. 16-23; Anditya Mattoo, *National Treatment in the GATS: Corner-Stone or Pandora's Box?*, Journal of World Trade, Vol.31, No.1

elements for determining the consumer tastes and the end-use of the products depend on the substitutability of the products for the consumers or in the given market.[209] Thus, differences in the method of supply are relevant for the likeness analysis when consumers perceive the service supplied through different means are not substitutable or when the services supplied through different means are not used for performing similar functions in the given market.

The determination of whether electronically delivered services are like the services distributed through non-electronic means, therefore, depends on the competitive relationship between the services at issue and on all the available evidence as whole. The means of delivery is only one of the constituents in a holistic likeness analysis. Some commentators believe that the purpose of the measures should also be taken into consideration under Article XVII due to the conflict of interests relating to Internet-related trade measures.[210] However, the 'aim and effect' test has been affirmatively rejected by WTO panels and the Appellate Body under both the GATT and the GATS.[211] Nevertheless, based on the WTO jurisprudence, there might be more space for regulatory distinctions under the 'less favourable treatment' analysis, which extend the application of Article XVII:3 to both *de jure* and *de facto* discriminatory measures.

b. Less Favourable Treatment

In the meaning of Article XVII of the GATS, the different treatment between like domestic and foreign services and service suppliers violates national treat-

(1997), pp. 25-26; and Krajewski & Engelke, Article XVII GATS National Treatment. In: Rüdiger Wolfrum, Peter Tobias Stoll and Clemens Feinäugle (eds), *WTO -- Trade in Services*, Netherlands: Kononklijke Brill NV (2008), pp. 403-404.

[209] Appellate Body Report, *European Communities – Measures Affecting Asbestos and Asbestos-Containing Products* (cited as *EC -- Asbestos*), WT/DS135/AB/R (5/April/ 2001), para. 117.

[210] *See* Mireille Cossy, *Determining "likeness" under the GATS: Squaring the circle?*, World Trade Organization – Economic Research and Statistics Division, Staff Working Paper ERSD-2006-08, September 2006; *see* also Joost Pauwelyn, Comment: The unbearable lightness of likeness. In: Marion Panizzon, Nicole Pohl and Pierre Sauve (eds.), *GATS and the Regulation of International Trade in Services*, Cambridge: Cambridge University Press, pp. 358-369.

[211] Panel Report, *Japan – Taxes on Alcoholic Beverages* (cited as *Japan – Alcoholic Beverage II*), WT/DS8/R & WT/DS10/R & WT/DS11/R (11/July/1996), para. 6.16. Appellate Body Report, *European Communities – Regime for the Importation, sale and distribution on bananas* (cited as *EC -- Bananas III*), WT/DS27/AB/R (25/September/ 1997), para. 241.

ment obligation only when such treatment modifies the condition of competition in the relevant market to the detriment of foreign services and service suppliers. Article XVII:2 and XVII:3 directly indicate national treatment obligations covers both *de jure* and *de facto* discriminations as the obligations apply to both formally different and formally identical measures.

While *de jure* discrimination generally refers to measures that discriminate foreign services or service suppliers exclusively on their origins, the concept of *de facto* discrimination is less clear. Much attention is given to the issue whether a non-protectionist policy with a protectionist effect constitutes a *de facto* discrimination and violates national treatment obligations.[212] In other words, whether regulatory distinctions should be taken into account when assessing the meaning of 'less favourable treatment' under Article XVII. The legal certainty on this issue is especially critical for Internet-related services, as any origin-neutral measure that restricts the electronic means of service supply might constitute detriment impact on the foreign services and service providers. For example, in *US – Gambling*, the US claimed that the measures at issue, which prohibit all gambling and betting services on the Internet, are not in violation of national treatment obligations since they do not distinguish services and service suppliers based on the origin.

Despite the lack of systematically applicable standards for less favourable treatment under the GATS, few elements need to be considered to establish a *de facto* discrimination argument. First, a challenged measure must not differentiate the foreign and domestic services or service suppliers on a basis of origin, but on a neutral purpose, such as health or human rights considerations. Second, the measure must modify the competitive opportunities for foreign services or service suppliers. However, neither the GATT nor the GATS further specify the meaning of modifying competitive opportunities. Third, in determining less favourable treatment, the complaining party must prove that the whole group of like foreign service suppliers is accorded less favourable treatment when compared to the treatment accorded to the whole group of like domestic service

---

[212] *See* James Flett, *WTO Space for National Treatment Regulation: Requiem for a Diagonal Vector Test*, Journal of International Economic Law, Vol.16, Iss.1, pp. 37-90 (March 2013); Joost Pauwelyn, Comment: The unbearable lightness of likeness. In: Marion Panizzon, Nicole Pohl and Pirrre Sauve (eds.), *GATS and the Regulation of International Trade in Services*, Cambridge: Cambridge University Press, pp. 358-369; Nicolas F. Diebold, *Non-Discrimination in International Trade in Service – Likeness in WTO/GATS*, Cambridge University Press (2010), pp. 32-83; and Federico Ortino, The Principles of Non-Discrimination and Its Exceptions in GATS: Selected Legal Issues. In: Kern Alexander and Mads Andenas, *The World Trade Organization and Trade in Services*, Leiden; Boston: Matinus Nijhoff (2008), pp. 173-204.

suppliers in the given market.[213] Finally, a detrimental effect alone is not sufficient to establish a less favourable treatment argument if the effect cannot be "explained by factors or circumstances unrelated to the foreign origin of the product".[214]

In order to achieve a reasonable balance between trade liberalization and regulatory autonomy, it is argued that the true objective of a measure must play a decisive role in determining *de facto* discrimination for a less favourable treatment analysis. The rationale of the argument is that it is not by mechanically comparing the likeness that could complete the holistic assessment of national treatment obligation but by enquiring into the real objective of the measures.[215] In the case of *de facto* discrimination, no facts are *per se* excluded. As the Appellate Body indicated in *US – Clove Cigarette*, in order to determine whether a measure discriminates against a group of imported products, a panel must carefully scrutinize the design, architecture, revealing structure, operation and application of the measure, and in particular whether the measure is even-handed.[216] Therefore, a panel needs to weigh and balance all the relevant evidence to determine whether a WTO Member is able to prove that the detrimental effect is explained by the factors or circumstances unrelated to the foreign origin of the services or service suppliers.[217]

Applying this approach to electronically delivered services, the different treatment between electronic and non-electronic delivery services does not violate a Member's national treatment obligation, *per se*. A panel has to examine whether the services supplied through different means are in a competitive relationship in a given market and whether the distortive effect on the foreign ser-

---

[213] Appellate Body Report, *European Communities – Measures Affecting Asbestos and Asbestos-Containing Products* (cited as *EC -- Asbestos*), WT/DS135/AB/R (5/April/2001), para. 100.

[214] Appellate Body Report, *Dominican Republic – Measures Affecting the Importation and Internal Sale of Cigarettes* (cited as *Dominican Republic -- Cigarettes*), WT/DS 302/AB/R (25 April 2005), para. 96.

[215] *See* James Flett, *WTO Space for National Treatment Regulation: Requiem for a Diagonal Vector Test*, Journal of International Economic Law, Vol.16, Iss.1, pp. 37-90 (March 2013); and Joost Pauwelyn, Comment: The unbearable lightness of likeness. In: Marion Panizzon, Nicole Pohl and Pirrre Sauve (eds.), *GATS and the Regulation of International Trade in Services*, Cambridge: Cambridge University Press, pp. 358-369

[216] Appellate Body Report, *United States – Measures Affecting the Production and Sale of Clove Cigarettes* (cited as *US – Clove Cigarettes*), WT/DS406/AB/R (4 April 2012), para. 182.

[217] *See* Joost Pauwelyn, Comment: The unbearable lightness of likeness. In: Marion Panizzon, Nicole Pohl and Pirrre Sauve (eds.), *GATS and the Regulation of International Trade in Services*, Cambridge: Cambridge University Press, pp. 358-369.

vices and service suppliers could be explained by factors unrelated to the foreign origin. This approach seems to coincide with the principle of technological neutrality and with the panels and the Appellate Body's decisions in *US – Clove Cigarettes*, *US – Tuna II*, and *EC – Approval and Marketing of Biotech Products*.[218] Consequently, it is up to a panel to conduct a weighing and balancing process on the basis of all the presented facts to determine whether a measure constitutes a *de facto* discrimination and affords less favourable treatment to foreign services or service suppliers.

E. GATS Article XIV (a) General Exceptions Clause

US – Gambling is the first WTO case considering public morals exceptions under Article XIV(a) of the GATS. Due to the similarity to Article XX of the GATT, both the panel and the Appellate Body in *US – Gambling* depended heavily on the well-established GATT case law to support their decisions. Therefore, for a WTO Member to deviate from its substantive obligations under the GATS to pursue a legitimate objective, the restrictive measure must comply with the two-tier test required in Article XIV.

A measure must, first, fall within the ambit of one of the provisions set out in paragraph (a) of Article XIV. If the measure is provisionally justified, second, it needs to meet the requirements of the chapeau. The chapeau requires that the measure should not apply in a manner which constitutes arbitrary or unjustifiable discrimination between countries where the like conditions prevail or constitutes a disguised restriction on trade in services. The criteria set out in the chapeau is not intended to apply to the content of a measure but to the manner in which the measure is applied.[219] The purpose of the chapeau is to delineate a line between a Member's right to regulate and another Member's rights under the GATS.[220]

---

[218] Appellate Body Report, *United States – Measures Concerning the Importation, Marketing and Sale of Tuna and Tuna Products* (cited *as US – Tuna II*), WT/DS 381/AB/R (16 May 2012), para. 313-321. Panel Report, *European Communities – Measures Affecting the Approval and Marketing of Biotech Products* (cited as *EC – Biotech Products*), WT/DS291/R (21 November 2006), para. 7.2514.

[219] Panel Report, *United States – Measures Affecting the Cross-Border Supply of Gambling and Betting Services* (cited as *US – Gambling*), WT/DS285/R (10 November 2004), para. 6.581.

[220] Appellate Body Report, *United States – Measures Affecting the Cross-Border Supply of Gambling and Betting Services* (cited as *US – Gambling*), WT/DS285/AB/R (7 April 2005). When analyzing the requirements of the chapeau of Article XIV, para. 339.

In *US – Gambling*, the US invoked Article XIV (a) and (c) to justify its market access commitment violation. The US claimed that the laws are necessary to protect public morals and/or public order within the meaning of Article XIV (a). The Appellate Body ruled that the US restrictive measures qualified as necessary to protect public morals or public order, and only the Interstate Horseracing Act is not compatible with the requirements of the chapeau.[221] One can see from the succeeding analysis that both the panel and the Appellate Body did not apply an exceedingly restrictive test in determining the necessity of the measures for pursuing a legitimate aim and the requirements of the chapeau.[222] This approach might have a significant impact on the digital trade in services. Because of the unique characteristics of the Internet, many Internet-related trade restrictive measures are implemented by the WTO Member States for the protection of public morals, cultural diversity, national security, and fundamental human rights. Consequently, the rights and obligations of WTO Members in digital trade will partially depend on how a panel applies or interprets the general exceptions under Article XIV of the GATS.

a. Necessary to Protect Public Morals and Maintain Public Orders

To provisionally justify an otherwise WTO-inconsistent measure under Article XIV(a), a WTO member must show that the measure at issue is necessary to protect public morals or to maintain public orders. In *US – Gambling*, the panel clarified that the content of public morals and public orders "can vary in time and space, depending upon a range of factors, including prevailing social, cultural, ethical and religious values".[223] The panel further defined that 'public morals' denotes "standards of right and wrong conduct maintained by or on behalf of a community or nation"[224], and 'public orders' refers to "the preservation of the fundamental interests of a society, as reflected in public policy and

[221] Having found that the measures were provisionally justified under Article XIV(a), the Appellate Body exercised judicial economy and did not address the exception claim under Article XIV(c).

[222] *See* Sacha Wunsch-Vincent, *The Internet, cross-border trade in services, and the GATS: lessons from US – Gambling*, World Trade Review, 5:3 (2006), pp. 347-351; *see* also Mira Burri, Designing future-oriented multilateral rules for digital trade. In: Pierre Sauvé and Martin Roy (eds), *Edward Elgar Research Handbook on Trade in Services*, Edward Elgar (2015), pp. 331-356.

[223] Panel Report, *United States – Measures Affecting the Cross-Border Supply of Gambling and Betting Services* (cited as *US – Gambling*), WT/DS285/R (10 November 2004), para. 6.461.

[224] Ibid., para. 6.465.

law".[225] The Appellate Body upheld the panel's decision that the objectives of the US laws, which are intended to prevent money laundering, organized crime, fraud, underage gambling, and impulsive gambling addiction, fall within the scope of public morals and/or public orders under Article XIV(a).[226] In addition, the Appellate Body recognized that deference should be given to the Members to decide the level of protection with respect to the objective pursued under Article XIV(a), even if the desired level of protection would eliminate the whole service from the market.

In order to determine whether the US measures are "necessary" within the meaning of Article XIV(a), the panel and the Appellate Body followed the well-established standards in *Korea – Beef* and *EC – Asbestos*, which considered the general exceptions clause under Article XX of the GATT.[227] The Appellate Body stated that the process of determining the 'necessity' of a measure includes examining the importance of the interests or values that the measure is designed to protect, the restrictive impact of the measure on international trade and the contribution of the measure to the end pursued. Lastly, the measure is necessary only if no less trade-restrictive alternative is reasonably available.

i. The Necessity Test

When considering whether the US measures are designed to protect 'public morals' or to maintain 'public order', the panel first noticed that "Members should be given some scope to define and apply for themselves the concepts of "public morals" and "public order" in their respective territories, according to their own systems and scales of values".[228] Therefore, the panel concluded that since gambling activities could be limited for public policy considerations, the measures prohibiting gambling and betting services fall within the scope of Article XIV(a).[229] The panel further assessed the importance of the interests or values that the US laws are intended to protect. After examining the evidence

---

[225] Ibid., para. 6.467.
[226] Appellate Body Report, *United States – Measures Affecting the Cross-Border Supply of Gambling and Betting Services* (cited as *US – Gambling*), WT/DS285/AB/R (7 April 2005), paras. 296-299.
[227] *See* Chapter 1, pp. 71-73.
[228] Panel Report, *United States – Measures Affecting the Cross-Border Supply of Gambling and Betting Services* (cited as *US – Gambling*), WT/DS285/R (10 November 2004), para. 6.461.
[229] Ibid., paras 6.473-6.474.

submitted by the US, the panel recognized that preventing organized crimes and protecting health risks serve vital societal interests.[230]

The panel continues to determine the extent to which the US measures contribute to the realization of the ends pursued. Based on the material provided by the US, the measures at issue seek to address concerns pertaining to money laundering, organized crime, fraud, underage gambling, and pathological gambling. The panel considered that the Wire Act, the Travel Act, and the Illegal Gambling Business Act must contribute, at least to some extent, to addressing those concerns.[231] Finally, although the panel identified that the interests protected by the US measures are very important societal interests and the measures materially contribute to the realization of the ends pursued, the panel also found that the measures in question have a significant impact on trade. In this regard, the panel went on to examine whether a WTO-consistent or less trade-restrictive alternative measure exists.

ii. Reasonably Available WTO Consistent Alternatives

The necessity analysis is comprehended by comparing the measures at issue with less restrictive alternatives, and the interests pursued must be considered when assessing the availability of possible alternative measures. In *US – Gambling*, the Appellate Body stated:

> "A comparison between the challenged measure and possible alternatives should then be undertaken, and the results of such comparison should be considered in the light of the importance of the interests at issue. It is on the basis of this 'weighing and balancing' and comparison of measures, taking into account the interests or values at stake, that a panel determines whether a measure is 'necessary' or, alternatively, whether another, WTO-consistent measures is 'reasonably available'."[232]

The Appellate Body overturned the panel's decisions on reasonably available WTO-consistent alternatives. The panel is of the opinion that since the US had not engaged in consultations with Antigua before and while implementing its prohibitions on the cross-border supply of gambling and betting services, the

[230] Ibid., para. 6.492.
[231] Ibid., para. 6.494.
[232] Appellate Body Report, *United States – Measures Affecting the Cross-Border Supply of Gambling and Betting Services* (cited as *US – Gambling*), WT/DS285/AB/R (7 April 2005), para. 307.

US did not explore and exhaust all reasonably available WTO-compatible alternatives. The Appellate Body disagreed with the panel and emphasized that a Members' right to regulate under Article XIV is the Member's sovereign prerogative to determine the level of protection of what they consider appropriate for the relevant objectives. A reasonable alternative, therefore, cannot be only theoretically in nature but must be the measure that would achieve a Member's desired level of protection with respect to the objective pursued under Article XIV (a) of the GATS.[233]

Further, to build a *prima facie* case, it is the party who invokes the general exceptions provision needs to demonstrate that the measures at issue are necessary to achieve the objectives relating to public morals or public order. According to the Appellate Body, however, this burden of proof is reasonably limited since it is the complainant who bears the burden of identifying the possibility of reasonably available alternatives. Only when the complaining party raises a WTO-consistent alternative measure, the responding party then needs to demonstrate the proposed alternative is not reasonably available.[234]

In sum, the Appellate Body disagreed with the panel's necessity analysis for several reasons. First, it is Antigua, the complaining party, who bears the burden of raising a WTO-consistent alternative measure, not the US, the responding party. Second, the panel erred in relying on consultations as an alternative measure that is reasonably available for the US to protect the interests pursued. Conforming to the Appellate Body's opinions, engaging in consultations with Antigua is not an appropriate alternative for the panel to consider since "consultations are by definition a process, the results of which are uncertain and therefore not capable of comparison with the measure at issue in this case".[235] After recognizing that the US made its *prima facie* case of necessity within the meaning of GATS Article XIV(a), and Antigua failed to identify a reasonably available alternative measure, the Appellate Body concluded that the US measures are necessary and, therefore, provisionally justified.[236]

---

[233] Ibid., para. 308. The panel in *US – Clove Cigarettes* decided that listing two dozen possible alternative measures is insufficient to establish a prima facie case if the proposed alternative measures do not show that such measures could make an equivalent contribution to the achievement of the objective at the level of protection sought by the defendant. Panel Report, *United States – Measures Affecting the Production and Sale of Clove Cigarettes* (cited as *US – Clove Cigarettes*), WT/DS406/R (2 September 2011), para. 7.423.

[234] Ibid., para. 309-311.

[235] Ibid., para. 317.

[236] Ibid., para. 326.

b. Chapeau

As previously discussed, since the purpose of the chapeau is to prevent the misuse of general exceptions under the GATS, the focus of the chapeau, by its express terms, is on the application of a measure that is found to be inconsistent with one of the obligations under the GATS. In *US – Gambling*, the panel applied a standard of consistency to determine whether the measures at issue are applied in a non-discriminatory manner. When considering the alleged enforcement of the Wire Act, Travel Act, and Illegal Gambling Business Act against domestic remote suppliers of gambling and betting services, the panel found that the evidence provided by the US was 'inconclusive' and the US failed to show that the manner in which it enforced its prohibition on the remote supply of gambling and betting services is consistent with the requirements of the chapeau. Furthermore, the panel also believed that the Interstate Horseracing Act, which provides a possible exemption of domestic remote suppliers for horseracing betting services, is not applied in a consistent manner between domestic suppliers and suppliers from other Members.[237]

The Appellate Body did not reject the consistency standard under the chapeau. Nevertheless, the Appellate Body reversed the panel's decisions regarding the non-enforcement of the measures. According to the Appellate Body, to decide whether the enforcement of the law constitutes an arbitrary or unjustifiable discrimination between domestic and foreign service suppliers, the evidence taken into consideration needs to be based on the overall number of suppliers, on patterns of enforcement, and on the reasons for particular instances of non-enforcement.[238] Therefore, the panel's consideration of isolated instances of the US non-enforcement of the relevant laws was insufficient to rebut the US defense under the chapeau and to support its finding of "inconclusive" evidence.[239] The Appellate Body, however, upheld the panel's decision on the finding of inconsistent application of the Interstate Horseracing Act since the measure exempts only domestic suppliers of remote betting services for horse racing from the prohibitions in the Wire Act, the Travel Act and the Illegal Gambling Business Act.[240]

---

[237] Panel Report, *United States – Measures Affecting the Cross-Border Supply of Gambling and Betting Services* (cited as *US – Gambling*), WT/DS285/R (10 November 2004), para. 6.566-6.607.

[238] Appellate Body Report, *United States – Measures Affecting the Cross-Border Supply of Gambling and Betting Services* (cited as *US – Gambling*), WT/DS285/AB/R (7 April 2005), para. 356.

[239] Ibid., para. 368.

[240] Ibid., para. 369.

F. Conclusions on US – Gambling

Although it remains questionable whether the WTO is an optimal forum for dealing with various controversial issues relating to the Internet, the *US – Gambling* case has provided some promising answers to the unsolved disputes on the cross-border delivery of services.[241] First, *US – Gambling* reassures the applicability of the WTO and GATS obligations to electronic cross-border delivery services. By adopting the principle of technological neutrality, the panel and the Appellate Body emphasized that in WTO law, products or services should not be differentiated from other products or services based on the means of delivery. Therefore, all the GATS provisions, either under general obligations or specific commitments, are applicable to the supply of services through electronic means. The panel also confirmed that services supplied through electronic means should be considered as mode 1 cross-border supply of services. The application of technological neutrality principle within a mode of supply brings legal clarity to future litigations.

Second, in *US – Gambling*, in accordance with the rules of treaty interpretation of the Vienna Convention, the adjudicating bodies have adopted an evolutionary approach to deciding the extent and the scope of a Member's specific commitments in its GATS Schedule. The panel and the Appellate Body confirmed that since a Member's GATS Schedule serves as an integral part of the Agreement, it is the common intentions of the Members, rather than the intent of an individual Member, that counts in order to ascertain the meaning of a Member's commitments. Consequently, to interpret the meaning of the terms in a specific service sector of a Member's GATS Schedule, a panel needs to examine the ordinary meaning to be given to the terms of a Schedule in their context and in the light of their object and purpose.

Third, both the panel and the Appellate Body in *US – Gambling* adopted relatively flexible approaches in determining the requirements of 'necessity' and 'chapeau' under Article XIV of the GATS. According to WTO case law, for a measure to be necessary to fulfill the objective pursued, the measure must be indispensable in relation to the policy objective.[242] In every case, a process of weighing and balancing a series of factors needs to be applied. The process of weighing and balancing reflects deference towards regulatory autonomy. This approach is welcome in the light of the relatively restricting and limited scope

---

[241] *See* Sacha Wunsch-Vincent, *The Internet, cross-border trade in services, and the GATS: lessons from US – Gambling*, World Trade Review, 5:3 (2006), pp. 319-355.

[242] Appellate Body Report, *Korea – Measures Affecting Imports of Fresh, Chilled and Frozen Beef* (cited as *Korea -- Beef*), WT/DS161/AB/R & WT/DS169/AB/R (11 December 2000), para. 161.

of GATS Article XIV and the evident tension between regulatory autonomy and trade liberalization.

Notwithstanding its contribution, the panel and the Appellate Body's decision in *US – Gambling* attracted certain criticism and left some questions unanswered. The most controversial aspect of the case is when the adjudicating bodies considered the interpretation of Article XVI on market access. Most critiques focused on the issue that the "total prohibition" on online gambling services in the case should be categorized as a "regulatory requirement" subject to GATS Article VI:4/5 domestic regulations instead of as a "quantitative limitation" on services or service suppliers in the form of numerical quota. Although it is still questionable whether a total prohibition on electronic delivery of services should be treated as a mere technical standard due to the considerable impact of the Internet on trade in services[243], to clarify the line between the rules on market access and domestic regulations is necessary for the preservation of Members' regulatory autonomy.

Some unanswered questions from *US – Gambling* were clarified by the *China – Audiovisual Products* case. An analysis of the case is presented in Section III. *China – Audiovisual Products* is a broad and complex dispute and it is the first case where the panel and the Appellate Body attempted to draw a line between the GATT and the GATS. The WTO adjudicating bodies gave a great amount of deliberation to China's trading rights commitments, i.e., China's Accession Protocols. Furthermore, the Appellate Body's opinion on the application of the general exceptions clause under Article XX of the GATT draws attention to the protection of cultural products, which is closely related to the Chinese Internet censorship case study provided in Chapter 4.

---

[243] *See* Joost Pauwelyn, *Rien ne Ve Plus? Distinguish Domestic Regulation from Market Access in GATT and GATS*, World Trade Review 4:2 (2006), pp. 131-170.
Joost Pauwelyn argued that domestic regulations, in particular qualification, technical, or licensing requirements, cannot be found to violate Article XVI as a market access restriction simply because they have a quantitative effect. Pauwelyn further illustrated the point by the example of a taxi driver's license. The argument is that if following the *US-gambling* path, a requirement for taxi drivers to pass a driving test, which results in some taxi drivers off the market, would constitute market access restriction because of its quantitative effect.

III. GATT Application – The *China -- Audiovisual Products* Case

In April 2007, the US filed a broad-based dispute against a series of Chinese laws and regulations affecting both trade in goods and services. The laws and regulations in question involve limitations on the importation and distribution of various publications and audiovisual products, including books, newspapers, periodicals, videocassettes, DVDs, sound recordings, and films for theatrical release. Specifically, the US alleged that Chinese measures regarding the internal sale and distribution of audiovisual entertainment products and reading materials were in violation of China's obligations under the GATT, the GATS, and China's WTO Accession Protocol.[244]

A. The Background and Summary of the Case: China – Audiovisual Products

The first issue in *China – Audiovisual Products* is China's trading rights commitments under the Accession Protocol. When China joined the WTO, it made several commitments in the Protocol of Accession. The US claimed that China's restrictive measures were in violation of its commitments to liberalize trading rights for all enterprises in China. In response, in accordance with the right to regulate under paragraph 5.1 of the Accession Protocol, China argued that the measures at issue are "the result of a selection process which limits the number of importation entities but could be justified in order to implement an effective and efficient content review mechanism".[245] China contested that the measures should be justified under Article XX of the GATT. The panel found certain provisions in China's measures were inconsistent with paragraphs 1.2 and 5.1 of China's Accession Protocol obligations and paragraphs 83(d), 84(a) and 84(b) of China's Accession Working Party Report.

---

[244] Under the WTO legal system, acceded members can be required to abide by additional and more stringent rules of conduct than its original members. The scope and content of such rules are country-specific and are set out in the protocol of accession. When China acceded to the WTO in 2001, it agreed that, in paragraph 5.1 and 5.2 of Accession Protocol, within three years after accession "all enterprises in China", and "all foreign individuals and enterprises, including those not invested or registered in China", would have the right to import and export all goods throughout its custom territory, except for a list of products reserved for state trading in Annex 2A of the Accession Protocol.

[245] Panel Report, *China – Measures Affecting Trading Rights and Distribution Services for Certain Publications and Audiovisual Entertainment Products* (cited as *China – Audiovisual Products*), WT/DS363/R (12 August 2009), para. 7.331

To justify the restrictive measures under Article XX(a) of the GATT, China claimed that its measures govern the importation of cultural goods, which are unique in the way that they may have a potentially serious impact on societal and individual morals. China further explained that the content review mechanism, which is operated through a number of selected import entities, is necessary to protect public morals under GATT Article XX(a) because the measures are in conformity with the necessity test and are not applied in an arbitrary or unjustifiable manner.[246] On the contrary, the US argued that the measures at issue are too far distant from the pole of indispensability to qualify as necessary within the meaning of Article XX(a).[247] By assuming arguendo that Article XX(a) applies to the Accession Protocol, the panel decided that China has neither made a *prima facie* case that measures at issue are necessary nor demonstrated that the alternative measure put forward by the US is not genuine or not reasonably available in the light of the interests pursued. The panel concluded, therefore, that the Chinese measures are not justified under Article XX(a) of the GATT.

The US further claimed that Chinese measures also violate China's market access and national treatment obligations under Article XVI and Article XVII of the GATS. The US asserted that the restrictions on the distribution of reading materials and sound recordings in electronic form, as well as the distribution of audiovisual home entertainment products, are inconsistent with China's commitments on GATS Article XVI and Article XVII, respectively. In the panel's opinion, the inscription of "sound recording distribution services" under the heading of Audiovisual Services (Sector 2.D) of China's service Schedule extends to the distribution of sound recordings in non-physical form, i.e., through electronic means. The panel held that China's measures prohibiting foreign-invested entities from engaging in the distribution of sound recordings in electronic form were inconsistent with national treatment obligations under Article XVII. The panel further found that the measures at issue were also inconsistent with China's market access obligations under Article XVI.

Finally, the US claimed that certain Chinese measures in relation to the distribution of imported reading materials, sound recordings, and films for theatri-

---

[246] Ibid., paras. 7.711-7.716.

[247] The Appellate Body in *Korea – Beef* case stated:

> 161…., the reach of the word "necessary" is not limited to what which is "indispensable" or "of absolute necessity" of "inevitable". … the term "necessary" refers, in our view, to a range of degree of necessity. At one end of this continuum lies "necessary" understood as "indispensable"; at the other end, is "necessary" taken to mean as "making contribution to." *We consider that "necessary" measure is, in this continuum, located significantly closer to the pole of "indispensable" than to the opposite pole of simply "making contribution to".* (emphasis added).

cal release are also in violation of national treatment obligations under Article III:4 of the GATT (internal regulations). The panel first confirmed that the analysis of 'likeness' between imported and domestic products should be done on a case-by-case basis and "a determination of 'likeness' under Article III:4 of the GATT 1994 is fundamentally a determination about the nature and extent of a competitive relationship between and among products".[248] The panel emphasized that the term 'affecting' in Article III:4 has been interpreted to have a broad scope of application. In other words, the word "affecting" covers both measures that either directly regulate the sale of domestic and imported like products or indirectly create incentives or disincentives that might adversely modify the conditions of competition between domestic and foreign products.[249]

As for the requirements of less favourable treatment in the meaning of Article III:4, the panel stated that the determination of whether the measures at issue modify the conditions of competition in the relevant market to the detriment of imported like products must be based on a "close scrutiny of the fundamental thrust and effect of the measure itself".[250] After a holistic analysis of China's national treatment obligations under the GATT, the panel found that certain Chinese measures affecting the distribution of imported reading materials were inconsistent with Article III:4. These findings were not appealed.

The Panel Report was circulated in August 2009, and three aspects of the Report were appealed by China. First, China contested that the Accession Protocol, which applies only with respect to trade in goods, should not apply to measures concerning films for theatrical release and unfinished audiovisual products since the measures in question regulate the content of films and the services related to such content. Secondly, China appealed the panel's analysis and findings on the issue of "necessity" in the meaning of Article XX(a) of the GATT. Lastly, China disputes the panel's finding that "Sound recording distribution services" in China's GATS Schedule includes the distribution of sound recordings through electronic form, especially through the Internet. The Appellate Body upheld all the panel's decisions, and the Appellate Body Reports were adopted by the WTO Dispute Settlement Body on 19 January 2010.

Each of the three appealed issues will be discussed respectively in the following section since they exemplify various problems of the lack of adequate regulatory responses for new types of trade in services and goods brought about by the new technologies. The first section discusses the question of whether a product is a 'good' or a 'service' in the context of digital trade. The line be-

[248] Ibid. para. 7.1445.
[249] Ibid. para. 7.1440.
[250] Ibid. paras. 7.1467-7.1473.

tween goods and services is gradually blurred because many of the new technologies did not exist at the time the GATT/GATS were drafted. A prudential interpretation on this subject is critical since the obligations under the GATT and the GATS are very different.[251] Second, the Appellate Body has adopted an evolutionary approach to defining the scope of a WTO Member GATS Schedule and strengthened the principle of technological neutrality under the GATS. Finally, the last section examines the panel and the Appellate Body's findings on general exceptions under Article XX(a), which has significant implications for the censorship regime. Although the Appellate Body in *China – Audiovisual Products* did not directly regulate on the issue of censorship, China was requested to undertake a systemic reform on its censorship (content review) mechanism to comply with its WTO obligations. In this sense, the practice of the WTO adjudicating bodies plays a critical role in confining legal conditions in the digital age.

B. Measures Subject to Trade in Goods and Trade in Services Simultaneously

In *China – Audiovisual Products*, the panel found that China's measures pertaining to films for theatrical release under Article 30 of the *Film Regulation* and Article 16 of the *Film Enterprise Rule* are inconsistent with its Accession Protocol.[252] On appeal, China argued that the panel erred in finding that China's Accession Protocol commitments apply to the measures at issue since the 'right to trade' guaranteed by the Protocol is the right to import and export 'goods'. According to China, the provisions of the measures regulate the content of films and the services associated with the importation of such content, not the importation of goods. China claimed that "films for theatrical release are not goods because they are exploited through a series of services because the commercial value of films for theatrical release lies in the revenue generated by these ser-

[251] *See* Paola Conconi and Joost Pauwelyn, *Trading Culture: Appellate Body Report on China – Audiovisuals (WT/DS363/AB/R. adopted 19 January 2010)*, World Trade Review, 10:1, pp. 95-118 (2011).

[252] In the light of the similarity of the two provisions at issue and China's arguments regarding the applicability of its trading rights commitments to them, the panel found that the reasons that led to its conclusion on Article 30 of the *Film Regulation* also applied, *mutatis mutandis*, to Article 16 of the *Film Enterprise Rule*. Therefore, both the panel and the Appellate Body focused the analysis on Article 30 of the *Film Regulation*.

vices and because the delivery material containing the content of films are mere accessories of such services and have no commercial value of their own".[253]

The US, in response, argued that China's interpretation would transform virtually all goods into services because "the vast majority of goods are commercially exploited through a series of associated services".[254] In addition, the US took the examples of Article III:10 and Article IV of the GATT, which deal with cinematographic films, to support its claim that films for theatrical release are considered as goods. The US also referred to the international classification of products under the Harmonized System and China's WTO Schedule of Concession for goods. Both of the documents contain a heading for "cinematographic film" with embedded content.[255]

Due to the lack of specific definitions of 'goods' and 'services' under the WTO agreements, the boundaries between the GATT and the GATS are inherently unclear. Nevertheless, the issue presented in front of the Appellate Body in *China – Audiovisual Products* is whether a measure that regulates trade in services may simultaneously be subject to the obligations for trade in goods. From the succeeding analysis, one can perceive that the Appellate Body focused not only on the substantive content of the measure involved, but also on its impact on international trade in goods and services. This methodology might be in conformity with the Appellate Body's mandate; nevertheless, the decision could result in some inconsistency when applying the rule to digitally delivered products.

a. Physical Nature of the Products

Before considering whether China's trading rights commitments are applicable to the measures at issue, the Appellate Body first referred to the findings in the previous cases concerning the application of the GATT and the GATS. In *Canada – Periodicals*, the Appellate Body found that 'a periodical is a good comprised of two components: editorial content and advertising content. Both components can be viewed as having services attributes, but they combine to form a physical product – the periodical itself'.[256] The Appellate Body confirmed that

[253] Appellate Body Report, *China – Measures Affecting Trading Rights and Distribution Services for Certain Publications and Audiovisual Entertainment Products* (cited as *China – Audiovisual Products*), WT/DS363/AB/R (21 December 2009), para. 173.
[254] Ibid.
[255] Ibid.
[256] Appellate Body Report, *Canada – Certain Measures Concerning Periodicals* (cited as *Canada – periodicals*), WT/DS31/AB/R (30 June 1997), p. 17.

"the entry into force of the GATS, as Annex 1B of the WTO *Agreement*, does not diminish the scope of application of the GATT 1994".[257] In *EC – Bananas III*, the Appellate Body observed that the GATT and the GATS are not mutually exclusive. On a case-by-case basis, a particular measure could be found to fall within the scope of the GATT and that of the GATS. The determination depends on the nature of the measure at issue.[258]

Given that China's trading rights commitments apply to trade in goods, the Appellate Body in *China – Audiovisual Products* was asked to examine whether the Chinese measures, which regulate trade in services, could also affect WTO Members' right to trade goods, and, therefore, be subject to the obligations under both the GATS and the Accession Protocol. The Appellate first upheld the panel's finding that China's trading rights commitments apply to measures concerning trade in "all good".[259] Thus, the applicability of China's Accession Protocol is triggered when the measure concerns who may import a good.[260] When considering whether Article 30 of the Film Regulation regulates who may import goods, the Appellate Body stated:

> "... where the content of a film is carried by physical delivery materials, Article 30 of the *Film Regulation* will inevitably regulate who may import goods for the plain reason that the content of a film is expressed through, and embedded in, a physical good."[261]

China argued that any effects resulting from the measure at issue on trade in goods are merely "incidental and practical" and not subject to its trading rights commitments. The Appellate Body first recognized that content and goods, and the regulations thereof, are not mutually exclusive.[262] The Appellate Body disagreed with China and decided that the effect of the measures on who may import goods is inevitable, rather than incidental and "the mere fact that the import transaction involving hard-copy cinematographic films may not be an "essential feature" of the exploitation of the relevant film" does not preclude the applica-

[257] Ibid., p. 19.

[258] Appellate Body Report, *European Communities – Regime for the Importation, sale and distribution on bananas* (cited as *EC -- Bananas III*), WT/DS27/AB/R (25/September/1997), para. 221.

[259] Appellate Body Report, *China – Measures Affecting Trading Rights and Distribution Services for Certain Publications and Audiovisual Entertainment Products* (cited as *China – Audiovisual Products*), WT/DS363/AB/R (21 December 2009), para. 196.

[260] Ibid.

[261] Ibid., para. 188.

[262] Ibid., para. 195

tion of China's trading rights commitments to the Film Regulations".[263] In conclusion, the Appellate Body upheld Pane's finding that since Article 30 of the Film Regulation has a 'necessary' effect on who may engage in importing of hard-copy cinematographic films, the regulation is subject to China's Accession Protocol.

b. The Implications for Electronically Delivered Products

As mentioned at the beginning of this chapter, it is questionable whether content that was previously provided by a physical medium, but now can be downloaded and kept in digital form is a good or a service. The controversy is raised by either the inherently unclear division between the GATT and the GATS, or by different political and economic interests of WTO Members.[264] Although it may be plausible to treat digitally delivered products as 'goods' and subject to the GATT in order to avoid the potential conundrum that different obligations are applied to two "like products" on the basis of different methods in which the products are presented, it is far from conclusive to make the assumption based on this reason alone.[265]

The Appellate Body's opinion in *China – Audiovisual Products* might induce more confusion than clarity by focusing on the tangible nature of a product in determining whether a measure is subject to the GATT or the GATS. According to the Appellate Body, when the content of a film is carried by physical delivery materials (hard-copy film reel), the measure would inevitably affect the importation of goods. Put differently, if a measure has an effect on the importation of the tangible component of a product, the measure is subject to the WTO Agreement concerning trade in goods, irrespective of whether the tangible component constitutes an 'essential feature' of the value of the product.

Therefore, if a film for theatrical release no longer needs to be exported/imported by a cinematographic reel but can be delivered through digital means, any restrictions on the electronically delivered films are exclusively

---

263 *See* Sacha Wunsch-Vincent, Trade Rules of the Digital Age (2008). In: Marion Panizzon, Nicole Pohl and Pierre Sauve (eds.), *GATS and the Regulation of International Trade in Services*, Cambridge: Cambridge University Press, pp. 497-529.

264 *See* Sacha Wunsch-Vincent, *The WTO, the Internet and Trade in Digital-Products: EU-US Perspectives*, North America: Hart Publishing (2006), pp. 35-80.

265 *See* Stewart A. Baker et al., *E-Products and the WTO*, 35 Int. Lawyer 5, 6(2001); and *See* also Tim Wu, *The World Trade Law of Censorship and Internet Filtering*, Chicago Journal of Int'l Law, Vol.7, Issue 1 (2006).

subject to the GATS.[266] That is to say, China's Accession Protocol would be applicable no more since there is no tangible component in the process of the transaction. If the classification system under the GATT is available only to the extent that the imported products must have physical attributes,[267] a measure that regulates the films imported through physical reel will be subject to both the GATS and the GATT respectively, while a measure that regulates the film imported through the Internet will only need to comply with the obligations under the GATS. Consequently, two identical products will be subject to two different obligations due to the different means of delivery.

Choosing the legal framework for digitally delivered products between the GATT and the GATS is a daunting task not only because of the different level of liberalization under the two Agreements, but also the various political and economic interests each WTO Member intends to pursue. For example, the US and the EU have very different opinions on how to classify digitally delivered products. The US, a dominant country in producing and exporting digital related-products, argued that the GATT is a preferable forum since the degree of trade liberalization is more encompassing under the GATT than the GATS.

The quantitative restrictions and discriminatory regulations are mandatorily prohibited under the GATT, whereas market access and national treatment obligations under the GATS only exist to the extent a WTO Member made specific commitments to a particular sector or sub-sector of services in its GATS Schedule. The US also claimed that the principle of technological neutrality indicates the nature of a product should not depend on a different method of distribution.[268] The EC, on the contrary, motivated by economic and cultural diverse interests, contended that any electronic delivery should be treated as services and subject to the scope of the GATS because digitally delivered products do not have physical attributes and Members have more regulatory autonomy under the GATS to protect cultural differences.[269]

[266] *See* Joost Pauwelyn, *Squaring Free Trade in Cultural Goods and Services with Chinese Censorship: The WTO Appellate Body Report on China – Audiovisual*, Melbourne Journal of International Law, 11(1), pp. 119-140 (2010); and Paola Conconi and Joost Pauwelyn, *Trading Culture: Appellate Body Report on China – Audiovisuals (WT/DS363/AB/R. adopted 19 January 2010)*, World Trade Review, 10:1, pp. 95-118 (2011).

[267] *See* Rolf H. Weber, *Digital Trade in WTO-Law – Taking Stock and Looking Ahead*, Asian Journal of WTO & Int'l Health Law and Policy (AJWH), Vol.5:1 (2010).

[268] For a comprehensive analysis, *see* Sacha Wunsch-Vincent, *The WTO, the Internet and Trade in Digital-Products: EU-US Perspectives*, North America: Hart Publishing (2006), pp. 35-80.

[269] Ibid.

Technological innovation has made it difficult to classify a product based on intuition alone. The purpose here, therefore, is not to provide a solution for this classification issue but to point out that focusing on the tangible nature of a product would inevitably categorize electronically delivered products as services and result in legal uncertainty when a product is able to be delivered by both electronic and non-electronic means. On the one hand, on a multilateral level, no substantial progress had been made during the past ten years with respect to the classification of digital products. On the other hand, on the bilateral and regional level, some movements can be seen from the Preferential Trade Agreements (PTAs) negotiations lead by the US.[270] Given the increasing number of electronically delivered products in the global economy, the WTO adjudicating bodies will be asked to clarify on the classification problem in the near future. A panel needs to look beyond the tangibility criterion and take into account the ordinary meaning of terms in both the GATT and the GATS, the context of the agreements, the basic WTO principles, and the economic activities in the given market to make a holistic analysis.[271]

C. *Confirmation of Technological Neutrality under the GATS*

Pursuant to Article 31 and Article 32 of the Vienna Convention, in order to define the scope of 'Sound recording distribution services', the panel examined the ordinary meaning of 'sound recordings' and 'distribution services' and assessed the context of China's GATS Schedule, the GATS provisions, and the GATS Schedule of other Members. The panel further verified the objects and purposes of the GATS and had recourse to other supplementary means of interpretation to give meaning to 'sound recording distribution services'.[272] The pan-

[270] For example, the binding bilateral Free Trade Agreements (FTAs) between the US and Chile implements the E-Commerce Chapter, which is directly applicable to electronically delivered content products. Bypassing addressing the classification problems, the E-Commerce Chapters directly specify the applicability of national treatment obligations to certain digital products and both parties should accord no less favourable treatment to like physically and electronically delivered content products.

[271] *See* Stewart A. Baker et al., *E-Products and the WTO*, 35 Int. Lawyer 5, 6(2001); Joost Pauwelyn, *Squaring Free Trade in Cultural Goods and Services with Chinese Censorship: The WTO Appellate Body Report on China – Audiovisual*, Melbourne Journal of International Law, 11(1), pp. 119-140 (2010); *see* also Sam Fleuter, *The Role of Digital Products Under the WTO: A New Framework for GATT and GATS Classification*, Chicago Journal of International Law, Vol.17, No.1, 5 (2016).

[272] Panel Report, *China – Measures Affecting Trading Rights and Distribution Services for Certain Publications and Audiovisual Entertainment Products* (cited as *China – Audiovisual Products*), WT/DS363/R (12 August 2009), paras. 7.1168- 7.1247.

el concluded that the entry "Sound recording distribution services", under the heading of "Audiovisual Services" in sector 2.D of China's Schedule, extends to the distribution of sound recordings through non-physical means, i.e., the Internet. Regarding the technological neutrality argument brought by the US, the panel stated that there is no need for the further invocation of the principle of technological neutrality since the core meaning of China's commitment on 'sound recording distribution services' covers the distribution of audio content in electronic form.[273]

On appeal, China argued that the panel erred in interpreting the entry "Sound recording distribution services" in its Schedule as it encompassed distribution of the services through electronic means. To begin its analysis, the Appellate Body emphasized that "interpretation pursuant to the customary rule codified in Article 31 of the Vienna Convention, is ultimately a holistic exercise that should not be mechanically subdivided into rigid components".[274] The Appellate Body upheld the panel's findings for several reasons. First, the Appellate Body was not persuaded by China's claim that the panel erred in its consideration of dictionary definitions of the terms 'sound recordings' and 'distribution'. According to the dictionary meaning of the term 'sound recordings', the panel found that "the term "recording" cannot be limited to sound embedded on physical media, but refers to the content, regardless of the technology of storage or distribution of the sound".[275] As for the term 'distribution', the panel is of the opinion that 'distribution' could be understood as "the dispersal of things of value, and that this can involve tangible or intangible products".[276]

Second, when considering the context analysis of the panel, the Appellate Body agreed with the panel's observation that if China intended to cover exclusively the distribution of audiovisual products in physical form, it would have scheduled the services under the sector 4.D Distribution Service, where the distribution of physical goods is generally covered, instead inserting the services in question under the sector 2.D Audiovisual Services. Additionally, the Appellate Body found the term "distribution" in China's Schedule is formulated in such a way as used in Article XVIII (b) of the GATS, which includes the production, *distribution*, marketing, sale, and delivery of a *service*. In conclu-

---

[273] Ibid., paras. 7.1256-7.1258.

[274] Appellate Body Report, *China – Measures Affecting Trading Rights and Distribution Services for Certain Publications and Audiovisual Entertainment Products* (cited as *China – Audiovisual Products*), WT/DS363/AB/R (21 December 2009), para. 348.

[275] Panel Report, *China – Measures Affecting Trading Rights and Distribution Services for Certain Publications and Audiovisual Entertainment Products* (cited as *China – Audiovisual Products*), WT/DS363/R (12 August 2009), para. 7.1176.

[276] Ibid., para. 7.1181.

sion, the Appellate Body upheld panel's contextual interpretation that China's commitment to "Sound recording distribution services" includes the electronic distribution of sound recordings.[277]

Third, the Appellate Body examined whether the panel's interpretation is inconsistent with the principle of progressive liberalization under the preamble of the GATS. China claimed that the principle of progressive liberalization does not allow a panel to interpret the terms of a WTO Members GATS Schedule based on the contemporary meaning at the time of interpretation since this approach will expand the scope of the Member's commitments in its Schedule. The Appellate Body disagreed with China and considered that the terms in China's GATS Schedule are "sufficiently generic that what they apply to may change over time".[278] The Appellate Body further stated:

> "... the terms of GATS specific commitments based on the notion that ordinary meaning to be attributed to those terms can only be the meaning that they had at the time the Schedule was concluded would mean that very similar or identically worded commitments could be given different meanings, content, and coverage depending on the date of their adoption or the date a Member's accession to the treaty. *Such interpretation would undermine the predictability, security, and clarity of GATS specific commitments*, which are undertaken through successive rounds of negotiation, and which must be interpreted in accordance with customary rules of interpretation of public international law. (emphasis added)."[279]

Finally, the Appellate Body considered China's claims that panel's approach to Article 32 of the Vienna Convention was "fundamentally flawed from the outset". The Appellate Body noted that the purpose of treaty interpretation under Article 31 and Article 32 of the Vienna Convention is to ascertain the common intention of all the contracting parties, not one member alone, and the circumstances of the conclusion of the treaty are relevant in finding this common intention.[280] Thus, the Appellate Body concluded that the panel did not err in simply finding that "certain circumstances of the conclusion of the treaty did not exclude the possibility that China's GATS commitments also extended to the

---

[277] Appellate Body Report, *China – Measures Affecting Trading Rights and Distribution Services for Certain Publications and Audiovisual Entertainment Products* (cited as *China – Audiovisual Products*), WT/DS363/AB/R (21 December 2009), paras. 358-385.

[278] Ibid., para. 396.

[279] Ibid., para. 397.

[280] Ibid., para. 405.

electronic distribution of sound recordings".[281] The Appellate Body upheld the panel's overall conclusion that the entry "Sound recording distribution services" under the heading 2.D "Audiovisual Services" extends to the distribution of sound recording in non-physical form, notably through the Internet.

Although both the US and China discussed the applicability of technological neutrality to the measures at issue, the panel avoided the issue by merely mentioning that the principle of technological neutrality is not a concern in the dispute. Accordingly, the Appellate Body made no reference to the principle. Nevertheless, both the panel and the Appellate Body have adopted an evolutionary approach to treaty interpretation and explored the meaning of respective terms in relation to their contemporary meaning. The impact of this dynamic interpretative method on the future cases regarding Internet-related services should not be underestimated since whether WTO law could accommodate to the trade in digital age depends to a large extent on how a panel interprets the terms of the provisions that are drafted in 1995 when the development of the ICTs was not foreseeable by the negotiators.

D. General Exception under Article XX(a) of the GATT

China invoked Article XX(a) of the GATT to justify its WTO-inconsistent measures which restrict the right to import certain products exclusively to wholly state-owned Chinese enterprises. China claimed that its measures established a system of selection of import entities which are able to provide an effective content review mechanism for imported cultural goods. According to China, in order to protect its citizens from the negative impact of the content of imported cultural goods, particularly those that depict or vindicate violence or pornography, an effective content review mechanism and the selection of import entities by Chinese authorities are necessary to the realization of the high level of public moral protection that China intended to pursue.[282]

One of the reasons the *China – Audiovisual Products* case attracted a great deal of attention from commentators is that it raises a sensitive political issue referring to the Chinese government's censorship control over the importation of foreign cultural products.[283] Some optimistic human rights proponents had

---

[281] Ibid., para. 409.

[282] Panel Report, *China – Measures Affecting Trading Rights and Distribution Services for Certain Publications and Audiovisual Entertainment Products* (cited as *China – Audiovisual Products*), WT/DS363/R (12 August 2009), paras. 4.113-4.420.

[283] *See* Panagiotis Delimatsis, The Puzzling Interaction of Trade and Public Morals in the Digital Era. In: Mira Burri & Thomas Cottier, *Trade Governance in the Digital Age*

hoped the findings of the adjudicating bodies could open the Chinese market access to content-related products and ultimately enhance freedom of information and expression in China. In some ways, the case shows the opposite. Although both the panel and the Appellate Body applied dynamically interpretative methods to decide whether the measures are necessary to protect 'public morals', they took an expansive view of the concept by merely "assuming" that the imported materials "could have a negative impact on 'public morals' in China". By not touching the substantive content of 'public morals', the Appellate Body missed the opportunity to interpret the term in the light of international legal norms and standards. One commentator pointed out that "*China – Audiovisual* may be a legal win for the US Government, it is not a win for freedom of speech".[284]

a. The Scope of Public Morals

The panel began its analysis under Article XX of the GATT by first considering whether the challenged measures are designed to address public moral concerns. The panel first noted that the US did not specifically contest that the measures in question are not measures to protect public morals. In contrast, what the US challenged is the means China has chosen to achieve its objective of protecting public morals.[285] The panel further looked towards the Appellate Body's decision in *US – Gambling* regarding public morals exception under GATS Article XIV(a). It recognized that as for the similarity between two provisions, the interpretative approach of GATS Article XIV(a) is applicable to the purpose GATT Article XX(a) analysis. Consequently, the panel emphasized that the term public morals "denotes standards of right and wrong conduct maintained by or on behalf of a community or nation", and members "should be given some scope to define and apply for themselves the concepts of 'public morals' … in

---

World Trade Forum, Cambridge University Press (2012), pp. 276-296; Elanor A. Mangin, *Market Access in China – Publications and Audiovisual Materials: A Moral Victory with a Silver Lining*, Berkeley Technology Law Journal, Vol.25, I:1(2010), pp. 279-310; and Julia Ya Qin, *Pushing the Limits of Global Governance: Trading Rights, Censorship, and WTO Jurisprudence – A Commentary on the China – Publication Case*, Chinese Journal of International Law, Vol.10 (2011), pp. 271-322.

284 Joost Pauwelyn, *Squaring Free Trade in Cultural Goods and Services with Chinese Censorship: The WTO Appellate Body Report on China – Audiovisual*, Melbourne Journal of International Law, 11(1) (2010), p. 135.

285 Panel Report, *China – Measures Affecting Trading Rights and Distribution Services for Certain Publications and Audiovisual Entertainment Products* (cited as *China – Audiovisual Products*), WT/DS363/R (12 August 2009), paras. 7.756 & 7.763.

their respective territories, according to their own system and scales of values."[286]

According to the Chinese regulations, as set forth in Article 26 of the *Publications Regulation*, no publication may contain content that, for example, 'jeopardizes the solidarity, sovereignty, and territorial integrity of the nation', 'divulges national secrets, jeopardizes national security or injures the national glory and interest', 'propagates evil cults or superstition', 'jeopardizes social morality or fine cultural traditions of nationalities' and is 'otherwise prohibited by laws, administrative regulations, and provisions of the State.'[287] Article 27 of the *Publication Regulation* prevents minors from accessing illegal and unethical publications and audiovisual products.[288] China claimed that the dissemination of the listed content would have a negative impact on public morals in China and the measures at issue are designed to protect Chinese cultural and traditional values.

The panel noted that it is up to each WTO member to determine what level of protection is appropriate in the given situation and China has adopted the high level of protection of public morals for its territory in respect to the relevant products.[289] The panel further recognized that "the content and scope of the concept of "public morals" can vary from Member to Member, as they are influenced by each Members' prevailing social, cultural, ethical and religious values".[290] In the light of above elements and in the absence of the contestation from the US, the panel had no difficulty to assume that "each of the prohibited types of content listed in China's measures is such that, if it were brought into China as part of a physical product, it could have a negative impact on "public morals" in China within the meaning of Article XX(a) of the GATT 1994".[291]

b. Necessary to Protect Public Morals

Notwithstanding the fact that the relative importance of Chinese measures in pursuing its objective policies is presumed, the panel was not persuaded that the measures are necessary to protect public morals within the meaning of Article

---

[286] Ibid., para. 7.759. The panel reiterated that the content of public morals for members can vary in time and space, depending upon a range of factors, including prevailing social, cultural, ethical and religious values.
[287] Ibid., para. 7.760
[288] Ibid., para. 7.761.
[289] Ibid., paras. 7.816-7.819.
[290] Ibid., para. 7.763.
[291] Ibid.

XX(a) of the GATT. On appeal, China contested several panel's findings on the 'necessity' analysis. China believed that the panel erred in concluding that some of the Chinese measures made no material contribution to the protection of public morals, in extending the restrictive effect of the provisions to 'those wishing to engage in importing', and in deciding the alternative proposed by the US is reasonably available to China.[292] Based on the standards of 'necessity' test established by previous WTO cases, the Appellate Body weighed and balanced the contribution of China's measures to the protection of public morals in China, the restrictive effect of the measures on international commerce, and the availability of a genuine alternative.

i. The Contribution of the Measures to Protect Public Morals

Before examining whether the challenged Chinese measures contribute to the realization of public morals in China, the Appellate Body first recalled the findings from previous cases that, in the process of weighing and balancing a series of factors, "the greater the contribution a measure makes to the objective pursued, the more likely it is to be characterized as necessary".[293] To determine whether a measure contributes to the achievement of the objective pursued, the Appellate Body noted that the contribution is not limited to the 'actual contribution' as the contribution of a measure may not be immediately observable in the short-term. The Appellate Body recited the opinion from *Brazil – Retreated Tyres*, which stated:

> "... a panel might conclude that [a measure] is necessary on the basis of a demonstration that [it] is apt to produce a material contribution to the achievement of its objective. This demonstration could consist of quantitative projections in the future, or quantitative reasoning based on a set of hypotheses that are tested and supported by sufficient evidence."[294]

The Appellate Body agreed with the panel's findings that state ownership requirement and the exclusion of foreign-invested enterprises did not contribute to the protection of public morals in China. According to the Appellate Body, since enterprises with private investment would also be able to attract qualified personnel to conduct content review properly, China did not provide sufficient

---

[292] Appellate Body Report, *China – Measures Affecting Trading Rights and Distribution Services for Certain Publications and Audiovisual Entertainment Products* (cited as *China – Audiovisual Products*), WT/DS363/AB/R (21 December 2009), para.234.
[293] Ibid., paras. 250-252.
[294] Ibid., para. 253.

evidence to prove "a connection between the exclusive ownership of the State in the equity of an import entity and that entity's contribution to the protection of public morals in China".[295] Furthermore, based on similar reasons, the Appellate Body found that the complete exclusion of particular types of enterprises in China from engaging in the importation of the relevant products did not make a material contribution to the protection of public morals.[296] As for the State plan requirement, the Appellate Body reversed the panel's findings on the basis that the panel wrongly assumed that the requirement imposing a limitation on the number of import entities could make a material contribution to the protection of public morals.[297] In sum, according to the Appellate Body, none of the appealed measures make a material contribution to the protection of public morals in China.

ii. The Restrictive Effect on International Trade

Moving to the next step of the necessity test, the Appellate Body considered the restrictive effect of the measures at issue on international commerce. China appealed that the panel erred in including an assessment of the effect on those wishing to engage in importing since the panel's decision placed an 'unsustainable burden of proof' on China. The Appellate Body noted that the text of Article XX(a) does not provide explicit guidance on evaluating whether the restrictive effect assessment is limited to the effect on imports of the relevant products or could extend to the effect on importers or potential importers.[298] By looking into the chapeau of Article XX and the preamble of the GATT, the Appellate Body is of the view that the restrictive effect test must be undertaken in the light of the measure at issue, the specific obligation of covered agreements that the challenged measure infringes, and the defence being invoked.[299]

Based on this approach, the Appellate Body first looked into China's Accession Protocol and found that the right to trade granted by China's obligation under paragraph 5.1 of the Accession Protocol concerns not only the question of what can be traded but more directly to 'who' is entitled to engage in trading. Thus, considering the nature of the specific obligation, the Appellate Body agreed with the panel to take into account the restrictive effect on beneficiaries of the right to trade. Additionally, the Appellate Body disagreed with China that

---

[295] Ibid., para. 268.
[296] Ibid., paras. 268-269 & 277-278.
[297] Ibid., paras. 296-299.
[298] Ibid., para. 303.
[299] Ibid., para. 306.

the inclusion of the restrictive effect of a measure to those wishing to engage in the importation places 'an unsustainable burden of proof' on China. The Appellate Body recognized that by adopting the most restrictive measures, which *a priori* deprive certain enterprises of the right to trade, China needs to ensure its measures are carefully designed not to constitute an unnecessarily restrictive effect on international trade.[300] In other words, the less trade restrictive the measure, the easier it can be considered as necessary. For all the reasons above, the Appellate Body concluded that the panel does not err in its analysis regarding the restrictive effect of the Chinese measures on international trade.

iii. The Reasonable Alternative Measure

Following the well-established case law, if a panel's analysis yields a preliminary conclusion deduced from the weighing and balancing process that a measure is necessary, the necessity of the measure must be confirmed by comparing the measure with possible alternatives in the light of the importance of the interests or values at stake. On appeal, China contested that the panel erred in finding the alternative measure proposed by the US, which suggested that giving sole responsibility for conducting a content review to the Chinese government would constitute a genuine alternative, is reasonably available. China argued that the proposed alternative is merely theoretical in nature and would impose an undue and excessive burden on China. According to China, the proposed alternative measure would impose undue financial and administrative burden, would require China to engage in tremendous restructuring, would cause substantial technical difficulties, and would make it impossible to double check the content at the customs level.[301]

The Appellate Body first recalled that an alternative measure might be considered not to be reasonably available if it is merely theoretical (e.g., where the responding party is not capable of taking it), or if the measure imposes an undue financial or technical burden on the Member. Also, a proposed alternative measure might be considered not to be reasonably available if it could not preserve the responding party's right to achieve the desired level of protection with

---

[300] Ibid., para. 310. When considering the restrictive effect of a specific measure, the Appellate Body emphasized:

> ..., if a Member chooses to adopt a very restrictive measure, it will have to ensure that the measure is carefully designed so that the other elements to be taken into account in weighing and balancing the factors relevant to an assessment of the "necessity" of the measure will "outweigh" such restrictive effect.

[301] Ibid., para. 322.

respect to the objective policy pursued under Article XX of the GATT.[302] The Appellate Body further reiterated the findings in *US – Gambling* and stated that it is the complaining party who bears the burden of identifying possible alternative measures that the responding party could have taken.

The Appellate Body agreed with the panel that the evidence submitted by China did not demonstrate that the alternative proposed by the US couldn't make a material contribution to the realization of its desired high level of public morals protection.[303] The Appellate Body recognized that "adopting any alternative measure will, by definition, involve some change, and this alone does not suffice to demonstrate that the alternative would impose an undue burden".[304] In this regard, the Appellate Body upheld panel's finding that the measure at issue could not be considered necessary in the light of the fact that "at least one of the alternative measures proposed by the United States is an alternative "reasonably available" to China".[305]

E. Indications for the Protection of Public Morals in the Digital Age

The decisions of the panel and the Appellate Body in *China – Audiovisual Products* on the public morals exception might have a profound influence on the development of Internet policies at both the national and international levels. By having little difficulty in establishing the link between China's censorship measures and the protection of public morals under Article XX(a) of the GATT, the adjudicating bodies' opinions were criticized for neglecting to consider the fact that the Chinese measures may violate the fundamental principles of internally recognized human rights. In addition, by agreeing with the US that giving sole responsibility for conducting a content review to the Chinese government could constitute a genuine alternative measure, the Appellate Body's decision might result in a more restrictive censorship regime on imports in comparison with the current state-trusted entities content review system.[306]

---

[302] Ibid., para. 318.
[303] Ibid., paras. 324-326.
[304] Ibid., para. 328.
[305] Ibid., para. 332.
[306] *See* Panagiotis Delimatsis, *Protecting Public Morals in a Digital Age: Revisiting the WTO Rulings on US – Gambling and China – Publications and Audiovisual Products*, Journal of International Economic Law, Vol.14, No.2 (2011), pp. 257-293; Joost Pauwelyn, *Squaring Free Trade in Cultural Goods and Services with Chinese Censorship: The WTO Appellate Body Report on China – Audiovisual*, Melbourne Journal of International Law, 11(1), pp. 119-140 (2010); and Julia Ya Qin, *Pushing the Limits of Global Governance: Trading Rights, Censorship, and WTO Jurisprudence – A Commentary*

However, it is understandable that the WTO adjudicating bodies intended to avoid ruling on the thorny 'trade versus public morals' issue. The debate regarding the contradictive values between promoting free trade and protecting public morality existed prior to the establishment of the WTO and the derogation from the substantive obligations is not a unique notion in international trade law. For instance, based on the conception that no right is absolute, most fundamental human values codified in modern human rights law are limited to the extent of protecting public morals, national security or the rights of others.

Nevertheless, how to balance a Member's regulatory autonomy in protecting morality and its obligations under international law is a challenging task for the adjudicate branch of the WTO. A panel needs to weigh, on the one hand, how much deference should be given to the Member States to protect vital social interests in accordance with national values. On the other hand, the panel should have sufficient latitude at its disposal to prevent a far-reaching public morals application and maintain the consistency of the trading system, taking into account the collective purposes within the international legal systems.[307]

The advances in information and communication technology complicate the already tangled public morals and public order issues under the WTO. The borderless and transnational nature of the Internet and the increasing participation of the Internet intermediaries in the international forum are challenging the components of state sovereignty in various aspects. Consequently, it is unsurprising that WTO Member States have strong interests in harnessing the changes brought about by the Internet with regulatory responses.[308]

Although these technologies are acting as a significant driving force for modern innovation and economic growth, the regulatory control, accompanied by often burdensome and disproportionate regulations, is becoming a common phenomenon. To deviate from the substantive international obligations, nation states have increasingly justified their restrictive censorship measures for the purposes of protecting public morals or maintaining public order. The *China – Audiovisual Products* case reflects this conundrum, and the WTO adjudicating bodies missed the opportunity to clarify how much margin of appreciation

---

on the China – Publication Case, Chinese Journal of International Law, Vol.10 (2011), pp. 271-322.

[307] *See* Nicolas F. Diebold, *The Morals and Order Exceptions in WTO Law: Balancing the Toothless Tiger and the Undermining Mole*, Journal of Economic Law, Vol.11, No.1 (2007), pp. 43-74.

[308] *See* Mira Burri & Thomas Cottier, Introduction: Digital technologies and international trade regulation (2012). In: Mira Burri and Thomas Cottier (eds.), *Trade Governance in the Digital Age – World Trade Forum*, Cambridge University Press, pp. 1-14.

should be given to the Members to define the content of morality within their territory.

A Member's discretion in determining the scope of public morality under both Article XX(a) of the GATT and Article XIV(a) of the GATS should be subject to the standard of review under the WTO.[309] While there is no explicit language in the DSU regarding how to apply the standard of review when a panel is called upon to examine a Member State's measure, the Appellate Body's opinions in *EC – Hormones* may shed some light. The Appellate Body explained that, by taking Article 11 of the DSU into consideration[310], when applying a standard of review, a panel should not give a complete deference to WTO Members, nor should the panel have a complete *de novo* determination to substitute its own findings for those of the national authority.[311] However, various variants are conceivable between the spectrums of these two extreme parameters, which were not explicitly mentioned by the Appellate Body.[312] In general, the application of the standard of review is case-specific, and in order to make an objective assessment, a panel should be able to examine a Member's measures in accordance with the ordinary meaning to be given to the terms, in their context, and in the light of their objects and purposes.

---

[309] *See* Matthias Oesch, Standards of Review in WTO Dispute Resolution, Journal of International Economic Law, Vol.6, No.3 (2003), pp. 635-659; John H. Jackson, *Sovereignty, the WTO, and Changing Fundamentals of International Law*, New York: Cambridge University Press (2006), pp. 169-172; and Steven P. Croley & John H. Jackson, *WTO Dispute Procedures, Standard of Review, and Deference to National Governments*, The American Journal of International Law, Vol.90 (1996), pp. 193-213.

[310] Article 11 of the DSU seems to be the most suitable legal basis for the application of standard of review in the WTO system. It stipulates:

> The function of panels is to assist the DSB in discharging its responsibilities under the Understanding and the covered agreements. Accordingly, a panel should make an objective assessment of the matter before it, including and objective assessment of the facts of the case and the applicability of and conformity with the relevant covered agreements, and make such other findings as will assist the DSB in making the recommendations or in giving the rulings provided for in the covered agreements.

[311] Appellate Body Report, *EC Measures Concerning Meat and Meat Products (Hormones)* (cited as *EC – Hormones*), WT/DS26/AB/R and WT/DS48/AB/R (16 January 1998), para. 117.

[312] Ibid.

IV. Conclusion

Given that purpose of the book is to address Internet censorship measures under the international regulatory framework, Chapter 3 is intended to examine whether WTO laws possess the necessary flexibility and resilience to accommodate the changes brought about by the new ICTs in international trade. Since the GATT and the GATS were drafted at the time when the impact of the Internet and E-commerce on international trade was not foreseeable by most of the negotiators, the interaction between digital technologies and trade regulations is unclear. Additionally, the unique characteristics of the Internet, along with complex economic, political, and cultural interests of nation states, challenge WTO law in many perspectives. Yet, from the materials covered by the chapter, strong evidence can be found in the WTO jurisprudence that, in the light of the principle of technological neutrality and in terms of an evolutionary approach in treaty interpretation, the WTO dispute settlement system still plays a crucial role in defining the legal scope of digital trade.

Based on the analysis in *US – Gambling* and *China – Audiovisual Products*, both the panel and the Appellate Body agreed that the WTO obligations should not be differentiated by the means of the delivery, and the meaning of a term should not be interpreted on the basis of the storage or distribution technologies but rather on the nature of its content. The application of the principle of technological neutrality in the context of WTO law has two significant indications for the development of trade in the digital age. First, it confirms that all the GATS provisions, either with respect to general obligations or specific commitments, are applicable to the supply of services through electronic means. Second, the principle establishes that in determining the 'likeness' of products or services within the meaning of the national treatment obligation under Article III of the GATT and Article XVII of the GATS, a panel should focus on the attributes of the products or services *per se*, rather than on the means by which they are delivered. Therefore, different methods of supply do not, by themselves, make the products or services unlike. The panel needs to examine the nature and extent of the competitive relationship between the domestic and foreign products or services in the given market.

Furthermore, in the two WTO cases, the adjudicating bodies adopted an evolutionary approach in treaty interpretation, which provides the basic principles for the Internet censorship analysis in Chapter 4. First, when determining the extent and scope of WTO Members' specific commitments in the GATS Schedule, the panel and the Appellate Body confirmed that since a Member's GATS Schedule serves as an integral part of the WTO Agreement, in accordance with the customary rules of treaty interpretation under Articles 31 and 32 of the Vienna Convention, it is the common intentions of the Members, rather than the intent of an individual Member, that count in order to ascertain the meaning of a Member's commitments. The Appellate Body further explained that most of the terms in a Member's GATS Schedule are sufficiently generic that what they apply to may change over time and, therefore, the meaning of a term should be explored within its contemporary meaning at the time of interpretation. Since many Internet-related services, such as search engines and social networks, did not exist at the time that WTO Members negotiated their GATS commitments, it is through this dynamic interpretative mechanism that WTO law can still appropriately adapt to the changes brought about by the new technologies.

Secondly, the evolutionary approach in treaty interpretation is also reflected in *US – Gambling* and *China – Audiovisual Products* when the panel and the Appellate Body interpreted the public morals exceptions under Article XX(a) of the GATT and Article XIV(a) of the GATS. The term 'public morals' was defined as "standards of right and wrong conduct maintained by or on behalf of a community or nation". The panel recognized that the meaning to be given to this term can vary in time and space, depending on prevailing social, cultural, ethical, and religious values. It can be perceived from the case reviews that the WTO panels tried to avoid a collision with 'trade and public morals' issues since great deference has been given to the Members to define the content of morality and decide the desired level of protection.

However, according to Article 11 of the DSU, such deference is not absolute and must be subject to the standard of review in future WTO disputes. Under the standard of review in WTO law, a balance must be established between granting discretion to WTO Members and ensuring the security and predictability of the trading system. As concluded in Chapter 1, in order to make an 'objective assessment', a panel should take into account general principles of law and other international law to determine the genuine meaning of the terms in the WTO agreements. The WTO adjudicating bodies, therefore, should be able to weigh and balance all the evidence and then determine whether a Member is acting in good faith to pursue its legitimate objectives.

Chapter 4. China Case Study

The importance of the China case study to understanding the relations between government Internet censorship measures and international law can be analyzed from several perspectives. First, having 688 million Internet users by the end of 2015, China has the most Internet users of any country in the world. Unsurprisingly, China also has the biggest E-commerce market. Given its authoritarian politics, many human rights advocates had optimistically expected that the Internet would bring political and social reforms to China's democratic development. Scholars believed that the very distinctive and decentralized technical characteristics of the Internet have the competence to promote political revolution.[1] Nevertheless, since the Internet was first installed in China, the Chinese government has shown its determination and capability to govern this new information technology while taking advantage of the economic prosperity it can bring.

Secondly, whereas the Internet infrastructure and Internet-related services in China have experienced unprecedented growth in terms of scale and quality,[2] the Internet environment in China remains one of the most oppressive in the world due to the comprehensive and multilayered Internet censorship mechanisms. In 2010, the Chinese authority published its first White Paper on Internet policy and emphasized that "within Chinese territory, the Internet is under the jurisdiction of Chinese sovereignty".[3] The same conception of state sovereignty over the sphere of the Internet was reiterated by State President Xi Jinping on several occasions. Efficiently controlling the Internet has become the central political ideology of China to prevent threats to national security and social values. At both political and economic levels, the Chinese government's grip on the Internet has been tightened over the past few years.

Thirdly, in the name of protecting morality or security, the Chinese government has implemented pervasive legal and technical mechanisms for online censorship to suppress political dissidents and restrict foreign companies from doing business in China. Irrespective of the legitimate objectives, by controlling the free flow of information and restricting Internet-related trade in goods and services, any Internet-related restrictive measures will inevitably have adverse

---

[1] *See* Yochai Benkler, *The Wealth of the Networks: How Social Production Transforms Markets and Freedom*, New Haven: Yale University Press (2006), pp. 10-11.

[2] *See* Jyh-An Lee and Ching-Yi Liu, *Forbidden City Enclosed by the Great Firewall: The Law and Power of Internet Filtering in China*, Minn. J. L. Sci. & Tech., Vol.13:1 (2012), pp. 125-151.

[3] The Information Office of the State Council of the People's Republic of China, *White Paper – The Internet in China* (8 June 2010).

impacts on human rights and international trade.[4] Nation states are no longer unitary subjects in international relations and the governance of the Internet requires international cooperation. Countries imposing comprehensive legal and technical restraints on the Internet need to justify their restrictions in conformity with international legal norms and principles.

Section I of Chapter 4 provides a background study of Internet development in China. The Internet was officially introduced into China in 1994. Notwithstanding this late beginning, the number of Internet users and online markets are increasing rapidly in the past two decades. The explosive growth of the Internet in China does not necessarily guarantee political liberalization and a free market. Section II introduces the Internet censorship mechanisms adopted by the Chinese authorities at all levels of government to monitor and control Internet content and users' activities. The sophisticated technical surveillance from the backbone of the Internet to local service providers, combined with self-censorship and criminalization of online behaviors, might cause limitations on people's enjoyment of rights on the Internet and on international trade.

Sections III and IV, therefore, discuss the extent to which China's Internet censorship measures will potentially violate international human rights law and WTO law. Based on the analysis in Chapter 2, Section III first examines whether the restrictions on the free flow of information and arbitrary collection of personal information constitute intrusions to a person's right to freedom of expression and information and the right to privacy. Section III further analyzes the notion of Internet sovereignty. Generally speaking, national sovereignty applies to cyberspace. Living in the middle of a transition, where sovereignty seems to be the direction in which Internet governance is heading, therefore, the debate on Internet governance should no longer be whether countries have the legitimate right to proclaim sovereignty over the Internet, but how to define the boundary between a state's sovereign authority and its commitments and obligations in international law. Next, on the basis of the analysis in Chapter 3, Section IV provides a *Google – China* scenario as a research baseline for discussing Internet censorship measures in the context of WTO law and examines whether the WTO is an adequate forum to address the measures at issue. Put differently, Section IV intends to study whether a panel has the competence to address the collective purposes of the international trade regime to carry out the responsibility for the consequences of its practices.

---

[4] *See* Ada Bogliolo Piancastelli de Siqueira, *It's in the Way That You Use It: Revisiting Trade and Human Rights in the Case of Online Censorship*, Southwestern Journal of Int'l Law, Vol.20 (2013), pp. 39-79.

I. Internet Development in China

Since the earliest stage of Internet development in China, the Chinese government has realized the potential trade opportunities which the Internet could bring to economic modernization and growth. Consequently, authorities at various levels have been actively involved in expanding the relevant underlying infrastructures and initiating E-commerce projects.[5] Despite the continuous expansion of Internet populations and markets, Internet-related infrastructure, platforms, or online business forums are dominated either by state-owned entities or indigenous companies.

A. The Arrival of the Internet and Mobile Users in China

Early in April 1994, at the Sino-US Joint Committee on Scientific and Technological Cooperation conference, China gained the formal approval of the National Science Foundation (NSF) to be connected to the Internet. On April 20, 1994, Sprint, a US company, put 64 kbps international lines into operation for connecting the National Computing and Networking Facility of China[6] (NCFC) to the Internet.[7] This event was marked as the birth of China's earliest global Internet. In 2008, the number of Internet users in China surpassed those in the US for the first time, reaching 298 million by the end of the year. By the end of 2015, China had roughly 688 million Internet users, an increase of 39.51 million over the previous year, and the Internet penetration rate had reached 50.3%.[8]

---

[5] *See* Anonymous, *China and the Internet – An Uphill Fight for Freedom*, Harvard International Review (2009), pp. 68-73.

[6] National Computing and Networking Facility of China (NCFC) was a high-tech information infrastructure project among the "key discipline development projects" supported by the World Bank. NCFC was also financed by State Development Planning Commission, Chinese Academy of Science, National Natural Science Foundation of China, and State Education Commission. The ultimate purpose of the project was to build up the backbone network of China and three academic networks.

[7] *See* Tai, Zixue, *The Internet in China: Cyberspace and Civil Society*, New York: Routledge (2006), pp. 119-160.

[8] China Internet Network Information Center (CNNIC), *37th Statistical Survey Report on the Internet Development in China* (January 2016).

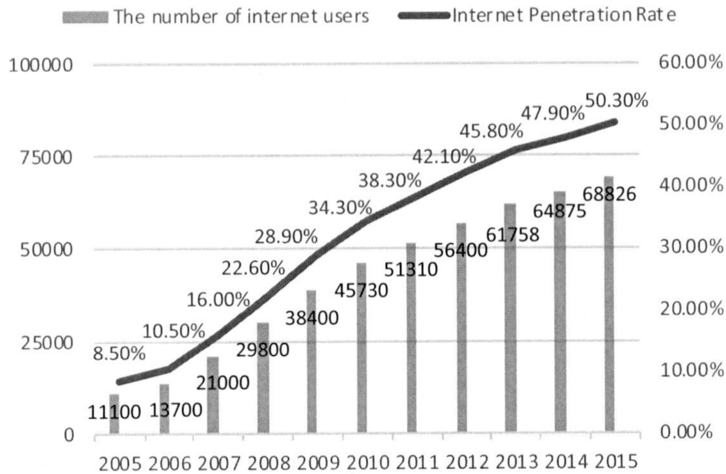

Figure 1. The Number of Chinese Internet Users and Internet Penetration Rate (Source: CNNIC Statistical Survey on Internet Development in China 2015.12)

Additionally, the growing number of mobile Internet users consolidates the influence of the Internet on the economy and society in China. In December 2015, the number of mobile Internet users in China reached 620 million, and over 90% of Internet users in China used their mobile phones to access it.[9] According to a survey carried out by the China Internet Network Information Center (CNNIC), 18.5% of Internet users, about 127 million people, were connected to the Internet only through mobile networks in 2015. Mobile phone are the most prominent devices to boost the growth of Internet users. In addition, the mobile Internet has shaped new forms of social life, changed consumer behavior, and created innovative business models.

In 2015, Internet users spend an average of 26.2 hours on the Internet per week in China.[10] Consequently, fueled by the massive number of active Netizens, Chinese cyberspace is brimming with personal Internet applications. Instant messaging, search engines, Internet news, online videos, online music, E-payments, and online shopping are the most popular online applications and have been growing steadily in the past years (*see* Table 1). Instant messaging is the most used Internet application in China. The suppliers of mainstream instant messaging applications have shifted development direction from basic commu-

[9] Ibid.

[10] Ibid.

nication needs to a comprehensive platform connecting all sorts of daily living services, such as mobile payment and taxi services. WeChat (微信), QQ, Momo (陌陌), WangXin (旺信), and Youni (有你) are the most popular mobile instant messaging applications in China.

	2015		2014		
Application	**The number of users (1000)**	**The percentage of Internet users using the applications**	**The number of users (1000)**	**The percentage of Internet users using the applications**	**Annual growth rate**
Instant messaging	62, 480	90.7%	58,776	90.6%	6.2%
Search engine	56,623	82.3%	52,223	80.5%	8.4%
Internet news	56,440	82.0%	51,894	80.0%	8.8%
Online video	50,391	73.2%	43,298	66.7%	16.4%
Online music	50,137	72.8%	47,807	73.7%	4.9%
E-payment	41,618	60.5%	30,431	46.9%	36.8%
Online shopping	41,325	60.0%	36,142	55.7%	14.3%
Online games	39,148	56.9%	36,585	56.4%	7.0%
Online banking	33,639	48.9%	28,214	43.5%	19.2%
E-mail	25,847	37.6%	25,178	38.8%	2.7%

Table 1. Usage Rate of Internet Applications by Chinese Internet Users 2014-2015 (Source: China Internet Network Information Center 2016)

In addition, online search engines are among the most used Internet services in China. By the end of 2015, China search engine users reached 566 million.[11] In the era of information explosion, search engines have become an effective means for Internet users to locate relevant information instantly. Baidu, founded by Robin Lin and Eric Xu in 2000, has a monopoly on China's online search market since it partakes more than 80% of the Chinese search engine market share. In 2015, Baidu was listed as the number of 11 worldwide innovative

[11] Ibid.

company by Forbes and its total revenues in the fiscal year of 2015 were RMB 66.382 billion ($10.248 billion).[12] Besides search engine services, the company also runs an E-commerce platform with online payment tools and develops and markets web application software. However, the company is also known for its stringent self-censorship system that complies with the Chinese government's Internet policy standards.

B. E-commerce

The Internet is a vehicle of trade. Since the advent of the Internet in China, the Chinese authority has recognized the future trade opportunities brought by the E-commerce, and government at various levels has been actively involved in initiating and promoting E-commerce projects.[13] The result is the explosive growth of the online market. In 2013, China had 302 million online customers and the volume of transactions was over RMB 1.85 trillion ($268 billion), and by the end of 2015, the number of online shoppers increased to 413 million.[14]

China's online shopping market is characterized by its B2C (business-to-consumer) and C2C (consumer-to-consumer) structure. B2C online shopping is a platform providing direct business activities between manufacturers and end consumers, and C2C is a platform that allows consumers to buy and sell products on the Internet.[15] Online shopping has become a prevalent phenomenon of online behavior and many Chinese Internet users are buying products on a regular basis through different web portals. In addition, the growth of B2C and C2C markets has been reinforced by the development of online payment methods, such as credit cards and third-party payment companies.

Despite the ever-expanding market, the Chinese online shopping forum is dominated by indigenous companies (*see* Figure 2), especially the Alibaba Group. Alibaba, founded in 1999, was the first B2C website company in China. In 2014, the Alibaba Group held the world record for the largest US-listed initial public offering and raised $25 billion in its debut on the first day. The Alibaba Group provides online marketplaces for B2B (business-to-business),

---

[12] Fornes, *The World's Most Innovative Companies* (2015). Available at https://www.forbes.com/companies/baidu/. (accessed 01 March 2016)

[13] *See* Tom Birtwistle, *The Rise of China's Silicon Dragon*, PwC's Experience Centre (June 2016).

[14] China Internet Network Information Center, *2015 中国网络购物市场研究报告* (*2015 China Internet Commerce Market Research Report*).

[15] Maurice Blanchard, *Market Study – China E-commerce*, Switzerland Global Enterprise (2014).

B2C, as well as C2C models, and dominates the Chinese E-commerce industry.[16] Tmall (天貓), an online retailer and spin-off from the Alibaba Group, owns over 50% of B2C market share. Tmall has over 50,000 shops that sell over 70,000 brands. Jing Dong (京东), the second biggest online retailer in China, occupies more than 20% of the online shopping market share and has expanded its services with Enterprise Resource Planning (ERP) to supply O2O (online-to-offline) cooperation.[17] China's online shopping market is growing mature and ripe for the future development.

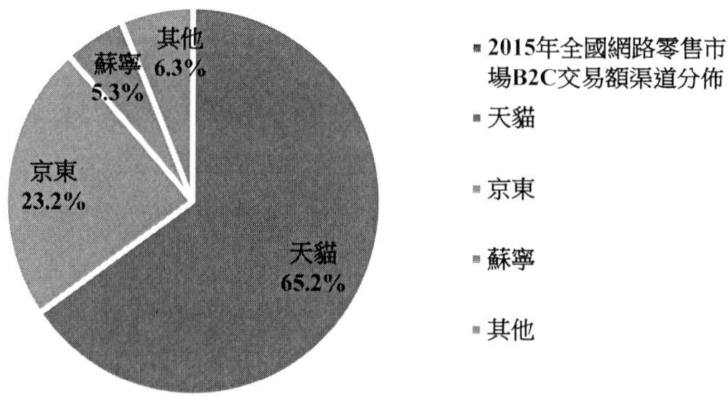

Figure 2. Structure of China Online Shopping B2C Market Share in 2015 (Tmall (天貓) 65.2%; Jing Dong (京东) 23.2%; Suning (苏宁易购) 5.3%; Others (其他) 6.3%) (Source: China Internet Network Information Center 2015)

Notwithstanding the vigorous development of the Internet market in China, foreign companies have various difficulties entering the Chinese online market due to strict regulatory requirements.[18] For example, any foreign or domestic enterprise that wants to register a Chinese national top domain (.cn) or to establish a China-based website needs to apply for an Internet Content Provider (ICP) license. A website hosted on a server in China must, by law, have an ICP li-

[16] Ibid.

[17] China Internet Network Information Center, *2015 中国网络购物市场研究报告* (*2015 China Internet Commerce Market Research Report*).

[18] Min Jiang, *Internet Companies in China – Dancing between the Party Line and the Bottom Line*, the Institut français des relations internationales (Ifri) Center for Asia Studies, Asia Visions 47 (January 2012).

cense number before it can be accessed online. The ICP licensing system was implemented in accordance with Decrees Nos.291 and 292 of the State Council of the PRC, i.e., the People's Republic of China Telecommunications Regulations and the Methods for the Administration of Internet-Based Information Service in China. ICP licenses are issued by the Ministry of Industry and Information Technology of PRC (MIIT) and approved at provincial level.[19]

There are two types of ICP license: non-commercial and commercial. An applicant must first apply for an ICP filing, known as 'Bei'an' (備案), regardless of whether the site is non-commercial or commercial in scope. After obtaining an ICP filing, the licensee will be eligible to host the website on a China-based server for information usage only. A non-commercial license is open to both domestic and foreign invested companies, and a commercial ICP license is mandatory for companies wishing to conduct online advertising, E-commerce, and other lucrative online activities.[20] A commercial ICP license was previously only available to Chinese companies or a joint venture company in which the foreign equality ratio in E-commerce business was less than 50%. Since June 2015, a wholly foreign-owned enterprise has been allowed to apply for a commercial ICP license.[21]

[19] In accordance with 中华人民共和国国务院令(第２９１号) (Decree No. 291 of the State Council of People's Republic of China), the Regulation of Telecommunications of the People's Republic of China has been adopted at the 31st regular meeting of the State Council on 20 September 2000.

[20] 中华人民共和国国务院令(第２９2号) 互联网信息管理办法 (Decree No.291 of the State Council of People's Republic of China).

[21] Richard Hoffmann, *WFOE can now apply for a commercial ICP license for E-commerce business*, ECOVIS Beijing (24 June 2015). Available at http://www.ecovis.com/focus-china/foreigners-can-now-enter-the-chinese-e-commerce-industry/. (accessed 15 March 2016)

II. The Chinese Internet Censorship Mechanisms

In a speech given at the Paul H. Nitze School of Advanced International Studies at Johns Hopkins University on March 8, 2000, President Bill Clinton argued that through new ICTs, the US will benefit economically from greater access to the Chinese market and liberty will spread in China.[22] Commentating on China's efforts to regulate the Internet, Clinton described such efforts as being like "trying to nail Jell-O to the wall".[23] On January 21, 2010, Secretary Hillary Clinton delivered a speech on Internet freedom and the future of global freedom of expression in Newsum, Washington DC. She emphasized the U.S. government's commitment to promoting Internet freedom and condemned countries that had erected electronic barriers to prevent their people from accessing portions of the world's networks.[24] Secretary Clinton's speech came a week after the cyber-attack from China targeting Google and at least 30 other Internet companies and email accounts of human rights activists.

However, nearly two decades later, the Jell-O is still on the wall. The Chinese government has demonstrated its fortitude, and that it is capable of constructing a virtual shield around the Chinese authoritarian regime on the Internet. Six months after Secretary Clinton's remarks, the Chinese State Council Information Office published its first White Paper on Internet policy. While guaranteeing citizens' freedom of speech on the Internet, the White Paper proclaimed the importance of ensuring Internet security and maintaining sovereign power over the Internet within the Chinese territory. According to the White Paper, the Chinese government believes:

---

[22] In the speech, President Bill Clinton stated:

> "In the new century, liberty will spread by cell phone and cable modem." "We know how much the Internet has changed America, and we are already an open society. Imagine how much it could change China."

[23] Clinton also stressed that "now, there's no question China has been trying to crack down on the Internet – good luck. That's sort of like trying to nail Jell-O to the wall. By I would argue to you that there to do that just proves how real these changes are and how much they threaten the status quo. It's not an argument for slowing down the effort to bring China into the world, it's an argument for accelerating that effort. In the knowledge economy, economic innovation and political empowerment, whether anyone likes it or not, will inevitably go hand in hand".

[24] Hillary Rodham Clinton, *Remarks on Internet Freedom*, US Department of State (21 January 2010). Available at http://www.state.gov/secretary/rm/2010/01/135519.htm. (accessed 29 March 2016)

> "The Internet is an important infrastructure facility for the nation. Within Chinese territory, the Internet is under the jurisdiction of Chinese sovereignty. The Internet sovereignty of China should be respected and protected. Citizens of the People's Republic of China and foreign citizens, legal persons and other organizations within Chinese territory have the right and freedom to use the Internet; at the same time, they must obey the laws and regulations of China and conscientiously protect Internet security."[25]

Additionally, the White Paper stressed that protecting the safe flow of Internet information is the prerequisite of the free flow of information on the Internet. Therefore, no organization or individual is allowed to produce, duplicate, or disseminate information that subverts state power and jeopardizes national unification. The terms used to describe illegitimate online information are ambiguous and could be broadly defined. With arbitrary interpretation, any content and information disseminated on the Internet could be deemed as harmful to state security, state interests, and societal stability.

Moreover, the Chinese government has adopted a series of laws, executive orders, and directives to conduct comprehensive Internet censorship to ensure its cyberspace sovereignty. At both the political and economic level, under the leadership of President Xi, the government's grip on Internet control has tightened over the past years. As Mr. Xi declared in an internal speech at the National Propaganda and Ideology Work Conference in August 2013, "the Internet has become the main battlefield for the struggle for public opinion".[26] He further underlined:

> "Anti-China forces in the western countries have been trying to utilize the Internet to "topple China". Couple years ago, western political leaders claimed that "with the Internet, we will have ways to deal with China" or "with the widespread usage of the Internet, the West would be able to embrace socialist countries in their arms." From the US monitoring programs, such as "PRISM" and "Xkeyscore", it is hard for people to imagine the scale and the power of their Internet capability. In the battlefield of the In-

---

[25] The Information Office of the State Council of the People's Republic of China, *White Paper – The Internet in China* (8 June 2010).

[26] 网传习近平8•19 讲话全文：言论方面要敢抓敢管敢于亮剑, China Digital Times (4 Novermber 2013). Available at http://chinadigitaltimes.net/chinese/2013/11/网传习近平8•19 讲话全文：言论方面要敢抓敢管敢/ (accessed 08 April 2016)

ternet, our ideology security and political safety depend directly on if we can withstand and win this battle."[27]

A. The Great Firewall: Blocking and Filtering Online Content

With the assistance of Western Internet companies,[28] China has established the most sophisticated censorship mechanism, known as the 'Great Firewall' or 'Golden Shield'.[29] The Great Firewall is used to monitor all information flowing across the 'Chinese border'. China's gateways to the international Internet are controlled by nine state-run operators at the backbone of the infrastructure in Beijing, Shanghai, and Guangzhou. Through these centrally controlled systems, the Chinese authorities can effectively filter and cut off all cross-border information.[30] At each checkpoint, Chinese Internet carriers, such as China Telecom and the China Union, have deployed devices that can discard or redirect electronic information packages passing through their routers when sensitive or controversial keywords are detected.[31] A limited number of international entry points, coupled with subscription and license requirements, give the Chinese government the technologies and capabilities to analyze, manipulate, and control Internet traffic on a widespread scale.

The centralized control of international gateways and the irregular blockage of the local Internet have had a profound impact on the domestic political situation and global economy. Domestically, for example, in 2009, China shut down access to the entire communication system in Xinjiang Uighur Autonomous Region for ten months after an outburst of ethnic violence in the regional capital,

[27] The original text of the transcript, "西方反华势力一直妄图利用互联网"扳倒中国"，多年前有西方政要就声称"有了互联网，对付中国就有了办法"，"社会主义国家投入西方怀抱，将从互联网开始"。从美国的"棱镜"、"X—关键得分"等监控计划看，他们的互联网活动能量和规模远远超出了世人想象。在互联网这个战场上，我们能否顶得住、打得赢，直接关系我国意识形态安全和政权安全。"

[28] *See* Derek Bambauer, Cool Tools for Tyrants; *The Latest American Technology Helps the Chinese Government and other Repressive Regimes Clamp Down*, Legal Affair (Jan-Feb 2005). For example, routers manufactured by Cisco, an American based Internet technology company, comprised a large part of the Chinese Internet backbone and Internet filtering technologies.

[29] *See* Christopher Stevenson, *Breaching the Great Firewall: China's Internet Censorship and the Quest for Freedom of Expression in a Connected Wor*ld, Boston College International & Comparative Law Review, Vol.30 (2007), pp. 531-558.

[30] *See* Jyh-An Lee and Ching-Yi Liu, *Forbidden City Enclosed by the Great Firewall: The Law and Power of Internet Filtering in China*, Minn. J. L. Sci. & Tech., Vol.13:1 (2012), pp. 125-151.

[31] Ibid.

Urumqi.[32] Since then, authorities have implemented several smaller-scale shutdowns in the area whenever tension between the Uyghur ethnic minority and the Chinese government has risen. In June 2012, after Chinese security forces opened fire on a crowd of Muslim protesters in Xinjiang's southern Hotan city, most residents had no access to the Internet and WeChat, a popular Chinese instant messaging application, for a few weeks.[33] In September 2014, during the month of Ramadan, the Internet was disconnected and text message services were disabled across Shache County in Xinjiang.[34]

Internationally, by blocking IP addresses, China has efficiently blocked major foreign websites and platforms from its market. Equipped with a blacklist of undesirable IP addresses, without much involvement of Internet intermediaries, routers at checkpoints can drop all packets destined to the blocked IP address, which contains the address of a sensitive website like www.nytimes.com or Google's public Domain Name Server (DNS).[35] The blacklist is periodically leaked online but it has never been officially released. Video-sharing platforms and social media websites such as YouTube, Facebook, Twitter, and Google+ have not been accessible to Chinese Internet users. While those worldwide popular international Internet applications are blocked in China, indigenous equivalents are thriving and attracting millions of users in the Chinese market. Therefore, the combination of IP blocking technology and DNS tampering strategy[36] has seriously hindered foreign companies' business share in China while promoting the development of similar domestic service suppliers. For instance, Google held 24% of Chinese search engine market share and Baidu held 3% in

---

[32] Edward Wong, *After Long Ban, Western China is Back Online,* New York Times (14 May 2010). Available at http://www.nytimes.com/2010/05/15/world/asia/15china.html. (accessed 20 April 2016)

[33] Andrew Jacobs, *Over News of Clash, a Shroud of Silence in Xinjiang*, New York Times (26 August 2013). Available at http://www.nytimes.com/2013/08/27/world/asia/over-news-of-clash-a-shroud-of-silence-in-xinjiang.html. (accessed 20 April 2016)

[34] Siman Denyer, *China's war on terror becomes all-out attack on Islam in Xinjiang*, Washington Post (19 September 2014). Available at https://www.washingtonpost.com/world/chinas-war-on-terror-becomes-all-out-attack-on-islam-in-xinjiang/2014/09/19/5c5840a4-1aa7-4bb6-bc63-69f6bfba07e9_story.html. (accessed 28 April 2016)

[35] *See* Steven J. Murdoch & Ross Anderson, Tool and Technology of Internet Filtering. In: Ronald Deibert, John Palfrey, Rafal Rohozinski, and Jonathan Zittrain, *Access Denied: The Practice and Policy of Global Internet Filtering*, the MIT Press (January 2008).

[36] Most Internet communication uses domain names instead of IP addresses. DNS tempering involves falsifying the response returned by the DNS server. The DNS server accessed by users is given a list of banned domain names. When a computer requests the corresponding IP address, the server can trick the user with a false IP address.

2002. In 2014, the Baidu search engine accounted for 88.7 % of the market while Google's market share had dwindled to 2.2%.[37] (*see* Figure 3).

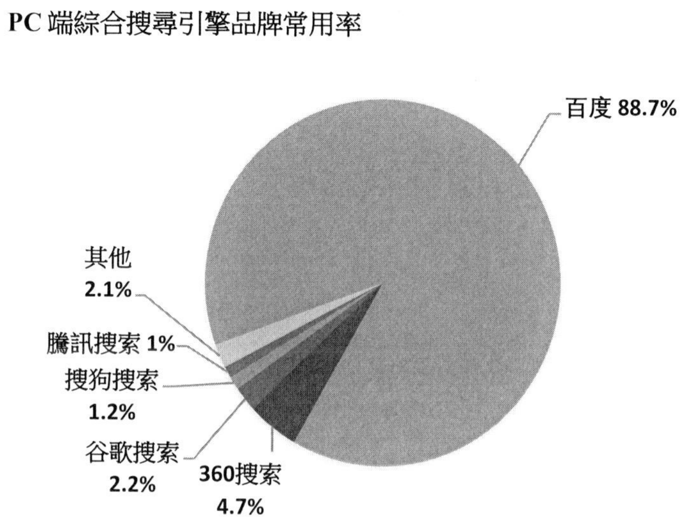

Figure 3. Search Engine Market Share Statistics
(Baidu (百度) 88.7%; 360 Search (搜索) 4.7%; Google (谷歌)2.2%; Sogou (搜狗); Tencent (腾讯) 1.0%; Others (其他)2.1%)
(Source: CNNIC Statistical Survey on Internet Development in China)

Except for blocking IP addresses or DNS, online content filtering technologies adopted by the Chinese government are heterogeneous, depending on timing, technology, and geographic regions.[38] The authorities use both automatic and manual resources to control information on the Internet. Automatic filtering technologies, such as deep pack inspection (DPI) and intrusion detection systems (IDS),[39] are constantly implemented to inspect the contents of packages. If sensitive keywords, like Taiwan independence or human rights, are detected by

[37] China Internet Network Information Center (CNNIC), *中国互联网络发展状况统计报告* (January 2015).

[38] Freedom House, *Freedom on the Net – China* (2014).

[39] Richard Clayton, Steven J. Murdoch, and Robert N. M. Watson, Ignoring the Great Firewall of China. In: Danezis G., Galle P. (eds), *Privacy Enhancing Technologies*, Lecture Notes in Computer Science, Vol.4258, Springer, Berlin, Heidelberg (2006).

the systems, the package will be dropped automatically.[40] The range of the filtered content could be from a website to a term in an e-mail. Such granular filtering mechanisms allow the Chinese authorities to conduct a more accurate but less noticeable censorship of the Internet.[41] In addition, Chinese government agencies and private companies employ thousands of people to manually monitor online activities. For example, the 50 Cent Party, paid at the rate of 50 cents RMB per post, are web commentators hired and trained by governmental units to steer online discussion of sensitive topics and report users who have posted offending statements on the Internet.[42]

B. Self-censorship: Individuals and Private Corporations

Besides technological censoring mechanisms, the Chinese government has successfully fostered a self-censorship phenomenon on the Internet. ISPs are responsible to monitoring and filtering content on their networks and Internet users are subject to financial or criminal penalties if they post or disseminate unlawful information online. These mandatory obligations at every layer of Internet access, from ISPs and ICPs to the end users, constitute the most efficient but severe Internet censorship mechanism.

a. Internet Service Providers and Internet Content Providers

ISPs and ICPs are required by law to monitor the content on their platforms and websites, to delete harmful information, to store users' information and activities, and to hand in personal data to the state authorities when requested. Companies failing to comply with the censorship regulations might face warnings, financial penalties, temporary shutdown, and license revocation. As a result, many private Internet companies implement self-censorship instruments to conform with the Internet regulations and avoid possible punishments.[43]

---

[40] *See* Jyh-An Lee and Ching-Yi Liu, *Forbidden City Enclosed by the Great Firewall: The Law and Power of Internet Filtering in China*, Minn. J. L. Sci. & Tech., Vol.13:1 (2012), pp. 125-151.

[41] Ben Wagner, *Deep Packet Inspection and Internet Censorship: International Convergence on an 'Integrated Technology of Control'*, Global Voices Advocacy Defending Free Speech Online (2009).

[42] *See* Ron Deibert, John G. Palfrey, Rafal Rohozinski and Jonathan Zittrain (eds.), *Access Contested: Security, Identity, and Resistance in Asia Cyberspace*, OpenNet Initiative, International Development Research Centre and the MIT Press (December 2011).

[43] *See* Haiping Zheng, *Regulating the Internet: China's Law and Practice*, Beijing Law Review, Vol.4, No.1 (2013), pp. 37-41.

For instance, Article 20 of the Measures for Managing Information Services stipulates that Internet Information Service (IIS) providers and ISPs are directly responsible for producing, reproducing, releasing, or disseminating forbidden information listed in Article 15 on their services.[44] If commercial IIS providers violate Article 20, the licensing authorities could suspend the service operations or revoke the operating licenses. For non-commercial IIS providers, the licensing authorities could temporarily or permanently shut down platforms and websites.[45] The nine categories of information in Article 15 include:

> 1. Information that goes against the basic principles set in the Constitution;
> 2. information that endangers national security, divulges state secrets, subverts the governmental authority, and undermines national integrity;
> 3. Information that infringes the honor and interests of the state;
> 4. Information that instigates ethnic hatred or ethnic discrimination, or that under mines the unity of the people;
> 5. Information that undermines state's religion policies, or that preaches the teachings of evil cults or that promotes feudalistic and superstitious beliefs;
> 6. Information that disseminates rumors, disturbs social order, or undermines social stability;
> 7. Information that spreads pornography or other salacious materials; promotes gambling, violence, homicide or terrorism; instigated crimes;
> 8. Information that insults or slanders other people, infringes upon other people's legitimate rights and interests;
> 9. Other information prohibited by the law or administrative regulations.

Similar regulations are applied to electronic bulletin board services, Internet news service providers, and Internet audio and video service providers.[46] The

[44] Measures for Managing Internet Information Services (互联网信息服务管理办法) was issued by the State Council on 25 September 2000, effective on 1 October 2000. Available at http://www.cac.gov.cn/2000-09/30/c_126193701.htm (in Chinese). (accessed 08 May 2016)

[45] Ibid. (The original regulation is: （一）反对宪法所确定的基本原则的；（二）危害国家安全，泄露国家秘密， 颠覆国家政权， 破坏国家统一的；（三）损害国家荣誉和利益的；（四）煽动民族仇恨、民族歧视、破坏民族团结的；（五）破坏国家宗教政策，宣扬邪教和封建迷信的；（六）散布谣言，扰乱社会秩序，破坏社会稳定的；（七）散布淫秽 、色情、 赌 博、暴力、凶 杀 、恐怖或者教唆犯罪的； （ 八 ） 侮辱或者 诽 谤他人，侵害他人合法权益的；（九）含有法律、行政法规禁止的其他内容的。)

[46] Article 9 & Article 17 of the Rules on the Management of Internet Electronic Bulletin Service and Article 2 of the Provisions on the Administration of News Information Services impose similar liabilities on ISPs and Internet content providers to conduct censorship on their platforms and websites.

latest Cyber Security Law of People's Republic of China, enacted in November 2016, intensifies the burden of private ISPs and ICPs to support and promote cyber security. As stipulated in Article 21 of the Cyber Security law, in order to fulfill the responsibility to protect cyber security, network operators shall:[47]

> 1. establish internal security management system and operating rules, ascertain persons responsible for cyber security, and fulfill cybersecurity protection responsibility;
> 2. adopt technical measures to prevent computer viruses, cyber-attacks, network intrusion, and other actions endangering cyber security;
> 3. adopt technical measures to monitor and record network operational statute and cybersecurity incidents. Following the relevant regulations, the record should be stored no less than six months;
> 4. adopt data classification, important data back-up, and encryption measures;
> 5. comply with other obligations provided by law or administrative regulations.

The broad and inexplicit phrases of the regulations, along with criminal penalties and license revocation, have forced ISPs to employ automated and human monitors to censor and delete content on their platforms. For example, Sina Weibo, the biggest microblogging website in China, conducts comprehensive internal censorship to comply with the Chinese government's requirements. A survey which tried to quantify Weibo's internal censorship policies indicates that Weibo employs 'defense-in-depth' in its strategy for filtering and removing sensitive content.[48] According to the research, 30% of the total deletions happened within 30 minutes of the information being posted and 90% occurred within 24 hours of publication.[49] Active users with a certain number of followers are usually under scrutiny, and sensitive topics in public discussion or topics related to state power often have a very short lifetime in the forum.[50]

---

[47] 中华人民共和国网络安全法 (Cybersecurity Law of People's Republic of China) was promulgated on 7 November 2016, not yet effective. Available at http://www.cac.gov.cn/2016-11/07/c_1119867116_2.htm (in Chinese). (accessed 12 May 2016)

[48] *See* Tao Zhu, David Phipps, Adman Pridgen, Jedidiah R. Crandall and Dan S. Wallach, *The Velocity of Censorship: High-Fidelity Detection of Microblog Post Deletions*, 22nd USENIX Security Symposium in Washington, D.C. (August 2013).

[49] Ibid.

[50] Ibid.

b. Individuals

Individuals are also subject to the government's self-censorship regime. China has implemented a series of regulations requiring Internet users to register real personal identities to gain access to certain Internet services. Anonymity is a prominent feature of Internet freedom since it allows users to make public comments freely and without fearing the consequential punishments in the physical world.[51] Real-name registration requirements could fundamentally change the open nature of the Internet and encourage self-censorship in the broader public. Nevertheless, in the name of maintaining national security and public order or preventing cybercrimes, China has enacted local and national regulations, forcing ISPs to confirm a person's real identify before providing their services.[52]

On December 28, 2012, at the 30th Committee Meeting of the National Peoples' Congress Standing Committee, the Communist Party of China (CCP) passed the Decision of the Standing Committee of the National People's Congress on Strengthening Online Information Protection to strengthen the legal basis for real-name registration for most ISPs and ICPs in China.[53] Article 6 of the Decision mandates that "network service providers shall require users to provide real identity information when signing agreements or confirming the provision of services to supply website access services, to supply fixed telephone, mobile phone, and other surfing formalities, or to supply information publication services to users".[54]

The real-name registration requirement has become an official national law and a legal obligation for all websites and ISPs in China.[55] In February 2015,

[51] *See* Jyh-An Lee & Ching-Yi Liu, *Real-name Registration Rules and the Fading Digital Anonymity in China*, Washington International Law Journal, Vol.25, No.1 (2015).

[52] King-wa Fu, Chung-hong Chan & M. Chau, *Assessing Censorship on Microblogs in China: Discriminatory Keywords Analysis and the Real Name Registration Policy*, IEEE Internet Computing (May-June 2013), p. 43.

[53] 全国人大常委会关于加强网络信息保护的决定 (Decision of the Standing Committee of the National People's Congress on Strengthening Online Information Protection) is promulgated by the Standing Committee on 28 December 2012. Available at http://www.cac.gov.cn/2012-12/29/c_133353262.htm (in Chinese). (accessed 22 May 2016)

[54] Article 6 stipulated:

> 六、网络服务提供者为用户办理网站接入服务，办理固定电话、移动电话等入网手续，或者为用户提供信息发布服务，应当在与用户签订协议或者确认提供服务时，要求用户提供真实身份信息。

[55] *See* Jyh-An Lee & Ching-Yi Liu, *Real-name Registration Rules and the Fading Digital Anonymity in China*, Washington International Law Journal, Vol.25, No.1 (2015).

the government passed the Provisions on the Administration of Internet User Account Name, which obliges ISPs, according to the principle of 'real name backstage, voluntary choice front stage', to require users to authenticate themselves before registering for an account.[56] Alibaba, Tencent, Baidu, Sina Weibo, and other network companies were reported to have deleted more than 60,000 accounts on various platforms to comply with the new regulations.[57] Moreover, mobile phone SIM card buyers had to have their ID card examined by electronic ID readers after September 1, 2015 on pain of having their account closed.[58]

C. Criminalization of Online Activities

Vague provisions in China's Criminal Code, Criminal Procedure Law, Law on Guarding State Secrets, Cyber Security Law, and laws governing printing and publications give prosecutors wide range of discretion in imprisoning citizens for wrongful online activities.[59] In 2010, the Chinese government amended the 1989 Law on Guarding State Secrets to require ISPs, ICPs, and other public information network operators to support public security, national security and prosecutorial organs in investigating leaked state secrets on their websites or platforms.[60] The Chinese authorities, however, adopted a relatively broad view of information deemed to be state secrets. According to Article 9 of the Law on Guarding State Secrets, state secrets are categorized as matters involving national defense, foreign affairs, national security, infrastructure, and other matters that are classified as state secrets by the national State Secrets Bureau.[61] In

[56] 互联网用戶账号名称管理规定 (Provisions on the administration of Internet User Account Name) is promulgated on 4 February 2015, effective 1st March 2015. Available at http://www.cac.gov.cn/2015-02/04/c_1114246561.htm (in Chinese). (accessed 23 May 2016)

[57] Paul Carsten, *China Censorship sweep deletes more than 60,000 Internet Accounts*, Robert Birsel (ed.), Reuters (February 2015). Available at http://www.reuters.com /article/us-china-internet-censorship-idUSKBN0LV16S20150227. (accessed 23 May 2016)

[58] Staff Reporter, Real-Name SIM Registration to be Enforced in China Sept. 1, Want China Times (28 August 2015).

[59] Freedom House, *Freedom on the Internet – China* (2014).

[60] 中华人民共和国保守国家秘密法 (Law on Guarding State Secrets). The amendment was promulgated on 29 April 2010, effective 1 October 2010. Available at http://www.stats.gov.cn/zjtj/tjfg/xgfxfg/201510/t20151028_1262977.html (in Chinese). (accessed 28 May 2016)

[61] Article 9 of the Law on Guarding State Secrets stipulates state secrets shall include the following:

such cases, Internet service operators are required to immediately cease the transmission of the information, maintain the records, and report the incident to the responsible government departments.

Moreover, an amendment to the Criminal Law, effective 1 November 2015, mandated criminal penalties for a maximum of seven years imprisonment for those who disseminate false information or misinformation on the Internet or any other social media.[62] In addition, the Cyber Security Law of China strengthens self-censorship and real-name registration requirements for Internet service operators and requires them to support security agencies in violation investigations. Article 47 further mandates network operators to reinforce management of information published by users. Accordingly, if prohibited information is detected, ISPs and ICPs shall immediately stop the transmission of the information, employ handling methods to prevent the information from spreading, maintain the records, and report to the relevant competent departments.[63]

Many Internet users and activists in China have been detained and imprisoned in the past years. In 2009, Liu Xiaobo, 2010 Nobel Peace Prize Winner, was sentenced to 11 years in jail on the charge of 'inciting subversion of state power' for publishing three articles on the Internet.[64] In 2012, Cao Haibo, a cybercafé employee in the southwestern city of Kunming, was sentenced to eight years in prison for posting pro-democracy articles online.[65] In 2014, Gao

(1) secret matters concerning major policy decisions on state affairs; (2) secret matters in the building of national defense and in the activities of the armed forced; (3) secret matters in diplomatic activities and in activities related to foreign countries, as well as secrets to be maintained as commitments to foreign countries; (4) secret matters in national economic and social development; (5) secret matters concerning science and technology; (6) secret matters concerning activities for safeguarding state security and investigation of criminal offenses; and (7) other matters that are classified as state secrets by the national State Secrets Bureau.

[62] 中华人民共和国刑法修正案(九) (The Amendment (IX) to the Criminal Law of the People's Republic of China) was promulgated on 29 August 2015, effective 1 November 2015. Available at http://law.npc.gov.cn/FLFG/flfgByID.action?flfgID=35091146&zlsxid=08 (in Chinese) (accessed 03 June 2016)

[63] 中华人民共和国网络安全法 (Cybersecurity Law of People's Republic of China) was promulgated on 7 November 2016, not yet effective. Available at http://www.cac.gov.cn/2016-11/07/c_1119867116_2.htm (in Chinese). (accessed 08 June 2016)

[64] Sharon Hom, *Google and Internet control in China: A nexus between Human Rights and Trade?*, Hearing before the Congressional-Executive Commission on China (24 March 2010), pp. 11-13.

[65] Andrew Jacobs, China: Café Owner Sentenced Over Online Messages, New York Times (1 November 2012). Available at http://www.nytimes.com/2012/11/02/world/asia/china-cafe-owner-sentenced-over-online-messages.html?_r=0. (accessed 22 June 2016)

Yu, a 70-year-old Chinese journalist, was detained and sentenced to seven years in prison on a charge of providing state secrets to foreign websites. The leaked document was an internal Communist Party report that warned senior officials to be cautious about the subversive 'seven mistaken ideologies', including human rights and press freedom.[66] According to Reporters Without Borders, more than 100 journalists and bloggers are currently detained by the Chinese authorities.[67]

---

[66] *See* Freedom House, *Freedom on the Net – China* (2015); Doug Bolton, *Chinese journalist Gao Yu jailed for seven years for leaking a Communist Party document about crackdown on press freedom*, Independent (17 April 2015). Available at http://www.independent.co.uk/news/world/asia/chinese-journalist-gao-yu-jailed-for-seven-years-for-leaking-a-communist-party-document-about-10184078.html. (accessed 26 June 2016)

[67] Reporters Without Borders is an international non-governmental organization promotes and supports freedom of information and freedom of the press. Available at https://rsf.org/en. (accessed 26 June 2016)

III. Internet Sovereignty and Potential Human Rights Violations

Many scholars optimistically believed that the worldwide expansion of the Internet would constitute a liberating force and lead to the demise of repressive regimes as people were able to access information and ideas around the world via innovative technologies.[68] Nevertheless, China's Internet filtering and censorship mechanisms have successfully toppled the idealistic concepts that Internet freedom would bring freedom of speech and information to the people and that political transformation would be an evitable outcome for authoritarian countries if they were to embrace the new technologies.[69] Nevertheless, China's Internet infrastructures and policies have been carefully designed to promote economic growth and maintain state control simultaneously.[70]

China's Internet censorship regime has received considerable attention from the international community, with political and economic accusations.[71] In response, China has referred to the conflict as an issue of cultural diversity. For instance, after Secretary Hillary Clinton's speech on Internet freedom, which specifically addressed China as a state that threatens "the free flow of information"[72], Chinese media swiftly denounced the US government's criticisms and argued that the US government was endeavoring to impose information

[68] *See* Shanthi Kalathil & Taylor C. Boas, *Open Networks, Closed Regimes: The Impact of the Internet on Authoritarian Rule,* Carnegie Endowment for International Peace, Washington D.C. (2003), pp. 1-12.
[69] *See* Jennifer Shyu, *Speak No Evil: Circumventing Chinese Censorship*, San Diego L. Rev., Vol.45 (2008), pp. 215-216.
[70] *See* Lijun Tang & Peidong Yang, *Symbolic Power and the Internet: The Power of a 'Horse'*, Media, Culture & Society, Vol.33(5) (2011), pp. 675-691; Shubo Li, *The Online Public Space and Popular Ethos in China*, Media, Culture & Society, Vol.32 (1) (2010), pp. 63-83; and Jyh-An Lee and Ching-Yi Liu, *Forbidden City Enclosed by the Great Firewall: The Law and Power of Internet Filtering in China*, Minn. J. L. Sci. & Tech., Vol.13:1 (2012), pp. 125-151; *see* also Katherine Tsai, *How to Create International Law: the Case of the Internet Freedom in China*, Duke Journal of Comparative & International Law, Vol.21 (2011), pp. 401-430.
[71] *See* Jyh-An Lee and Ching-Yi Liu, *Forbidden City Enclosed by the Great Firewall: The Law and Power of Internet Filtering in China*, Minn. J. L. Sci. & Tech., Vol.13:1 (2012), pp. 125-151.
[72] Hillary Rodham Clinton, *Remarks on Internet Freedom*, US Department of State (21 January 2010). Available at http://www.state.gov/secretary/rm/2010/01/135519.htm. (accessed 29 June 2016)

imperialism upon China by requesting universal access to an open Internet.[73] Some government-owned or affiliated media criticized the concept of 'freedom of speech' as an "aggressive political and diplomatic strategy, rather than a desire for moral values".[74] In 2012, at the UN Human Rights Council meeting in Geneva, China reiterated that freedom of expression on the Internet is far from absolute.[75]

Recently, under the leadership of State President Xi, the Chinese authorities have tightened their grip on Internet policies by proclaiming the notion of Internet Sovereignty. According to the White Paper mentioned earlier, the Chinese government believes that within the context of international law, each nation state should have the right to regulate the Internet within its territory.[76] In June 2014, the *People's Daily* published a set of interviews with Chinese experts on Internet security.[77] The report focused on the concept of Internet sovereignty. Although they had different perspectives, the experts agreed on the core message that each nation should have the authority to govern the Internet as it sees fit.[78] While acknowledging the difficulty of defining boundaries for cyberspace, Wang Jun, the vice dean of the Marxism School of Mizu University, pointed out that:

---

[73] *See* Opinion, *The Real Stake in 'Free Flow of Information*', Global Times (22 January 2010). Available at http://www.globaltimes.cn/content/500324.shtml. *See* also Comment, *Internet Safety, Order*, China Daily (23 January 2010). Available at http://www.chinadaily.com.cn/cndy/2010-01/23/content_9365529.htm. (The newspaper stressed that it is Internet technology that has expedited economic and political reform in China, and it is the Internet that has broadened the channels for Chinese people's freedom of speech tremendously. Therefore, it sounds ridiculous to accuse China of restricting Chinese people's freedom of speech.) Both Global Times and China Daily are state-affiliated news media. (accessed 5 July 2016)

[74] Ibid.

[75] William New, UN Human Rights Council Rallies on Right to Internet Freedom of Expression, Intellectual Property Watch (29 February 2012). Available at https://www.ip-watch.org/2012/02/29/un-human-rights-council-rallies-on-right-to-internet-freedom-of-expression/. (accessed 5 July 2016)

[76] The Information Office of the State Council of the People's Republic of China, *White Paper – The Internet in China* (8 June 2010).

[77] 王远, *人民日报权威论坛：网络主权，一个不容回避的议题*,人民日报 (23 June 2014). Available at http://opinion.people.com.cn/n/2014/0623/c1003-25183666.html (in Chinese). (accessed 11 July 2016)

[78] Ibid. Shannon Tiezzi, China 'Sovereign Internet', The Diplomat (24 January 2014). Available at http://thediplomat.com/2014/06/chinas-sovereign-internet/. (accessed 11 July 2016)

> "Although cyberspace has no national boundaries, network infrastructure has borders. Internet users have their home counties. Internet enterprises and intermediaries normally belong to specific countries. Therefore, Internet infrastructure within a country's territory, ISPs and websites registered in that country and its Internet users are subject to the nation's sovereignty. No countries have the right to interfere."[79]

In several official speeches, Mr. Xi also emphasized the importance of Internet sovereignty and considered the concept to be a pillar of the CCP's approach to the Internet in the international sphere. In December 2015, at the opening ceremony of the 2nd World Internet Conference in Wuzhen,[80] Mr. Xi reiterated in his opening keynote remarks that in order to push forward the revolution of the global Internet management system, all countries should respect the sovereignty of every country on the Internet. Mr. Xi stated:

> "We need to respect each country's right to choose their methods of cyber development, cyber administration, and Internet public policy independently and to participate in the international cyber space management equally. We should never seek network hegemony, interfere in other nations' internal affairs and never engage, indulge, or support cyber activities that harm other countries national security."[81]

On the surface, the Chinese approach to Internet governance might seem to have certain merits and conform to the norms of international law. Based on the analysis in Chapter 2, the rights to freedom of expression and privacy are not absolute but subject to limitations. Nevertheless, in the context of internationally recognized human rights law, any restrictions on people's fundamental rights must be provided by law, serve one of the legitimate purposes expressly enu-

---

[79] The original text read as 网络空间虽然没有国界，但网络基础设施有国界，网民有祖国，网络公司或网络中介组织往往具有国家属性。因此，一国领土范围的网络设施，在一国境内注册备案的网络服务商和网站，一国的网民也属该国主权管辖范围，他国无权干涉。

[80] The World Internet Conference is annually held by the Cyberspace Administration of China and Zhejiang Provincial People's government. The first conference was held on 19-21 November 2014. Despite China's efforts to stress the country's leadership role in global Internet governance during the conference, the international community did not participate enthusiastically. In 2014, only eight foreign governments sent high-level representatives and most private participants were Chinese companies.

[81] Live report: opening ceremony of the 2ed World Internet Conference. Available at http://www.wuzhenwic.org/2015-12/16/c_47521.htm. (accessed 20 August 2016)

merated in the relevant text, and be necessary to the aim pursued.[82] In addition, in modern international relations, due to globalization and growing interdependence between countries, a nation's sovereign right is not absolute and must be bound by its obligations to the international community and to its people.[83]

Against this background, the following section first examines whether China's Internet censorship mechanisms undermine its people's freedom of expression and information and right to privacy, which are protected under the UDHR and the ICCPR. Second, the traditional definition of state sovereignty and Internet sovereignty are discussed respectively. While the concept of sovereignty is still the center of almost all thinking concerning international relations, the notion of absolute sovereign rights has been challenged from various aspects. A power-oriented assertation of state sovereignty in the contemporary international relations is highly controversial. The advent of the ICT complicates the already tangled issue of sovereignty. Because of the unique open nature of the Internet, any national Internet-related regulations would have extra-territorial effects on other nations. Therefore, if Chinese Internet censorship measures severely constrain individuals' rights guaranteed under international human rights law, consideration must be given to whether a nation enjoys full authority to regulate the Internet without interference or whether there is a boundary limiting the application of the sovereign rights to the digital world.

A. In Violation of International Human Rights Law

According to the analysis in Chapter 2, arbitrary and disproportionate Internet censorship mechanisms implemented by the government authorities either violate individuals' rights to freedom of expression and information, or intercept an individual's right to privacy, or both. However, like most values in modern democratic society, both rights are not absolute but subject to limitations. According to well-developed general international standards, to determine the level of protection that human rights should enjoy is to determine the proportionate equilibrium of interests between individuals and the public since the concept of balance is an attribute of a 'good governance.[84]

---

[82] *See* Chapter 2 I.A.b.

[83] *See* Johan D. van der Vyver, Sovereignty. In: Dinah Shelton (ed.), *The Oxford Handbook of International Human Rights Law*, Oxford University Press (2013).

[84] *See* Amitai Etzioni, The Limits of Privacy, New York: Basic Books (1999).
(Amitai Etzioni argues that "good societies carefully balance individual rights and social responsibilities, autonomy and the common good, privacy concerns for public safety and public health, rather than allow one value or principle to dominate. Once we accept the concept of balance, the question arises as to how we are to determine whether

Proclaimed by the United Nation Human Rights Council (UNHRC), the notion that "the same rights that people have offline must also be protected online"[85] has been widely accepted at international, regional, and national level. Due to the unique characteristics of ICTs, while individuals are able to access information and knowledge that was previously unattainable, information controllers, either public authorities or private entities, are able to acquire personal information that it was impossible or unfeasible to obtain in the past.[86] Accordingly, when governments implement any Internet censorship mechanisms in the name of public order or national security to restrict the realization of people's fundamental rights online, they must bear in mind their international obligations and commitments as well.[87]

China represents a controversial case in the context of Internet censorship and human rights violations. Whereas the Chinese constitution explicitly guarantees the right to freedom of information and expression, the right to privacy, the right to engage in academic research, and the right against unlawful searches,[88] the Chinese government maintains the world's most sophisticated Internet censorship mechanisms to control information on the Internet.

Using censoring technologies to control the flow of information on the Internet without transparency and due process violates international human rights law for protecting and promoting freedom of expression and the right to privacy.

---

our polity is off balance and in what direction it needs to move, and to what extent, to restore balance.")

[85] United Nations General Assembly, Resolution adopted by the Human Rights Council, *26/13 The Promotion, Protection and Enjoyment of Human Rights on the Internet*, A/HRC/RES/26/13 (14 July 2014).

[86] *See* UN Human Rights Council, *Report on the Special Rapporteur on the Promotion and Protection of the Right to Freedom of Opinion and Expression, Frank La Rue*, UN General Assembly, A/HRC/17/27 (15 May 2011).

[87] *See* Molly Land, *Toward an International Law of the Internet*, Harvard International Law Journal, Vol. 54 (2) (Summer 2013), pp. 393-458.

[88] People's right to freedom of expression and the right to engage in academic research are regulated in Article 35 and Article 47 of Constitution of the People's Republic of China respectively. The right to privacy is guaranteed in Article 40. However, the governmental authorities enjoy extensive discretion of investigation and censorship of personal communication when state security or public security is concerned. Article 40 of the Constitution provides:

> The freedom and privacy of correspondence of citizens of the People's Republic of China are protected by law. No organization or individual may, on any ground, infringe upon the freedom and privacy of citizens' correspondence except in cases where, to meet the needs of state security or of an investigation into criminal offences, public security or prosecutorial organs are permitted to censor correspondence in accordance with procedures prescribed by law.

Chinese Internet censorship mechanisms, such as filtering or blocking online content, are generally not prescribed by law. Even if the censorship is authorized by government Internet policies or regulations, most of the terms are not formulated with sufficient precision to enable citizens to foresee the consequences which a given action may entail. This lack of clarity also gives the Chinese authorities great discretion in interpreting and applying the measures arbitrarily in any specific circumstances. Furthermore, criminalization of online activities or a total shutdown of Internet access for a certain period of time would be deemed unnecessary since they are neither the least restrictive methods to the rights at issue nor proportionate to the protected interests. Lastly, the lack of possible review by a judicial or independent body for the blocked or removed content jeopardizes the values of accountability and due process guaranteed by modern international human rights law.[89]

For example, forced self-censorship and intermediary liability severely undermine the fulfillment of an individual's right to freedom of expression and privacy since they often lead to an over-broad private censorship.[90] The recently enacted Cyber Security Law intensifies the legal obligations of private ISPs to adopt technological methods to keep Internet users' records for no less than six months,[91] and Article 24 of which obliges network operators to require users to provide real identity information when registering for the services.[92] Also, the lately adopted Counterterrorism Law requires ISPs to supply law enforcement agencies with encryption keys and keep the records of each user's online time, user accounts, IP addresses, phone numbers, and other information for 60 days and provide personal information to the authorized government authorities when required.[93] The governmental authorities at various levels have used the

---

[89] *See* UN Human Rights Council, *Report on the Special Rapporteur on the Promotion and Protection of the Right to Freedom of Opinion and Expression, Frank La Rue*, UN General Assembly, A/HRC/17/27 (15 May 2011).

[90] Ibid.

[91] 中华人民共和国网络安全法 (Cybersecurity Law of People's Republic of China) was promulgated on 7 November 2016, not yet effective. Available at http://www.cac.gov.cn/2016-11/07/c_1119867116_2.htm (in Chinese). (accessed 25 August 2016)

[92] Article 24 of the Cybersecurity Law stipulates:

> Network operators handling network access and domain registration services for users, handling stationary or mobile phone network access, or providing users with information publication or instant messaging services, shall require users to provide real identity information when signing agreements with users confirming provision of services. When users do not provide real identity information, network operators must not provide them with relevant services.

[93] 中华人民共和国反恐怖主义法 (Counterterrorism Law of the People's Republic of China), Order of the President of the People's Republic of China, No. 36 (27 December

information obtained from the ISPs to prosecute or detain Internet users for their online activities.[94]

It is evident that the purposes of some of the measures are not to protect public morals, cultural diversity, and national security or to maintain public order but to prevent political dissidents from expressing their opinions in a public forum. These rigorous regulations, together with the indeterminate meaning of the terms therein, exert chilling effects on freedom of expression and cause unlawful interference in a person's private life and privacy. However, China has claimed that each country should have the authority to determine its internal affairs without interference from other countries, and the same rule of state sovereignty applies to the Internet.

B. State Sovereignty

Ironically, the term 'Internet sovereignty' originated in the mid-nineties with a completely opposite meaning to the definition given by the Chinese government. It might seem naïve now; however, proponents of Internet freedom generally believed that because of the separation from doctrines tied to territorial jurisdictions, distinct new rules would evolve in the new spaces. Therefore, Internet freedom advocates claimed that nations had to respect the unique character of cyberspace and its set of rules.[95] The reality is, as technology advances, so do the nation states. Many of the descriptive requirements for cyberspace sovereignty in the 1990s were only possible given a highly fragmented network.[96] Clearly, China, which has the most centralized Internet operating system in the world, does not match this description.

Generally speaking, the notion of national sovereignty applies to cyberspace. A UN report on Developments in the Field of Information and Telecommunications in the Context of International Security concluded that "state sovereignty and international norms and principles that flow from sovereignty apply to State conduct of ICT-related activities, and to their jurisdiction over ICT infrastruc-

2015), Article 19. Available at http://big5.gov.cn/gate/big5/www.gov.cn/zhengce/2015-12/28/content_5029899.htm. (accessed 28 August 2016)

[94] *See* Chapter 4.II.D.

[95] *See* David R. Johnson and David Post, *Law and Borders – The Rise of Law in Cyberspace*, Stanford Law Review, Vol.48 (1996), p.1367; *see* also Stephen Taylor, *Erosion of National Sovereignty by 21st Century Technology*, International Business Center (2003).

[96] *See* Timothy S. Wu, *Cyber Sovereignty? – the Internet and the International System*, Harvard Journal of Law & Technology, Vol.10, No.3 (1997), p. 648.

ture within their territory".[97] Based on the UN report, Chinese scholars and President Xi Jinping reiterated that Internet sovereignty has been recognized by the UN as a legitimate authority of a nation on cyberspace. Nevertheless, the assertions neglected to mention that the report also emphasized that "state efforts to address the security of ICTs must go hand-in-hand with respect for human rights and fundamental freedoms set forth in the Universal Declaration of Human Rights and other international instruments" and "states must meet their international obligations regarding internationally wrongful acts".[98]

Therefore, within the context of Internet governance, a state's sovereign power should be limited by its international obligations. Against this background, the following section first examines the traditional concept of state sovereignty and its application to the Internet. The Westphalian sovereign system has been challenged in the process of globalization, and states are not unitary actors in the interdependent world in which we live today.[99] The governance of the Internet requires new thinking about the concept of state sovereignty. The section further examines whether the Chinese version of Internet sovereignty is conductive to Internet governance.

a. Westphalia Sovereignty and Internet Sovereignty

The traditional concept of sovereignty is defined as supreme and independent authority in government as claimed by a state in a defined territory.[100] This conception of sovereignty has been increasingly challenged by some, while being asserted by others, especially in the sphere of cyberspace. Opponents of Internet sovereignty have claimed that the creation and function of the Internet is based on a decentralized establishment, which requests interoperability among gov-

---

[97] United Nations, General Assembly, *Group of Governmental Experts on Developments in the Field of International and Telecommunications in the Context of International Security – Note by the Secretary General*, A/68/98 (24 June 2013), para. 20.

[98] Ibid. After recognizing the state sovereignty to the Internet, the UN further stated that:

> 21. State efforts to address the security of ICTs must go hand-in-hand with respect for human rights and fundamental freedoms set forth in the Universal Declaration of Human Rights and other international instruments.
>
> 23. States must meet their international obligations regarding internationally wrongful acts attributable to them. States must not use proxies to commit internationally wrongful acts. States should seek to ensure that their territories are no used by non-State actors for unlawful use of ICTs.

[99] Rolf H. Weber, *New Sovereignty Concepts in the Age of Internet*?, Journal of Internet Law, Vol.14, Issue 2 (2010), p. 12-20.

[100] *See* Kal Raustiala, *Rethinking the Sovereignty Debate in International Economic Law*, Journal of International Economic Law, Vol.6, No.4 (2003), pp. 841-878.

ernments, private sector developers, service providers and individuals; therefore, no state can exercise absolute sovereign right in such a transnational community.[101] However, in the name of protecting national security or morality and maintaining economic sustainability, the practice of erecting borders around 'cyber territory' is being observed across the world.[102] While We are living in the middle of a transition that sovereignty is the inevitable direction Internet governance is heading to, the boundary of the sovereign power in the digital age remains undetermined.

i. The Erosion of the Traditional Concept of Sovereignty

The notion of state sovereignty is the basic concept of modern international law and has many various meanings and implications.[103] For decades, the term sovereignty represented the idea of absolute authority in the political community within a state's territory. In the 16th century, the concept of sovereignty was first introduced by Jean Bodin, who is considered the founder of the modern theory of sovereignty, as a political theory linking states with their sovereign rights.[104] Bodin's concept of sovereignty is equally captured in the Latin adage: *Summa in cives ac subdiots legibusque solute potest* (Sovereignty is the supreme power over citizens and subordinates, which [supreme power] is not subject to the law).[105] In the 16th century, the term sovereignty referred to the absolute supremacy of the ruling monarch.[106]

The modern concept of sovereignty and the notion of a 'nation state' began with the Peace Treaty of Westphalia of 1648, which ended the Thirty Years War in Europe.[107] Although it did not explicitly describe the term 'sovereignty', the

---

[101] *See* Rolf H. Weber, *New Sovereignty Concepts in the Age of Internet*?, Journal of Internet Law, Vol.14, Issue 2 (2010), p. 12-20; *see* also David R., Johnson & David Post, *Law and Bordered – The Rise of Law in Cyberspace*, Stanford Law Review, Vol. 48 (1996), pp. 1367- 1402.

[102] Chris C. Demchak and Peter Dombrowski, *Rise of a Cyber Westphalian Age*, Strategic Study Quarterly (Spring 2011), pp. 32-61.

[103] *See* John H. Jackson, *Sovereignty, the WTO, and Changing Fundamentals of International Law*, New York: Cambridge University Press (2006), pp. 57-78.

[104] *See* Johan D. van der Vyver, Sovereignty. In: Dinah Shelton (eds), *The Oxford Handbook of International Human Rights Law*, Oxford University Press (2013).

[105] *See* Julian H Franklin, *Jean Bodin and the Rise of Absolutist Theory*, Cambridge University Press (1973).

[106] Ibid.

[107] The Treaty of Westphalia was essentially a peace treaty intending to end the religious conflict in Europe after 30 years' war between Holy Roman Emperor and the king

Treaty recognized the principle of sovereign power and the equality of states.[108] Each party to the treaty agreed to respect the exclusive territorial rights, political independence, equality under international law, and right to conduct foreign policy of all other parties.[109] Modern Europe, as a continent of sovereign states, was established. Over time, the terms of the Peace Treaty of Westphalia were shaped into what is called "Westphalian sovereignty" today, i.e., the absolute right of sovereign states.[110]

European rulers embraced sovereignty as a means to stabilize Europe in the 17th century. The principle continued to be the driving force behind the decolonization movement and the transformation of international relations after the Second World War.[111] The UN Charter of 1945 endorsed the notion of sovereign equality in Article 2, which stipulated that "the United Nations is based on the sovereign equality of all its members".[112] The 1970 Declaration on Principles of International Law Concerning Friendly Relations and Co-operation Among States in Accordance with the Charter of the United Nations (1970 Declaration) reiterated that "no State or group of States has the right to intervene, directly and indirectly, for any reason whatever, in the internal or external affairs of any other State" and "every State has an inalienable right to choose its political, economic, social and cultural systems, without interference in any form by other State".[113]

of France and their respective allies. The signing of the treaty resulted in a decentralized sovereignty-dominated body politic in Europe. When the Roman Empire vanished, kings, princes, or dukes in Switzerland, Netherlands, Germany, France, Austria, Spain, etc. exercised their secular authority over their territory to control internal affairs, including choice of religion. *See* Derek Croxton, *The Peace of Westphalia of 1648 and the Origins of Sovereignty*, The International History Review, Vol.21, No.3 (September 1999), pp. 569- 591.

108 Ibid.

109 *See* Stephen D. Krasner, *Sovereignty: Organized Hypocrisy*, Princeton University Press (1999), pp. 1-25.

110 *See* John H. Jackson, *Sovereignty, the WTO, and Changing Fundamentals of International Law*, New York: Cambridge University Press (2006).

111 Winston P. Nagan & Aitza M. Haddad, *Sovereignty in Theory and Practice*, San Diego Int'l L. J., Vol.13 (2012), pp. 429-520 (453-460).

112 United Nations, *Charter of the United Nations*, 24 October 1945, 1 UNTS XVI, Art. 2, para. 1.

113 United Nations General Assembly Resolution, *1970 Declaration on Principles of International Law Concerning Friendly Relations and Co-operation Among States in Accordance with the Charter of the United Nations*, A/RES/25/2625 (24 October 1970). Both statements are described under the title: *The principle concerning the duty not to*

From the historical, political, legal, and economic perspectives, sovereignty has been a source of international stability for more than two hundred years. Nevertheless, during this period of time before the digital era, sovereignty was never static but a changing phenomenon in various policy, academic, and political constituents.[114] Richard K. Ashley argued that "in effect, sovereignty is a practical category whose empirical contents are not fixed but evolve in a way reflecting the active practical consensus among coreflective statesmen".[115] The central subject of sovereignty has shifted from monarch to nation states and to the people. The argument of inherent sovereign rights has also transferred from a focus on the supreme and absolute right of the rulers to the conception of an allocation of power among nation states in the interdependent global community.[116] Therefore, the concept of sovereignty is complex and has been the subject of continuous contestation and debate.

Professor Stephan Krasner, an eminent scholar who described the concept of sovereignty as organized hypocrisy, labeled four types of sovereignty. Krasner explained:

> "The term sovereignty has been commonly used in at least for different ways: domestic sovereignty, referring to the organization of public authority within a state and to the level of effective control exercised by those holding authority; interdependence sovereignty, referring to the ability of

intervene in matters within the domestic jurisdiction of any State, in accordance with the Charter.

[114] *See* Stephen D. Krasner, Problematic Sovereignty. In: Stephen D. Krasner (ed.), *Problematic Sovereignty – Contested Rules and Political Possibility*, Columbia University Press, New York (2001), pp. 1-23; *see* also Wiston P. Nagan & Aitza M. Haddad, *Sovereignty in Theory and Practice*, San Diego Int'l L. J., Vol.13 (2012), pp. 429-520; *see* also Janice E. Thomson, *State Sovereignty in International Relations: Bridging the Gap Between Theory and Empirical Research*, International Studies Quarterly, Vol.39 (1995), pp. 213-233.

[115] *See* Richard K. Ashley, *The Poverty of Neorealism, International Organization*, Vol.38, No.2 (Spring 1984), pp. 272-273.

[116] *See* Janice E. Thomson, *State Sovereignty in International Relations: Bridging the Gap Between Theory and Empirical Research*, International Studies Quarterly, Vol.39 (1995), pp. 213-233; and Vlad Alexandru Voicescu & Nicu-Râzvan Dobârceanu, *Sovereignty and Integration in Modern Era. Perspectives*, Law Review: Judicial Doctrine & Case-law, Vol.2, Issue 4 (Oct.-Dec. 2012), pp. 1-10; *see* also Stephen D. Krasner, Problematic Sovereignty. In: Stephen D. Krasner (ed.), *Problematic Sovereignty – Contested Rules and Political Possibility*, Columbia University Press, New York (2001), pp. 1-23; and Robert Howse, Sovereignty, Lost and Found. In: Wenhua Shan, Penelope Simons and Dalvinder Singh (eds.), *Redefining Sovereignty in International Economic Law*, Hart Publishing, USA Portland (2008), pp. 61-75.

> public authorities to control transborder movements; international legal sovereignty, referring to the mutual recognition of states or other entities; and Westphalian sovereignty, referring to the exclusion of external actors from domestic authority configurations. These four meanings of sovereignty are not logically couples, nor have they covaried in practice."[117]

The term sovereignty embraces notions of (*inter alia*) supremacy of domestic authority, the political independence of a nation to carry out foreign and domestic policies over its territory and people, equality of states, self-determination, freedom of the nation from external intervention (foreign or international force or otherwise), mutual recognition, free consent in international relations (explicit or implicit), and controls over movement across borders. Therefore, what sovereignty signifies is not a well-defined body of rights and obligations of a state but a changing frame of reference, determined by the factors and processes in different political or economic forms at different periods of time.[118] Although the components of sovereignty have never been determined, together, at least to a certain extent, they provided a predictable foundation for the successful implementation of international law.[119]

Nevertheless, given the degree of interdependence in the political and economic relations between nation states and the emergence of international human rights movements, many of the components of sovereignty have been criticized as outdated. Some scholars have argued that the concept of sovereignty never was and never will be absolute.[120] Some have even contended that the usage of sovereignty in international relations is "an illegitimate offspring" since the concept does not encourage global cooperation but isolation.[121] For example, some countries, in the name of political independence and territorial impermeability, have refused to respect the universally recognized norms of human rights. As Louis Henkin pointed out: "The banner of sovereignty still waves ominously

---

[117] Stephen D. Krasner, *Sovereignty: Organized Hypocrisy*, Princeton University Press (1999), p. 9.

[118] *See* Vaughan Lowe, Sovereignty and International Economic Law. In: Wenhua Shan, Penelope Simons and Dalvinder Singh (eds.), *Redefining Sovereignty in International Economic Law*, Hart Publishing, USA Portland (2008), pp. 77-84.

[119] Richard N. Haass, *Sovereignty, Existing Rights, Evolving Responsibilities*, Remarks at the School of Foreign Services and the Mortara Center for International Studies, Georgetown University (14 January 2003).

[120] *See* John H. Jackson, Sovereignty: Outdated Concept or New Approaches. In: Wenhua Shan, Penelope Simons and Dalvinder Singh (eds.), *Redefining Sovereignty in International Economic Law*, Hart Publishing, USA Portland (2008), pp. 3-26.

[121] *See* Louis Henkin, *That "S" Word: Sovereignty, and Globalization, and Human Rights, Et cetera*, Fordham Law Review, Vol.68 (1999).

over all human rights issues; the mantra of sovereignty is still intoned against human rights. Sovereign states accept international human rights standards, if they wish to, when they wish to, to the extent they wish to."[122]

The recent development in global governance, especially the emerging tendency of cooperation among states after the Second World War, indicates the need for alternative thinking on the purpose and role of sovereignty in the contemporary era.[123] Many scholars have argued that globalization, the evolving concept of human rights, and the advance in information technologies have all challenged the traditional Westphalian sovereign power of a state to exclude external actors from domestic structures within its territory.[124] The establishment of the UN, the WTO, the World Bank, and other international organizations has imposed restrictions on state sovereignty since those institutions often govern matters traditionally addressed at the domestic level. States are legally obliged to comply with the obligations of treaties or customary international laws that they have agreed to.[125] A research essay supplementing to the report of the International Commission on Intervention and State Sovereignty noted:

> "Sovereignty has been eroded by contemporary economic, cultural, and environmental factors. Interference in what would previously have been regarded as internal affairs – by other states, the private sector, and non-state actors – has become routine. However, the preoccupation here is not these routine matters but the potential tension when the norm of state sovereignty and egregious human suffering coexist."[126]

Regardless of the controversy, the concept of sovereignty has shaped and dominated international relations for more than two hundred years. It has always been the fundamental norm of international law and the foundation of the world order. For example, the notion of self-determination, one of the most

---

[122] Ibid., p. 5.

[123] *See* Kal Raustiala, *Rethinking the Sovereignty Debate in International Economic Law*, Journal of International Economic Law, Vol.6, No.4 (2003), pp. 841-878.

[124] *See* Janice E. Thomson, *State Sovereignty in International Relations: Bridging the Gap Between Theory and Empirical Research*, International Studies Quarterly, Vol.39 (1995), pp. 213-233.

[125] *See* John H. Jackson, Sovereignty: Outdated Concept or New Approaches. In: Wenhua Shan, Penelope Simons and Dalvinder Singh (eds.), *Redefining Sovereignty in International Economic Law*, Hart Publishing, USA Portland (2008), pp. 3-26.

[126] ICISS, *The Responsibility to Protect – Research, Bibliography, Background (Supplementary Volume to the Report of the International Commission on Intervention and State Sovereignty)*, International Development Research Centre (2001), pp. 5-13.

prominent components of state sovereignty, was transformed into a universal right and recognized as a writ for obtaining decolonization in the second half of the 20th century.[127] State consent, whether implicit or explicit, is still regarded as a prerequisite for imposing international obligations on states.[128] Consequently, while the concept of Westphalian sovereignty is not plausible in this interdependent and globalized world, sovereignty will continue to play a vital role in modern international relations. Therefore, the fundamental issue should be to what extent a state can legitimately claim sovereignty and under what circumstances this sovereign power should be delegated to the international community.

Respecting international obligations and emphasizing international cooperation will contribute to a greater accountability in global governance.[129] Ashley argues that sovereignty "involves not only the possession of self and the exclusion of others but also the limitation of self in respect of others, for its authority presupposes the recognition of others who, per force of their recognition, agree to be so excluded".[130] Therefore, while claiming its right to govern as a nation within the context of international law, a state should also observe its responsibilities and obligations to other nations and to its people. As Henkin correctly pointed out:

> "we have to avoid the temptations of traditional sovereignty. The autonomy – the "privacy" of states – is an important value, but not as an iron curtain. We cannot insist what we do at home is no one else's business, even if we do it in the name of religion or in the name of some other values. A decent respect for the opinions of mankind, you will remember, was our undertaking from our nation's birth, and we have to honor that as part of our sovereignty.

---

127 *See* Thomas M. Frank, *The Emerging Right to Democratic Governance*, The American Journal of International Law, Vol. 86 (1992), pp. 46-91 (52-54).

128 *See* John H. Jackson, *Sovereignty, the WTO, and Changing Fundamentals of International Law*, New York: Cambridge University Press (2006), pp. 57-78; and *see* also Johan D. van der Vyver, Sovereignty. In: Dinah Shelton (eds), *The Oxford Handbook of International Human Rights Law*, Oxford University Press (2013).

129 *See* Thomas Cottier, *Multilayered Governance, Pluralism and Moral Conflict*, Indiana Journal of Global Legal Studies, Vol.16, No.2 (Summer 2009), pp. 647-679.

130 Richard K. Ashley, *The Poverty of Neorealism, International Organization*, Vol.38, No.2 (Spring 1984), pp. 225-286 (272).

Sovereignty as a right to do as one pleases is part of the concept, but not sovereignty as anarchy, not sovereignty as resistance to cooperation. And not sovereignty as immunity."[131]

ii. Internet Sovereignty

The nature and origin of the Internet were based on the ideology that the Internet should be treated as a global common and no traditional sovereign states could assert jurisdiction over this borderless space.[132] The early Internet architects and pioneers believed the Internet represented an anti-authoritarian, non-hierarchical, and anti-government sphere whose innovation could only be led and shaped by a self-organized community. They further claimed that revolution of this technology would be too flexible and too rapid for any government which tried to regulate it.[133]

The ideology of the Internet was proved to be myth. Countries around the world have used the same technology that built the Internet to erect borders in cyberspace. The role of governments in the Internet has changed. The growth of E-commerce and the transformation of social life to cyberspace demonstrate the necessity of a rule-based environment where human behaviors are involved. The surprising and shocking incidents of Stuxnet in 2010[134] and Edward Snowden in 2013[135] revealed the secure vulnerability of the interconnected digital world. Although the characteristics of the Internet are profoundly different from those of physical space, it is undeniable that what happens in the 1 and 0 binary

[131] Louis Henkin, *That "S" Word: Sovereignty, and Globalization, and Human Rights, Et cetera*, Fordham Law Review, Vol.68 (1999), p. 12-13.
[132] *See* Timothy S. Wu, *Cyber Sovereignty? – the Internet and the International System*, Harvard Journal of Law & Technology, Vol.10, No.3 (1997), p. 648; *see* also David R., Johnson & David Post, *Law and Bordered – The Rise of Law in Cyberspace*, Stanford Law Review, Vol. 48 (1996), pp. 1367- 1402.
[133] *See* David R., Johnson & David Post, *Law and Bordered – The Rise of Law in Cyberspace*, Stanford Law Review, Vol.48 (1996), pp. 1367- 1402.
[134] Stuxnet, as a malicious piece of software, targeted the program controlling centrifuges in Iranian nuclear reprocessing plants. Spread by infected USB thumb divers, Stuxnet bypassed Internet security controls and infiltrated many Windows operating systems. The infection of Stuxnet lasted for at least two years, and the scope and complexity of national security challenges posed by cyberspace created a new level of insecurity.
[135] Edward Joseph Snowden, a former Central Intelligence Agency employee, leaked 'several' classified documents from the National Security Agency in 2013. The exact size of Snowden's disclosed information is unknown, but it raised a serious surveillance concerns among nation states.

sphere has real consequences in the real world.[136] A free Internet is essential to facilitate innovation, but regulatory control is also necessary to moderate the adverse effects the Internet might have on society.

In principle, the doctrine of national sovereignty applies to cyberspace as it does to real space. The erection of virtual borders and the increasing requests for a stable and secure online environment have led governments to legitimately declare themselves cyberspace authorities. First, despite the fact that the Internet has been regularly referred to as a trans-border infrastructure, Internet governance is far from borderless.[137] As previously discussed, the concept of sovereignty depends fundamentally on the defined territory. While it seems impossible to claim a territory in a space that does not exist, the underlying infrastructures are built in the physical world and people who participate in online activities reside within the territory of a sovereign state. In other words, a cyber border for every country is within technological reach.[138]

Secondly, the increasing and prospective threats to national security and social values on the Internet provide nation states legitimate reasons to claim authority in the virtual world. In order to maintain societal stability, ensure economic growth, and protect national and international security, states increasingly exercise control over Internet infrastructure and corresponding activities within their sovereign territories.[139] The Chinese government has implemented the most sophisticated filtering and surveillance system at its international Internet gateways to fight social disharmony, fraud, piracy, gambling, pornography, and Western subversive influence. The European Union has promulgated Internet data protection regulations to prevent the misuse or abuse of citizens' personal information. The US has declared cyber threats to be the most vital national security concern and has issued the US Cyber Command to create a

---

[136] *See* Georgios I. Zkos, *Demolishing State's Sole Power over Sovereignty and Territory via Electronic Technology and Cyberspace*, Journal of Internet Law, Vol. 17, Issue:5 (November 2013), pp. 3-17.

[137] *See* Jack Goldsmith and Tim Wu, *Who Controls the Internet? Illusions of a Borderless World*, Oxford University Press, New York (2006); *see* also Min Jiang, *Chinese Internet Sovereignty*, Instantané 2012 – PolitisLab' A CEIS Project on Public Affairs and Communication (2011).

[138] *See* David R., Johnson & David Post, *Law and Bordered – The Rise of Law in Cyberspace*, Stanford Law Review, Vol. 48 (1996), pp. 1367- 1402.

[139] *See* Eric Talbot Jensen, *Cyber Sovereignty: The Way Ahead*, Texas International Law Journal, Vol.50 (2) (2015), pp. 273-302.

cyber safety wrapper around critical military assets and to establish a virtual border for the nation.[140]

Accordingly, states continuously exercise their control over cyberspace and Internet activities based on the principle of territorial sovereignty. Nevertheless, even in the concrete world, the notion of absolute sovereignty is no longer plausible. Although states might still inevitably play a central role in Internet governance, internally or externally, the unique interoperable characteristic of this transnational online community makes it impossible to fully rely on one country to protect the overall public interest.[141] The fact that most Internet infrastructure is built or owned by private actors and any national Internet-related regulations would easily generate extraterritorial effects reflects an urgent need for cooperation at the international level.[142]

In addition, when considering Internet sovereignty, it is crucial to deliberate on state obligations corresponding to sovereign power. The reciprocal nature of rights and obligations in international law is a generally accepted assumption.[143] In other words, state sovereignty in the context of Internet governance should be considered along with states' obligations to recognize the sovereignty of other states,[144] the obligations of non-intervention,[145] the obligations to maintain the open character of cyberspace/ the Internet, the obligations to cooperatively en-

---

[140] *See* Chris C. Demchak and Peter Dombrowski, *Rise of a Cybered Westphalian Age*, Strategic Studies Quarterly, Vol. 5, (1) (2011), pp. 31-62.

[141] *See* Rolf H. Weber, *New Sovereignty Concepts in the Age of Internet?*, Journal of Internet Law, Vol.14, Issue 2 (2010), pp. 12-20.

[142] Châteua de Bossey, *Report of the Working Group on Internet Governance*, Working Group on Internet Governance (WGIG) (June 2005). WGIG defined the concept of Internet governance as:

> Internet governance is the development and application by Government, the private sector and civil society, in their respective roles, of shared principles, norms, rules, decision-making procedures, and programmes that shape the evolution and use of the Internet.

[143] *See* Martti Koskenniemi, Doctrines of State Responsibility. In: James Crawford, Alain Pellet, and Simon Olleson (eds.), *The Law of International Responsibility*, Oxford Commentaries on International Law (2010), p. 45 (47-48).

[144] *See* Wolff Heintschel von Heinegg, Legal Implications of Territorial Sovereignty in Cyberspace. In: C. Czosseck, R. Ottis and K. Ziolkowski (eds.), *2012 4th International Conference on Cyber Conflict*, NATO CCD OCE Publications, Tallinn (2012), pp. 7-19.

[145] I.C.J., *Case Concerning Military and Paramilitary Activities in and against Nicaragua*, ICJ Rep. 14 (1986) para. 202. The ICJ stated, "between independent States, respect for territorial sovereignty is an essential foundation of international relations ..., and international law requires political integrity also to be respected."

sure cyber security,[146] and the obligations for the realization of fundamental human rights protections. It is through international cooperation that nation states can meet and satisfy the new challenges brought about by the new technologies. If the notion of sovereignty is a changing frame of reference in international relations,[147] the outdated absolute sovereignty does not comply anymore with the needs of a global governance framework in the digital age.[148]

b. The Chinese Version of Internet Sovereignty

From the release of the White Paper on Internet Policy to the recently enacted Cyber Security Law of China, the Chinese government has tightened its control of Internet governance toward an unprecedented comprehensive but specific system. As Mr. Xi reiterated that "China allows no compromise on cyberspace sovereignty",[149] China has been criticized for leading the Internet toward a digital authoritarianism.[150]In response to criticism from other countries, the Chinese government has rigorously proclaimed that its Internet-related measures are in line with core Chinese values, and that state sovereignty on the Internet empowers the government to regulate the people and activities within its territory.

As discussed above, this approach, based on the antiquated concept of Westphalian sovereignty,[151] is unable to offer effective solutions for Internet governance. The assertion of unconstrained sovereign power exclusively based on territoriality often fails to answer the questions of allocation of power, since state power is frequently delegated to a multitude of treaties, customary international norms, and institutions by which states share their power in the international legal system.[152] In the interdependent and globalized world, it is difficult,

---

[146] Eric Talbot Jensen, *Cyber Sovereignty: The Way Ahead*, Texas International Law Journal, Vol.50, Issue: 2 (2015), pp. 273-302 (280-289).

[147] *See* Vaughan Lowe, Sovereignty and International Economic Law. In: Wenhua Shan, Penelope Simons and Dalvinder Singh (eds.), *Redefining Sovereignty in International Economic Law*, Hart Publishing, USA Portland (2008), pp. 77-84.

[148] *See* Rolf H. Weber, *New Sovereignty Concepts in the Age of Internet?*, Journal of Internet Law, Vol.14, Issue 2 (2010), p. 12-20.

[149] Live report: opening ceremony of the 2ed World Internet Conference. Available http://www.wuzhenwic.org/2015-12/16/c_47521.htm. (accessed 01 September 2016)

[150] *See* Fredrik Erixon and Hosuk Lee-Makiyama, *Digital Authoritarianism: Human Rights, Geopolitics and Commerce*, ECIPE Occasional Paper, No. 5 (2011).

[151] *See* John H. Jackson, *Sovereignty, the WTO, and Changing Fundamentals of International Law*, New York: Cambridge University Press (2006), pp. 70-76.

[152] *See* Joel Trachtman, *Cyberspace, Sovereignty, Jurisdiction, and Modernism*, Indiana Journal of Global Legal studies, Vol:5, Issue:2 (1998), pp. 561-582.

if not impossible, for one state, acting alone, to provide the policy outcomes that are desired by the people. Innovative computing technologies compress the time and space of social interaction so profoundly that any proclamation of state sovereignty over the Internet exclusively based on territorial borders will turn out to be invalidated.[153] In the context of Internet governance, actions by one nation can easily constrain and influence the internal affairs of others. The assertion of an absolute sovereign right over the Internet will, therefore, inevitably interfere with the sovereignty of other countries.

The Chinese vision of Internet sovereignty - absolute monopoly - will be challenged domestically and internationally. From the domestic perspective, the modern concept of sovereignty has gravitated from the power of the state towards the sovereignty of the people.[154] The strict regulations focusing on individuals' responsibilities to the state rather than the protection of individuals' rights on the Internet undermined the legitimacy of state sovereignty resting upon the will and consent of its people.[155] From the international perspective, since many of the new challenges brought about by the Internet can only be settled through international cooperation, submitting to international law and allocating sovereign power to international institutions will actually serve as a means to reaffirm state sovereignty.[156]

In sum, state sovereignty applies to cyberspace; however, the application of sovereignty must comply with a nation's international commitments and obligations. Section IV, therefore, examines whether the Internet control and censorship mechanisms adopted by the Chinese government are in violation of the WTO, especially the GATS. The Internet and related technologies have contributed to the fast growth of electronic delivery services. Since the stability of the economic system depends on good governance, Internet-related restrictive measures, which have unanticipated reverse effects on international trade, need

---

[153] *See* Oreste Pollicino and Marco Bassini, The Law of the Internet between Globalization and Localization. In: Miguel Maduro, Kaarlo Tuori, and Suvi Sankari (eds.), *Transnational Law – Rethinking European Law and Legal Thinking*, Cambridge University Press, United Kingdom (2014), pp. 346-380 (326-328).

[154] *See* John H. Jackson, *Sovereignty, the WTO, and Changing Fundamentals of International Law*, New York: Cambridge University Press (2006), pp. 70-76.

[155] *See* Min Jiang, *Chinese Internet Sovereignty*, Instantané 2012 – PolitisLab' A CEIS Project on Public Affairs and Communication (2011).

[156] *See* Kal Raustiala, *Rethinking the Sovereignty Debate in International Economic Law*, Journal of International Economic Law, Vol.6, No.4 (2003), pp. 841-878.

to comply with the rules of international trade law.[157] In the absence of an international standard of Internet governance, the *Google – China* scenario presented in Section IV intends to analyze whether, by taking into account human welfare and social justice, the WTO is the appropriate forum to settle the censorship issues on the Internet.

157 *See* Susan Ariel Aaronson, *The Digital Trade Imbalance and its Implications for Internet Governance*, Global Commission on Internet Governance, No. 25 (January 2016).

IV. Potential WTO Agreement Violations (Specifically under the GATS)

China, having the most Internet users in the world, is considered to be among those countries which have the most influence on Internet policies. Nevertheless, Internet censorship mechanisms adopted by the Chinese government restrict international trade in various situations. Released in April 2016, the office of the United States Trade Representative (USTR) listed Chinese Internet censorship as a trade barrier for the first time in its annual report on the challenges faced by US exporters in the foreign market.[158] According to the report, Chinese measures impose severe restrictions on a wide range of foreign ICT goods and services with an apparent long-term goal of replacing these with domestic products.[159] The report further indicated that "over the past decade, China's filtering of cross-border Internet traffic has posed a significant burden on foreign suppliers, hurting both Internet sites themselves, and users who often depend on them for their businesses".[160] Therefore, the debates over Internet censorship should focus on barriers to Internet freedom as well as on barriers to free trade.[161]

Taking the *Google – China* incident as a research baseline, the following section considers the possibility of challenging the Chinese Internet censorship measures before the WTO adjudicating bodies. Based on the analysis in Chapter 3, section IV first analyzes whether China has undertaken specific commitments in its GATS Schedule as regards the services provided by Google, after which it examines specific obligations of market access and national treatment under the GATS. The analysis further discusses whether the comprehensive Chinese Internet censorship measures violate the transparency obligation or nullify the reasonable expectations of other WTO Members respectively. If any of the obligations is violated, the last issue is whether China could have deviated from its substantive obligations under the GATS to protect public morals or maintain public order within the meaning of Article XIV (a) of the GATS.

---

[158] *See* Ambassador Michael B.G. Froman, *2016 National Trade Estimate Report on Foreign Trade Barriers*, Office of the United States Trade Representative (April 2016), pp. 81-95.

[159] Ibid., p. 84.

[160] Ibid., p. 91.

[161] *See* Ritika Patni & Nihal Joseph, *WTO Ramifications of Internet Censorship: The Google – China Controversy*, NUJS Law Review, Vol. 3 (2010), pp. 337-363 (337-339).

A. The Google – China Controversy

As the largest search engine in the world, Google is a company trusted by millions of users to protect their personal information and conducts its business under the motto of 'Don't be Evil'.[162] Although it has expanded into many countries and hosted domain names in over 150 countries on its search engine, Google has faced serious obstacles to providing its services in the Chinese market. From 1999 to 2002, the US-based Google.com was available to Chinese users, as it was to users from other countries.[163] Working entirely from its headquarters in California, Google was able to provide a Chinese-language search interface without the interference of any censorship mechanisms adopted by the Chinese government.[164] By the end of 2002, the company had a 25% share of the Chinese online search market share.[165]

On September 3, 2002, Google disappeared for two weeks and the users searching for Google.com were instead redirected to Baidu, a rival Chinese search site.[166] Although it is clear that Google was blocked by the Chinese government through the Great Firewall, the real reasons for the blockage were unknown. Since then, Google has been blocked in China from time to time and its market share dropped from 25% to 19.2% in 2006 while Baidu blossomed from a 3% market share in 2002 to 63.7% in fall 2006.[167]

Given the economic potential of the expanding Chinese Internet market, in January 2006, Google launched google.cn to escalate operations in China at the price of conducting self-censorship. In response to criticisms from human rights advocates, Google justified its decision on the basis that a censored service is better than no service at all. For example, in a public announcement made at the

162 'Don't be evil' is the ethical standard of Google's code of conduct. As Google explained, "Googlers generally apply those words to how we serve our users. But "Don't be evil" is much more than that. Yes, it's about providing our users unbiased access to information, focusing on their needs and giving them the best products and services that we can. But it's also about doing the right thing more generally – following the law, acting honorably, and treating co-workers with courtesy and respect."

163 Kristina Wilson, Yaneli Ramos, and Daniel Harvey, *Google in China – "The Great Firewall"*, the Kenan Institute for Ethics at Duke University (2006).

164 Clive Thompson, *Google's China Problem (and China's Google Problem)*, The New York Times Magazine (23 April 2006). Available at http://www.nytimes.com/2006/04/23/magazine/23google.html. (accessed 02 September 2016)

165 Ibid.

166 Johan Lagerkvist, After the Internet, *Before Democracy – competing Norms in Chinese Media and Society*, Peter Kang AG, Bern: Switzerland (2010), p. 232.

167 Ibid.

time of the launch of Google.cn, Andrew McLaughlin, Google's senior policy counsel, explained:

> "Filtering our search results clearly compromises our mission. Failing to offer Google search at all to a fifth of the world's population, however, does so far more severely. Whether our critics agree with our decision or not, due to the severe quality problems faced by users trying to access Google.com from within China, this is precisely the choice we believe we faced."[168]

After reentering the Chinese market, the future of Google.cn seemed promising since Google's search market share was driven up to 35% within three fiscal years.[169] On January 12, 2010, however, Google announced its intention to end self-censorship on its services in China and to pull out of the Chinese market.[170] Since the beginning of 2009, Google has received several accusations from the Chinese government and been shut down several times for failing to remove pornographic content from its search results whereas thousands of Chinese pornography websites remained easily accessible through other domestic service providers.[171] The final incident that resulted in Google's announcement that it was withdrawing from the Chinese market was a series of sophisticated and organized cyber-attacks targeting US companies in December 2009.

The attacks, named 'Operation Aurora', were aimed at more than twenty US companies, including Google.[172] Google reported that the Gmail accounts of several Chinese human rights activists were compromised as well as some of Google's intellectual properties relating to the design of its websites' algorithms

---

[168] Andrew McLaughlin, Google in China, Google Official Blog (27 January 2006). Available at https://googleblog.blogspot.de/2006/01/google-in-china.html. (accessed 05 September 2016)

[169] Anonymous, *A Dual Trace Approach to Challenging Chinese Censorship in the WTO: The (Future) Case of Google and Facebook*, Michigan Journal of International Law, Vol.34, Issue:4 (2013), pp. 857-892 (860-865).

[170] Google.com, *A New Approach to China*, Google Official Blog (12 January 2010). Available at https://googleblog.blogspot.tw/2010/01/new-approach-to-china.html. (accessed 07 September 2016)

[171] Anonymous, *A Dual Trace Approach to Challenging Chinese Censorship in the WTO: The (Future) Case of Google and Facebook*, Michigan Journal of International Law, Vol.34, Issue:4 (2013), pp. 857-892 (860-865).

[172] Ibid.

and operating systems.[173] Despite repeatedly denials from Beijing, Google and the US State Department publicly suggested that the Chinese government was responsible for the attacks.[174] After fruitless negotiations between Google and China, on March 22, 2010, the company announced that it would close Google.cn and reroute Chinese users to its uncensored Chinese search engine based in Hong Kong.[175]

Google's unprecedented decision is a symbolic sign of how Internet censorship can constitute barriers to international trade and undermine the business environment for foreign companies while continuously providing advantageous competitive opportunities for domestic companies.[176] On the day Google announced its decision to shut down Google.cn, Baidu's Nasdaq stock rose to $64.01, or 16.6%.[177] Similarly, the stocks of Sina (新浪) and Sogou (搜狗), the third and fourth search engines in China, also increased 4.9% and 6.2%.[178] According to statistics from CNNIC, in 2014, the Baidu search engine accounted for 88.7% of the Chinese market while Google's market share had dwindled to 2.2%.[179] Furthermore, while YouTube, a wholly-owned subsidiary of Google, has remained permanently blocked since 2009, its major local competitors, Tudou (土豆) and Youku (优酷), are thriving and gaining market share. Facebook, Twitter, Instagram, and other major Western popular websites or applications are confronting similar difficulties when expanding their market in China.

---

173 Google.com, *A New Approach to China*, Google Official Blog (12 January 2010). Available at https://googleblog.blogspot.tw/2010/01/new-approach-to-china.html. (accessed 07 September 2016)

174 Jon M. Garon, *Searching Inside Google: Cases, Controversies and the Future of the World's Most Provocative Company*, Loyola of Los Angeles Entertainment Law Review, Vol. 30, Issue: 3 (2010), pp. 429-475 (470).

175 Justine Lau, *A History of Google in China*, Financial Times (9 July 2010). Available at http://www.ft.com/cms/s/0/faf86fbc-0009-11df-8626-00144feabdc0.html?ft_site=falcon. (accessed 15 September 2016)

176 Cynthia Liu, *Internet Censorship as a Trade Barrier: A Look at the WTO Consistency of the Great Firewall in the Wake of the China – Google Dispute*, Georgetown Journal of International Law, Vol.42 (2011), pp. 1199-1240 (1200-1207).

177 Jordan Calinoff, *Beijing's Foreign Internet Purge – Is web censorship just an excuse to drive out foreign competition and give a boost to Chinese brands?*, Foreign Policy (15 January 2010). Available at http://foreignpolicy.com/2010/01/15/beijings-foreign-internet-purge/. (15 September 2016)

178 Ibid.

179 China Internet Network Information Center (CNNIC), *中国互联网络发展状况统计报告* (January 2015).

B. *Applying the GATS to Chinese Internet Censorship Measures*

According to the analysis in Chapter 3, on the basis of the principle of technological neutrality and evolutionary interpretation, the panels and the Appellate Body in *US – Gambling* and *China – Audiovisual Products* agreed that the GATS obligations and commitments undertaken in 1994 are applicable to the electronic delivery of services through mode 1 cross-border supply.[180] Therefore, when considering whether Chinese Internet censorship measures constitute barriers to foreign Internet service providers supplying their services in the Chinese online market, the GATS rules should apply to the measures at issue. It should be noticed that the purpose of the GATS is, on the one hand, to promoted progressive liberalization of trade in services and, on the other hand, to respect WTO Members' regulatory autonomy to protect vital social values. How to draw the balance between different interests is always a controversial issue in WTO jurisprudence.

a. China's Specific Commitments and Online Content Services

In the *Google – China* scenario, the first issue is whether China has undertaken commitments as regards the services provided by Google since the specific obligations of the GATS can only apply to a Member's measures affecting trade in services when the Member makes a commitment to a specific sector or subsector of the services in its GATS Schedule. The subsequent section first illustrates how to classify the services at issue, such as search engines, video sharing websites, and e-mails, in the current classification system under the GATS. Second, it discusses whether, if the services are categorized under one of the service sectors or sub-sectors, China has made the full commitments on both market access and national treatment obligations under GATS Articles XVI and XVII.

[180] WTO Trade in Service, *Work Programme on Electronic Commerce -- Progress Report to the General Council*, Work Programme on Electronic Commerce, S/L/74 (27 July 1999), para. 4; and Panel Report, *United States – Measures Affecting the Cross-Border Supply of Gambling and Betting Services* (cited as *US – Gambling*), WT/DS285/R (10 November 2004), para. 6.285. The panel stated:

> … mode 1 under the GATS encompasses all possible means of supplying services from the territory of one WTO Member into the territory of another WTO Member. Therefore, a market access commitment for mode 1 implies the right for other Members' suppliers to supply a service through all means of delivery, whether by mail, telephone, Internet etc., unless otherwise specified in a Member's Schedule.

i. Classification of Online Services in WTO Members' GATS Schedule

To determine the applicability of the GATS to Internet services is complicated since the Internet and Internet-related services were in their infancy (or did not even exist) and attracted little attention from the negotiators when the GATS was concluded in 1995.[181] Nevertheless, the panel and the Appellate Body in both *US – Gambling* and *China – Audiovisual Products* adopted an evolutionary approach to interpreting the meaning of the terms in WTO Members' GATS Schedule.[182] According to the WTO adjudicating bodies, under Article XX:3 of the GATS, the Schedule of a Member forms an integral part of the GATS. Therefore, in order to ascertain the meaning of a concession in a Member's Schedule, the scope of a specific commitment should be interpreted according to the common intention of the parties and in conformity with the customary rules of treaty interpretation, i.e. Articles 31 and 32 of the Vienna Convention.[183]

According to the case review provided in Chapter 3, the Appellate Body conducted its classification analysis on the basis of the 1993 Scheduling Guidelines and the W/120 system (and correspondent CPC).[184] However, it is a tricky task for a panel to determine which sector or sub-sectors cover those of Google's services at issue since neither the W/120 nor CPC makes direct reference to many Internet services, and some new online services often lack equivalent offline predecessors.[185] For example, a search engine could belong to either 'data-processing services', listed under W/120 1-B 'Computer and Related Services', or 'on-line information and database retrieval services', listed under W/120 2-C 'Telecommunication Services'.[186] For some WTO Members, the

[181] *See* Ritika Patni & Nihal Joseph, *WTO Ramifications of Internet Censorship: The Google – China Controversy*, NUJS Law Review, Vol. 3 (2010), pp. 337-363.

[182] *See* Tim Wu, *The World Trade Law of Censorship and Internet Filtering*, Chicago Journal of International Law, Vol.7, No.1 (1st June 2006), pp. 263-287.

[183] Appellate Body Report, *United States – Measures Affecting the Cross-Border Supply of Gambling and Betting Services* (cited as *US – Gambling*), WT/DS285/AB/R (7 April 2005), para. 159.

[184] *See* Mitsuo Matsushita, Thomas J. Schoenbaum, Petros C. Mavroidis and Michael Hahn, *The World Trade Organization – Law, Practice, and Policy (Third Edition)*, Oxford University Press, United Kingdom (2015), pp. 555-632 (586-589).

[185] Brian Hindley and Hosuk Lee-Makiyama, *Protectionism Online: Internet Censorship and International Trade Law,* ECIPE Working Paper, No.12 (2009), p. 10.

[186] The advance of the ICT complicated the problems of service classification. Many Internet-related services can be scattered in different sectors or subsectors and there could be overlaps between computer services, value-added telecommunication services, and audiovisual services.

commitments under both sectors are completely different. For future WTO disputes considering Internet-related services, the level of liberalization of market access and national treatment will depend on how the adjudicating bodies interpret the meaning of the terms in a Member's Schedule.

While a pragmatic way to classify an Internet-related service is by negotiating consistent commitments to avoid conflicting obligations, this approach is not a practical option in a short time.[187] Consequently, by looking into the current classification system and depending on the principle of technical neutrality, Google's services, i.e. search engine and video sharing website, should be categorized under CPC 843 Data Processing Services for several reasons.

Pursuant to Articles 31 and 32 of the Vienna Convention, it is necessary to take into account the ordinary meaning of 'data processing services', the context of the treaty, and other supplementary means to determine the scope of the service sector at issue. First, the ordinary meaning of the term 'data process services' is similar to search engine and other Internet-related services.[188] Panels and the Appellate Body generally first look at the dictionary definitions of the contested term to determine its ordinary meaning. The Shorter Oxford English Dictionary describes 'data processing' as "the performance by automatic means of any operations on empirical data, such as classifying or analyzing them".[189] Merriam-Webster's Collegiate Dictionary defines the term as "the converting of raw data to machine-readable form and its subsequent processing (as storing, updating, combining, rearranging, or printing out) by a computer".[190] The New Oxford American Dictionary states 'data processing' is "a series of operation on data, esp. by a computer, to retrieve, transform, or classify information".[191] Chambers' 21st Century Dictionary refers to 'data processing' as "computing the performance of operations on data by a computer system, especially the arrangement of a large amount of data into a more useful form according to specified rules and procedures".[192]

Google's search engine is built upon a series of data operations by a computer system to provide the most relevant and authoritative results from millions of

---

[187] *See* Ruosi Zhang, *Covered or Not Covered: That is the Question – Services Classification for Specific Commitments under the GATS*, World Trade Organization Economic Research and Statistics Division (7 December 2015).

[188] Brian Hindley and Hosuk Lee-Makiyama, *Protectionism Online: Internet Censorship and International Trade Law*, ECIPE Working Paper, No.12 (2009)

[189] Shorter Oxford English Dictionary, Fifth Edition, Oxford University Press (2002).

[190] Merriam-Webster's Collegiate Dictionary, Eleventh Edition, Merriam-Webster (2005).

[191] The New Oxford American Dictionary, Oxford University Press (2001).

[192] Chamber's 21st Century Dictionary, Chambers (1999).

web pages for subsequent processing. At the most basic level, there are three logical components in the operation of search engines: web crawling, indexing, and searching. Search engines retrieve web pages from the html and store all the information in an index database for use in later queries. When a person enters key words into a search engine, the engine examines its index and provides a listing of the best corresponding web page links according to its criteria.[193] Sergey Brin and Lawrence Page, the founders of Google, stated in a research paper that "Google is designed to crawl and index the Web efficiently and produce much more satisfying search results than the existing system".[194] Google, in order to produce high precision results, uses an iterative algorithm to calculate a quality ranking, called PageRank, for each web pages and utilizes the link structure of the Web to improve search results.[195] Therefore, according to the dictionary definitions, the ordinary meaning of 'data processing services' is very close to search engine services.

The second step to ascertain the meaning of 'data processing services' is to look into the context of the treaty or other supplementary means. According to both the 1993/ 2001 Scheduling Guidelines, CPC is a supplementary means to refine the exact meaning of the sectors or sub-sectors in the W/120 when the list does not provide a detailed explanation.[196] The explanatory note in the CPC details Group 843 into following:

843	Data Processing Services
8431	84310 Input preparation services Data recording services such as key punching, optical scanning or other methods of data entry.
8432	84320 Data Processing and tabulation services

---

[193] Waman S. Jawadekar, *Knowledge Management: Text & Cases*, Tata McGraw Hill Education Private Ltd, New Delhi (2011), p. 278.

[194] Sergey Brin and Lawrence Page, *The Anatomy of a Large-Scale Hypertextual Web Search Engine*, Seventh International World-Wide Web Conference (WWW 1998) (1998).

[195] *See* Ibid., pp. 3-5.

[196] 1993 Scheduling Guidelines explicitly referred CPC number as a supplementary means of clarifying the meaning of a specific service sector or sub-sector. In paragraph 16, it states:

> The legal nature of a schedule as well as the need to evaluate commitments, require the greatest possible degree of clarity in the description of each sector or sub-sector schedule. In general, the classification of sectors and sub-sectors should be based on the Secretariat's revised Services Sectoral Classification List. Each sector contained in the Secretariat's list is identified by the corresponding Central Product Classification (CPC) number. Where it is necessary to refine further a sectoral classification, this should be done on the basis of the COC or other internationally recognized classification.

Services such as data processing and tabulation services, computer calculating services, and rental services of computer time.

8433 84330 Time-sharing services
This seems to be the same type of services as 84320. …

Based on the CPC, 8432 is the only possible service sub-sector that covers search engine or video sharing services for two reasons. First, although the 'data processing services' listed under CPC 8432 do not explicitly refer to services delivered through electronic means, on the basis of the principle of technology neutrality, the term should include services provided via the Internet if those services are within the meaning of 'data processing'.[197] In *China – Audiovisual Products*, the panel concluded that the entry 'Sound Recording Distribution Services', under the heading of 'Audiovisual Services' in sector 2.D of China's Schedule, extends to the distribution of sound recordings through the Internet. The panel found that "the term "recording" cannot be limited to sound embedded on physical media, but refers to the content, regardless of the technology of storage or distribution of the sound".[198] The Appellate Body upheld the panel's decision by stating that the terms in China's GATS Schedule are "sufficiently generic that what they apply to may change over time".[199] As a result, by processing a heavy amount of information into a readable format for others to access or retrieve such information through electronic means, search engine services and other Internet services satisfy the condition of CPC 8432 Data Processing Services.

Second, the CPC was revised after 1991 and CPC 1.0 was adopted by the United Nations Statistics Division in 1998.[200] According to the explanatory note in CPC 1.0, almost all online services are confined to the subcategories of Online Information Provision Services (CPC 843). The group includes database

[197] *See* Cynthia Liu, *Internet Censorship as a Trade Barrier: A Look at the WTO Consistency of the Great Firewall in the Wake of the China – Google Dispute*, Georgetown Journal of International Law, Vol.42 (2011), pp. 1199-1240 (1222-1225).

[198] Panel Report, *China – Measures Affecting Trading Rights and Distribution Services for Certain Publications and Audiovisual Entertainment Products* (cited as *China – Audiovisual Products*), WT/DS363/R (12 August 2009), para. 7.1181.

[199] Appellate Body Report, *China – Measures Affecting Trading Rights and Distribution Services for Certain Publications and Audiovisual Entertainment Products* (cited as *China – Audiovisual Products*), WT/DS363/AB/R (21 December 2009), para. 396.

[200] Report of the Secretary General, *International Economic and Social Classification*, United Nations Economic and Social Council, E/CN.3/2000/17 (8 December 1999). Particular attention in CPC 1.0 revised version was paid to ensure that the structure of CPC adequately reflects the development of new technologies in the services sector of the economy.

services; provision of information on a web-site; provision of on-line data retrieval services from databases and other information to all or a limited number of users; and provision of on-line information by content providers. Search engines services can be categorized, *inter alia*, under database services. In addition, the Technical Subgroup on Classifications Statistics Division of the United Nations, which works closely with the WTO Secretariat, published Registry Entry # 946 on 30 June 2000. The publication stated clearly that web search portals are classified in CPC subclass 84300 (on-line information provision services).[201]

In sum, those of Google's services at issue should be considered as 'Data Processing Services' under CPC Group 843. The following section examines whether China has made specific commitments as regards the relevant service sectors. The legal basis for analyzing the *Google – China* scenarios depends on the premise that the services at issue are categorized as 'data processing services' under CPC Group 8432 and on fact that China has undertaken full market access and national treatment commitments in mode 1 supply of service on the service sector.

ii. China's GATS Commitments

In the Concession Schedule, China has included the following services in its commitments under 1-B Computer and Related Services:

a. Consultancy services related to the installation of computer hardware (CPC 841)
b. Software implementation services (CPC 842)
c. Data Processing services (CPC 843)
   - Input preparation services (CPC 8431)
   - Data processing and tabulation services (CPC 8432)
   - Time-sharing services (CPC 8433)

Based on the previous analysis, China has committed to 'None' for modes 1, 2, and 3 on both market access and national treatment obligations under 'Data processing and tabulation services' in W/120 1-B-c.[202] In other words, any

[201] Technical Subgroup on Classification, Interpretation: Web Search Portals – Registry Entry # 946, United Nations Statistic Division (30 June 2000). Available at https://unstats.un.org/unsd/cr/registry/regri.asp?Rid=946. (accessed 28 September 2016)
[202] Working Party on the Accession of China, Report of the Working Party on the Accession of China, WT/ACC/CHN/49/Add.2 (1 October 2001).

quantitative limitations of Chinese Internet-related restrictive measures, which fall under the six categories listed in Article XVI:2, will constitute a market access violation. likewise, a full commitment to national treatment obligation in Chinese GATS Schedule 1-B-c implies that Chinese measures should treat foreign services and service suppliers no less favourable than like domestic services and service suppliers.

China could argue that the revised CPC 1.0 should not be considered a supplementary means to interpret the GATS Schedule since the changes in CPC 1.0 have not been replicated in the WTO legal framework and the term 'data processing' of the GATS CPC system should not apply to search engine services since such services emerged only after the negotiation of its GATS Schedule and its accession to the WTO. Nevertheless, the WTO adjudicating bodies in *US – Gambling* and *China – Audiovisual Products* reiterated that the task of ascertaining the meaning of a concession in a Member's GATS Schedule involves identifying the common intention of the Members.[203] The Appellate Body in *China – Audiovisual Products* emphasized that if the term in a Member's Schedule is 'sufficiently generic', the interpretation of the term must be based on the contemporary meaning at the time of interpretation.[204] The Appellate Body further confirmed that technical feasibility at the time of service commitment would constitute a circumstance relevant to the interpretation under Article 32 of the Vienna Convention.[205] Therefore, if search engines or other Internet-related services were feasible for China before the entry into force of its GATS Schedule, China will not be able to claim that it was not its intention to commit to the services at issue or that the W/120 and CPC were drafted at the time when most Internet services did not exist.

Search engines and other Internet-related services might not have been technically feasible at the time when the GATS was drafted; nevertheless, search engines not only existed but were also widely used in China before China's accession to the WTO in late 2001. For example, the 6th Statistical Report on Internet Development in China, released on July 1 2000, reported that e-mail and search engine services are two of the most used services on the Internet in

---

[203] Appellate Body Report, *European Communities – Customs Classification of Certain Computer Equipment* (cited as *EC – Computer Equipment*), WT/DS62/AB/R WT/DS67/AB/R WT/DS68/AB/R (5 June 1998), para. 84

[204] Ibid., para. 397.

[205] Panel Report, *China – Measures Affecting Trading Rights and Distribution Services for Certain Publications and Audiovisual Entertainment Products* (cited as *China – Audiovisual Products*), WT/DS363/R (12 August 2009).

the Chinese market.[206] Furthermore, in 2000, the Chinese government and State Council issued a series regulation to govern telecommunication services and the content of the Internet.[207] Therefore, it is evident that the Chinese government was fully aware of the existence of the Internet and Internet services when its Accession Protocol was approved by the WTO on 10 November 2001. In sum, since China did not exclude search engine services from W/120 1-B-c (CPC843) or include the services in other sectors or sub-sectors, it is reasonable to presume that China has undertaken a full commitment on the services at issue under W/120 1-B-c (CPC843).

b. Market Access Violation (Article XVI of the GATS)

The market access obligation under Article XVI aims at measures which restrict trade in services through the application of quantitative limitations. Consequently, the market access barriers can be either discriminatory or non-discriminatory in nature. Article XVI does not require a comparison of the treatment between domestic and foreign services or service suppliers. Furthermore, the 2001 Scheduling Guidelines emphasizes that "all measures falling under any of the categories listed in Article XVI:2 must be scheduled, whether or not such measures are discriminatory according to the national treatment standard of Article XVII."[208] Article XVI covers, therefore, both discriminatory and non-discriminatory measures. In addition, the reference to 'no less favourable treatment' under Article XVI:1 requires a comparison between the standard of the treatment described in a Member's Schedule and the actual treatment of the foreign services or service suppliers.

The panel and the Appellate Body in *US – Gambling* confirmed that when a Member schedules a full market access commitment for a given service sector under one mode of supply, a prohibition on one, several, and all means of delivery would be considered as a limitation on market access for that mode unless

---

[206] China Internet Network Information Center (CNNIC), *6th Statistical Survey Report on the Internet Development in China* (1 July 2000).

[207] State Council of People's Republic of China, *Regulation on Telecommunication of the People's Republic of China*, Decree No. 291 (20 September 2000) and State Council of People's Republic of China, *Regulation on Internet Information Service of the People's Republic of China*, Decree No. 292 (20 September 2000).

[208] WTO Council of Trade in Services, Guidelines for the Scheduling of Specific Commitments under the General Agreement on Trade in Services, S/L/92 (28/March/2001), para. 8.

explicitly stated otherwise in its Schedule.[209] The adjudicating bodies further concluded, not without contested, that a total prohibition on the remote supply of gambling and betting services constitutes a quantitative restriction listed in Article XVI:2(a) and (c)[210], even if the limitation is not expressed with reference to numerical units. The Appellate Body asserted that "it is clear that the thrust of sub-paragraph (a) is not on the *form* of limitations, but on their numerical, or quantitative nature".[211] Therefore, limitations in the form of 'numerical quota' within Article XVI:2(a) should be interpreted as limitations having the characteristics of a number. Accordingly, a total prohibition on one, several, and all means of delivery is equivalent to zero quota and a measure of quantitative nature within the meaning of Article XVI:2(a).

Based on this standard, Chinese Internet censorship measures that completely block foreign Internet service or service suppliers would amount to a 'total prohibition' and 'zero quota' on all means of delivery and violate China's market access obligation under Article XVI:2 (a) and (c) of the GATS. Similar to the US measures in *US – Gambling*, none of the Chinese Internet restrictive measures are stated in numerical form.[212] Nevertheless, a complete blockage on Google's search services and YouTube video streaming services amounts to a zero quota and is prohibited under Article XVI:2 (a) and (c). Since China has made a full market access commitment under mode 1 cross-border supply of services, any measure prohibiting one, several, or all means of cross-border delivery will reduce the opportunities for foreign suppliers using those means of delivery to supply services to zero.

---

[209] Panel Report, *United States – Measures Affecting the Cross-Border Supply of Gambling and Betting Services* (cited as *US – Gambling*), WT/DS285/R (10 November 2004), para. 6.285. The panel emphasized that "a market access commitment for mode 1 implies the right for other Members' suppliers to supply a service through all means of delivery, whether by mail, telephone, Internet, etc., unless otherwise specified in a Member's Schedule.".

[210] *See* Chapter 3 I.B.b.i

[211] Appellate Body Report, *United States – Measures Affecting the Cross-Border Supply of Gambling and Betting Services* (cited as *US – Gambling*), WT/DS285/AB/R (7 April 2005), para. 232.

[212] *See* Cynthia Liu, *Internet Censorship as a Trade Barrier: A Look at the WTO Consistency of the Great Firewall in the Wake of the China – Google Dispute*, Georgetown Journal of International Law, Vol.42 (2011), pp. 1199-1240.

c. National Treatment Violation (Article XVII of the GATS)

Under Article XVII of the GATS, in order to comply with the national treatment obligation, a WTO Member shall "accord to services and service suppliers of any other Member, in respect of all measures affecting the supply of services, treatment no less favourable than that it accords to its own like services and service suppliers". Article XVII:2 and 3 further stipulate that formally identical or formally different treatment might both constitute the meaning of 'less favourable treatment' if it "modifies the conditions of competition" to the detriment of the foreign services or service suppliers. In other words, national treatment obligation of trade in services covers both *de jure* and *de facto* discrimination since the purpose of Article XVII is to guarantee equal competitive opportunities for foreign services and service suppliers in comparison to like domestic services and service suppliers.[213]

Four elements need to be examined to determine whether China's Internet censorship measures comply with its national treatment obligations under GATS Article XVII. The elements are: (1) whether China has undertaken a national treatment commitment in the relevant service sector and/ or mode of supply; (2) whether the measure at issue affects the supply of services; (3) whether the domestic and foreign services and service suppliers are like services or like service suppliers; and (4) whether the measure accords no less favourable treatment to both domestic and foreign services and service suppliers.

i. Specific Commitments

The scope of each WTO Member's national treatment obligation depends on its specific commitments in the service Schedule with respect to the services sector at issue and subject to the conditions, limitations or qualifications listed in the Schedule. Based on the previous analysis, China has undertaken a full national treatment commitment under W/120 1-B-c (CPC 843) 'Computer and Related Services'. Thus, Chinese Internet censorship measures should not modify the conditions of competition to the detriment of foreign services and service suppliers in the relevant market.

---

213 Panel Report, *China – Certain Measures Affecting Electronic Payment Services* (cited as *China – Electronic Payment*), WT/DS413/R (16/July/2012), para. 7.700.

ii. Measures Affecting the Supply of Services

The second element of national treatment obligation under the GATS Article XVII is whether the measures at issue affect the supply of services. The meaning of the term 'measure' is significant in the *Google – China* analysis since many of the Internet blocking, filtering, and censorship mechanisms conducted by the Chinese government are based on opaque or non-transparent policies and practices. To what extent Chinese Internet censorship mechanisms will constitute actionable measures under the GATS depends on the legal standards relating to the identification of the measures being challenged. Article XXIII of the GATS stipulates that a WTO Member may seek assistance from the DSU in cases where a Member considers that another Member does not abide by its obligations and/or specific commitments under the GATS.[214]

Having recourse to the provisions of the DSU, Article 3.3 of the DSU provides:

> The prompt settlement of situations in which a Member considers that any benefits accruing to it directly or indirectly under the covered agreements are being impaired *by measures taken by another Member* is essential to the effective functioning of the WTO and the maintenance of a proper balance between the rights and obligations of Members. (emphasis added)

Referring to the establishment of a panel, Article 6.2 of the DSU provides:

> The request for the establishment of a panel shall be made in writing. It shall indicate whether consultations were held, identify the *specific measures* at issue and provide a brief summary of the legal basis of the complaint sufficient to present the problem clearly. (emphasis added)

Consequently, the relevant 'nexus' must exist between the responding Member and the measures. In other words, the measures at issue must be attributed to the Member to satisfy Article 3.3 of the DSU.[215] Besides, "the measure must be the *source* of the alleged impairment, which is, in turn, the *effect* resulting from

---

[214] Article XXIII of the GATS (Dispute Settlement and Enforcement) provides:
1. If any Member should consider that any other Member fails to carry out its obligations or specific commitments under this Agreement, it may with a view to reaching a mutually satisfactory resolution of the matter have recourse to the DSU.

[215] Appellate Body Report, *United States – Sunset Review of Anti-dumping Duties on Corrosion-resistant Carbon Steel Flproducts from Japan* (cited as *US – Corrosion-resistant Steel Sunset Review*), WT/DS244/AB/R (15 December 2003), para. 81.

the existence or operation of the measures".[216] In the *US – Gambling* case, when considering whether the 'total prohibition' can constitute an autonomous measure that can be challenged *per se,* the Appellate Body is of the opinion that "without demonstrating the source of the prohibition, a complaining party may not challenge a 'total prohibition' as a 'measure', *per se*, in dispute settlement proceedings under the GATS."[217]

Additionally, since Article 3.3 and Article 6.2 of the DSU are general provisions governing the content of panel requests, they must be read together with relevant provisions contained in the concerned WTO agreements, i.e. the GATS.[218] The relevant GATS provisions read as:

> Article I:3 (a) of the GATS
> "Measures by Members" means measures taken by:
> (i) central, regional or local governments and authorities; and
> (ii) non-governmental bodies in the exercise of powers delegated by central, regional or local governments or authorities.
>
> Article XXVIII of the GATS
> For the purpose of this agreement:
> (a) "measures" means any measure by a Member, whether in the form of a law, regulation, rule, procedure, decision, administrative action, or any other form
> (b) "supply of a service" includes the production, distribution, marketing, sale and delivery of a service;
> (c) "measures by Member affecting trade in services" include measures in respect of
> (i) the purchase, payment or use of a service;
> (ii) the access to and use of, in connection with the supply of a service, services which are required by those Members to be offered to the public generally;
> (iii) the presence, including commercial presence, of persons of a Member for the supply of a service in the territory of another Member;

---

[216] Appellate Body Report, *United States – Measures Affecting the Cross-Border Supply of Gambling and Betting Services* (cited as *US – Gambling*), WT/DS285/AB/R (7 April 2005), para. 121.
[217] Ibid., para. 126.
[218] Panel Report, *United States – Measures Affecting the Cross-Border Supply of Gambling and Betting Services* (cited as *US – Gambling*), WT/DS285/R (10 November 2004), para. 6.150.

The reference to 'any other form' in Article XXVIII paragraph (a) indicates a broad interpretation of the term 'measures' in the context of the GATS since it is not limited to a particular form. In *US – Corrosion-Resistant Steel Sunset Review*, the Appellate Body, in discussing the meaning of term 'measure' under WTO law, concluded that a measure could be any act or omission attributed to a WTO Member or any instruments of a Member containing rules or norms, irrespective of how or whether those rules or norms are applied in a particular instance. The Appellate Body stated:

> "In addition, in GATT and WTO dispute settlement practice, panels have frequently examined measures consisting not only particular acts applied on to a specific situation, but also of acts setting forth rules or norms that are intended to have general and prospective application. In other words, *instruments of a Member containing rules or norms could constitute a "measure", irrespective of how or whether those rules or norms are applied in a particular instance*. This is so because the disciplines of the GATT and the WTO, as well as the dispute settlement system, are *intended to protect not only existing trade but also the security and predictability needed to conduct future trade*."[219] (emphasis added).

In general, according to the jurisprudence regarding the interpretation in the context of the DSU and the purpose of the relevant WTO agreements, the term 'measure' should be read in a broad manner under Article XVII to include not only the laws and regulations of a Member, but other governmental actions as well.[220] The panel in *China – Audiovisual Products* explained that a determination of whether something is a measure must be based on the content and substance of the instrument, and not merely on its form or nomenclature. The panel explained, "Acts setting forth rules or norms that are intended to have general and prospective application are measures subject to WTO dispute settlement".[221] The Internet censorship mechanisms adopted by the Chinese authorities, therefore, should be considered as 'measures' within the meaning of GATS

[219] Appellate Body Report, *United States – Sunset Review of Anti-dumping Duties on Corrosion-resistant Carbon Steel Flproducts from Japan* (cited as *US – Corrosion-resistant Steel Sunset Review*), WT/DS244/AB/R (15 December 2003), para. 82.

[220] Panel Report, *United States – Measures Affecting the Cross-Border Supply of Gambling and Betting Services* (cited as *US – Gambling*), WT/DS285/R (10 November 2004), paras. 6.152-6.174.

[221] Panel Report, *China – Measures Affecting Trading Rights and Distribution Services for Certain Publications and Audiovisual Entertainment Products* (cited as *China – Audiovisual Products*), WT/DS363/R (12 August 2009), para. 7.172.

Article XVII since a measure could be any act or omission attributed to a WTO Member or any instrument of a Member containing rules or norms, irrespective of how or whether those rules or norms are applied in a particular instance.

iii. Like Domestic and Foreign Services/ Service Suppliers

'Like services' and 'like service suppliers' are among the most controversial but crucial criteria in the context of national treatment under GATS Article XVII. While there are no explicit definitions of 'likeness', it is only the measure that treats 'like foreign services' or 'like foreign service suppliers' less favourable that will fall within the meaning of Article XVII:1 of the GATS. As discussed in Chapter 3, the WTO adjudicating bodies are of the opinion that the determination of likeness in the context of Article XVII is a determination about the nature and extent of a competitive relationship between services and service suppliers in the given market, and such a determination should be based on the evidence as a whole. Furthermore, in the light of the complexity of trade in services, determination of like services or service suppliers should be made on a case-by-case basis.

In the *Google – China* scenario, the foreign and domestic services or service suppliers in question should be considered as like services or service suppliers. In *EC – Asbestos*, the Appellate Body used four criteria to determine the 'likeness' between domestic and foreign products: the physical properties of the products, end-uses, consumer taste, and international classification of the products.[222] Although it is debatable whether transplanting the GATT approach into the GATS context is suitable, due to the intangibility of services activities and the fact that the regulation of services is generally more complex than that of goods,[223] these four parameters are still useful to determine whether the domestic and foreign services and service suppliers are in a competitive relationship with each other.

Thus, considering the physical properties of search engines and video sharing platforms, Google and Baidu are both built upon a series of operations of data by a computer system to provide the most relevant and authoritative results from millions of web pages for subsequent processing. YouTube and Youku are not only similar in their names but also in design since they both provide video sharing platforms, of which the content is generated by Internet users. It is diffi-

---

[222] Ibid., para. 101.

[223] *See* Mireille Cossy, *Determining "likeness" under the GATS: Squaring the circle?*, World Trade Organization – Economic Research and Statistics Division, Staff Working Paper ERSD-2006-08, September 2006.

cult for China to argue that its domestic services and service suppliers are not like foreign services and service suppliers in the given market.

Second, based on 'consumer tastes' and 'end-uses', the services and service suppliers at issue should also be considered as like services and service suppliers. The Appellate Body in *EC – Asbestos* stated that the determination of 'end-uses' should consider the "extent to which products are capable of performing the same, or similar, function (end-uses)" and the 'consumers' taste and habits' should refer to "the extent to which consumers are – or would be – willing to choose one product instead of another to perform that end-use".[224] Consequently, to determine 'end-uses' and 'consumer tastes' is to determine the substitutability of the services in the given market. The application of these criteria will rely on the evidence as a whole and usually needs to be determined on a case-by-case basis. Statistics show that the market share of Chinese domestic Internet service providers usually rises when the services from foreign competitors are blocked, filtered, or slowed. Although more factual findings are required, it can be assumed that the domestic and foreign services and service providers at issue are substitutable in the given market and, therefore, are like services or like service providers in the context of the GATS.

iv. Less Favourable Treatment

Under Article XVII, different treatment of like services and service suppliers violates national treatment obligation only when such treatment modifies the condition of competition in the relevant market to the detriment of foreign services and service suppliers. That is to say, the less favourable treatment standard protects the expectation of equal competitive opportunities rather than the specific outcome on the internal market for both current and future trade.[225] GATS Article XVII:2 and XVII:3 cover both *de jure* and *de facto* discrimination as the obligation applies to both formally different and formally identical measures. While *de jure* discrimination refers to measures which have a reverse effect on foreign services or service suppliers based on the origin, the criteria to determine *de facto* discrimination are less clear.

---

[224] Appellate Body Report, *European Communities – Measures Affecting Asbestos and Asbestos-Containing Products* (cited as *EC -- Asbestos*), WT/DS135/AB/R (5/April /2001), para. 117.

[225] WTO Background Note by the Secretariat, *The Fundamental WTO Principles of National Treatment, Most-Favoured-Nation Treatment and Transparency*, WTO Working Group on the Interaction between Trade and Competition Policy, WT/WGTCP/W/ 114 (14/April/1999).

In *EC – Banana*, the panel stressed that, for *de facto* discrimination to be sustained, the comparison of less favourable treatment should be made between the whole group of foreign services and service suppliers and the whole group of like domestic services and service suppliers.[226] Generally, in the case of *de facto* discrimination, no facts are *per se* excluded. As the Appellate Body indicated in *US – Clove Cigarette*, in order to determine whether a measure discriminates against the group of imported products, a panel must carefully scrutinize the design, architecture, revealing structure, operation, and application of the measure, and in particular whether it is even-handed.[227] A panel needs to weigh and balance all the relevant evidence to decide whether the complaining party has met the burden of proving that the alleged measures treat foreign services and service suppliers less favourably than domestic services and services suppliers.[228] In addition, the wording of footnote 10 to Article XVII:1 clarifies that the standard of treatment no less favourable must be based on the impact on the conditions of competition that results from the contested measures rather than from 'inherent competitive disadvantages' as foreign services or service suppliers.[229]

One of the most controversial issues for the application of Article XVII is whether public policy objectives can be taken into consideration in the 'treatment no less favourable' analysis. For the balance between trade liberalization and Members' regulatory autonomy, many commentators have argued that the true objective of a measure must play a decisive role in determining *de facto* discrimination in the context of Article XVII since a holistic assessment of the national treatment obligation is not carried out by mechanically comparing likeness but by enquiring into the real objective of the measures.[230] The panel in

---

[226] Panel Report, *European Communities – Regime for the Importation, Sale and Distribution of Bananas* (cited as *EC – Bananas III*), WT/DS27/R/ECU (25/09/1997), paras. 7.332-7.338.

[227] Appellate Body Report, *United States – Measures Affecting the Production and Sale of Clove Cigarettes* (cited as *US – Clove Cigarettes*), WT/DS406/AB/R (4 April 2012). When analyzing less favourable treatment under TBT Article 2.1, para. 182.

[228] *See* Joost Pauwelyn, Comment: The unbearable lightness of likeness. In: Marion Panizzon, Nicole Pohl and Pirre Sauve (eds.), *GATS and the Regulation of International Trade in Services*, Cambridge: Cambridge University Press, pp. 358-369.

[229] Article XVII of the GATS footnote 10 states:

> Specific commitments assumed under this Article shall not be construed to require any Member to compensate for an inherent competitive advantage which result from the foreign character of the relevant services or service suppliers.

[230] *See* James Flett, *WTO Space for National Treatment Regulation: Requiem for a Diagonal Vector Test*, Journal of International Economic Law, Vol.16, Iss.1, pp. 37-90 (March 2013); and Joost Pauwelyn, Comment: The unbearable lightness of likeness. In:

Argentina – Financial Services described that because of the specific characteristics of trade in services and in the light of the specific circumstances of each dispute, relevant regulatory aspects could be taken into account when interpreting the term 'treatment no less favourable' under GATS Article II:1 and Article XVII.[231]

However, the Appellate Body rejected the panel's opinions and asserted that neither the text and context of Articles II:1 and XVII of the GATS nor the object and purpose of the GATS provide a legal basis to support the legal standard applied by the panel.[232] The Appellate body further stated that although no evidence relating to the regulatory aspects should *a priori* be excluded, it is when such evidence, subject to the particular circumstances, bears on the conditions of competition that it might be taken into account "as an integral part of a panel's analysis of whether the measure at issue modifies the conditions of competition to the detriment of like services or service suppliers of any other Member",[233] For the Appellate Body, the legal standard of national treatment under the GATS does not provide a separate step to consider the regulatory purpose of the measures, and the public policy objective would be better analyzed under the general exceptions in GATS Article XIV. The Appellate Body described:

> "This balance, too, reinforces the established legal standard for "treatment no less favourable" under the non-discrimination provisions of the GATS, that it, whether a measure modifies the conditions of competition to the detriment of like services or service suppliers of any other Member. Where a measure is inconsistent with the non-discrimination provisions, regulatory aspects or concerns that could potentially justify such a measure are more appropriately addressed in the context of the relevant exceptions. *Addressing them in the context of the non-discrimination provisions would upset the existing balance under the GATS*."[234](emphasis added).

Marion Panizzon, Nicole Pohl and Pirrre Sauve (eds.), *GATS and the Regulation of International Trade in Services*, Cambridge: Cambridge University Press, pp. 358-369

[231] Panel Report, *Argentina – Measures Relating to Trade in Goods and Services* (cited as *Argentina – Financial Services*), WT/DS543/R (30 September 2015), paras. 2.217 and 2.232.

[232] Appellate Body Report, *Argentina – Measures Relating to Trade in Goods and Services* (cited as *Argentina – Financial Services*), WT/DS453/AB/R (14 April 2016). The Appellate Body rejected the panel's articulation of the legal standard of treatment no less favourable. When concerning panel's analysis of 'regulatory aspects', para. 6.126.

[233] Ibid., para. 6.127.

[234] Ibid., para. 6.115.

Applying this legal standard to Chinese Internet censorship measures would suggest that a complaining party must prove that the Internet censorship measures adopted by the Chinese government modified the conditions of competition to the detriment of foreign Internet services or service suppliers within the meaning of GATS Article XVII. Whereas the commercial market in China is growing due to the development of ICT products and Internet services, the increasingly intricate Internet-related regulations and measures inhibit foreign participation in China's digital market.[235] As described above, the Chinese government has blocked or intercepted access to Google, YouTube, Facebook, Twitter, and other foreign social networks while their immediate domestic competitors continue to operate in the same fashion.[236]

For example, in addition to Google vs. Baidu, foreign microblogging site Twitter has faced the same difficulties in doing business in China. In the aftermath of the Ürümqi riots in July 2009, Twitter was completely blocked by the Chinese government in the name of national security. Nonetheless, in August 2009, Sina, one of the largest Chinese telecom company, launched a microblogging social network named Sina Weibo (新浪微博), which is nearly identical to Twitter.[237] In the absence of foreign competitors, the market share of Sina Weibo is booming. According to Charles Chao, CEO and Chairman of Sina, Weibo's registered accounts passed 400 million in 2012.[238] By the end of 2016, Weibo's monthly users grew to 313 million and its net revenue increased to \$212.7 million in Q4 2016.[239] Sina Weibo's major competitors in China include Tencent Weibo (腾讯微博), Sohu Weibo (搜狐微博), and NetEase Weibo (网易微博), which are all Chinese service suppliers.

---

[235] *See* Martina F. Ferracane and Hosuk Lee-Makiyama, *China's Technology Protectionism and Its Non-negotiable Rationales*, European Centre for International Political Economy (2017).

[236] *See* Anonymous, *A Dual Trace Approach to Challenging Chinese Censorship in the WTO: The (Future) Case of Google and Facebook*, Michigan Journal of International Law, Vol.34, Issue:4 (2013), pp. 857-892.

[237] *See* Cho-Wen Chu, *Censorship or Protectionism? Reassessing China's Regulation of Internet Industry*, International Journal of Social Science and Humanity, Vol. 7, No. 1 (January 2017).

[238] Sina Corporation, *Sina Reports Third Quarter 2012 Financial Results*, Sina News Release (15 November 2012). Available at http://phx.corporate-ir.net/phoenix.zhtml?c=121288&p=irol-newsArticle&ID=1759522&highlight=. (accessed 16 October 2016)

[239] China Internet Watch, *Weibo monthly active users grew to 313M in Q4 2016*. Available at https://www.chinainternetwatch.com/19847/weibo-q4-2016/. (accessed 17 October 2016)

Besides, the licensing requirements for ISPs in China might also accord less favourable treatment to foreign services or service providers in comparison to local equivalents. As discussed in Section I, to operate a website under the domain .cn in China, it is mandatory to obtain an ICP license issued by the MIIT. A Wholly Foreign Owned Enterprise (WFOE) has been allowed to apply for commercial ICP licenses since January 2015.[240] The official license application website of the MIIT, as well as the entire application process, is only available in Mandarin. The application procedure is lengthy and relatively untested. By 2016, only one WFOE had been granted a commercial ICP license.[241]

If a foreign Internet service provider is not granted an ICP license, the provider will lose its opportunities to get the benefits of hosting a website in China. The first and most significant advantage to hosting a website in China is the faster loading time. Websites hosted in China can be opened and accessed faster than websites hosted overseas. In a highly substituted business, like Internet services, any delaying or slowing down of access to websites can be reasonably expected to modify the conditions of competition to the detriment of foreign services or service suppliers by decreasing their ability to supply the services to local Internet users.[242] In addition, only by obtaining an ICP license can a website be promoted through PPC Advertising keyword purchase on search engines. A good ranking normally represents the authenticity and reliability of a website. It is difficult for a foreign Internet service provider to reach Chinese customers if it is not searchable on any of the search engines in China. It is evident that while foreign Internet service providers struggle to gain access to the Chinese Internet market, domestic companies' businesses are thriving in the biggest E-commerce market in the world.

In sum, with a full commitment to the national treatment obligation, Internet censorship measures adopted by the Chinese authorities are in violation of Arti-

---

[240] Ministry of Industry and Information Technology, *Notice of the Ministry of Industry and Information Technology on Removing the Restrictions of Foreign Equity Ratios in Online Data Processing and Transaction Processing (Operating E-commerce) Business in China (Shanghai) Pilot Free Trade Zone* (*工业和信息化部关于在中国（上海）自由贸易试验区放开在线数据处理与交易处理业务（经营类电子商务）外资股权比例限制的通告*) (13 January 2015).

[241] Alex Philips, *Appling for an ICP License – Unlock Your Online Potential in China*, LNP China (22 September 2016). Available at https://www.lnpchina.com/china-made-easy/single-post/2016/09/21/applying-for-an-icp-license-the-key-to-hosting-your-websit e-in-china. (accessed 18 October 2016)

242 *See* Cynthia Liu, *Internet Censorship as a Trade Barrier: A Look at the WTO Consistency of the Great Firewall in the Wake of the China – Google Dispute*, Georgetown Journal of International Law, Vol.42 (2011), pp. 1199-1240.

cle XVII since the measures modified the conditions of competition to the detriment of foreign services or services suppliers and accorded less favourable treatment to services or service suppliers of other Members. Any justifications of the restrictive measures, such as the objectives to support public safety or protect public morals, should be considered under the general exceptions in Article XIV(a) of the GATS. The regulatory purpose of a measure, according to the WTO adjudicating bodies, is irrelevant in determining whether the measure is consistent with the national treatment obligations in the context of the GATS.

d. Transparency Violation (Article III and Article VI:1, 2 & 5 of the GATS)

As one of the most crucial requirements for good governance and one of the fundamental norms for trade in general, transparency is increasingly seen as an essential tool in the governance of international trade.[243] The principle of transparency requires governments to provide information regarding domestic laws and regulations, as well as the procedures for their application and administration.[244] The obligation to publish all relevant regulations is linked with the obligations relating to the impartial administration of such regulations and the right of review of decisions taken under them.[245] Regulatory transparency, therefore, is based on the belief that information asymmetry exacerbates power imbalance and might negatively impact the legitimacy and accountability of the regulatory authorities since only openness in the decision making processes will create greater compliance, less burdensome regulations, predictable conditions of market access, and, ultimately, a more efficient trading system.[246] As one commen-

---

[243] *See* Terry Collins – Williams and Robert Wolfe, *Transparency as a Trade Policy Tool: the WTO's Cloudy Windows*, World Trade Review Vol.9, No.4 (2010), pp. 551-581.

[244] *See* Panagiotis Delimatsis, *International Trade in Services and Domestic Regulations – Necessity, Transparency, and Regulatory Diversity,* Oxford University Press (2007), pp. 255-270.

[245] WTO Background Note by the Secretariat, *The Fundamental WTO Principles of National Treatment, Most-Favoured-Nation Treatment and Transparency*, WTO Working Group on the Interaction between Trade and Competition Policy, WT/WGTCP/W/114 (14/April/1999).

[246] The concept of transparency and domestic regulations *see* general OECD, Working Party of the Trade Committee, Strengthening Regulatory Transparency: Insights for the GATS from the Regulatory Reform Country Reviews, TD/TC/WP (99)43/FINAL (12/April/2000); Keiya Iida and Julia Nielson, Transparency in Domestic Regulation: Practices and Possibilities. In: Aaditya Mattoo and Pierre Sauvé, *Domestic Regulation and Service Trade Liberalization*, World Bank and Oxford University Press (2003), pp.

tator pointed out, "not only does transparency enhance predictability and legal certainty, but it also improves the accountability and legitimacy of regulatory authorities at all stages of regulatory policy making".[247]

Transparency is also imperative to the facilitation of trade in services. Together with the non-discrimination and market access obligations, transparency is one of the fundamental principles of WTO law.[248] The transparency requirements as regards domestic regulations are first and foremost important to the domain of trade in services as most barriers to trade in services arise from miscellaneous domestic laws, regulations, and practices. Lack of transparency will increase the complexity and uncertainty of supplying services.[249] Transparency in regulations and in their application and administration provides predictable conditions for foreign service suppliers to do business in the given market.[250]

The intricate structure of Chinese Internet censorship measures and the arbitrary application and interpretation of the vague terms in those measures explicitly violate China's GATS obligations under GATS Article III, transparency, and Article VI, domestic regulations. The possible violations are discussed in the following section respectively. It is worth mentioning in advance the importance of the transparency principle in the context of trade in services and its interaction with Members' right to regulate. The WTO Secretariat noted that in the area where the scope of discretionary government measures is comprehensive, transparency obligations serve to foster a rule-based approach to trade policy.[251] In the area of trade in service, especially Internet-related services,

7-27; and Rüdiger Wolfrum, Peter Tobias Stoll and Clemens Feinäugle (eds), *WTO -- Trade in Services*, Netherlands: Koninklijke Brill NV (2008).

[247] Panagiotis Delimatsis, *International Trade in Services and Domestic Regulations – Necessity, Transparency, and Regulatory Diversity,* Oxford University Press (2007), p. 257.

[248] WTO Background Note by the Secretariat, *The Fundamental WTO Principles of National Treatment, Most-Favoured-Nation Treatment and Transparency*, WTO Working Group on the Interaction between Trade and Competition Policy, WT/WGTCP/ W/114 (14/April/1999).

[249] Panagiotis Delimatsis, General Obligations and Disciplines Article III GATS (2008). In: Rüdiger Wolfrum, Peter Tobias Stoll and Clemens Feinäugle (eds), *WTO -- Trade in Services*, Netherlands: Koninklijke Brill NV, pp. 92-103.

[250] Panagiotis Delimatsis, *International Trade in Services and Domestic Regulations – Necessity, Transparency, and Regulatory Diversity,* Oxford University Press (2007), p. 257.

[251] WTO Background Note by the Secretariat, *The Fundamental WTO Principles of National Treatment, Most-Favoured-Nation Treatment and Transparency*, WTO Working Group on the Interaction between Trade and Competition Policy, WT/WGTCP/ W/114 (14/April/1999).

where national and international regulatory systems are not well developed, nations enjoy a great deal of discretion in determining the level of protection they intend to pursue. Regulatory transparency in this circumstance would play a vital role in preventing unnecessary barriers to trade in services and providing predictability of the trading system in the digital age.

i. Violation of Article III:1 of the GATS -- Transparency Obligation

The WTO Glossary defined transparency as the "degree to which trade policies and practices, and the process by which they are established, are open and predictable."[252] Therefore, two types of transparency obligations are listed in WTO law: obligations regarding publication and notification of relevant domestic measures and obligations regarding the administration and application of the measures.[253] Transparency obligations under the GATS cover both categories. GATS Article III contains the publication and notification requirements and GATS Article VI disciplines the administration and application of domestic regulations. The transparency obligations under the GATS provide the specific due process obligations where an authorization is sought.[254]

Article III is a general obligation of the GATS rules. The publication requirements contained in paragraph 1 and 2 of Article III oblige WTO Members to promptly publish or otherwise make publicly available, through websites, for example, all relevant measures of general application which pertain to or affect trade in services.[255] GATS Article III:3 concerns WTO Members' obligations to promptly notify the Council for Trade in Services, on an annual basis, of all new, or any changes to existing, laws, regulations or administrative guidelines significantly affecting trade in services. To comply with Article III:4, WTO Members shall also respond promptly to any request by another Member for information about measures falling within the scope of Article III:1. The exceptions to the transparency obligation can be found in GATS Article III *bis*, which allows Members to refuse to disclose confidential information. In other words, a

---

[252] WTO Glossary. Available at https://www.wto.org/english/thewto_e/glossary_e/glossary_e.htm. (accessed 22 October 2016)

[253] Transparency obligations can also be found in GATT Article X, Article 7 and Article 8 of the Agreement on Sanitary and Phytosanitary Measures (SPS), and Article 2 and Article 5 of the Agreement on Technical Barrier to Trade (TBT).

[254] Panagiotis Delimatsis, General Obligations and Disciplines Article III GATS (2008). In: Rüdiger Wolfrum, Peter Tobias Stoll and Clemens Feinäugle (eds), *WTO -- Trade in Services*, Netherlands: Kononklijke Brill NV, p. 95.

[255] *See* Chapter 3 I.B.a.ii.

Member has the right to suppress certain information which, if disclosed, would impede law enforcement or harm its essential social or security interests.

China's opaque and non-transparent Internet censorship measures, which have a severe negative economic impact on foreign services and service suppliers, might constitute violations of its transparency obligations under GATS Article III:1, Article III:2, and Article III:4. First, Article III:1 requires members to publish all relevant measures of general application promptly. In the case of China, most Internet filtering or blocking measures are not accessible to the public. The Chinese authorities preserve a list of IP, DNS, and Universal Resource Locater (URL) addresses that are blocked on a regular basis through the Great Firewall. The authorities also maintain a list of prohibited terms and phrases at the router level to determine which types of information are allowed to pass through the 'Chinese border'.[256]

While this censorship mechanism has sufficiently hindered foreign service providers in providing Internet-related services in the Chinese market, none of the lists are published through any appropriate medium. The foreign service providers have been deprived of the right to know the content of the measures and the chance to make better choices according to the change of policies.[257] As publication and notification requirements are essential to generate transparent good governance, the Chinese government has failed to meet its transparency obligations under Article III:1 and 2 at both national and international level by imposing non-transparent Internet censorship measures that significantly affect foreign Internet companies doing business in China.

China may also be in violation of its obligation under Article III:4 in the *Google – China* scenario. In 2011, the Office of the USTR, a governmental agency responsible for developing and recommending trade policies, made a formal submission through the WTO and asked the government of China to answer detailed questions relating to the censorship of the Internet.[258] However, the Chinese government provided no answers to any of the questions. Some of the requests from the USTR included:

---

[256] *See* Ritika Patni & Nihal Joseph, *WTO Ramifications of Internet Censorship: The Google – China Controversy*, NUJS Law Review, Vol. 3 (2010), p. 357.

[257] *See* Robert Wolfe, *Letting the Sun Shine in at the WTO: How Transparency Brings the Trading System to Life,* WTO Economic Research and Statistic Division (06 March 2013).

[258] Gilbert B. Kaplan, *China's Censorship of the Internet and Social Media: The Human Toll and Trade Impact*, Hearing before the Congressional-Executive Commission on China (17 November 2011).

> With respect to China's rules governing Web site blocking, who is responsible for determining when a Web site should be blocked? What are the criteria for blocking access? Where are the guidelines published? Who does the actual blocking? How can a service supplier know if their Web site has been blocked? Are decisions to block appealable?
>
> With respect to the broad nature of the eleven categories of content which Internet service providers may not disseminate: are there any criteria to determine when content falls within the eleven categories? Are government requests to filter specific terms communicated directly to Internet service providers? Are the same terms subject to filtering made available to Internet information service providers inside and outside of China?
>
> With respect to the preventing of "illegal information" as that term is used in the White Paper on the Internet in China: How is the illegal information defines? Does Internet content from outside of China go through a separate monitoring process for illegal information than Internet content created inside of China? If so, how so they differ?

GATS Article III:4 imposes an access-to-information obligation and provides an inquiry point where other Members can obtain information on domestic regulations.[259] The requested information may relate to measures of general application affecting the operation of the GATS, international agreements that a given Member is a signatory to, and measures that significantly affect trade in services covered by the Members' specific commitments in its GATS Schedule. In the light of the comprehensive Internet censorship measures, the wide range of their application, and severe adverse effects on foreign ISPs, all the requested information from the USTR concerning Internet censorship measures are within the meaning of GATS Article III:4. Given its failure to provide adequate information requested by the US government, China has violated its transparency obligations under Article III:4 of the GATS.

---

[259] *See* Panagiotis Delimatsis, General Obligations and Disciplines Article III GATS (2008). In: Rüdiger Wolfrum, Peter Tobias Stoll and Clemens Feinäugle (eds), *WTO -- Trade in Services*, Netherlands: Kononklijke Brill NV, pp. 92-103.

ii. Violation of Article VI:1, VI:2 and VI:5 of the GATS – Domestic Regulations

Considering the significant effects of regulatory barriers to trade in services, Article VI of the GATS directly addresses domestic regulations.[260] The primary intention of various requirements under Article VI is to create a transparent domestic regulatory decision making process and ensure WTO Members provide a reasonable, objective, and impartial administrative system for trade in services.[261] Article VI contains both procedural and substantive standards for measures that are neither discriminatory nor market access restrictive but might negatively impact trade in services. GATS Article VI is divided into two sections: due process procedural obligations under Article VI:1, 2, and 6; and a mandate to negotiate future disciples under Article VI:4 and 5.

Article VI:1 contains the general rule of administrative transparency and regulates that "all measures of general application affecting trade in services are administered in a reasonable, objective and impartial manner". The main objective of Article VI:1 is to prevent trade in services from being impeded by the arbitrary application and administration of domestic regulations. To ensure the consistency and predictability of administrative decisions, the obligation under GATS Article VI:1 embodies a fundamental standard of rule of law and good governance.[262] Unlike Article III:1, the scope of the provision is explicitly limited to sectors where specific commitments are undertaken by a WTO Member. Article VI:1 does not apply to the content of the measures but only to their administration.

Based on the principle of due process, Article VI:2 requires the maintenance or establishment of judicial, arbitral or administrative tribunals or procedures to review administrative decisions affecting trade in services and provide appropriate remedies if justified. Article VI:2 is not limited to measures in sectors with specific commitments but applies generally to all measures within the scope of the GATS. According to Article VI:2, administrative decisions must be

---

[260] *See* Jan Wouters and Dominic Coppens, GATS and Domestic Regulation: Balancing the Right to Regulation and Trade Liberalization. In: Kern Alexander and Mads Andenas, *The World Trade Organization and Trade in Services*, Leiden; Boston: Matinus Nijhoff (2008), pp. 207-262.

[261] *See* Panagiotis Delimatsis, *International Trade in Services and Domestic Regulations – Necessity, Transparency, and Regulatory Diversity,* Oxford University Press (2007), pp. 255-294 (286-270).

[262] *See* Markus Krajewskil, General Obligations and Discipline Article VI GATS. In: Rüdiger Wolfrum, Peter Tobias Stoll and Clemens Feinäugle (eds), *WTO -- Trade in Services*, Netherlands: Kononklijke Brill NV, pp. 165-196.

reviewed at the request of an affected foreign service supplier. However, without specific requirements of procedural and institutional structures, Article VI:2 leaves considerable discretion to WTO Members to decide how to proceed with the reviewing procedures.[263] In essence, the obligation to establish an objective and impartial review mechanism with appropriate remedies under Article VI:2 corresponds with the fundamental element of rule of law.

Against the background, the application and administration of China's Internet censorship measures do not comply with the requirements of Article VI:1 and Article VI:2 since the measures have not been administrated in a reasonable, objective, and impartial manner, and there is no official means of review or appeal for foreign Internet service providers once their websites are blocked or intercepted. The application of Internet censorship measures in China is anything but reasonable, objective, and impartial.[264] At different times, affected by different incidents, any information on the Internet could be considered as sensitive in the eyes of the Chinese authorities. Foreign Internet services outside the Great Firewall of China are blocked or delayed without official notices and ISPs operating locally may face revocation of licenses or shutdown of services if they fail to remove the 'forbidden' information or content on their platforms. While the Chinese Internet censorship measures apply to both domestic and foreign service suppliers, the 'self-censorship' requirement is particularly troublesome for foreign ISPs.[265] For example, in the absence an official master list to determine which information is allowed to be transmitted to Chinese users, foreign Internet companies, like Google, have to set up programs to test which terms or websites are blocked by the Chinese Great Firewall to establish their own blacklist.[266] Being arbitrary and unpredictable, Chinese Internet censorship measures are not administrated in accordance with the standard of the rule of law and are, therefore, in violation of GATS Article VI:1.

Moreover, without adequate institutions or procedures to review China's Internet censorship administrative decisions that seriously affect trade in Internet-related services, China also violates its general obligations under GATS Article

---

[263] Ibid.

[264] *See* Henry Gao, Googling for the Trade-Human Rights Nexus in China: Can the WTO Help? In: Mira Burri and Thomas Cottier (eds), *Trade Governance in the Digital Age*, Cambridge University Press (2012), pp. 247-275.

[265] Anonymous, *A Dual Trace Approach to Challenging Chinese Censorship in the WTO: The (Future) Case of Google and Facebook*, Michigan Journal of International Law, Vol.34, Issue:4 (2013), pp. 857-892.

[266] *See* Henry Gao, Googling for the Trade-Human Rights Nexus in China: Can the WTO Help? In: Mira Burri and Thomas Cottier (eds), *Trade Governance in the Digital Age*, Cambridge University Press (2012), pp. 247-275.

VI:2. According to the most recent report from the USTR to the US Congress, China currently blocks 11 of the top 25 global websites and the total number of blocked sites is estimated at 3,000.[267] While the number of blocked or filtered foreign websites is increasing every year,[268] the Chinese authorities have not provided any official means to review administrative decisions or methods for Internet service suppliers to appeal. Although Article VI:2 allows WTO Members to adopt any review system appropriate to their administrative or constitutional framework, it requires a certain degree of official procedural accountability for impartial reviews and remedies.[269] Accordingly, Chinese Internet censorship measures do not comply with Article VI:2.

The measures at issue might also violate Article VI:5 (a), which requires Members to not apply licensing and qualification requirements and technical standards that nullify or impair the specific commitments in a manner which:

> (i) does not comply with the criteria outlined in subparagraph 4 a), b) or c); and
> (ii) could not reasonably have been expected of that Member at the time the specific commitments in those sectors were made.

In accordance with Article VI:4, procedures, requirements, and standards shall be, *inter alia*:

> (a) based on objective and transparent criteria, such as competence and the ability to supply the service;
> (b) not more burdensome than necessary to ensure the quality of the service;
> (c) in the case of licensing procedures, not in themselves a restriction on the supply of the service.

As discussed above, Chinese censorship measures are vague or opaque and applied in an arbitrary and non-transparent manner. There are no objective criteria and even if such criteria do exist, they are not accessible to the public and

---

[267] Office of the United States Trade Representative, *2017 National Trade Estimate Report on Foreign Trade Barriers* (2017), p. 99.

[268] For example, in the 2016 National Trade Estimate Report on Foreign Trade Barriers, from 2015-2016, 'only' 8 of the top 25 most trafficked global sites are blocked in China.

[269] *See* Cynthia Liu, *Internet Censorship as a Trade Barrier: A Look at the WTO Consistency of the Great Firewall in the Wake of the China – Google Dispute*, Georgetown Journal of International Law, Vol.42 (2011), pp. 1199-1240.

thus fail to meet the transparency required under Article VI:4 (a).[270] Although it is unclear whether the term 'unnecessary barriers to trade' in Article VI:4 aims to include the consideration of policy objectives or limit the examination to balancing the costs and benefits of the contested measures, the Chinese Internet censorship regime might still be more trade restrictive than necessary by imposing a great burden on foreign ISPs to speculate about the possible meaning of the 'prohibited terms' embedded in the comprehensive Internet-related regulations.

Pending the entry into force of the disciplines on Internet services regulations pursuant to Article VI:4, Article VI:5 provides the requirements laid down in Article VI:4 (a) – (c) in sectors in which a Member has undertaken specific commitments. According to Article VI:5 (a)(ii), even if a violation can be found under Article VI:4, the requirements and standards should be applied in a manner that could "not be reasonably have been expected of the Member at the time the specific commitments in those sectors were made". Put differently, the 'standstill' clause of Article VI:5(a)(ii) indicates that the provision is limited to measures which are adopted after a WTO Member undertook the specific commitments in its Schedule since all measures which were in place at the time of scheduling can be reasonably expected.[271]

Accordingly, China might argue that the list of information banned by the Chinese authorities has not changed much since the State Council promulgated Measures for the Administration of International Connection of Computer Information Network in 1997 and the censorship regime and the manner in which it operates is more or less the same today as it was before 2001.[272] However, the general application of Article VI:5(a)(ii) does not apply to the situation in China. It might be true that some of the Chinese Internet censorship measures pre-date the time of public commercial use of the Internet.[273] Nevertheless, most Inter-

[270] *See* Henry Gao, Googling for the Trade-Human Rights Nexus in China: Can the WTO Help? In: Mira Burri and Thomas Cottier (eds), *Trade Governance in the Digital Age*, Cambridge University Press (2012), pp. 247-275.
[271] *See* Markus Krajewskil, General Obligations and Discipline Article VI GATS. In: Rüdiger Wolfrum, Peter Tobias Stoll and Clemens Feinäugle (eds), *WTO -- Trade in Services*, Netherlands: Kononklijke Brill NV, pp. 165-196.
[272] *See* Henry Gao, Googling for the Trade-Human Rights Nexus in China: Can the WTO Help? In: Mira Burri and Thomas Cottier (eds), *Trade Governance in the Digital Age*, Cambridge University Press (2012), pp. 247-275.
[273] *See* Martina F. Ferracane and Hosuk Lee-Makiyama, *China's Technology Protectionism and Its Non-negotiable Rationales*, European Centre for International Political Economy (2017).

net-related restrictive measures have been implemented in the past decade.[274] Fifty-four measures entered into force after 2007 and more drafts are under negotiation for the purpose of enhancing a secure and controllable level of network products and services.[275] For example, the latest Cyber Security Law contains 79 articles and intensifies the burden of private ISPs and ICPs to support and promote cyber security. The wide-ranging and imprecise phrases of the regulations, together with criminal penalties and license revocations, make it hard to predict the overall effects of the restrictive measures on foreign ISPs. Consequently, since most Chinese Internet censorship measures were enacted after China's accession to the WTO, China cannot apply Article VI: 5(a)(ii) as a justification for its violation under Article VI: 5(a)(i).

e. Non-violation Compliant: Nullification and Impairment (GATS Article XXIII:3 & DSU Article 26)

The WTO DSU provides a distinctive feature for a Member's measures that might not amount to a violation of WTO treaty obligations but reduce the level of negotiated trade liberalization when the non-violations nullify or impair the legitimate expectations of another WTO Member. In the context of the GATS, the nullification and impairment requirements are used to address the diminution of services' market access commitments in the absence of an explicit violation of the GATS rules.[276] Article XXIII:3 of the GATS stipulates:

> If any Member considers that any benefit it could reasonably have expected to accrue to it under a specific commitment of another Member under Part III of this Agreement is being nullified or impaired as a result of the application of any measure which does not conflict with the provisions of this Agreement, it may have recourse to the DSU. If the measure is determined by the DSB to have nullified or impaired such a benefit, the Member af-

[274] Ibid.

[275] The Internet or computer-related regulations which are under negotiations or seeking for opinions include Critical Information Infrastructure Security Protection Regulations, National Intelligence Law of the People's Republic of China, Internet News Information Service Management Regulations, Regulations for Internet Content Management Administration Law Enforcement Procedures, Encryption Law of the People's Republic of China, Measures for the Security Review of Internet Products and Services, and etc.

[276] *See* Marion Panizzon, How Human Rights Violations Nullify and Impair GATS Commitments. In: Marion Panizzon, Nicole Pohl and Pirre Sauve (eds.), *GATS and the Regulation of International Trade in Services*, Cambridge: Cambridge University Press, pp. 534-560.

> fected shall be entitled to mutually satisfactory adjustment on the basis of paragraph 2 of Article XXI, which may include the modification or withdrawal of the measure…

GATS Article XXIII:3 determines the application of non-violation claims of trade in services, which is based on the jurisprudence that developed around elements of non-violation complaints in Article XXIII:1 lit.b of the GATT at the time of the Uruguay Round negotiations.[277] The drafter of the GATT conceived Article XXIII as a vague and open-ended mechanism to ensure that Members' reasonable expectations of negotiated concessions would not be upset by unforeseen circumstances.[278] Due to the broad and flexible nature of the provision, when considering GATT Article XXIII:1 lit.b, both the panel and the Appellate Body reiterated several times that non-violation claims should be made with caution and treated as an exceptional instrument of the dispute settlement.[279]

Since no GATS Article XXIII:3 case has so far been brought before the WTO adjudicating bodies, the jurisprudence analysis of non-violation complaints under GATT Article XXIII:1 is significant and relevant when considering the nullification and impairment requirements under GATS Article XXIII:3. In *Japan – Film*, the panel recognized a three-part structure for the complaining party to bring a successful non-violation claim. First, there must be an application of a measure by a WTO Member. The second element requires the existence of benefits which other Members could reasonably have expected to improve market-access opportunities from the relevant tariff concessions.[280] Third, the benefits accruing to the complaining Member must be nullified or impaired as a result of the application of a measure by another WTO Members. In other words, the complaining party must demonstrate "a clear correlation between the measures and the adverse effect on the relevant competitive relationships".[281] In

---

[277] GATT Article XXIII provides in pertinent part:

> If any contracting party should consider that any benefit accruing to it directly or indirectly under this Agreement is being nullified or impaired or that the attainment of any objective of the Agreement in being impeded as the result of
> (a) the failure of another contracting party to carry out its obligations under this Agreement,
> (b) the application by another contracting party of any measure, whether or not it conflicts with the provisions of this Agreement, or
> (c) the existence of any other situation

[278] *See* Robert W. Staiger and Alan O. Sykes, *Non-Violation*, Journal of International Economic Law, Vol.16 (2013), pp. 741-775.

[279] Panel Report, *Japan – Measures Affecting Consumer Photographic Film and Paper* (cited as *Japan -- Film*), WT/DS44/R (31 March 1998), para. 10.36.

[280] *See* the detailed analysis in Ibid., paras. 10.42-10.89.

[281] Ibid., para. 10.82.

addition, in order to determine the meaning of 'reasonable anticipations', the panel established a rebuttal presumption that the measures existing at the time of the tariff negotiations at issue are presumed to have been anticipated by WTO Members.[282]

In *EC – Asbestos*, the Appellate Body reiterated the notion that the remedy for non-violation claims should be "approached with caution and should remain an exceptional remedy".[283] The Appellate Body upheld the panel's findings that Article XXIII:1(b) even applies to measures falling within the scope of general exceptions under GATT Article XX(b) to pursue health objectives since the Article refers to 'any measure'. The Appellate Body cited the panel's opinions from *EEC – Oilseeds*[284] and concluded:

> "... Once again, we look to the text of Article XXIII:1(b), which provides that "the application by another Member of any measure" may give rise to the cause of action under that provision. The use of the word "any" suggests that measures of all types may give rise to such a cause of action. The text does not distinguish between, or exclude, certain types of measure. Clearly, therefore, the text of Article XXIII:1(b) contradicts the European Communities' argument that certain types of measures, namely, those with health objectives, are excluded from the scope of application of Article XXIII:1(b)."[285]

In *Korea – Government Procurement*, the panel introduced a non-violation remedy with the general good faith obligation under customary international law.[286] The panel believed that a non-violation claim under GATT Article XXIII:1 should be interpreted in conformity with the customary international law and, in particular, with the principle that the treaty commitment must be performed in good faith and comply with the object and purpose of the treaty as expressed in its terminology and the actual provisions as a whole. When consid-

---

[282] Ibid., paras. 10.79-10.81.

[283] Appellate Body Report, *European Communities – Measures Affecting Asbestos and Asbestos-Containing Products* (cited as *EC -- Asbestos*), WT/DS135/AB/R (5/April /2001), para. 186.

[284] Panel Report, *European Economic Community – Payment and Subsidies Paid to Processors and Producers of Oilseeds and Related Animal-Feed Proteins* (cited as *EEC -- Oilseeds*), L/6627-37S/86 (25 January 1990), para. 114.

[285] Appellate Body Report, *European Communities – Measures Affecting Asbestos and Asbestos-Containing Products* (cited as *EC -- Asbestos*), WT/DS135/AB/R (5/April /2001), para. 188.

[286] *See* Robert W. Staiger and Alan O. Sykes, *Non-Violation*, Journal of International Economic Law, Vol.16 (2013), pp. 741-775.

ering non-violation claims with the principle of customary international law, the panel stated:

> "7.93 In our view, the non-violation remedy as it has developed in GATT/WTO jurisprudence should not be viewed in isolation from general principles of customary international law. As noted above, the basic premise is that Members should not take actions, even those consistent with the letter of the treaty, which might serve to undermine the reasonable expectations of negotiating partners. This has traditionally arisen in the context of actions which might undermine the value of negotiated tariff concessions.
>
> 7.95 The non-violation doctrine goes further than just respect for the object and purpose of a treaty as expressed in its terminology. One must respect actual provision (i.e., concessions) as far as their material effect on competitive opportunities is concerned. It is an extension of the good faith requirement in this sense."[287]

In sum, according to the jurisprudence from GATT Article XXIII:1, to bring a successful non-violation claim, a complaining party has the burden of proving that a measure taken by a WTO Member nullified or impaired the reasonable expectations of the competitive opportunities from the negotiated tariff concessions. The expectations must be reasonable, in the sense of a rebuttal presumption that measures introduced after the tariff negotiations are assumed not to be anticipated by WTO Members. Last, a non-violation remedy must be interpreted against the backdrop of the principle of good faith embedded in the customary international law. In other words, treaty commitments must be performed in respect of the purpose and object of the Agreement and the actual provisions as far as their material effects on competitive opportunities are concerned.

How a panel interprets and applies the nullification and impairment requirements in the context of the GATS is crucial in the *Google – China* scenario since Article XXIII:3 is one of the few GATS provisions that could have space for considering non-trade values in the WTO legal system. As discussed in Chapter 1, since WTO law is a branch of international law specializing in trade disputes among its Member States, considering human rights as a single legal standing does not comply with the limited jurisdiction of a WTO panel.[288]

Nevertheless, in a nullification and impairment claim, a human rights violation could be treated as a factual finding element. A WTO Member could argue

[287] Panel Report, *Korea – Measures Affecting Government Procurement* (cited as *Korea – Government Procurement*), WT/DS163/R (1 May 2000).
[288] *See* Chapter 2 II.C.

that the economic efficiency of a market heavily depends on the free flow of information. The Chinese Internet censorship measures that constrain the freedom to access necessary information to do business, therefore, frustrate the expectations of a well-functioning market and upset the competitive opportunities of foreign service suppliers.[289] In the modern international trading system, the protection of human rights norms is indispensable in promoting economic growth and raising standards of living.[290] Thus, human rights protection should be able to serve as a more positive method of advancing free trade and, ultimately, the greater growth and development of humankind.

To determine whether the expectations are legitimate, a panel must take into account 'all measures' of the party making the concession that could have been reasonably anticipated at the time of the commitments.[291] Censorship is not unique to the Internet. Before China's accession to the WTO, many regulations had been enacted to prevent the dissemination of information for the purposes of protecting social values, national integrity, and national security. China might argue that to apply such regulations on the Internet at some point in the future should have been anticipated by WTO Members at the time of their concession since it is a nation's sovereign right to conduct censorship within its territory, either online or offline. Nevertheless, given the comprehensiveness of China's Internet censorship mechanisms, no WTO Member in 2001 could have reasonably anticipated such a suppressive Internet environment in China. Additionally, most Internet-related restrictive measures have been introduced during the past 10 years, and more new regulations are under negotiation.[292] According to the rebuttal presumption established by the panel in *Japan – Film*, foreign ISPs

---

[289] *See* Marion Panizzon, *How Close Will GATS Get to Human Rights?*, NCCR Trade Regulation (August 2006).

[290] World Bank, *World Development Report 2006: Equality and Development*, The International Bank for Reconstruction and Development, the World Bank and Oxford University Press (2005). The report emphasized that:

> By ensuring that institutions enforce personal, political, and property rights for all, including those currently excluded, countries will be able to draw on much larger pools of investors and innovators, and be much more effective in providing services to all their citizens. Greater equality can, over the long term, underpin faster growth.

[291] Panel Report, *Japan – Measures Affecting Consumer Photographic Film and Paper* (cited as *Japan -- Film*), WT/DS44/R (31 March 1998), para. 10. 61. (The panel stated: for expectations to be legitimate, they must take into account all measures of the party making the concession that could have been reasonably anticipated at the time of the concession.)

[292] *See* Martina F. Ferracane and Hosuk Lee-Makiyama, *China's Technology Protectionism and Its Non-negotiable Rationales*, European Centre for International Political Economy (2017).

should have reasonable expectations of a well-functioning and open online market in China.

These reasonable expectations, however, have been frustrated by the intensive Internet censorship measures adopted by the Chinese authorities. Google's withdrawing from the Chinese market is one of the prominent examples of how the restrictions on freedom of expression and the right to privacy could adversely impact foreign ISPs in delivering their services to Chinese Internet users. In addition, the arbitrary blockade of websites and strict self-censorship responsibilities imposed on ISPs also upset the competitive opportunities that have been reasonably expected from China's market access commitments.

Although non-violation claims should be considered an exceptional instrument in a WTO dispute, for the reasons stated above, it is very likely that a WTO Member could bring a successful nullification and impairment case under the GATS in the *Google – China* scenario. Besides, the opaque and ambiguous Internet censorship regulations and their broad applications have a negative impact on the object and purpose of the GATS *per se*. Under Article XXIII:3, treaty commitments must be performed in respect of the purpose and object of the Agreement. As described in the GATS preamble, 'transparency' and 'progressive liberalization' are explicit disciplines for trade in services.[293] The Chinese Internet censorship measures are anything but transparent and their applications have impaired economic growth and restrained technological innovation, both domestically and internationally.[294] It could thus be that the Chinese government has failed to implement its treaty commitments in good faith and is subject to a non-violation claim under Article XXIII:3 of the GATS.

d. Public Moral & Public Order Exceptions under GATS Article XIV (a)

Assuming that the Chinese Internet censorship measures are found to be in violation of any of the above discussed obligations, the last step is to consider whether China is able to justify the restrictive measures on the basis of public morals and public order exceptions under Article XIV(a) of the GATS. Since

---

[293] The second paragraph of the GATS Preamble emphasizes:

> Wishing to establish a multilateral framework of principles and rules for trade in services with a view to the expansion of such trade under conditions of transparency and progressive liberalization and as a means of promoting the economic growth of all trading partners and the development of developing countries;

[294] Testimony of Robert D. Atkinson (President of Information Technology and Innovation Foundation), *China's Technological Rise: Challenges to US Innovation and Security*, House Committee on Foreign Affairs Subcommittee on Asia and the Pacific (26 April 2017).

measures falling under Article XIV are exempt from all obligations of the GATS, the exceptions should be interpreted narrowly to avoid deliberate circumventions.[295] In *US – Gambling*, the Appellate Body adopted the two-tier test to determine whether a measure can be justified under Article XIV(a) of the GATS.

According to the Appellate Body, a measure must, first, fall within the ambit of one of the provisions set out in paragraphs (a) to (e) of Article XIV. If the measure is provisionally justified, it needs to meet the requirements of the chapeau. Thus, for Chinese Internet censorship measures to be justified as 'necessary to protect public morals or to maintain public order' under Article XIV(a), the Chinese government is obliged to prove first that the measures at issue are necessary to pursue the intended level of protection of the relevant objectives to build a *prima facie* case. If China can fulfill the necessity requirement, the burden of proof shifts to the complaining party to demonstrate possible less restrictive alternative measures. Secondly, the Chinese Internet censorship measures also need to satisfy the prerequisites under the chapeau of Article XIV, which requires that measures are not applied in a manner that could constitute arbitrary and unjustifiable discrimination or disguised restrictions on international trade.

In the *Google – China* scenario, restrictions on the freedom of information and expression might be analyzed from two different perspectives: first, although the protection of public morality is regarded as one of the core prerogatives of a nation state and the WTO adjudicating bodies normally render WTO Members great discretion to define the scope of 'public morals' within their territory, what the limitations are on such discretion if the underlying measures contradict people's fundamental rights guaranteed by international human rights law; and second, if the Internet censorship measures are considered to contribute to the protection of public morals, it is important to consider whether a panel is competent to make an overall comparison of all the interests at stake when analyzing the 'necessity' of the measures within the meaning of Article XIV(a).

[295] WTO Council of Trade in Services, Guidelines for the Scheduling of Specific Commitments under the General Agreement on Trade in Services, S/L/92 (28/March/2001), para. 20.

i. GATS Article XIV(a) -- Public Morals or Public Order

In *US – Gambling*, the panel stated that a Member who invokes Article XIV(a) exception clause must demonstrate two elements:[296]

> (a) the measure must be one designed to "protect public morals" or to "maintain public order"; and
> (b) the measure for which justification is claimed must be "necessary" to protect public morals or to maintain public order

Consequently, if China wants to justify its Internet censorship measures under Article XIV(a), it has the burden of proving that the measures at issue are intended to protect public morals or maintain public order and they make a material contribution to the achievement of the objectives. If China can make a *prima facie* case, the complaining party needs to demonstrate that other, less trade restrictive, alternatives are reasonably available. However, China still has the opportunity to prove that the purposed alternatives are theoretical in nature or too burdensome to implement.[297]

Public Morals

In *US – Gambling*, the panel has demonstrated its propensity for a broad deference to WTO Members when considering the concept of morality.[298] The panel defined the term 'public morals' as "standards of right and wrong conduct maintained by or on behalf of a community or nation".[299] The panel noted that "the content of [public morality] can vary in time and space, depending upon a range

---

[296] Panel Report, *United States – Measures Affecting the Cross-Border Supply of Gambling and Betting Services* (cited as *US – Gambling*), WT/DS285/R (10 November 2004), para. 6.449.
[297] Appellate Body Report, *United States – Measures Affecting the Cross-Border Supply of Gambling and Betting Services* (cited as *US – Gambling*), WT/DS285/AB/R (7 April 2005), para. 308.
[298] *See* Panagiotis Delimatsis, *Protecting Public Morals in a Digital Age: Revisiting the WTO Rulings on US – Gambling and China – Publications and Audiovisual Products*, Journal of International Economic Law, Vol.14, No.2 (2011), pp. 257-293.
[299] Panel Report, *United States – Measures Affecting the Cross-Border Supply of Gambling and Betting Services* (cited as *US – Gambling*), WT/DS285/R (10 November 2004), paras. 6.462-6.465.

of factors, including prevailing social, cultural, ethical and religious values".[300] In the later *China – Audiovisual Products*[301] and *EU – Seal Products*[302] cases, both the panel and the Appellate Body also showed a great respect for a Member's definition of public morals and decision on the level of protection.

It is clear that the WTO adjudicating bodies intended to avoid ruling on the sensitive issues between trade and other values. This attitude can also be found in other international or regional tribunals.[303] In the digital age, respecting each Member's moral standards with its own scale of values in important since it is more difficult to clearly describe a consensus concept of morality in contemporary global society.[304] However, a full discretion for WTO Members to define the exact content of 'public morals' might ultimately undermine the legitimacy and predictability of the GATS and the WTO.[305] Therefore, the discretion of a Member to determine the scale of public morality should not be absolute, but subject to judicial review. A panel's decision needs to depend on the nature of the legitimate aim and the application of the policy objectives.

Applying the standard to the *Google – China* scenario, while the Chinese government might have the right to determine the content of the morality it aims to protect within its territory, according to the panel and Appellate Body's opin-

---

[300] Ibid., para. 461. The panel further stated, "Members should be given some scope to define and apply for themselves the concepts of "public morals" and "public order" in their respective territories, according to their own system and scales of values."

[301] Panel Report, *China – Measures Affecting Trading Rights and Distribution Services for Certain Publications and Audiovisual Entertainment Products* (cited as *China – Audiovisual Products*), WT/DS363/R (12 August 2009), paras. 7.759, 7.762-7-763.

[302] Appellate Body Report, *European Communities – Measures Prohibiting the Importation and Marketing of Seal Products* (cited as *EC – Seal Products*), WT/DS 400/AB/R & WT/DS 401/AB/R (22 May 2014), paras. 5.199-5.201.

[303] The similar notion of margin of appreciation is reflected in ECJ decisions. In the Henn and Darby case, the Court, when considering the justification on the grounds of public morality, ruled that "in principle, it is for each Member State to determine in accordance with its own scale of values and in the form of selected by it the requirements of public morality in its territory." (ECJ Case 34/79, *Henn and Darby*, [1979] ECR 3795, para. 15.)

[304] Panagiotis Delimatsis, *Protecting Public Morals in a Digital Age: Revisiting the WTO Rulings on US – Gambling and China – Publications and Audiovisual Products*, Journal of International Economic Law, Vol. 14, No.2 (2011), pp. 257-293 (275).

[305] Jeremy C. Marwell, *Trade and Morality: The WTO Public Morals Exception after Gambling*, New York University Law Review, Vol. 81 (2006), pp. 802-842 (817). (The author stressed that the least trade restrictive standard and nondiscriminatory application of the measures should be able to cabin WTO Members from unilaterally defining their own public morality.)

ions, China needs to prove that the 'morals' are supported by the 'standards of right and wrong conduct maintained by or on behalf of a community or nation'. Thus, a WTO panel should be able to weigh the evidence submitted by China and determine whether the Chinese government is acting in good faith in pursuit of legitimate objectives and whether the majority of Chinese people endorse the moral values the government claims.[306]

Save for a few pornographic or racist websites, most foreign websites are blocked or filtered out of the Chinese Internet market because they might contain politically sensitive or 'Western ideology' information that could endanger the stability of the government.[307] If the morality to be evaluated by the standard of right and wrong is that of a community rather than that of the government, it is difficult for China to argue that deprivation of the freedom to access the most innovative information technology and the right to freely express one's opinions are the standards maintained by the community as a whole. In addition, the mere existence of laws or regulations that concern individuals' behavior does not necessarily reflect the standards endorsed by the community or nation.[308] Thus, China needs to demonstrate that it acted in good faith to pursue legitimate public morals.

Due to the political sensitivity, WTO Members are reluctant to bring up the censorship topic in a trade dispute. For example, in *China – Audiovisual Products*, the US did not specifically contest that the Chinese measures in question are designed to protect public morals but only challenged the means as not being necessary to achieve the pursued level of protection.[309] As a result, it is

---

[306] *See* Nicolas F. Diebold, *The Morals and Order Exceptions in WTO Law: Balancing the Toothless Tiger and the Undermining Mole*, Journal of Economic Law, Vol.11, No.1 (2007), pp. 43-74.

[307] *See* Cho-Wen Chu, *Censorship or Protectionism? Reassessing China's Regulation of Internet Industry*, International Journal of Social Science and Humanity, Vol.7, No.1 (January 2017).

[308] *See* Henry Gao, Googling for the Trade-Human Rights Nexus in China: Can the WTO Help? In: Mira Burri and Thomas Cottier (eds), *Trade Governance in the Digital Age*, Cambridge University Press (2012), pp. 247-275.

[309] In *China – Audiovisual Products*, the US pointed out "it is not challenging China's right to determine its desired level of protection. The United States is challenging the means China has chosen to achieve those ends. The United States is of the view that the means China has selected are not "necessary". More particularly, the United States considers that China has failed to demonstrate that the measures at issue are "necessary" within the meaning of Article XX(a)." (Panel Report, *China – Measures Affecting Trading Rights and Distribution Services for Certain Publications and Audiovisual Entertainment Products* (cited as *China – Audiovisual Products*), WT/DS363/R (12 August 2009), para. 7.808.)

highly possible that the issue related to the scope of public morals within the context of Internet censorship will not be challenged by other WTO Members, given the importance of censorship to the Chinese government. If the measures at issue are deemed to be measures intended to protect public morals or maintain public order, they still need to meet necessity test to be provisionally justified under GATS Article XIV(a).

Necessary to Protect Public Morals or to Maintain Public Order

Following the well-established case law under Article XX of the GATT, the panel and the Appellate Body in *US – Gambling* stressed that in determining whether a measure is necessary in the context of Article XIV(a) of the GATS, a process of weighing and balancing a series of factors needs to be applied. Albeit not identical in terms of content, the necessity test adopted by the WTO adjudicating bodies closely resembles the principle of proportionality developed in continental European law.[310] The test delineates the line between the importance of the policy objective and the negative trade impact of the measures. In other words, based on all the evidence before a panel, the more vital the societal value and the less heavy the trade impact of the measure, the more easily it can be considered as necessary in the context of Article XIV(a).

To evaluate whether a measure is necessary to protect public morals or maintain public order, a panel needs to weigh and balance:[311]

> (1) the relative importance of the interests or values that the challenged measure is intended to protect
> (2) the extent to which the challenged measure contributes to the realization of the end pursued by that measure;
> (3) the trade impact of the challenged measure

Accordingly, while a WTO Member might have the discretion to determine the scope of public morals or public order deemed appropriate for its society, a panel is competent to evaluate the importance of the policy objectives under the

[310] Thomas Cottier, Panagiotis Delimatsis, Nicolas F. Diebold, Article XIV GATS General Exceptions. In: Rüdiger Wolfrum, Peter Tobias Stoll and Clemens Feinäugle (eds), *WTO -- Trade in Services*, Netherlands: Kononklijke Brill NV, pp. 287-328 (315-316).
[311] Panel Report, *United States – Measures Affecting the Cross-Border Supply of Gambling and Betting Services* (cited as *US – Gambling*), WT/DS285/R (10 November 2004), para. 6.476.

necessity test.[312] Additionally, in order to undertake a holistic analysis of what is 'necessary' within the meaning of Article XIV(a), a panel must examine whether there are reasonable less restrictive alternatives available. An alternative measure needs to make an equivalent or better contribution to the realization of the end pursued but with less restrictive impact on those who wish to participate in the domestic market.[313]

Applying these standards to the Chinese Internet censorship measures, it is possible that the restrictive measures will satisfy the first two elements of the necessity test based on previous WTO case law. If China claims that the restrictive measures are designed to regulate cultural content and sensitive information which might endanger the stability of the society or the integrity of the country, it is likely that the panel will find the values that the challenged measures are intended to protect are vital. Regarding the contribution of the measures, if the ultimate purpose of the Chinese Internet censorship measures is to build a non-transparent censorship regime on the Internet and to prevent its people from accessing 'controversial' foreign websites,[314] completely blocking the services, intercepting traffic flow, filtering related content, and withdrawing licenses have all made material contributions to the end pursued.

Nevertheless, the Chinese measures at issue might fail the necessity test due to the significant trade impact on the foreign ISPs. The extensive blockage and arbitrary interception of foreign websites have affected a broad range of commercial services activities conducted through the Internet. The Appellate Body in *China – Audiovisual Products* pointed out that the assessment of the restrictive effect on international trade must be "undertaken in the light of the measure at issue, the specific obligation of covered agreements that the measure infringes, and the defense being invoked".[315] Furthermore, the impact could extend not

---

[312] *See* Nicolas F. Diebold, *The Morals and Order Exceptions in WTO Law: Balancing the Toothless Tiger and the Undermining Mole*, Journal of Economic Law, Vol.11, No.1 (2007), pp. 43-74; and *See* Jeremy C. Marwell, *Trade and Morality: The WTO Public Morals Exception after Gambling*, New York University Law Review, Vol.81 (2006), pp. 802-842 (805-807).

[313] Panel Report, *China – Measures Affecting Trading Rights and Distribution Services for Certain Publications and Audiovisual Entertainment Products* (cited as *China – Audiovisual Products*), WT/DS363/R (12 August 2009), para. 7.899.

[314] *See* Julia Ya Qin, *Pushing the Limits of Global Governance: Trading Rights, Censorship, and WTO Jurisprudence – A Commentary on the China – Publication Case*, Chinese Journal of International Law, Vol.10 (2011), pp. 271-322.

[315] Appellate Body Report, *China – Measures Affecting Trading Rights and Distribution Services for Certain Publications and Audiovisual Entertainment Products* (cited as *China – Audiovisual Products*), WT/DS363/AB/R (21 December 2009), para. 306.

only to the relevant imported products but also to the importers and potential importers.[316] Although more evidence is needed to evaluate the real adverse economic impact of the Chinese Internet censorship measures on foreign services and service suppliers, the evidence has shown that, in 2017, 11 of the top 25 global sites were blocked from the Chinese market and the total number of blocked foreign websites was estimated at 3,000.[317] While the ultimate effect on trade in *US – Gambling* was estimated to be about $ 21 million,[318] the Chinese Internet censorship measures might affect billions of dollars' worth of business.

Lastly, if China could make a *prima facie* case to demonstrate that restrictive measures are necessary to protect public morals or maintain public order under GATS Article XIV(a), the complaining party bears the burden of identifying the existence of any reasonably available alternatives to the contested measures that have a less detrimental impact on trade.[319] The Appellate Body in *US – Gambling* described how the interests pursued must be taken into consideration when assessing the availability of possible alternatives. Put differently, the alternative measure must be one that "would preserve for the responding Member its right to achieve its desired level of protection with respect to the objective pursued under paragraph (a) of Article XIV".[320] Nevertheless, a responding party can argue the alternative measure is not reasonably available if it is merely theoretical in nature or imposes an undue financial or technical burden on the Member.

In the current circumstance, the active filtering of search results and selective removing of sensitive content is less trade restrictive than a permanent blockade or temporary interception since the former would at least preserve the competitive opportunities for foreign Internet services or service suppliers in the Chinese Internet market.[321] If the purpose the Chinese government intended to pursue is to keep its citizens from accessing 'unwanted' information, a highly sophisticated filtering technology would be able to provide an equivalent contribu-

---

[316] Ibid., para. 303.

[317] Office of the United States Trade Representative, *2017 National Trade Estimate Report on Foreign Trade Barriers* (2017), p. 99.

[318] *United States – Measures Affecting the Cross-Border Supply of Gambling and Betting Services*, Recourse to Arbitration by the United Sates under Article 22.6 of the DSU, Decision by the Arbitrator, WT/DS285/ARB (21 December 2007), para. 3.189.

[319] Appellate Body Report, *United States – Measures Affecting the Cross-Border Supply of Gambling and Betting Services* (cited as *US – Gambling*), WT/DS285/AB/R (7 April 2005), para. 307.

[320] Ibid., para. 308.

[321] *See* Brian Hindley and Hosuk Lee-Makiyama, *Protectionism Online: Internet Censorship and International Trade Law,* ECIPE Working Paper, No.12 (2009).

tion to the achievement of the same level of protection. Furthermore, with regard to the self-censorship liability for private companies, instead of leaving the service providers to 'guess' the prohibited terms that need to be censored by law, the Chinese authorities could publish a list of phrases or links that are not allowed to be accessed or disseminated by the people. As previously mentioned, while it might be possible for big enterprises, like Google or Facebook, to conduct such research, many small foreign companies are rejected from the Chinese market simply because they lack the abilities or technologies to develop their own filtering lists.[322]

If a panel accepts the alternatives, China could still make a counterargument that the measures are theoretical in nature or would impose an undue financial or technical burden. Nevertheless, as a country with the most advanced Internet filtering mechanism in the world, China will find it difficult to make these arguments. First, China's gateways to the international Internet are controlled by nine state-run operators at the backbone of the infrastructure, which empowers the authorities to filter all cross-border information efficiently.[323] Second, the simple existence of the Great Firewall of China will make the technical and administrative burden of filtering a fairly weak argument.[324] Third, the CCP propaganda department and government agencies at all levels have employed approximately 20,000 to 50,000 people to manually monitor online content.[325] With all the technologies and human resources at hand, selective filtering is a less restrictive but reasonably available alternative measure for the Chinese government to pursue the intended public policies with the same level of protection.

ii. Chapeau under Article XIV of the GATS

If some of the Chinese Internet censorship measures successfully passed the necessity test within the meaning of Article XIV(a), it is highly unlikely they

---

[322] *See* Gilbert B. Kaplan, *China's Censorship of the Internet and Social Media: The Human Toll and Trade Impact*, Hearing before the Congressional-Executive Commission on China (17 November 2011).

[323] *See* Jyh-An Lee and Ching-Yi Liu, *Forbidden City Enclosed by the Great Firewall: The Law and Power of Internet Filtering in China*, Minn. J. L. Sci. & Tech., Vol.13:1 (2012), pp. 125-151.

[324] *See* Brian Hindley and Hosuk Lee-Makiyama, *Protectionism Online: Internet Censorship and International Trade Law,* ECIPE Working Paper, No.12 (2009).

[325] *See* Ron Deibert, John G. Palfrey, Rafal Rohozinski and Jonathan Zittrain (eds.), *Access Contested: Security, Identity, and Resistance in Asia Cyberspace*, OpenNet Initiative, International Development Research Centre and the MIT Press (December 2011).

can satisfy the requirements under the chapeau of the provision. Owing to the similar wordings of the chapeaux of GATS Article XIV and GATT Article XX, the extensive GATT case law was applied *mutatis mutandis* by the panel in *US – Gambling* when interpreting the chapeau under Article XIV.[326] In general terms, the chapeau is an anti-discrimination clause, the purpose of which is to prevent the misuse or abuse of the general exception clauses in the principle of good faith.[327] The interpretation or application of the chapeau is also a weighing and balancing process to find an appropriate equilibrium between the right of a Member to invoke a justification under Article XIV and its obligations to respect the rights of other Members undertaken under the Agreement.[328]

According to the chapeau, a restrictive but provisionally justified measure may not constitute: (1) arbitrary or unjustifiable discrimination between countries where the same conditions prevail; or (2) a disguised restriction on international trade. To reiterate, more evidence is required in the *Google – China* scenario for a panel to conduct a holistic weighing and balancing analysis since the application of the chapeau is on a case-by-case basis,[329] and the requirements set out in the chapeau apply only to the manner in which the measure is applied.[330] As can be seen from the subsequent analysis, the application of Internet censorship measures in China constitutes arbitrary or unjustifiable discrimination between domestic and foreign services or service suppliers.

---

[326] Panel Report, *United States – Measures Affecting the Cross-Border Supply of Gambling and Betting Services* (cited as *US – Gambling*), WT/DS285/R (10 November 2004), para. 6.571.

[327] *See* Arwel Davies, *Interpreting the Chapeau of GATT Article XX in Light of the 'New' Approach in Brazil – Tyres*, Journal of World Trade Law, Vol.43, No.3 (2009), pp. 507-539; *see* also Marion Panizzon, *Good Faith in the Jurisprudence of the WTO: The Protection of Legitimate Expectations, Good Faith Interpretation and Fair Dispute Settlement*, Oxford: Hart Publishing (2006), pp. 51-52.

[328] Appellate Body Report, *United States – Import Prohibition of Certain Shrimp and Shrimp Product* (cited as *US -- Shrimp*), WT/DS58/AB/R (12 October 1998), para. 159.

[329] Panel Report, *United States – Measures Affecting the Cross-Border Supply of Gambling and Betting Services* (cited as *US – Gambling*), WT/DS285/R (10 November 2004), para. 6.476.

[330] Ibid., para. 6.581. (The panel stated: the chapeau of Article XX of the GATT 1994 addresses not so much a challenged measure or its specific content, but rather the manner in which that measure is applied, with a view to ensuring that the exceptions of Article XX are not abused.)

Arbitrary Discrimination

The Appellate Body stated in *US – Shrimp* that three elements need to be considered in determining whether a measure is discriminatory within the meaning of the chapeau: (1) the application of the measure results in discrimination; (2) the discrimination must be arbitrary or unjustifiable in character; and (3) this discrimination occurs where like conditions prevail.[331] In the case, the US measures which required the countries applying for certification to export shrimp to the US were found to constitute arbitrary discrimination since the US applied its measures in a very rigid and inflexible manner without any regard for the conditions prevailing in the exporting countries.[332]

The Appellate Body further considered the certification process required by the US measures to constitute arbitrary discrimination because of the "lack of formal opportunity for an applicant country to be heard, or to respond to any arguments that may be made against it"[333]; the lack of the notice or reasons for denial; the lack of procedure review of, or appeal from, a denial of an application;[334] and the lack of basic fairness and due process.[335] Additionally, given that the conditions in various countries are often different, in order for a measure to be in compliance with the requirements of the chapeau, it should be flexible enough to take into account the specific conditions prevailing in exporting countries.[336]

Accordingly, a measure applied in a rigid and inflexible manner might constitute arbitrary discrimination under the chapeau of Article XIV. The Chinese Internet censorship measures, which are applied in an opaque and arbitrary manner, will be deemed to constitute arbitrary discrimination within the terms of the chapeau. Under the system of the Great Firewall, foreign websites have been blocked, filtered, and intercepted without any notice or reason. Not only is there a lack of review or appeal procedures, but there is no information at all that shows how the Chinese authorities make their decisions on conducting censorship online. In addition, the terms of the published Internet-related de-

---

[331] Appellate Body Report, *United States – Import Prohibition of Certain Shrimp and Shrimp Product* (cited as *US -- Shrimp*), WT/DS58/AB/R (12 October 1998), para. 150.

[332] Ibid., para. 177. (The Appellate Body is of the view that there is little or no flexibility in how United States officials make the determination for certification pursuant to the application provisions. Consequently, the rigidity and inflexibility constitute arbitrary discrimination within the meaning of the chapeau.

[333] Ibid., para. 180.

[334] Ibid.

[335] Ibid., para. 181.

[336] Ibid., para. 165.

crees, laws, and regulations are broad and comprehensive, and are applied in an arbitrary manner. The license application process is complicated and there is no review or appeal mechanism if the license is rejected or revoked. In sum, there is no due process or procedural guarantee in the application of the Chinese Internet censorship measures and, therefore, a panel would consider the measures to be applied in a manner constituting arbitrary discrimination between countries where the same conditions prevail.

V. Conclusion

The case study of China's Internet censorship measures presented a conundrum between a state's sovereign power and its obligations to the international community in the digital world. The ideology that the Internet will create its own territory free from the governments in the real world has proven illusionary, and the capabilities of the Internet are adapting to the existing rules and authorities. Claiming sovereignty over the Internet allows each country to adjust the online environment to its standards, ensuring autonomy and an overall diversity in various policies. Nevertheless, at the same time, government censorship measures undermine people's fundamental rights, reduce economic efficiencies, and limit innovations by eroding the open technical standards of the Internet. In the absence of international Internet governance standards, Chapter 4 is intended to delineate the boundaries of sovereign right on the Internet and stress a nation's obligations towards the international community.

The Chinese government has introduced a considerable number of Internet restrictive measures in the past decade. As shown in this chapter, the terms of the Internet-related regulations, directives, and policies are designed in vague and ambiguous manners, allowing the authorities to arbitrarily interpret or apply the rules to suit their purposes in any particular circumstances. The measures apply to a wide range of areas and have severely infringed people's rights to freedom of expression and information and intervened in the right to privacy. In the context of 'Internet sovereignty', China has regularly argued that within Chinese territory, the Internet is under the jurisdiction of the Chinese government and its authoritarian control over the Internet is to protect local values, state interests, and national security from 'foreign hostile forces'.

However, such an assertion of absolute Internet sovereignty neglects the issue of allocation of power in international relations and does not conform to the modern concept of sovereignty. The concept of sovereignty is never static but evolves in a way that reflects diverse economic and political constituents at different periods of time.[337] Therefore, the Chinese version of Internet sovereignty is controversial for two reasons. First, given the highly interdependent connections between nation states, the traditional concept of Westphalian sovereignty is not suitable for contemporary international relations. It is difficult for a state, acting alone without the cooperation of other participants in the system, to

---

[337] *See* Richard N. Haass, *Sovereignty, Existing Rights, Evolving Responsibilities*, Remarks at the School of Foreign Services and the Mortara Center for International Studies, Georgetown University (14 January 2003).

provide the adequate policies desired by the people.[338] Second, the assertion of absolute sovereignty over the Internet is a paradox since any local restrictive Internet policy will have an extra-territorial effect on the internal affairs of other countries. Due to the pervasive and transnational nature of the Internet, a proclamation of state sovereignty over it, exclusively based on territorial borders, will inevitably violate the sovereignty of other countries.

Based on the first three chapters, the *Google-China* scenario has offered a comprehensive analysis of how Chinese Internet censorship measures constitute barriers to trade within the context of the WTO, especially the GATS, and how to incorporate human rights standards into the WTO legal system. The analysis first found that the Chinese Internet-related measures violate the transparency obligations under Article III and Article VI:1,2, and 5 of the GATS. Article III contains prompt publication and notification requirements and Article VI:1,2, and 5 guarantee due process and assure domestic restrictions on the quality of services are no more burdensome than necessary. Because of the opacity and complexity of the Internet censorship mechanisms, foreign ISPs are constantly subject to arbitrary measures without administrative guidelines or procedural accountability. Therefore, the wide-ranging and inexplicit phrases of the regulations, in conjunction with possible criminal penalties and license revocation, place an undue burden on foreign ISPs to comply with Chinese Internet censorship measures.

Second, the analysis confirmed that Google services, including search engine, video sharing, and email services, are classified as 'Data Processing Services' under the W/120 1-B-c, of which China has undertaken full commitments on both market access and national treatment obligations in Mode 1 cross-border supply of services. With a full commitment on market access, a blockage on a foreign Internet service creates an obstacle to the domestic market and constitutes a quantitative restriction within the meaning of Article XVI. Chinese Internet censorship measures are also in violation of its national treatment obligation under Article XVII of the GATS since the measures accorded less favourable treatment to foreign services and service suppliers in comparison with domestic like services and service suppliers. Some of the Chinese Internet censorship measures are not enacted on the basis of origin but still resulted in *de facto* discrimination since they modified the conditions of competition to the detriment of foreign services and service suppliers.

---

[338] Abram Chayes and Antonia Handler Chayes, *The New Sovereignty: Compliance with International Regulatory Agreements*, Cambridge, Mass: Harvard University Press (1995), pp. 26-27.

Third, if Chinese Internet censorship measures are considered to be WTO-consistent, they might still nullify or impair other WTO Members' legitimate expectations of the negotiated level of trade liberalization under Article XXIII:3 of the GATS. The purpose of Article XXIII:3 is to ensure a Member's reasonable expectations from negotiated concessions are not upset by unforeseen circumstances. As discussed in Chapter 1, a human rights allegation cannot be brought in front of a WTO panel as a single legal standing. Under Article XXIII:3, however, a human rights violation could be treated as a factual element that upsets the reasonably expected market access commitments. First, since most of the restrictive measures on the Internet have been implemented since China's accession to the WTO, other Members should not have anticipated a repressive online market. Second, as the economic efficacy of a market heavily depends on the free flow of information, a WTO Member could argue that Chinese Internet censorship measures constrain the freedom of expression and information and frustrate the expectations of a well-functioning market.

Lastly, the analysis concluded that China is unable to justify its censorship measures on the basis of protecting public morals or maintaining public order under Article XIV(a) of the GATS. According to WTO jurisprudence, considering the significant impact of international trade and the existence of less restrictive alternatives, it is difficult for China to prove that the measures at issue are necessary within the meaning of Article XIV(a). More importantly, by adopting an evolutionary approach in treaty interpretation, Internet censorship measures that were clearly found to be incompatible with freedom of expression or the right to privacy should not be accepted within the scope of 'public morals'.

This conclusion is based on two arguments. First, pursuant to Article 31 and Article 32 of the Vienna Convention, a panel is competent to have recourse to the norms of human rights codified in internationally recognized human rights law and the rules of customary international law when giving meaning to the terms of the WTO agreements. Second, if 'public morals' denotes 'standards of right and wrong conduct maintained by or on behalf of a community or nation', it is not easy for China to argue that its measures, which deprives individuals of autonomy and dignity, reflect the standards endorsed by the community as a whole. The content of WTO law depends by and large on the interpretative choices of the WTO adjudicating bodies. Therefore, while taking into account the purpose and role of the international trade regime, a panel's decision should be conducted in consideration of a certain moral responsibility for the consequences of its practices. The integrity and predictability of the field of global trade governance will be closely related to the legitimacy of those consequences.

Conclusion

The Internet was born as a free medium that enables people from different locations to share information and ideas. The underlying characteristics of the Internet are its global integrity, free accessibility, interoperability, collaboration, and decentralized operation. As the technology evolved and innovated over time, the use of the Internet has surpassed its original design. The Internet today is a 'network of networks' that interconnects all platforms with different functions and applications. While the Internet and the services it provides continue to be the central elements in all facets of societal, political, and economic developments in the modern society, regulatory movements have emerged to respond to the conflict of interests it has brought about. The idea that this new information and communication technology will create a new territory free from state governments in the real world has turned out to be a myth. Although the Internet still preserves some of its unchangeable properties, due to its profound influence on human behavior, international trade, and state interests, the necessity for some legal frameworks to moderate its effects is inevitable.

However, Internet policies at all levels of government are subject to political and social as well as economic struggles. Whereas any country can claim jurisdiction over Internet infrastructures, online activities, and companies within its traditionally defined territory, no nation can genuinely control the Internet. Besides, the intrinsic global nature of the Internet and its associated opportunities for economic efficiency and human rights enhancement further complicate the issue of Internet governance. On the one hand, while all networks on the Internet are globally connected, they are also locally configured. On the other hand, any Internet-related domestic measures will have spillover effects in the international arena.

Consequently, the fundamental issue of Internet governance concerns whose laws should apply and whose rights should be protected. Due to the lack of unified values and standards, the current Internet policy environment is fragmented, or, as some scholars call it, balkanized.[1] Regardless of different rhetorical descriptions, the underlying debate on Internet governance is a longstanding dispute in the international legal system, namely the concept of state sovereignty.

[1] The Internet is created with the ideology of a unified community with no interference from the power of governments. The fragmentation or Balkanization of the Internet generally refer to the erosion of the universal accessibility and integrity of the Internet from technologies, interest groups, or governments. However, such an ideology sometimes underestimates the profound political and economic implications of the Internet and overlooks the fact that diversity is an inexorable result of human behavior.

A struggle for Internet governance, therefore, could be seen as a struggle for sovereignty in modern international relations. Since the traditional concept of absolute sovereignty is fading away due to the growing interdependence of contemporary societies,[2] it is highly questionable whether the notion of Internet sovereignty could provide sustainable solutions for the governance of cyberspace.

Of all the issues related to Internet governance, Internet censorship is one of the most controversial terrains in international politics and law. Internet censorship mechanisms are applied to intercept the information flow through or within a nation's borders. The main purpose of the online censorship system is to prevent citizens from accessing information that is deemed inappropriate by the government, whether it is to prevent illegal activities or to protect indigenous cultural values, national interests, or national security. While the motives for Internet censorship may seem righteous at first glance, sometimes censorship is implemented merely to eradicate political dissidents or to protect domestic enterprises. Although censorship is an old phenomenon, given the unique influence the Internet has on promoting individuals' fundamental rights and facilitating economic growth, the assertion of the complete authority of the state to act as it chooses would not be able to provide the policy outcomes that are desired by the people.

Although the concept of the absolute rights of the sovereign state has continuously been challenged, nation states remain the central participants in modern international relations.[3] Therefore, if sovereignty is a predestined direction in which Internet governance is heading, in preference to defying a state's sovereignty in the digital world, the book has attempted to define the boundaries and legitimacy of sovereign authorities on the Internet. The practical value of the Internet should not be arbitrarily determined by a particular state or territory, but by a more comprehensive community, whose interests and rights depend on how the rules are generated, interpreted, and implemented in the context of in-

[2] *See* Robert Howse, Sovereignty, Lost and Found. In: Wenhua Shan, Penelope Simons and Dalvinder Singh (eds.), *Redefining Sovereignty in International Economic Law*, Hart Publishing, USA Portland (2008), pp. 61-75; Kal Raustiala, *Rethinking the Sovereignty Debate in International Economic Law*, Journal of International Economic Law, Vol.6, No.4 (2003), pp. 841-878; and *see* also John H. Jackson, *Sovereignty, the WTO, and Changing Fundamentals of International Law*, New York: Cambridge University Press (2006), pp. 57-78.

[3] *See* Johan D. van der Vyver, Sovereignty. In: Dinah Shelton (eds), The Oxford Handbook of International Human Rights Law, Oxford University Press (2013).

ternational law. If "a global era requires global engagement",[4] the solutions to many pending problems related to Internet governance need to be allocated at international level. In other words, due to the political and legal externalities of national rules on the Internet, the specific structure of the Internet requires reconsideration of the role of sovereignty in the digital age.

Nevertheless, addressing regulatory framework to Internet governance at the international level is not without controversies. The difficulties arise from, on the one hand, the fragmentation of international law. On the other hand, new challenges brought about by the new ICTs contest the applicability of the existing international legal systems to the Internet. One of the main findings of the study is that although technological innovations reshape human behaviors to a certain extent, the content and subjects of legal relations on the Internet are still defined and confined by social values in the tangible world. While laws always struggle to keep pace with evolving technologies, with appropriate interpretative choices, the existing regulations should be flexible and resilient enough to accommodate technological changes in the information age.

The case study of China in Chapter 4 presented an overall analysis of how to address Internet censorship issues at the international level. While China has the most Internet users and the largest E-commerce market in the world, it also has the most sophisticated and comprehensive Internet censorship system. In 2010, the Chinese government published its first white paper on Internet policy and emphasized that "within the Chinese territory, the Internet is under the jurisdiction of Chinese sovereignty".[5] Since then, the government's grip on the Internet has tightened. More than 50 Internet-related restrictive measures have been implemented over the past decade, with a range of applications. These measures, combined with advanced filtering apparatus, have precipitated a highly censored and repressive online environment in China. The 'Great Firewall' of China allows Chinese authorities to monitor all information traffic flows across the 'Chinese border' at the backbone level. Packets containing sensitive keywords, such as Tibet and Taiwan independence or human rights, are dropped at the gateways. Major foreign websites, such as Facebook, Twitter, and Google, are blocked continuously from the Chinese market without adequate reasons. Addi-

[4] UN Secretary-General, Kofi Annan presented his annual report to the General Assembly and emphasized that a global era requires global engagement to protect people from the wrongdoing of governments. He also asserted, "State sovereignty, in its most basic sense, is being redefined by the forces of globalization and international cooperation." *See* Kofi A. Annan, *Secretary – General's Speech to the 54th Session of the General Assembly*, UN Document SG/SM/7136 (20 September 1999).

[5] The Information Office of the State Council of the People's Republic of China, *White Paper – The Internet in China* (8 June 2010).

tionally, pervasive measures, such as real-name registration and criminalization of online activities, successfully foster a self-censorship phenomenon among Internet users and Internet service/content providers.

Chinese Internet censorship policy is controversial in both the human rights and international trade regimes. From the human rights perspective, the right to freedom of expression and information and the right to privacy are severely restrained by the Chinese censorship mechanism. Freedom of expression and information is enshrined in Article 19 of the UDHR and the ICCPR as a right to hold opinions without interference, and the right to seek, receive, and impart information and ideas through any media regardless of frontiers. The right has been considered as necessary for government transparency and accountability and as a vital precondition for individual autonomy, self-expression, and self-fulfillment. The notion of the right to privacy is not universally understood in the same way but developed and shaped by social trends and available technologies. Nevertheless, the right to privacy is essential for personal dignity and self-determination. Article 12 of the UDHR stipulates that "no one should be subject to arbitrary interference with his privacy, family, home or correspondence of the law against such interference or attacks". Based on the analysis in Chapter 2, whereas the Internet empowers individuals' rights as no previous medium has, it also poses new threats to people's fundamental freedoms.

Therefore, freedom of expression and the right to privacy are not guaranteed by novel technologies but must be protected by policies and practices which support transparency and due process of law. In response to the constant interference in the exercise of individuals' rights on the Internet, many movements have been adopted to declare human rights in the online world. On June 29 2012, the UN adopted a grand resolution to promote the enjoyment of human rights on the Internet and affirmed that "the same rights that people have offline must also be protected online".[6] Additionally, it is generally recognized that the broad language "through any other media" used in both Article 19 of the UDHR and the ICCPR is considered to accommodate future technological developments, including the Internet.[7]

The assurance of freedom of expression and information on the Internet in positive human rights laws indicates that any limitations on a right online must

---

[6] United Nations General Assembly, 20th session, *Promotion and protection of all human rights, civil, political, economic, social and cultural rights, including the right to development: The promotion, protection and enjoyment of human rights on the Internet*, U.N. Doc. A/HRC/20/L.13 (29 June 2012).

[7] *See* Chapter 2 I.A.a.

comply with the principles of international human rights law.[8] That is to say, any restrictions on freedom of expression and information on the Internet must be prescribed by law and the law must be precise and adequately accessible to the public. The censorship measures must serve one of the legitimate purposes such as the rights of other, protecting national security and interest, and maintaining public morals and public order. The measures that restrict Internet access must be necessary and proportionate to pursue the legitimate policy objective. In other words, interfering measures must be the least restrictive to the right at issue and the benefit of the interference must be greater than the harm caused to individuals' right to hold opinions or to seek, receive, and impart information on the Internet.

The right to privacy on the Internet enjoys the same level of protection. Nevertheless, numerous new threats to the right to privacy are perceived due to the new information and communication technologies. The processing of personal data is one of the major challenges to privacy in the digital age. Information privacy is defined as the right of an individual to have some degree of control over his or her personal information in the pursuit of self-interest, without interference from who are in possession of those data. The large volume of personal information is collected by governments or Internet intermediaries, coupled with the advent of big data technology, means that the central issue of privacy in the modern information society is the relation between the right to privacy and data protection. Privacy and data protection might not be identical concepts; however, the principles underling data protection can be directly derived from the right to privacy. A person's right to privacy in the digital age, therefore, should be protected substantively ad procedurally against arbitrary or unlawful interference.

From the international trade perspective, Chinese Internet censorship measures constitute barriers to trade within the context of WTO, especially the GATS. To determine whether the GATS legal framework is applicable to digital trade, the WTO adjudicating bodies adopted an evolutionary approach to interpreting the scope of a WTO Member's specific commitments and clarified that Internet-related services should be categorized as cross-border supply of services (mode 1), as defined in Article I of the GATS. Based on the analysis in Chapter 3, panels and the Appellate Body adapted the GATS rules to the challenges posed by the new technologies, as can be observed in several aspects.

[8] The permissible limitations on freedom of expression and information are elaborated in numerous international human rights treaties and judgments of human rights courts. The three-part cumulative test is articulated in Article 19 & 29 of the UDHR, Article 19(3) of the ICCPR, Article 10(2) of the ECHR and Article 13(2) of the ACHR.

First, the panel and the Appellate Body confirmed that measures affecting the electronic delivery of services are measures affecting trade in services within the context of the GATS. Second, the principle of 'technological neutrality' was upheld in both the *US – Gambling* and *China – Audiovisual Products* cases, and, therefore, a full market access (GATS Article XVI) or national treatment (GATS Article XVII) commitment under mode 1 should encompass the supply of services through electronic means. Third, when examining the meaning of the terms in a WTO Member's GATS Schedule, the Appellate Body emphasized that if the terms are 'sufficiently generic', the content must be interpreted according to their contemporary meaning and in conformity with customary rules of treaty interpretation under Article 31 and Article 32 of the Vienna Convention.

Against this background, in a broad sense, Internet governance is a simple term without a simple definition and there is no single theory to solve all Internet-related issues. The deliberations of Internet censorship need to consider the conflict of interest, the multitude of stakeholders, and the regulatory balance between international and national legal systems. The case study of China, therefore, is not able to present the entire range of regulatory options available for governance in the digital age. Additionally, the issue of Internet censorship is more complicated than the *China – Google* scenario offered in Chapter 4. Nevertheless, the case study provided a starting point to demonstrate how the international regulatory approach is an adequate solution to Internet governance and why the assertion of the traditional sovereign power of states on the Internet is neither plausible nor legitimate in contemporary international relations.

The *Google – China* narrative exemplified how restrictive Internet policies could simultaneously have severe adverse impacts on individuals' fundamental freedoms and international trade. While the Chinese authority faces political struggles over diverging values on the Internet in the international sphere, those values are equally controversial within the domestic legal system. Internationally, Internet sovereignty was reiterated by State President Xi in several occasions to claim rights over the Internet within Chinese territory, and the Chinese government has frequently described the international pressure for a more liberated online environment as coming from 'foreign hostile forces' (境外敌对势力) to undermine the national security and stability of the society. The promotion of freedom of expression and information has been described as a Western ideological penetration that emasculates Chinese cultural values.

Nonetheless, the Chinese vision of Internet sovereignty is a paradox in two ways. First, the principle of sovereignty is never a static concept but has been a subject of continuous contestations. What sovereignty signifies is not a well-established body of rights and obligations of states but a changing frame of reference, determined by the factors and processes in different political and economic forms at different periods of time.[9] The traditional Westphalian sovereignty is discredited to a certain extent and unable satisfactorily to meet the multiple needs of society as a whole.[10] Given the political and economic interdependence of nation states and the emergence of international institutions after the Second World War, it is evident that the international legal system is undergoing a transformation, which requires reconsidering the essential concepts of sovereignty. The claim of absolute sovereign power, which ignores a nation's international obligations and obligations towards people, merely renders the argument a rhetorical embellishment that diverts attention from the real issues.[11]

Second, if the components of the traditional concept of sovereignty have been critically hindered by contemporary economic, social, and environmental constituents, revolutionized information and communication technology makes the supreme political authority of nation states even more fragile. Although it is undeniable that the growth of E-commerce and the transformation of social life into cyberspace require controls on human behavior, the unique interoperable characteristic of the Internet and the extraterritorial consequence of national Internet policies invalidate any proclamation of state sovereignty exclusively based on territory. 'Sovereignty' should not be applied as an antidote to the Chinese government's violation of essential human rights on the Internet. In fact, with technological innovation, the enhanced freedom of expression and information and exceptional threats to the right to privacy on the Internet urgently require governments to comply with the international human rights norms and principles set forth in positive human rights laws. The Chinese government is obliged to demonstrate its censorship measures are necessary, legitimate, and proportionate to the end pursued.

Domestically, a person's fundamental rights are guaranteed by the Chinese constitution. The right to freedom of expression and the press are protected in Article 35, the right to enjoy freedom of religious belief is promised in Article 36, the right to privacy is listed in Article 41, and the freedom to engage in sci-

---

[9] *See* Stephen D. Krasner, Problematic Sovereignty. In: Stephen D. Krasner (ed.), *Problematic Sovereignty – Contested Rules and Political Possibility*, Columbia University Press, New York (2001), pp. 1-23; *see* also Wiston P. Nagan & Aitza M. Haddad, *Sovereignty in Theory and Practice*, San Diego Int'l L. J., Vol.13 (2012), pp. 429-520; and also Janice E. Thomson, *State Sovereignty in International Relations: Bridging the Gap Between Theory and Empirical Research*, International Studies Quarterly, Vol.39 (1995), pp. 213-233.

[10] Ibid.

[11] *See* Stephen D. Krasner, *Sovereignty: Organized Hypocrisy*, Princeton University Press (1999), pp. 1-25.

entific research, literary and artistic creation, and other cultural pursuits is guaranteed in Article 47. Unsurprisingly, these constitutional rights are continuously encroached on by a wide variety of Internet-related regulations, especially when the terms of the regulations are often designed in a vague and ambiguous manner, providing authorized bodies with wide discretion to determine their meaning. For example, while the new Cybersecurity Law, National Security Law, and Counterterrorism Law require ISPs or ICPs to monitor and delete harmful information on their platforms and websites, the definition of 'harmful information' is esoteric. It could encompass information that endangers national security, divulges states secrets, infringes the honor and glory of the state, promotes evil cults, and distributes other information prohibited by laws or administrative regulations. The recently amended Criminal Law stipulates that people disseminating 'misinformation' on the Internet are subject to the criminal penalty of up to seven years in prison.

The Chinese government contested that it prevents its citizens from accessing major foreign websites or using foreign search engines to protect Chinese values from hostile alien ideologies. The argument has no legal validity if the merit the government intends to preserve is the interests of the state or the party, rather than the interests of the people. Regardless how virtuous it might be for any government to defend the integrity of its culture; cultural diversity is never the reason for a nation to withdraw from its obligations to respect the inherent dignity and equality of the individual. It is true that the culture or public morals of a society vary from place to place and the universal application of human rights without respecting cultural traits undermines cultural identity. Nevertheless, the notion of human rights does not only exist in Western culture. Some tenets of contemporary human rights or the concepts of a democratic society, such as equality and good governance, are reflected in Confucianism, which has deep roots in the formation of Chinese cultural, social, and political systems. The *minben* (民本) philosophy is analogous to the normative idea of popular sovereignty, and the typical expression of *minben* is that people alone are the foundation of a nation (*minwei bangben* 民為邦本). Chinese Internet censorship policies that concentrate on the power of the state rather on the rights of its citizens cannot be justified in the guise of preserving cultural diversity.

The *Google – China* scenario also presented a detailed analysis of how Internet censorship measures inhibit foreign participation in the Chinese digital market and how to incorporate human rights standards into a WTO dispute. In China, comprehensive legal and technical Internet censorship mechanisms have been implemented not only to filter sensitive political information but also to block foreign websites and intermediaries. The research in Chapter 4 showed that while major foreign Internet services and service providers are unable to reach Chinese Internet users, their domestic counterparts with similar, if not identical, functionalities dominated the market in every area, from instant messaging to social networks and E-commerce. After Google was forced to close the Google.cn search engine owing to the increasingly stringent censorship regulations and unwarranted interception of its service transmission, Baidu (百度), Google's most prominent domestic competitor, gained market share up to 88.7% in 2015.

Internet censorship measures adopted by the Chinese government might violate the GATS rules in three different situations. First, the intricate structure of Chinese Internet restrictive measures and the arbitrary application of the vague terms of the measures might violate China's general obligations of transparency under GATS Article III and Article VI:1, 2, and 5. Regulatory transparency plays a pivotal role in good governance and is a prerequisite for a healthy, predictable, and accountable market. Article III of the GATS requires China to promptly publish all relevant measures that pertain to or affect trade in services and notify the Council for Trade in Services of all new regulations or any amendments to existing laws and administrative guidelines which might have a significantly impact on trade in services. Whereas a series of sensitive terms or foreign websites are filtered and blocked through the Great Firewall on a regular basis, no guidelines or objective criteria are accessible to the public. Foreign Internet service providers are constantly subject to ambiguous and arbitrary measures that prevent them from entering the Chinese market.

Furthermore, Article VI: 1, 2, and 5 obligate China to administrate and apply its domestic regulations in a reasonable, objective, and impartial manner; to provide a reviewing procedure of administrative decisions at the request of affected service suppliers; and to guarantee that licenses and qualification requirements and technical standard are no more burdensome than necessary to ensure the quality of the services. Based on the research in Chapters 3 and 4, Chinese Internet restrictive measures do not comply with its transparency obligations since the measures are not administered under the standard of rule of law and there is no guarantee of an adequate degree of official procedure accountability. The lack of clarity and transparency around the exact extent to which restrictive measures might be applied imposes a significant burden on foreign Internet service providers to speculate about the true intentions of the regulations.

Second, China's Internet censorship measures also violate its specific obligations under Articles XVI and XVII of the GATS. To determine a violation of specific obligations, a panel must first decide whether China has undertaken explicit commitments to the services at issue, such as search engine, video streaming, and email services. Based on the principle of technological neutrality and the evolutionary approach of treaty interpretation, the services should be considered as 'Data Processing Services' under CPC Group 843 and W/120 1-B-c[12], according to which China has made a full commitment to both market access and national treatment obligations in cross-border supply of services.

To comply with its market access obligation under Article XVI, China should not restrict trade in services by applying quantitative limitations subsumed in the list of Article XVI:2. Quantitative restrictive measures are considered to be the most damaging methods of market access and are often deemed as protectionist. In *US – Gambling*, the Appellate Body concluded that when a Member scheduled a full market access commitment for a given service sector under mode 1 of supply, a prohibition on one, several, and all means of delivery would be considered as a quantitative limitation on the market access listed in Article XVI:2 (a) and (c). Although Chinese Internet censorship measures are not designed in a numerical manner, the complete blockage of foreign websites constitutes a limitation on the number of service suppliers to zero, which is in the form of 'numerical quota'. Consequently, with a full commitment on market access, the measures adopted by the Chinese authorities, which "totally prevent the use by service suppliers of one, several or all of means of delivery that are included in mode 1"[13], are in violation of GATS Article XVI:2 (a) and (c).

China also undertook a full commitment to national treatment obligation under Article XVII, which requires a WTO Member treats services and service suppliers of another Member no less favourable than it accords to domestic like services and service suppliers. Non-discrimination is the key concept in WTO law and the purpose of national treatment obligation under the GATS is to ensure equal competitive opportunities for foreign services and service suppliers. In the *Google – China* senior, it is evident that the domestic and foreign services are like services and the service suppliers are in a competitive relationship.

Nevertheless, it is less clear whether the Chinese Internet censorship measures accord foreign services and service suppliers less favourable than domestic services and service suppliers. While the measures at issue might not constitute *de jure* discrimination, they could be considered as *de facto* discrimination within the meaning of Article XVII:3. Although more factual findings

[12] *See* Chapter 4 IV.B.a.

[13] Panel Report, *United States – Measures Affecting the Cross-Border Supply of Gambling and Betting Services* (cited as *US – Gambling*), WT/DS285/R (10 November 2004), para. 6.338. Appellate Body Report, *United States – Measures Affecting the Cross-Border Supply of Gambling and Betting Services* (cited as *US – Gambling*), WT/DS285/AB/R (7 April 2005), para. 239.

are required, compared with the entire group of domestic services and service suppliers, Internet censorship mechanism adopted by the Chinese government modified the conditions of competition to the detriment of the entire group of foreign services and service suppliers. China might still argue that the measures do not *de facto* discriminate against foreign services or service suppliers if they are not protectionist by design. Nevertheless, in the recent *Argentina – Financial Services* case, the Appellate Body explained that the regulatory purpose could not convert the measures' detrimental impact on the conditions of competition into 'treatment no less favourable' since regulatory concerns are more appropriately addressed under general exceptions of Article XIV of the GATS.

Third, Chinese Internet censorship measures might be subject to the non-violation complaints under GATS Article XXIII:3. Article XXIII:3 applies to a WTO-consistent measure which nullifies or impairs other Members' reasonable expectations of negotiated concession under unforeseen circumstances. According to WTO jurisprudence, measures existed at the time of the tariff negotiations are presumed to have been anticipated by WTO Members. The WTO adjudicating bodies asserted that non-violation claims should be interpreted against the backdrop of good faith embedded in the customary international law.

In the case study, where China has undertaken a full commitment on market access, other Members should have reasonable expectations of an open and effectively functioning online market in China. Such expectations could be nullified or impaired by the comprehensive Internet censorship measures on several grounds. First, economic efficiency and market perfection depend on the free flow of information. Suppression of information will affect the functioning of the market and consequently reduce overall welfare. Second, many of the Internet-related regulations implemented after China's accession to the WTO imposed a heavy self-censorship responsibility on private Internet service suppliers and such a burden undermines the value of the negotiated concessions China undertook in its GATS Schedule. Lastly, the ambiguous Internet censorship measures are in contrast with the good faith obligation under the customary international law since the measures, which impair international economic growth and restrain technical innovations, frustrate the 'transparency' and 'progressive liberalization' objectives recognized in the Preamble of the GATS. However, whether Article XXIII:3 could proceed as a successful argument is questionable since the Appellate Body has reiterated several times that a non-discrimination claim should be applied with caution and treated as an exceptional instrument for a WTO dispute.

Third, if the Chinese Internet censorship measures violate one of the above-mentioned GATS provisions, the critical issue is whether China would be able to justify its restrictive measures on the basis of public morals exception under

Article XIV(a) of the GATS. General exception clauses allow WTO Members to deviate from their obligations under the GATS to pursue legitimate domestic policy objectives. To bring the argument under Article XIV(a), China has the burden of proving that the measures at issue are necessary to protect public morals and meet the requirements of the chapeau of Article XIV.

The prominence of the general exception clauses in the context of Internet censorship is not only because they provide a mechanism by which important state interests can find expression, but also because they present an appropriate forum to address human rights issues in the WTO legal system. Although no reference to human rights can be found in the WTO agreements, the content and scope of WTO law depends by and large on the forms of regulatory understanding and the interpretative choices of the WTO adjudicating bodies in specific circumstances and periods of time. If a panel has the competence to take into account human rights norms and standards based on customary rules of treaty interpretation in a dispute, human rights issues could be dealt with in a way that gives them substantive meanings within the trade regime.

Nevertheless, the legal nexus between trade and human rights at the international level is never clear due to the very different concepts of the two regimes. Since the adoption of the GATT in 1947 and the UDHR in 1948, the two international legal systems have evolved in a mutually isolated manner for decades. In the aftermath of World War II, in the pursuit of world peace, the idea of international cooperation among nation states emerged as one of the critical drivers for re-establishing the international order. Nevertheless, because of the various political ideologies and the embedded idea of liberalism, whereas the trade regime focused on dismantling barriers to international trade, the human rights regime dedicated more effort to liberty rights, i.e., civil and political rights. Trade and human rights have developed distinctively with their own mandates, institutions, and expertise.

Still, the connection between trade and human rights is inevitable in contemporary international relations, and the evolving nature of both regimes has led to the emergence of different storylines about the debates on interfacing trade regulations and human rights law. Trade and human rights are complementary to a certain degree. On the one hand, a predictable and secure international trade system provides economic prosperity that is necessary for the enjoyment of human rights. On the other hand, the comprehensive protection of human rights creates the essential conditions for stable market access. Social interests and international trade are inextricably intertwined and the actions of one regime will have consequences on actions in the other. Precisely this inherent connection has brought about the concerns of human rights advocates as to the impact of free trade on the development of essential human rights when the state of affairs changed internationally.

In the 1980s, globalization, technology innovation in communication and transportation, and the rise of developing countries contributed to the new thinking of the social impact of the international economic structure. The right to development and economic, social, and cultural rights attracted more attention in the human rights sphere. Consequently, claims regarding the negative impact of globalization emphasized the issues of the possible infringement of the protection of labor rights, the rights to health and environmental standards, and other social welfare and justice. Put differently, the common normative basis of the critiques of the global economic system was mainly associated with concerns about the social costs of bilateral and multilateral trade agreements.

The political struggle around trade issues accelerated in the 1990s, and the WTO inevitably became the center of the modern debate on the 'conflict' between trade and human rights.[14] The underlying considerations were comprehensive, and the actors involved were from a broad array of different areas with different political, social, and economic interests. Within the context of the WTO, the criticism was oriented toward the WTO's narrow mandate to trade liberalization and the concept of the fragmented international legal order. Greater coherence was called for to resolve the tension between trade and human rights.[15]

Considering the relations between trade and social values, it must first be understood that the nature, purpose, and mandate of the WTO are not limited to the free trade but contain collective purposes to increase global welfare and ensure sustainable development. Additionally, due to the indeterminacy of WTO law, the substantive content of WTO law depends on the interpretative choices of its adjudicating bodies. Thus, in a WTO dispute, the critical question is how and to what extent a panel is competent to consider a non-trade claim in

---

[14] UN Committee on Economic, Social and Cultural Rights, *Statement of the UN Committee on Economic, Social and Cultural Rights to the Third Ministerial Conference of the World Trade Organization (Seattle, 30 November to 3 December 1999)*, UN Doc. E/C.12/1999/9 (26 November 1999). The CESCR has called the WTO to "undertake a review of the full range of international trade and investment policies and rules in order to ensure that these are consistent with existing treaties, legislation and policies designed to protect and promote all human rights."

[15] The Office of High Commissioner for Human Rights, *5th WTO Ministerial Conference Cancùn Mexico* (10-14 September 2003). The High Commissioner stated that a human rights approach to the trade regime should aim at "the progressive introduction of trade policies that take into account the needs and rights of individuals and communities".

the dispute settlement procedure. According to the analysis in Chapter 2, the jurisdiction of a panel is defined and limited to claims made under the WTO 'covered agreements' and a panel's decision cannot add to or diminish a Member's obligations under the WTO. The limitation on the substantive jurisdiction of a WTO panel, however, does not necessarily equal a limitation on the applicable law available to the panel. In its very first appeal, *US – Gasoline*, the Appellate Body confirmed that, based on the reference in Article 3.2 of the DSU to customary rules of interpretation, the WTO is not to be read in clinical isolation from public international law. The panel in *Korea – Procurement* further emphasized that no basis in the DSU excludes rules of international law, other than rules of interpretation, from being applied.

In general terms, given the nature of WTO Agreement as a branch of public international law, WTO rules do not preclude any sources of international law from being applied in WTO dispute settlement proceedings, including customary international law, general principles of law, and human rights law. This approach indicates that, although the norms and standards of other international legal systems cannot be raised as independent legal arguments due to the limited jurisdiction of a WTO panel, they could be used to ascertain the meaning of imprecise terms and the intentions of the parties. Such an understanding is supported by WTO jurisprudence. Evidence can be found in the *Thailand – Cigarettes*, *EC – Asbestos*, and *US – Shrimp* cases when public health and environmental protection are at issue. In the long run, it is important to set out a sense of collective moral responsibility for the consequence of practices occurring within the international trade regime. Ultimately, the legitimacy of the WTO and the predictability of the multilateral trading system will depend on how the WTO carries out its responsibility.

Subsequently, if China tries to justify its Internet censorship measures under Article XIV(a) to protect public morals, a panel should be able to take into account the norms and principles of human rights when interpreting the meaning of 'public morals' and when determining the necessity of the measure to achieve the pursued ends. The panel in *US – Gambling* defined the term 'public morals' as "standards of right and wrong conduct maintained by or on behalf of a community or nation".[16] Both the panel and the Appellate Body have shown great deference to WTO Members in defining the scope of public morals and deciding the desired level of protection. It is understandable that the adjudicat-

[16] Panel Report, *United States – Measures Affecting the Cross-Border Supply of Gambling and Betting Services* (cited as *US – Gambling*), WT/DS285/R (10 November 2004), para. 6.462-6.465.

ing bodies have tried to avoid unduly intervening in the substantive regulatory prerogatives of WTO Members; however, as formerly argued, the regulatory autonomy of a nation state has been allocated to international governance to a certain extent to encompass the needs of the society as a whole. A panel should not give complete discretion to a Member to decide the meaning of 'public morals' but interpret the term by recourse to its ordinary meaning within the context, object, and purpose of the WTO. The Internet censorship measures that severely undermine individuals' fundamental rights would be contrary to the ordinary meaning of the morality concept since the term should be evaluated by the standards of right and wrong conduct of a community or a nation as a whole rather than that of the government.

If the censorship issue within the meaning of public morals is not challenged by WTO Members owing to its political sensitivity, Chinese Internet censorship measures will not satisfy the necessity test and the requirements of the chapeau under Article XIV (a). The *Korea – Beef* case introduced an innovative 'weighing and balancing' test to examine whether the measures at issue were necessary to pursue domestic policy objectives. A panel needs to examine the importance of the value the censorship measures intended to protect, the restrictive impact of the measures on international trade, and the contribution of the measures to the end pursued. A restrictive measure is necessary if there are no WTO-consistent reasonable alternatives. The Appellate Body emphasized that the more vital the common interests of values, the easier they will be to accept as necessary. Yet, it is unclear how a panel will weigh the relative importance of the measures and their contribution to the end pursued if China claims that the ultimate purpose of the measures is to build a non-transparent and suppressive online environment. However, given the severe impact of Chinese censorship measures on international trade and the possible alternatives to blockage, such as selective filtering, the measures will not satisfy the necessity requirement within the meaning of Article XIV(a).

The recent development of WTO jurisprudence began to draw attention to the procedural justice under the chapeau of GATS Article XIV. Under the chapeau, a disputed measure should not be applied in a manner that may constitute arbitrary or unjustifiable discrimination between countries where the same conditions prevail or a disguised restriction on international trade. In other words, the measure needs to be enforced in good faith with reference to the concept of good governance. Chinese Internet censorship measures, therefore, should be applied in conformity with the principles of transparency and due process to guarantee procedural fairness for other WTO Members. From the evidence provided in Chapter 4, most Chinese Internet censorship mechanisms, either the Great Firewall or regulatory restrictions, are formulated and implemented in a rigid and inflexible manner without legal remedies. Based on the strict procedure review adopted by the Appellate Body, it is highly unlikely China would be able to fulfill its obligations under the chapeau of Article XIV.

In sum, Internet censorship or Internet governance is a developing process involving social, political, and economic struggles from multilayer actors. The purpose of the book is to address the extent to which nation states can assert their sovereign authority on the Internet from the international legal perspectives. Two arguments can be drawn for the concluding remarks. First, the legitimacy of Internet sovereignty in the context of absolute regulatory autonomy or non-intervention is challenged in the course of globalization and growing interdependence. The open nature of the Internet and extra-territorial effects of Internet policies render the assertion of Internet sovereignty a paradox.

The underlying controversy of Internet governance, therefore, stems from the state-centric conception that is deeply rooted in the international legal and political structure. States are not unitary actors in contemporary international relations. The sovereign authority of a nation is constrained by its international obligations and obligations towards its own people. Whereas nation states are habitually reluctant to accept a direct restriction on sovereign power in areas of sensitive political and cultural conflicts, diverging and competing interests are anticipated in any venues and regimes of governance. In the area of Internet governance, any national policies would inevitably have extraterritorial outcomes. Therefore, a shift of governance at the international level is necessary to provide a coherent and consistent legal framework for regulating the Internet. States should adhere to their international responsibilities and respect the basic common values of individuals' fundamental freedoms before asserting authority over the Internet.

Second, international governance must be based on good governance and consider individuals as subjects under international law. A rule-oriented system with a procedural guarantee in the decision-making process is essential for an international institution to be legitimate in a pluralist society. To bring predictability and accountability into the international trade legal system, WTO adjudicating bodies should interpret and apply WTO rules in conformity with general international laws and the principles of international law. From the recent jurisprudence development, the panels and the Appellate Body have shown that WTO law is sufficiently elastic to accommodate Internet-related measures. In the context of Internet censorship, when various values are at stake a panel should have the competence to review all the relevant factors and balance different interests to realize the policy goals of the WTO. State interests should no longer be the guiding criteria within a judicial weighing and balancing process since state interests do not necessarily refer to policies that enhance the welfare of the people or promote the enjoyment of fundamental rights. Countries with a suppressed Internet environment will inevitably hinder their economy and technical innovation since, ultimately, the political and economic development of a country will depend on how people see their rights and interests are carried out by the government.

Bibliography

Books, Chapters, and Articles

Aaronson, Susan Ariel and Zimmermann, Jamie M., *Trade Imbalance: The Struggle to Weigh Human Rights Concerns in Trade Policymaking*, New York: Cambridge University Press (2007), 1-31.

---, *The Digital Trade Imbalance and its Implications for Internet Governance*, Global Commission on Internet Governance, No. 25 (January 2016).

Alexander, Kern and Andenas, Mads, *The World Trade Organization and Trade in Services*, Leiden; Boston: Matinus Nijhoff (2008).

Alston, Philip, *Resisting the Merger and Acquisition of Human Rights by Trade Law: A Reply to Pertersmann*, European Journal of International Law, Vol.13 (2002), 815-844.

---, *Core Labour Standards' and the Transformation of the International Labour Rights Regime*, European Journal of International Law, Vol. 15, No. 3 (2004), 457-521.

Andenas, Mads & Zleptnig, Stefan, *Proportionality and Balancing in WTO Law: A Comparative Perspective*, Cambridge Review of International Affairs, Vol.20, Issue:1 (2007), 71-92.

Andersen, Henrik, *Protection of Non-Trade Values in WTO Appellate Body Jurisprudence: Exceptions, Economic Arguments, and Eluding Questions*, Journal of International Economic Law, Vol. 18 (16 May 2015), 383-405.

Anonymous, *China and the Internet – An Uphill Fight for Freedom*, Harvard International Review (2009), 68-73.

Anonymous, *A Dual Trace Approach to Challenging Chinese Censorship in the WTO: The (Future) Case of Google and Facebook*, Michigan Journal of International Law, Vol.34, Issue:4 (2013), 857-892.

Ashley, Richard K., *The Poverty of Neorealism, International Organization*, Vol.38, No.2 (Spring 1984), 225-286.

Baker, et al Stewart A., *E-Products and the WTO*, International Lawyer, Vol.35, Issue:5 (2001).

Barterls, Lorand, *Applicable Law in WTO Dispute Settlement Proceedings*, Journal of Trade Law, Vol.35, No.3 (2001), 499-519.

Bambauer, Derek, *Cool Tools for Tyrants: The Latest American Technology Helps the Chinese Government and other Repressive Regimes Clamp Down*, Legal Affair (Jan-Feb 2005).

Benkler, Yochai, *The Wealth of the Networks: How Social Production Transforms Markets and Freedom*, New Haven: Yale University Press (2006).

Bernauer, Thomas, Elsig, Manfred and Pauwelyn, Joost, The World Trade Organization's Dispute Settlement Mechanism – Analysis and Problem's. In: Martin Daunton, Amrita Narlikar & Robert M. Stern (eds), *The Oxford Handbook on the World Trade Organization*, Oxford University Press (2012), 487-506.

Besson, Samantha, *The Morality of Conflict: Reasonable Disagreement and the Law*, Hart Publishing: Oxford and Portland, Oregon (2005).

Bierman, Leonard, Fraster Donald R. and Koari James W., *The General Agreement on Tariffs and Trade from Market Perspective*, University of Pennsylvania Journal of International Economic Law, Vol.17, Issue:3 (1996), 821-850.

Birtwhistle, Tom, *The Rise of China's Silicon Dragon*, PwC's Experience Centre (June 2016).

Biukovic, Ljiljana, Is There Policy Space for Human Rights Linkages in China's Trade and Investment Network. In: Daniel Drache and Lesley A. Jacobs (eds.), *Linking Global Trade and Human rights*, New York: Cambridge University Press (February 2014), 274-295.

Blanchard, Maurice, *Market Study – China E-Commerce*, Switzerland Global Enterprise (2014).

Bossche, Peter Van den and Zdouc Werner, *The Law and Policy of the World Trade Organization – Text, Cases and Materials*, New York: Cambridge University Press (2013).

---, and Prévost Denise, *Essentials of WTO Law*, United Kingdom, Cambridge University Press (2016).

Breining-Kaufmann, Christine, The Legal Matrix of Human Rights and Trade Law: State Obligation versus Private Rights and Obligations. In: Thomas Cottier, Joost Pauwelyn, and Elisabeth Bürgi (eds.), *Human Rights and International Trade*, New York: Oxford University Press (2005), 95-136.

Brin, Sergey and Page, Lawrence, *The Anatomy of a Large-Scale Hypertextual Web Search Engine*, Seventh International World-Wide Web Conference (WWW 1998) (1998).

Brownlie, Ian, *Principles of Public International Law*, Oxford University Press, 7th Edition (2008).

Burri, Mira & Cottier, Thomas, Introduction: Digital technologies and international trade regulation (2012). In: Mira Burri and Thomas Cottier (eds.), *Trade Governance in the Digital Age – World Trade Forum*, Cambridge University Press, 1-14.

---, Designing future-oriented multilateral rules for digital trade (2015). In: Pierre Sauvé and Martin Roy (eds), *Edward Elgar Research Handbook on Trade in Services*, Edward Elgar (2015), 331-356.

---, The International Economic Law Framework for Digital Age, ZeitSchrift für Schweizerisches Recht 135 (2015), 10-72.

Bygrave, Lee, *Data Protection Law: Approaching Its Rational, Logic, and Limits*, London/Hague/New York: Kluwer Law International (2002).

Carey, Peter, *Data Protection: A Practical Guide to UK and EU Law*, Oxford University Press: United Kingdom (2015).

Charnovitz, Steve, *The Moral Exception in Trade Policy*, Virginia Journal of International Law, Vol.38 (Simmer 1998), 689-716.

---, *The Globalization of Economic Human Rights*, Brooklyn Journal of International, Vol.9, No.1(1999), 113-124.

Chayes, Abram and Chayes, Antonia Handler, *The New Sovereignty: Compliance with International Regulatory Agreements*, Cambridge, Mass: Harvard University Press (1995), 26-27.

Chu, Cho-Wen, *Censorship or Protectionism? Reassessing China's Regulation of Internet Industry*, International Journal of Social Science and Humanity, Vol.7, No.1 (January 2017).

Clayton, Richard, Murdoch, Steven J., and Watson Robert N. M., Ignoring the Great Firewall of China. In: Danezis G., Golle P. (eds), *Privacy Enhancing Technologies*, Lecture Notes in Computer Science, Vol.4258, Springer, Berlin, Heidelberg (2006).

Cleveland, Sarah H., Human Rights Sanctions and the World Trade Organization (2001). In: Francesco Francioni (ed.), *Environment, Human Rights and International Trade*, Oxford and Portland: Hart Publishing (2001), 119-261.

Cohen, Julie E., *Examined Lives: Information Privacy and the Subject as Object*, Stanford Law Review, Vol.52 (2000), 1371-1483.

Coliver Sandra, *The Article 19 Freedom of Expression Handbook: International and Comparative Law, Standards, and Procedures*, Article 19: London (1993).

Conconi, Paola and Pauwelyn, Joost, *Trading Culture: Appellate Body Report on China – Audiovisuals (WT/DS363/AB/R. adopted 19 January 2010)*, World Trade Review, Vol.10, Issue:1 (2011), 95-118.

Conrad, Christiane R., *Processes and Production Methods (PPMs) in WTO Law: Interfacing Trade and Social Goals*, New York: Cambridge University Press (2011).

Cooper, Richard N., Trade Policy as Foreign Policy. In: Robert M. Stern (ed.), *US Trade Policies in Changing World Economy*, MIT Press (January 1987), 291-336.

Cossy, Mireille, *Determining "likeness" under the GATS: Squaring the circle?*, World Trade Organization – Economic Research and Statistics Division, Staff Working Paper ERSD-2006-08 (September 2006).

Cottier, Thomas, *Trade and Human Rights – A Relationship to Discover*, Journal of International Economic Law, Vol.5, No.1 (2002), 111-132.

---, Pauwelyn, Joost, and Bürgi, Elisabeth, Linking Trade Regulation and Human Rights in International Law: An Overview. In: Thomas Cottier, Joost Pauwelyn, and Elisabeth Bürgi (eds.), *Human Rights and International Trade*, New York: Oxford University Press (2005), 1-26.

--- and Oesch, Matthias, *International Trade Regulation: Law and Policy in the WTO, the European Union and Switzerland,* Berne: Staempfli Publishers Ltd. (2005), 108-118.

---, Delimatsis, Panagiotis & Diebold, Nicolas F., Article XIV GATS General Exceptions (2008). In: Rüdiger Wolfrum, Peter Tobias Stoll and Clemens Feinäugle (eds), *WTO -- Trade in Services*, Netherlands: Kononklijke Brill NV, 287-328.

---, *Multilayered Governance, Pluralism and Moral Conflict*, Indiana Journal of Global Legal Studies, Vol.16, No.2 (Summer 2009), 647-679.

Croley, Steven P. & Jackson John H., *WTO Dispute Procedures, Standard of Review, and Deference to National Governments*, The American Journal of International Law, Vol.90 (1996), 193-213.

Croxton, Derek, *The Peace of Westphalia of 1648 and the Origins of Sovereignty*, The International History Review, Vol.21, No.3 (September 1999), 569- 591.

Damme, Isabelle Van den, *Treaty Interpretation by the WTO Appellate Body*, The European Journal of International Law Vol.21 no.3 (2010), 605-648.

Danagher, Luke, *An Assessment of the Draft Data Protection Regulation: Does it Effectively Protect Data?*, European Journal of Law and Technology, Vol. 3, No.3 (2012).

Davies, Arwel, *Interpreting the Chapeau of GATT Article XX in Light of the 'New' Approach in Brazil – Tyres*, Journal of World Trade Law, Vol.43, No.3 (2009), 507-539.

Deibert, Ronald, The Geopolitics of Internet Control: Censorship, Sovereignty, and Cyberspace (2009). In: Chadwick A and Howard PN (eds.), *Routledge Handbook of Internet Politics*, London: Routledge (2009).

---, Palfrey, John G., Rohozinski, Rafal and Zittrain, Jonathan (eds.), *Access Contested: Security, Identity, and Resistance in Asia Cyberspace*, OpenNet Initiative, International Development Research Centre and the MIT Press (December 2011).

Delimatsis, Panagiotis, *Don't Gamble with GATS – The Interaction between Article VI, XVI, XVII, and XVIII GATS in the Light of the US – Gambling Case*, Journal of World Trade, Vol.40, Issue: 6 (2006), 1059-1080.

---, *International Trade in Services and Domestic Regulations – Necessity, Transparency, and Regulatory Diversity,* Oxford University Press (2007).

---, *Due Process And 'Good' Regulation Embedded in the GATS – Disciplining Regulatory Behaviour in Services Through Article VI of the GATS*, Journal of International Economic Law Vol.10, Issue:1 (2007), 13-50.

---, *Determining the Necessity of Domestic Regulations in Services – The Best is Yet to Come*, The European Journal of International Law Vol.19, No.2 (2008), 365-408.

---, *Protecting Public Morals in a Digital Age: Revisiting the WTO Rulings on US – Gambling and China – Publications and Audiovisual Products*, Journal of International Economic Law, Vol.14, No.2 (2011), 257-293.

---, The Puzzling Interaction of Trade and Public Morals in the Digital Era (2012). In: Mira Burri & Thomas Cottier, *Trade Governance in the Digital Age World Trade Forum*, Cambridge University Press (2012), 276-296.

Demchak, Chris C. and Dombrowski, Peter, *Rise of a Cybered Westphalian Age*, Strategic Studies Quarterly, Vol. 5, Issue:1 (2011), 31-62.

Desmedt, Axel, *Proportionality in WTO Law*, Journal of International Economic Law, Vol.4, Issue: 3 (1 September 2001), 441-480.

Dibbell, Julian, *My Tiny Life, Crime and Passion in a Virtual World*, New York: Henry Holt and Company (1998).

Diebold, Nicolas F., *The Morals and Order Exceptions in WTO Law: Balancing the Toothless Tiger and the Undermining Mole*, Journal of Economic Law, Vol.11, No.1 (2007), 43-74.

---, *Non-Discrimination in International Trade in Service – Likeness in WTO/GATS*, Cambridge University Press (2010).

---, *Non-discrimination and the Pillars of International Economic Law – Comparative*

Analysis and Building Coherency, IILJ Emerging Scholars Paper No.18 (2010).

Dijk, Peter J Van P. and Hoof, G.J.H Van, *In Theory and Practice of the European Convention onHuman Rights*, Report of the Committee of Ministers, Kluwer Law: The Hague (1990).

Djordjevic, Margareta, *Domestic Regulation and Free Trade in Services – A Balancing Act*, Legal Issues of Economic Integration Vol.29, Issue:3 (2002), 305-322.

Dommen, Caroline, Safeguarding the Legitimacy of Multilateral Trading System: The Role of Human Rights Law. In: Frederick M Abbott, Christine Greining-Kaufmann, and Thomas Cottier (eds.), *International Trade and Human Rights: Foundations and Conceptual Issues*, University of Michigan: The World Trade Forum, Vol.5 (2006), 121-132.

Donnelly, Jack, *Cultural Relativism and Universal Human Rights*, Human Rights Quarterly, Vol.6, No.4 (November 1984), 400-419.

Dutton, William, Dopatka Anna, Hills Michael, Law Ginette and Nash Victoria, *Freedom of Connection – Freedom of Expression: The Changing Legal and Regulatory Ecology Shaping the Internet*, Oxford Internet Institute, UNESCO (19 August 2011).

Erixon, Fredrik and Lee-Makiyama, Hosuk, *Digital Authoritarianism: Human Rights, Geopolitics and Commerce*, ECIPE Occasional Paper, No. 5 (2011).

Etzioni, Amitai, *The Limits of Privacy*, New York: Basic Book (1999).

Ewing-Chow, Michael, *First Do No Harm: Myanmar Trade Sanctions and Human Rights*, Northwestern Journal of International Human Rights Vol.5, Issue:2 (Spring 2007), 53-180.

Fazioglu, Muge, *Forget Me Not, The Clash of the Right to the Forgotten and Freedom of Expression on the Internet*, International Data Privacy Law, Vol.3, No.3 (2013), 149-157.

Ferracane, Martina F. and Lee-Makiyama Hosuk, *China's Technology Protectionism and Its Non-negotiable Rationales*, European Centre for International Political Economy (2017).

Flauss, Jean-Françosi, *The European Court of Human Rights and the Freedom of Expression*, Indiana Law Journal, Vol.84, Issue:3 (2009) 809-850.

Flett, James, *WTO Space for National Treatment Regulation: Requiem for a Diagonal Vector Test*, Journal of International Economic Law, Vol.16, Issue: 1(March 2013), 37-90.

Fleuter, Sam, *The Role of Digital Products Under the WTO: A New Framework for GATT and GATS Classification*, Chicago Journal of International Law, Vol.17, No.1, 5(2016), 153-177.

Frank, Thomas M., *The Emerging Right to Democratic Governance*, The American Journal of International Law, Vol.86 (1992), 46-91.

Franklin, Julian H, *Jean Bodin and the Rise of Absolutist Theory*, Cambridge University Press (1973).

Frowein, Jochen Abr., *Freedom of Expression under the European Convention on Human Rights,* in Monitor/inf. 3, Council of Europe (1997).

Fu, King-wa, Chan, Chung-hong & Chau, M., *Assessing Censorship on Microblogs in China: Discriminatory Keywords Analysis and the Real Name Registration Policy*, IEEE Internet Computing (May-June 2013).

Gagnier, Christina, Regulating the Man Behind the Curtain. In: Future of the Privacy Forum, *Big Data and Privacy: Making Ends Meet*, Stanford Law School the Center of Internet and Society (2013), 35-38.

Gao, Henry S., Googling for the Trade-Human Rights Nexus in China (2012): Can the WTO Help? In: Mira Burri and Thomas Cottier (eds), *Trade Governance in the Digital Age*, Cambridge University Press (2012), 247-275

---, *Can WTO Law Keep Up with the Internet?*, 33 Legal Studies Research Paper of Singapore Management University School of Law (2014).

Garon, Jon M., *Searching Inside Google: Cases, Controversies and the Future of the World's Most Provocative Company*, Loyola of Los Angeles Entertainment Law Review, Vol.30, Issue: 3 (2010), 429-475.

Goldsmith, Jack & Wu, Tim, *Who Controls the Internet? Illusion of a Borderless World*, Oxford: Oxford University Press (2006).

Grabenwarter, Christoph, *European Convention on Human Rights Commentary*, C.H. Beck oHG, Hart, Nomos, Heibing Lichtenhahn Verlag, München (2014).

Grote, Rainer, Dispute Settlement and Enforcement Article XXIII GATS (2008). In: Rüdiger Wolfrum, Peter Tobias Stoll and Clemens Feinäugle (eds), *WTO -- Trade in Services*, Netherlands: Kononklijke Brill NV (2008), 489-505.

Gunasekara, Gehan, *Paddling in Unison or Just Paddling? International Trends in Reforming Information Privacy Law*, International Journal of Law and Technology, Vol.22, No.2 (2014), 141-177.

Guzman, Andrew, Pauwelyn, Joost and Hillman, Robert W., *International Trade Law*, Aspen Publisher (2009).

Haass, Richard N., *Sovereignty, Existing Rights, Evolving Responsibilities*, Remarks at the School of Foreign Services and the Mortara Center for International Studies, Georgetown University (14 January 2003).

Hathaway, Melissa E., *Connected Choices: How the Internet is Challenging Sovereign Decisions*, American Foreign Policy Interests, Vol.36 (2014), 300-313.

Heintschel von Heinegg Wolff, Legal Implications of Territorial Sovereignty in Cyberspace (2012). In: C. Czosseck, R. Ottis and K. Ziolkowski (eds.), *2012 4th International Conference on Cyber Conflict*, NATO CCD OCE Publications, Tallinn (2012), 7-19.

Hert, Paul, A Human Rights Perspective on Privacy and Data Protection Impact Assessments. In: D Wright and P De Hert, *Privacy Impact Assessment*, Dordrecht Heidelberg London New York: Springer (2012), 33-59.

Henkin, Louis, *That "S" Word: Sovereignty, and Globalization, and Human Rights, Et cetera*, Fordham Law Review, Vol.68 (1999), 1-14.

Hestermeyer, Holger, *Human Rights and the WTO – The Case of Patents and Access to Medicines*, New York: Oxford University Press (2007).

Hilf, Meinhard, *Power, Rules and Principles – Which Orientation for WTO/GATT Law?*, Journal of International Economic Law, Vol.4, Issue:1 (1 March 2001), 111-130.

Hindley, Brian and Lee-Makiyama, Hosuk, *Protectionism Online: Internet Censorship and International Trade Law,* ECIPE Working Paper, No.12 (2009).

Hom, Sharon, *Google and Internet control in China: A nexus between Human Rights and Trade?*, Hearing before the Congressional-Executive Commission on China (24 March 2010).

Hosein, Gus, Privacy as Freedom. In: In: Rikke Frank Jørgenen, *Human Rights in Global Information Society*, The MIT Press: Cambridge, Massachusetts, London, England (2006), 121-147.

Howse, Robert and Mutua Makau, *Protecting Human Rights in a Global Economy: Challenges for the World Trade Organization*, International Centre for Human Rights and Democratic Development (April 2000).

--- and Tuerk Elisabeth, The WTO Impact on Internal Regulations – A Case Study of the Canada – EC Asbestos Dispute. In de Burca, G. and Scott, J. (ends), *the EU and the WTO: Legal and Constitutional Issues*, Oxford: Hart Publishing (2001), 283-328.

---, *Back to the Court After Shrimp/Turtle? Almost but not Quite Yet: India's Short Lived Challenge to Labor and Environment Exceptions in the European's Union's Generalized System of Preferences*, American University International Law Review, Vol.18, Issue:6 (2003), 1333-1381.

---, Sovereignty, Lost and Found (2008). In: Wenhua Shan, Penelope Simons and Dalvinder Singh (eds.), *Redefining Sovereignty in International Economic Law*, Hart Publishing, USA Portland (2008), 61-75.

Jackson, John H., *The Puzzle of GATT: Legal Aspects of a Surprising Institution*, 1 Journal of World Trade Law 2 (1967).

---, *World Trade and the Law of GATT: A legal Analysis of the General Agreement on Tariffs and Trade*, Bobbes-Merrill (1969).

---, *The World Trading System: Law and Policy of International Economic Relations*, Cambridge, MIT Press (1989).

---, *The WTO Dispute Settlement Understanding – Misunderstandings on the Nature of Legal Obligation*, The American Journal of International Law, Vol.91, Issue:1 (Jan. 1997), 60-64.

---, *The WTO 'Constitution' and Proposed Reforms – Seven 'Mantras' Revisited, Journal of International Economic Law*, Vol.4 (2001), 67-78.

---, Davery William J. & Sykes, Jr. Alan O., *Legal Problems of International Economic Relations: Cases, Materials and Text (4th Edition)*, St. Paul, MN: Thomason West (2002).

---, *Sovereignty, the WTO, and Changing Fundamentals of International Law*, United Kingdom: Cambridge University Press (2006).

---, Reflections on the Possible Research Agenda for Exploring the Relationship between Human Rights Norms and International Trade Rules. In: In: Frederick M Abbott, Christine Greining-Kaufmann, and Thomas Cottier (eds.), *International Trade and Human Rights: Foundations and Conceptual Issues*, University of Michigan: The World Trade Forum, Vol.5 (2006), 19-28.

---, *Reflection on the Trade and Peace Relationship*. In: Padideh Ala'I, Tomer Brounde and Colin Picker (eds), *Trade as Guarantor of Peace, Liberty, and Security?*, Washington, DC: The American Society of International Law (2006), 23-32.

---, Sovereignty: Outdated Concept or New Approaches (2008). In: Wenhua Shan, Penelope Simons and Dalvinder Singh (eds.), *Redefining Sovereignty in International Economic Law*, Hart Publishing, USA Portland (2008), 3-26.

---, *The Evolution of the World Trading System – The Legal and Institutional Context*. In: Daniel Bethlehem, Isabelle van Damme, Donald McRae, and Rodney Neufeld (eds.), *The Oxford Handbook of International Trade Law*, New York: Oxford University Press (January 2009), 31-50.

Jawadekar, Waman S., *Knowledge Management: Text & Cases*, Tata McGraw Hill Education Private Ltd, New Delhi (2011).

Jensen, Eric Talbot, *Cyber Sovereignty: The Way Ahead*, Texas International Law Journal, Vol.50, Issue: 2 (2015), 273-302.

Jiang, Min, *Chinese Internet Sovereignty*, Instantané 2012 – PolitisLab' A CEIS Project on Public Affairs and Communication (2011).

---, *Internet Companies in China – Dancing between the Party Line and the Bottom Line*, the Institut français des relations internationales (Ifri) Center for Asia Studies, Asia Visions 47 (January 2012).

Johnson, David R. and Post, David, *Law and Borders – The Rise of Law in Cyberspace*, Stanford Law Review, Vol.48 (1996), 1367-1402.

Joseph, Sarah, *Blame It to the WTO? A Human Rights Critique*, New York: Oxford University Press (2011).

Jørgenen, Rikke, The Right to Express Oneself and to Seek Information. In: Rikke Frank Jørgenen, *Human Rights in Global Information Society*, The MIT Press: Cambridge, Massachusetts, London, England (2006), 53-71.

Kalathil, Shanthi & Boas, Taylor C., *Open Networks, Closed Regimes: The Impact of the Internet on Authoritarian Rule,* Carnegie Endowment for International Peace, Washington D.C. (2003).

Kikelly, Ursula, *The right to respect for private and family life – A guide to the implementation of Article 8 of the European Convention on Human Rights*, Council of Europe, Strasburg Cedex (2001).

King, Gary, Pan Jennifer, and Roberts Margaret E., *How Censorship in China Allows Government Criticism but Silences Collective Expression,* American Political Science Review, Vol.107, No.2 (May 2013), 326-343.

King, Nancy J. and Kalupahana Kishani, *Choosing Between Liberalization and Regulatory Autonomy under GATS: Implications of US – Gambling for Trade in Cross-Border Services*, Vand. J.Transnat'l L. 1189, Vol. 40 (November 2007), 1192-1298.

Koh, Harold Hongju, *How is International Human Rights Law Enforced?*, Indiana Law Journal, Vo. 74, Issue:4 (1 October 1999), 1397-1417.

Koskenniemi, Martti, Doctrines of State Responsibility. In: James Crawford, Alain Pellet, and Simon Olleson (eds.), *The Law of International Responsibility*, Oxford Commentaries on International Law (2010), 45-52.

Kozma, Julia, The United Nations Human Rights System: The Genesis and Role of the Human Rights Council and the High Commissioner for Human Rights. In: Anja Mihr and Mark Gibney, *The SAGE Handbook of Human rights (Volume 2)*, Los Angles: SAGE Publications (2014), 555-574.

Krajewski, Markus, *National Regulation and Trade Liberalization in Services – The Legal Impact of the General Agreement on Trade in Services (GATS) on National Regulatory Autonomy*, Kluwer Law International (2003).

---, *Playing by the Rules of the Game? Specific Commitments after US – Gambling and Betting and Current GATS Negotiations*, Legal Issues of Economic Integration, Vol.32, Issue:4 (2005), 417-447.

---, General Obligations and Discipline Article VI GATS (2008). In: Rüdiger Wolfrum, Peter Tobias Stoll and Clemens Feinäugle (eds), *WTO -- Trade in Services*, Netherlands: Kononklijke Brill NV (2008), 165-196.

Krasner, Stephen D., *Sovereignty: Organized Hypocrisy*, Princeton University Press (1999), 1-25.

---, Problematic Sovereignty (2001). In: Stephen D. Krasner (ed.), *Problematic Sovereignty – Contested Rules and Political Possibility*, Columbia University Press, New York (2001), 1-23.

Kuner, Christopher, *The European Commission's Proposed Data Protection Regulation: A Copernican Revolution in European Data Protection Law*, Bloomberg BNA Privacy and Security Law Report, 11 PVLR 06 (02 June 2012), 1-15.

Lagerkvist, Johan, *After the Internet, Before Democracy – competing Norms in Chinese Media and Society*, Peter Kang AG, Bern: Switzerland (2010).

Land, Molly, *Toward an International Law of the Internet*, Harvard International Law Journal, Vol.54, No.2 (Summer 2013), 393-458.

Lang, Andrew T.F., Inter-regime Encounters. In: Sarah Joseph, David Kinley, and Jeff Waincymer (eds.), *The World Trade Organization and Human Rights – Interdisciplinary Perspectives*, Cheltenham: Edward Elgar Publishing (2009),163-180.

Lassen, Eva Maria, Universalism and Relativism (2014). In: Anja Mihr and Mark Gibney, *The SAGE Handbook of Human rights (Volume 1)*, Los Angles: SAGE Publications (2014), 39-55.

Lee Jyh-An and Liu Ching-Yi, *Forbidden City Enclosed by the Great Firewall: The Law and Power of Internet Filtering in China*, Minn. J. L. Sci. & Tech., Vol.13, Issue:1 (2012), 125-151.

---, *Real-name Registration Rules and the Fading Digital Anonymity in China*, Washington International Law Journal, Vol.25, No.1 (2015).

Lee Tuthill and Martin Roy, GATS Classification Issues for Information and Communication Technology Services (2012). In: Mira Burri and Thomas Cottier, *Trade Governance in the Digital Age*, Cambridge: Cambridge University Press, 157-178.

Leitner, Kara and Lester, Simon, *WTO Dispute Settlement 1995-2013 – A statistical-Analysis*, Journal of International Economic Law, Vol.17, Issue: 1 (2014), 191-201.

Leroux, Eric H., From Periodicals to Gambling: A review of systemic issues addressed by WTO adjudicatory bodies under the GATS (2008). In: Marion Panizzon, Nicole Pohl, and Pierre Sauvé, *GATS and the Regulation of International Trade in Services*, Cambridge University Press, 236-275.

Lessig, Lawrence, *Code and Other Laws of Cyberspace*, New York: Basic Books (1999).

Lewis, James A., *Sovereignty and the Role of Government in Cyberspace*, Brown Journal of World Affairs, Vol.16, Issue: 2 (2010), 55-65.

Li, Shubo, *The Online Public Space and Popular Ethos in China*, Media, Culture & Society, Vol.32, Issue:1 (2010), 63-83.

Lim, Young Joon and Sexton, Sarah E., *Internet as a Human Right: A Practical Legal Framework to Address the Unique Nature of the Medium and to Promote Development*, Wash J.L. Tech. & Arts, Vol.7 (2012), 295-318.

Liu, Cynthia, *Internet Censorship as a Trade Barrier: A Look at the WTO Consistency of the Great Firewall in the Wake of the China – Google Dispute*, Georgetown Journal of International Law, Vol.42 (2011), 1199-1240.

Lowe, Vaughan, Sovereignty and International Economic Law (2008). In: Wenhua Shan, Penelope Simons and Dalvinder Singh (eds.), *Redefining Sovereignty in International Economic Law*, Hart Publishing, USA Portland (2008), 77-84.

Luff, David, Convergence: A buzzword to remain? (2012), In: Mira Burri and Thomas Cottier (eds.), *Trade Governance in the Digital Age – World Trade Forum*, Cambridge: Cambridge University Press, 65-90.

Mackinnon, Rebecca, *Consent of the Networked – The Worldwide Struggle for Internet Freedom*, New York: Basic Books (2012).

Macovei, Monica, *A Guide to the Implementation of Article 10 of the European Convention on Human Rights,* Human Rights Hand Book, No.2, Second Edition, Council of Europe (2004).

Mangin, Elanor A., *Market Access in China – Publications and Audiovisual Materials: A Moral Victory with a Silver Lining*, Berkeley Technology Law Journal, Vol.25, Issue:1(2010), 279-310.

Marceau, Gabrielle, *WTO Dispute Settlement and Human Rights*, European Journal of International Law, Vol.13, No.4 (2002), 753-814.

Marwell, Jeremy C., *Trade and Morality: The WTO Public Morals Exception After Gambling*, New York University Law Review, Vol.81, 802-842.

Matsushita, Mitsou, Thomas J. Schoenbaum, Petros C. Mavroidis and Michael Hahn, *The World Trade Organization – Law, Practice, and Policy (Third Edition)*, Oxford University Press, United Kingdom (2015).

Mattoo, Anditya, *National Treatment in the GATS: Corner-Stone or Pandora's Box?*, Journal of World Trade, Vol.31, No.1 (1997).

--- and Sauvé, Pierre, Domestic Regulation and Trade in Services: Key Issues (2003). In: Aaditya Mattoo and Pierre Sauvé, *Domestic Regulation and Service Trade Liberaliza-*

tion, World Bank and Oxford University Press (2003), 1-7.

McBeth, Adam, *International Economic Actors and Human Rights*, Oxford: Routledge (2010).

McCrudden Christopher, *International Economic Law and the Pursuit of Human Rights: A Framework for Discussion of the Legality of 'Selective Purchasing' Laws under the WTO Government Procurement Agreement*, Journal of International Economic Law, Vol.2, Issue:1 (March 1999), 3-48.

Mcgonagle, Tarlach, The Development of Freedom of Expression and Information within the UN: Leaps and Bounds or Fits and Starts?. In: Tarlach McGonagle & Yvonne Donders, *The United Nations and Freedom of Expression and Information Critical Perspectives*, Cambridge University Press (June 2015), 1-52.

McRae, Donald M., *The WTO in International Law: Tradition Continued or New Frontier?*, Journal of International Economic Law, Vol.3, Issue:1 (1 March 2000), 27-41.

Meltz, Eli A, *No Harm, No Foul? "Attempted" Invasion of Privacy and the Tort of Intrusion Upon Seclusion*, Fordham Law Review, Vol.83, Issue: 6 (2015), 3431-3470.

Mendel, Toby, The UN Special Rapporteur on Freedom of Opinion and Expression: Progressive Development of International Standards Relating to Freedom of Expression. In: Tarlach McGonagle & Yvonne Donders, *The United Nations and Freedom of Expression and Information Critical Perspectives*, Cambridge University Press (June 2015), 235-268.

---, Puddephatt, Andrew, Wagner, Ben, Hawtin, Dixie and Torres, Natalia, *Global Survey on Internet Privacy and Freedom of Expression*, United Nations Educational, Scientific and Cultural Organization (2012).

Mitchell, Andrew D., *Proportionality and Remedies in WTO Disputes*, The European Journal of International Law, Vol.17, No.5 (2006), 985-1108.

Murdoch, Steven J. & Anderson, Ross, Tool and Technology of Internet Filtering (2008). In: Ronald Deibert, John Palfery, Rafal Rohozinski, and Jonathan Zittrain, *Access Denied: The Practice and Policy of Global Internet Filtering*, the MIT Press (January 2008), 57-72.

Nagan, Wiston P. & Haddad, Aitza M., *Sovereignty in Theory and Practice*, San Diego Int'l L. J., Vol.13 (2012), 429-520.

Nanz, Patrizia, Democratic Legitimacy and Constitutionalism of Transnational Trade Governance: A View from Political Theory (2006). In: Christian Joerges and Ernst-Ulrich Pertersmann (eds.), *Constitutionalism, Multilevel Trade Governance and Social Regulation*, Oxford and Portland, Oregon: Hart Publishing (2006), 59-82.

Narlikar, Amrita, *The World Trade Organization: A Very Short Introduction*, New York: Oxford University Press (2005).

Natens, Bregt, *Regulatory Autonomy Constraints From the National Treatment Obligation in GATS*, Leuven Centre for Global Governance Studies, No.30 (February 2015).

Nattoo, Aaditya, *China's Accession to the WTO: The Services Dimension*, World Bank Policy Research Working Paper, No. 2932 (November 2002).

Nicolaïdis, Kalypso. & Trachtman J.P., From Policed Regulation to Managed Recognition in GATS (2000). In: P. Sauvé and R.M. Stern (eds.), *GATS 2000 – New Directions in Services Trade Liberalization*, 241-283.

Oesch, Matthias, *Standards of Review in WTO Dispute Resolution*, Journal of International Economic Law, Vol.6, No.3 (2003), 635-659.

O'Flaherty, Michael, International Covenant on Civil and Political Rights: Interpreting Freedom of Expression and Information Standards for the Present and the Future. In: Tarlach McGonagle & Yvonne Donders, *The United Nations and Freedom of Expression and Information Critical Perspectives*, Cambridge University Press (June 2015), 55-88.

Ortino, Federico, WTO Jurisprudence on De Jure and De Facto Discrimination. In: Federico Ortino and Ernst-Ulrich Pertersmann, *The WTO Dispute Settlement System 1995-2003*, Kluwer Law International (2004).

---, *Treaty Interpretation and the WTO Appellate Body Report in US – Gambling: A Critique*, Journal of International Economic Law, Vol.9, Issue:1 (January 2006), 117-148.

---, The Principles of Non-Discrimination and Its Exceptions in GATS: Selected Legal Issues (2008). In: Kern Alexander and Mads Andenas, *The World Trade Organization and Trade in Services*, Leiden; Boston: Matinus Nijhoff (2008), 173-204.

Padilla, David J., *The Inter-American Commission on Human Rights of the Organization of American States: A Case Study*, American University International Law Review, Vol.9, Issue:1 (1993), 95-115.

Panizzon, Marion, *How Close Will GATS Get to Human Rights?*, NCCR Trade Regulation (August 2006).

---, *Good Faith in the Jurisprudence of the WTO: The Protection of Legitimate Expectations, Good Faith Interpretation and Fair Dispute Settlement*, Oxford: Hart Publishing (2006).

---, How Human Rights Violations Nullify and Impair GATS Commitments (2008). In: Marion Panizzon, Nicole Pohl and Pirrre Sauve (eds.), *GATS and the Regulation of International Trade in Services*, Cambridge: Cambridge University Press (2008), 534-560.

Patni, Ritika & Joseph, Nihal, *WTO Ramifications of Internet Censorship: The Google – China Controversy*, NUJS Law Review, Vol. 3 (2010), 337-363.

Pauwelyn Joost, *The Role of Public International in the WTO: How Far Can We Go?*, The American Journal of International Law, Vol.95 (2001), 535-578.

---, *Rien ne Ve Plus? Distinguish Domestic Regulation from Market Access in GATT and GATS*, World Trade Review 4:2 (2006), 131-170.

---, Comment: The unbearable lightness of likeness (2008). In: Marion Panizzon, Nicole Pohl and Pirrre Sauve (eds.), *GATS and the Regulation of International Trade in Services*, Cambridge: Cambridge University Press, 358-369.

---, *Squaring Free Trade in Cultural Goods and Services with Chinese Censorship: The WTO Appellate Body Report on China – Audiovisual*, Melbourne Journal of International Law, Vol.11, Issue:1 (2010), 119-140.

Peer, Steve, Hervey, Tamara, Kenner, Jeff, and Ward, Angela, *The EU Charter of Fundamental Rights – A Commentary*, Hart Publishing: United Kingdom (2014).

Petersmann, Ernst-Ulrich, Multilevel Trade Governance in the WTO Requires Multilevel Constitutionalism. In: Christian Joerges and Ernst-Ulrich Pertersmann (eds.), *Constitutionalism, Multilevel Trade Governance and Social Regulation,* Oxford and Portland, Oregon: Hart Publishing (2006), 5-57.

---, International Trade Law, Human Rights and Customary International Rule on Treaty Interpretation. In: Sarah Joseph, David Kinley, and Jeff Waincymer (eds.), *The World Trade Organization and Human Rights – Interdisciplinary Perspectives*, Cheltenham: Edward Elgar Publishing (2009), 69-90.

---, The Promise of Linking Trade and Human Rights. In: Daniel Drache and Lesley A. Jacobs (eds.), Linking Global Trade and Human rights, New York: Cambridge University Press (February 2014), 46-64.

Phelan, Diarmuid Rossa, *Right to Life of the Unborn v Promotion of Trade in Services: The European Court of Justice and the Normative Shaping of the European Union,* The Modern Law Review, Vol.55, No.5 (September 1992), 670-689.

Pollicino, Oreste, European Judicial Dialogue and the Protection of Fundamental Rights in the New Digital Environment: An Attempt at Emancipation and Reconciliation: The Case of Freedom of Speech. In: Morano-Foadi Sonia and Vickers Lucy (eds.), *Fundamental Rights in the EU: A Matter for Two Courts,* Hart Publishing: United Kingdom (March 2015), 93-114.

--- and Bassini, Marco, The Law of the Internet between Globalization and Localization (2014). In: Miguel Maduro, Kaarlo Tuori, and Suvi Sankari (eds.), *Transnational Law – Rethinking European Law and Legal Thinking*, Cambridge University Press, United Kingdom (2014), 346-380.

Prosser, William L., *Privacy*, California Law Review, Vol.48, Issue:3 (1960), 383-423.

Qin, Julia Ya, *Pushing the Limits of Global Governance: Trading Rights, Censorship, and WTO Jurisprudence – A Commentary on the China – Publication Case*, Chinese Journal of International Law, Vol.10 (2011), 271-322.

---, Grinstein, Georges G. and Wierse Andreas, *Information Visualization in Data Mining and Knowledge Discovery*, Morgen Kaufman Publisher: San Francisco (2002).

Renucci, Jean-François, *Introduction to the European Convention on Human Rights – The Rights Guaranteed and the Protection Mechanisms*, Council of Europe Publishing (2005).

Randall, Maya Hertig, *Human Rights Within a Multilayered Constitution: The Example of Freedom of Expression and the WTO*, Max Planck Yearbook of United Nations Law, Volume 26 (2012), 183-280.

Raustiala, Kal, *Rethinking the Sovereignty Debate in International Economic Law*, Journal of International Economic Law, Vol.6, No.4 (2003), 841-878.

Robinson, Neil, Graux, Hans, Botterman, Maarten and Valeri, Lorenzo, *Review of EU Data Protection Directiev: Summary*, Information Commissioner's Office (May 2009).

Roth, Kenneth, *Defending Economic, Social and Cultural Rights: Practical Issues Faced by an International Human Rights Organization,* Human rights Quarterly, Vol.26, No.1 (2004), 64-73.

Schermers, Henry, Different Aspects of Sovereignty (2002). In: Gerald Kreijen, Marcel Brus, Jorris Duursma, Elizabeth De Vos, and John Dugard (eds.), *State Sovereignty and International Governance*, Oxford University Press (2002).

Sen, Amartya, Development as Freedom, New York: Oxford University Press (1999).

Shi, JingXia, *Free Trade and Cultural Diversity in International Law*, United Kingdom: Hart Publishing (2013).

Shyu, Jennifer, *Speak No Evil: Circumventing Chinese Censorship*, San Diego L. Rev., Vol.45 (2008), 211-249.

Siqueira, Ada Bogliolo Piancastelli De, *It's in the Way that You Use It: Revisiting Trade and Human Rights in the Case of Online Censorship*, Southwestern Journal of Int'l Law, Vol. 20 (2013), 39-79.

Sohn, Louis B., *The New International Law: Protection of the Rights of Individuals Rather Than States*, The American University Law Review, Vol.32, No.1 (1982), 1-64.

Staiger, Robert W. and Sykes Alan O., *Non-Violation*, Journal of International Economic Law, Vol.16 (2013), 741-775

Stefanick, Lorna, *Controlling Knowledge: Freedom of Information and Privacy Protection in a Networked World*, Edmonton: Athabasca University Press (2011).

Stevenson, Christopher, *Breaching the Great Firewall: China's Internet Censorship and the Quest for Freedom of Expression in a Connected Wor*ld, Boston College International & Comparative Law Review, Vol.30 (2007), 531-558.

Stoll, Peter-Tobias and Schorkopf, Frank, *WTO – World Economic Order, World Trade Law*, Max Planck Institute for Comparative Public Law and International Law, Leiden/Boston The Netherlands: Martinus Nijhoff Publishers (2006).

Taneja, Harsh and Wu, Angela Xiao, *Does the Great Firewall Really Isolate the Chinese? Integrating Access Blockage with Cultural Factors to Explain Web User Behavior*, The Information Society, Vol.30 (2014), 297-309.

Tang, Lijun & Yang, Peidong, *Symbolic Power and the Internet: The Power of a 'Horse'*, Media, Culture & Society, Vol.33, Issue:5 (2011), 675-691.

Taylor, Robert H., Pathways to the Present. In: Kyaw Yin Hlaing, Rober H. Taylor, and Tin Maung Maung Than (eds.), *Myanmar: Beyond Politics to Societal Imperatives 1* (2005), 1-16.

Taylor, Stephen, *Erosion of National Sovereignty by 21st Century Technology*, International Business Center (2003).

Thomson, Janice E., *State Sovereignty in International Relations: Bridging the Gap Between Theory and Empirical Research*, International Studies Quarterly, Vol.39 (1995), 213-233.

Trachtman, Joel, *Cyberspace, Sovereignty, Jurisdiction, and Modernism*, Indiana Journal of Global Legal studies, Vol:5, Issue:2 (1998), 561-582.

---, *The Domain of WTO Dispute Resolution*, Harvard International Law Journal, Vol.40 (1999), 333-370.

---, Negotiation on Domestic Regulation and Trade in Services (GATS Article VI): A Legal Analysis of Selected Current Issues. In Ernst-Ulrich Petersmann and James Harrison, *Reforming the World Trading System: Legitimacy, Efficiency, and Democratic Governance*, Oxford: Oxford University Press (2005).

Tsai, Katherine, *How to Create International Law: the Case of the Internet Freedom in China*, Duke Journal of Comparative & International Law, Vol.21 (2011), 401-430.

Tzanou, Maria, *Data Protection as a Fundamental Right Next to Privacy? 'Reconstructing' a not so New Right*, International Data Privacy Law, Vol.3, No.2 (2013), 88-100.

Usama, Fayyad, *The Digital Physics of Data Mining*, Communications of ACM, Vol. 44, Issue: 3 (March 2001), 62-65.

Vázquez, Carlos Manuel, *Trade Sanctions and Human Rights – Past, Present and Future,* Journal of International Economic Law, Vol.6, Issue:4 (2003), 797-839.

Vincent, R.J., *Human Rights and International Relations*, New York: Cambridge University Press (1986).

Voicescu, Vlad Alexandru & Dobârceanu, Nicu-Râzvan, *Sovereignty and Integration in Modern Era. Perspectives*, Law Review: Judicial Doctrine & Case-law, Vol.2, Issue 4 (Oct.-Dec. 2012), 1-10.

Vranes, Erich, *The WTO and Regulatory Freedom: WTO Disciplines on Market Access, Non-Discrimination and Domestic Regulation Relating to Trade in Goods and Services*, Journal of International Economic Law, Vol.12, No.4 (2009), 953-987.

Vyver, Johan D Van den., Sovereignty (2013). In: Dinah Shelton (eds.), *The Oxford Handbook of International Human Rights Law*, Oxford University Press (2013).

Wafa, Tim, *Global Internet Privacy Rights - A Pragmatic Approach,* University of San Francisco Intellectual Property Law Bulletin, Vol.13 (31 May 2009), 131-159.

Wagner, Ben, *Deep Pocket Inspection and Internet Censorship: International Convergence on an 'Integrated Technology of Control'*, Global Voices Advocacy Defending Free Speech Online (2009).

Waldo, James, Lin, Herbert S., and Millett, Lynette I. (eds), *Engaging Privacy and Information Technology in a Digital Age*, Washington, DC: The National Academic Press (2007).

---, Lin Herbert S., and Millett Lynette I., *Thinking About Privacy: Chapter 1 of "Engaging Privacy and Information Technology in Digital Age"*, Journal of Privacy and Confidentiality, Vol.2, No.1 (2010), 19-50.

Wang, Wei, *On the Relationship Between Market Access and National Treatment Under the GATS*, The International Lawyer Vol. 46, No.4 (Winter 2012), 1045-1065.

Wang, Zhizheng, *Systematic Government Access to Private-Sector Data in China, International Data Privacy Law*, Vol.2, No.4 (2012), 220-229.

Warren, Samuel and Brandeis, Louis, *The Right to Privacy*, Harvard Law Review 193, Vol.4, No.5 (15 December1980), 193-220.

Weaver, Russell L., *The Fourth Amendment, Privacy and Advancing Technology,* Mississippi Law Journal, Vol.80, No.3 (2011), 1131-1227.

---, Partlett, David F. and Cole, Mark D., Protecting Privacy in a Digital Age. In: Dieter Dörr and Russell L. Weaver, *The Right to Privacy in the Light of Media Convergence: Perspectives From Three Continent*, De Gruyter: Berlin (2012), 1-30.

---, and Friedland, Steven I., Privacy and the Fourth Amendment. In: Dieter Dörr, Russell L. Weaver (eds.), *Perspectives on Privacy: Increasing Regulation in the USA, Canada, Australia and European Countries*, De Gruyter: Berlin (2014), 1-17.

Weber, Rolf H., *Digital Trade in WTO-Law – Taking Stock and Looking Ahead*, Asian Journal of WTO & Int'l Health Law and Policy (AJWH), Vol.5, No.1 (March 2010), 1-24.

---, *New Sovereignty Concepts in the Age of Internet*?. Journal of Internet Law, Vol.14, Issue 2 (2010), 12-20.

---, *Transborder data transfer: concepts, regulatory approaches and new legislative initiatives*, International Data Privacy Law, Vol. 3, Issue: 2 (May 2013), 117-130.

---, *Digital Trade and E-Commerce: Challenges and Opportunities of the Asia-Pacific Regionalism*, Asian Journal of WTO & Int'l Health Law and Policy (AJWH), Vol. 10:32 (2015), 321-348.

Weil, Prosper, *Towards Relative Normativity in International Law?, The American Journal of International Law*, Vol.77, No.3 (July 1993), 413-442.

Whelan, Daniel J., The Two Covenants and the Evolution of Human Rights. In: Anja Mihr and Mark Gibney, *The SAGE Handbook of Human rights (Volume 1)*, Los Angles: SAGE Publications (2014), 123-144.

Wilson, Kristina, Ramos, Yaneli, and Harvey, Daniel, *Google in China – "The Great Firewall"*, the Kenan Institute for Ethics at Duke University (2006).

Wolfrum, Rüdiger, Stoll, Peter Tobias and Feinäugle, Clemens (eds), *WTO -- Trade in Services*, Netherlands: Kononklijke Brill NV (2008).

Wouters, Jan and Coppens, Dominic, GATS and Domestic Regulation: Balancing the Right to Regulation and Trade Liberalization. In: Kern Alexander and Mads Andenas, *The World Trade Organization and Trade in Services*, Leiden; Boston: Matinus Nijhoff (2008), 207-262.

Wu, Tim, *The World Trade Law of Censorship and Internet Filtering*, Chicago Journal of Int'l Law, Vol.7, Issue 1 (2006), 263-387.

---, *The Master Switch – The Rise and Fall of Information Empires*, New York: Alfred A. Knopf (2010).

Wu, Timothy S., *Cyber Sovereignty? – The Internet and the International System*, Harvard Journal of Law & Technology, Vol.10, No.3 (1997), 648-666.

Wunsch-Vincent, Sacha, *The WTO, the Internet and Trade in Digital-Products: EU-US Perspectives*, North America: Hart Publishing (2006).

---, *The Internet, cross-border trade in services, and the GATS: lessons from US – Gambling*, World Trade Review, Vol.5, Issue:3 (2006), 319-355.

---, Trade Rules of the Digital Age (2008). In: Marion Panizzon, Nicole Pohl and Pirrre Sauve (eds.), *GATS and the Regulation of International Trade in Services*, Cambridge: Cambridge University Press (2008), 497-529.

---, Toward Coherent Rules for Digital Trade (2012). In: Mira Burri and Thomas Cottier, *Trade Governance in the Digital Age*, Cambridge: Cambridge University Press (2012).

Zagel, Gudrun, *The WTO and Trade-Related Human Rights Measures: Trade Sanctions vs. Trade Incentives*, Austrian Review of International and European Law, Vol.9 (2004), 119-153.

---, *WTO & Human Rights: Examining Linkages and Suggesting Convergence*, International Development Law Organization, Vol.2, No.2 (2005).

Zheng, Haiping, *Regulating the Internet: China's Law and Practice*, Beijing Law Review, Vol.4, No.1 (2013), 37-41.

Zhu, Tao, Phipps, David, Pridgen, Adman, Crandall, Jedidiah R. and Wallach, Dan S., *The Velocity of Censorship: High-Fidelity Detection of Microblog Post Deletions*, 22nd USENIX Security Symposium in Washington, D.C. (August 2013).

Zixue, Tai, *The Internet in China: Cyberspace and Civil Society*, New York: Routledge (2006).

Zkos, Georgios I., *Demolishing State's Sole Power over Sovereignty and Territory via Electronic Technology and Cyberspace*, Journal of Internet Law, Vol. 17, Issue:5 (November 2013), 3-17.

Zlepting, Stefan, The GATS and Internet-Based Services: Between Market Access and Domestic Regulation. In: Kern Alexander and Mads Andenas, *The World Trade Organization and Trade in Services*, Leiden; Boston: Matinus Nijhoff (2008), 381-410.

DOCUMENTS FROM INTERNATIONAL ORGANIZATIONS

European Centre for International Political Economy (ECIPE), *The Economic Importance of Getting Data Protection Right: Protecting Privacy, Transmitting Data, Moving Commerce*, Report of the US Chamber of Commerce (2014).

European Commission, *Proposal for a Regulation of the European Parliament and of the Council on the protection of individuals with regard to the processing of personal data on the free movement of such data (General Data Protection Regulation)*, 25.1.2012, COM (2012) 11 final, 2012/2011 (COD) (25 January 2012).

European Union Agency for Fundamental Rights, *Handbook on European data protection law*, Luxemburg: Publication Office of the European Union (2014).

European Union, *Directive 95/46/EC of the European Parliament and of the Council on the Protection of Individuals with Regard to the Processing of Personal Data and on the Free Movement of Such Data* (24 October 1995).

---, *Charter of Fundamental Rights of the European Union*, 2012/C 326/02 (26 October 2012).

The Global Network Initiative, *2014 Annual Report Protecting and Advancing Freedom of Expression and Privacy in Information and Communication Technologies*, GNI (2014).

The Organization for Economic Co-operation Development (OECD), Working Party of the Trade Committee, Strengthening Regulatory Transparency: Insights for the GATS From the Regulatory Reform Country Reviews, TD/TC/WP (99) 43/FINAL

(12/April/2000).

---, *Recommendation of the Council Concerning Guidelines Governing the Protection of Privacy and Transborder Flows of Personal Data* (23 September 1980) (The Guidelines were update in 2013).

The White House, *Consumer Data Privacy in a Networked World: A Framework for Protecting Privacy and Promoting Innovative in the Global Digital Economy*, Washington (February 2012).

United Nations

United Nations, *Charter of the United Nations*, 1 UNTS XVI (34 October 1945).

---, *Statute of the International Court of Justice* (18 April 1946).

---, *Proclamation of Teheran – Final Act of the International Conference on Human Rights*, UN Doc. A/CONF. 32/41 at 3 (13 May1986).

---, *Vienna Declaration and Programme of Action*, UN Doc. A/CONF. 157/23 (25 June 1993).

UN Committee on Economic, Social and Cultural Rights (CESCR), *General Comment No.3: The Nature of States Parties' Obligation (Art.2, Para. 1, of the Covenant)*, E/1991/23 (14 December 1990).

---, *General Comment No.8 (1997) – The Relationship between Economic Sanctions and Respect for Economic, Social and Cultural Rights*, E/C.12/1997/8 (12 December 1997).

---, *Statement of the UN Committee on Economic, social and Cultural Rights to the Third Ministerial Conference of the World Trade Organization (Seattle, 30 November to 3 December 1999)*, UN Doc. E/C.12/1999/9 (26 November 1999).

---, *Social and Cultural Rights, General Comment No 14: The Right to the Highest Attainable Standard of Health (Article 12 of the Covenant)*, UN doc. E/C.12/2000/4 (11 August 2000).

UN Human Rights Committee, (HRC) *CCPR General Comment No.16: Article 17 (Right to Privacy), The Right to Respect of Privacy, Family, Home and Correspondence, and Protection of Honour and Reputation* (8 April 1988).

---, *General Comment no.31 [80], The nature of the general obligation imposed on States Parties to the Covenant*, CCPR/C/32/Rev.1/Add.13 (26 May 2004).

---, *CCPR General Comment No.27: Article 12 (Freedom of Movement)*, CC/PR/C/21/ /Rev.1/Add.9 (2 November 1999).

---, *General Comment No. 34, Article 19: Freedoms of Opinion and Expression*, U.N. Doc. CCPR/C/GC/34 (12 September 2011).

UN Human Rights Council, *Institution-building of the United Nations Human Rights Council*, A/HRC/RES/5/1 (18 June 2007).

---, *Report on the Special Rapporteur on the Promotion and Protection of the Right to Freedom of Opinion and Expression, Frank La Rue*, UN General Assembly, A/HRC/17/27 (15 May 2011).

---, *Report of the Special Rapporteur on the Promotion and Protection of the Right to Freedom of Opinion and Expression, Frank La Rue*, UN General Assembly, A/HRC/23/40 (17 April 2013).

---, *The Right to Privacy in the Digital Age: Report of the Office of the United Nations High Commissioner for Human Rights*, A/HRC/27/37 (30 June 2014),

UN Human Rights Council Working Group on the Universal Periodic Review, *National Report Submitted in Accordance with Paragraph 5 of the Annex to Human Rights Council Resolution 16/21: China*, A/HRC/WG.6/17/CHN/1 (5 August 2013).

UNESCO, *The 2005 Convention on the Protection and Promotion of the Diversity of Cultural Expression (Convention on Cultural Diversity)* (adopted on 20 October 2005).

---, *Keynotes to Foster Inclusive Knowledge Societies: Access to Information and Knowledge, Freedom of Expression, Privacy, and Ethics on a Global Internet*, United Nations Education, Scientific and Cultural Organization (2015).

UN Info. & Comm. Tech. Task Force, WTO, *E-Commerce and Information Technologies: From the Uruguay Round Through the Doha Development Agenda: A Report for the UN ICT Task Force,* (2005).

UN General Assembly, *Universal Declaration of Human Rights*, A/RES/3/217A(III) (10 December 1948).

---, *Optional Protocol to the International Covenant on Civil and Political Rights*, United Nations, Treaty Series, Vol. 999, p.171 (19 December 1966).

---, *1970 Declaration on Principles of International Law Concerning Friendly Relations and Co-operation Among States in Accordance with the Charter of the United Nations*, A/RES/25/2625 (24 October 1970).

---, *Peaceful Settlement of Dispute Between States*, A/RES/37/10 (15 November 1982).

---, *Convention on the Law of the Sea* (10 December 1982).

---, *Second Optional Protocol to the International Covenant on Civil and Political Rights, Aiming at the Abolition of the Death Penalty*, A/RES/44/128 (15 December 1989).

---, *Guidelines for the Regulation of Computerized Personal Data Files*, A/RES/45/95 (34 December 1990).

---, *High Commissioner for the Promotion and Protection of All Human Rights: Resolution adopted by the General Assembly*, A/RES/48/141 (20 December 1993).

---, *Human Rights Council: Resolution adopted by the General Assembly on 15 March 2006*, A/RES/60/251 (3 April 2006).

---, *The Right of Everyone to the Enjoyment of the Highest Attainable Standard of Physical and Mental Health*, A/61/338 (13 September 2006).

---, *Optional Protocol to the International Covenant on Economic, Social and Cultural Rights: Resolution/ adopted by the General Assembly*, A/Res/63/117 (5 March 2009).

---, *Group of Governmental Experts on Developments in the Field of International and Telecommunications in the Context of International Security – Note by the Secretary General*, A/68/98 (24 June 2013).

UN Office of the High Commissioner for Human Rights, *Review of the composition, organization and administrative arrangements of the Sessional Working Group of the Governmental Experts on the Implementation of International Covenant on Economic, Social and Cultural Rights*, Economic and Social resolution 1985/17 (1985).

United States International Trade Commission, *The Economic Effects of Significant U.S. Import Restraint (Sixth Update)*, Investigation No. 332-325, Publication 4095 (August 2009).

World Bank, *World Development Report 2006: Equality and Development*, The International Bank for Reconstruction and Development, the World Bank and Oxford University Press (2005).

World Trade Organization

General Agreement on Trade and Tariff, *Differential and more Favourable Treatment Reciprocity and Fuller Participation of Developing Countries*, Doc. L/4903 (28 November 1979).

Hong Kong Ministerial Declaration, WT/MIN(5)/Dec, 22 December 2005.

WTO, *15 Years of the Information Technology Agreement: Trade, Innovation and Global Production Networks*, Geneva: World Trade Organization (2012).

WTO Agreement: Marrakesh Agreement Establishing the World Trade Organization, 1867 U.N.T.S. 154, 33 I.L.M 1144 (15 April 1994).

WTO Agreement on the Application of Sanitary and Phytosanitary Measures, 1869 U.N.T.S. 493.

WTO Agreement on Technical Barriers to Trade, 1868 U.N.T.S 120.

WTO, *Briefing note: The Expansion of Trade in Information Technology Products (ITA Expansion)* (16 December 2015).

WTO Committee on Specific Commitments, Note by the Secretariat, Additional Commitments under Article XVIII of the GATS, S/CSC/W34 (16 July 2002).

WTO Council for Trade in Services, Disciplines on Domestic Regulation in the Accountancy Sector, S/L/64 (17 December 1998).

---, Background Note by the Secretariat, *Computer and Related Services*, S/C/W/45 (14 July 1998).

---, Note by the Secretariat, The Work Programme on Electronic Commerce, S/C/W/68 (16 November 1998).

---, Note by the Secretariat, Article VI:4 of the GATS: Disciplines on Domestic Regulation Applicable to All Services, S/C/W/96 (1 March 1999).

---, Work Programme on E-Commerce – Interim Report to the General Council, S/C/8 (31 March 1999).

---, Decision on Domestic Regulation – adopted by the Council for Trade in Services on 26 April 1999, S/L/70 (28 April 1999).

---, Negotiation on Trade in Services, TN/S/36 (21 April 2011).

---, Guidelines for the Scheduling of Specific Commitments under the General Agreement on Trade in Services, S/L/92 (28 March 2001).

WTO General Council, Dedicated Discussion on Electronic Commerce Under the Auspices of the Central Council on 15 June 2001, Summary by the Secretariat of the Issues Raised, WT/GC/W436, 6 July 2001.

WTO General Council, Declaration on the Expansion of Trade in Information Technology Product, WT/L/956 (28 July 2015)

WTO Ministerial Conference, Ministerial Declaration on Trade of Information Tech-

nology Products, WT/MIN (96)/16 (13 December 1996).
---, Work Programme on Electronic Commerce, Decision of 7 December 2013, WT/MIN(13), WT/L/907 (11 December 2013).
WTO, Ministerial Declaration on Global E-Commerce, WT/MIN(98)/DEC/2, 20 May 1998.
WTO, Report to the 17 November 2009 meeting of the General Council, Work Programme on Electronic Commerce, Dedicated Discussions under the auspices of the General Council, WT/GC/W/613, (9 November 2009).
WTO, The Fundamental WTO Principles of National Treatment, Most-Favoured-Nation Treatment and Transparency, Background Note by the Secretariat, WT/WGTCP/W/114 (14 April 1999).
WTO Trade in Service, Guidelines for the Scheduling of Specific Commitments Under the General Agreement on Trade in Services (GATS), S/L/92 (28 March 2001).
WTO WPDR, Communication from Australia, Necessity and Transparency, S/WPDR/W/8 (15 September 2000).
---, Communication from the European Communities and their Member States, Domestic Regulation: Necessity and Transparency, S/WPDR/W/14 (1 May 2001).
---, Note by the Secretariat, Report on the Meeting Held on 2 October 2001, S/WPDR/M/13 (21 November 2001).
---, Note by the Secretariat, Report on the Meeting Held on 4 December 2002, S/WPDR/M/19 (29 January 2003).
---, Note by the Secretariat, "Necessity Test" in the WTO, S/WPDR/W/27/Add.1 (18 January 2011).
---, *Disciplines on Domestic Regulation Pursuant to GATS Article VI:4*, Chairman's Progress Report, S/WPDR/W/45 (14 April 2011).
---, Note by Secretariat, Report on the Meeting Held on 3 July, S/WPDR/M/12 (16 August 2001).
WTO, Working Programme on Electronic Commerce, WT/L/274, 30 September 1998.
---, Decision of 17 December 2011, WT/L/843 (19 December 2011).
Understanding on Rules and Procedures Governing the Settlement of Disputes Art. 1, Marrakesh Agreement Establishing the World Trade Organization, Annex 2, 1869 U.N.T.S. 401 (15 April 1994).

TABLE OF CASES

EUROPEAN COURT OF HUMAN RIGHTS

European Court of Human Rights, *Handyside v. the United Kingdom*, Application No. 5493/72, Series A no.24 (7 December 1976).
---, *Sunday Times v. United Kingdom (No.1)*, Application No. 6538/74 (26 April 1979)
---, *Dudgeon v. The United Kingdom*, Application No. 7525/76 (22 October 1981).
---, *Leander v. Sweden*, Application No. 9248/81, Series A no. 116 (23 March 1987).

---, *Malone v. United Kingdom*, Application No. 8691/79 (2 August 1984).
---, *Müller and Others v. Switzerland,* Application No. 10737/84, Series A no. 133 (24 May 1988).
---, *Groppera Radio AG and others v. Switzerland*, Application No. 10890/84, Series A no. 173 (28 March 1990).
---, *Sunday Times v. United Kingdom (No.2)*, Application No. 13166/87 (26 November 1991).
---, Observer and Guardian v. the United Kingdom, Application No. 13585/88 (26 November 1991).
---, *Margareta and Roger Andersson v. Sweden*, Application No. 12963/87 (25 February 1992).
---, *Open Door Counseling Ltd and Dublin Well Women Centre Ltd and others v. Ireland*, Application No. 14234/88, Series A 264 A (29 October 1992).
---, Niemietz v. Germany, Application No. 13710/88 (16 December 1992).
---, *Otto-Preminger-Institut v. Austria*, Application No. 13470/87, Series A no. 295-A (20 September 1994).
---, *Murray v. The United Kingdom*, Application No. 14310/88 (28 October 1994)
---, *Olsson v. Sweden*, Application No. 10465/83 (March 1998).
---, *Hertel v. Switzerland*, ECHR 59/1997/843/1049 (25 August 1998).
---, *Rotaru v. Romania*, Application No. 28324/95 (4 May 2000).
---, *Association Ekin v. France*, Application No. 39288/98 (17 July 2001).
---, *Perna v. Italy*, Application No. 48898/99 (6 May 2003).
---, Von *Hannover v. Germany*, Application No. 59320/00 (24 June 2004).
---, *Chauvy and Others v. France*, Application No. 64915/01 (29 June 2004).
---, *Stoll v. Switzerland*, Application No. 69698/01 (10 December 2007).
---, *S & Marper v. The United Kingdom*, Application No. 30562/04 (04 December 2008).
---, *Társaság a Szabadságjogokért v. Hungary*, Application No. 37374/05 (14 April 2009).
---, *Aleksey Ovchinnikov v. Russia*, Application No. 24061/04 (16 December 2010).
---, *Yildiim V. Turkey*, Application No. 3111/10 (12 December 2012).
---, *Fredrik Neij and Peter Sunde Kolmisoppi v. Sweden*, Application No. 40397/12 (19 February 2013).

EUROPEAN COURT OF JUSTICE

ECJ Case C-159/90, *The Society for the Protection of Unborn Children Ireland Ltd v. Stephen Grogan*, ECR I-4658 (1991).
--- C-112/00 *Eugen Schmidberger, Internationale Transporte und Planzüge v. Republic Österreich,* ECJ I-5659 (2003).
--- C-542/06, *Heinz Huber v. Bundesrepublik Deutschland* (16 December 2008).
--- C-92/09 and C-93/09, *Volker und Markus Sheck GbR and Hartmut Eifert v. Land Hesen* (9 September 2010).
--- C-316/09, *MSD Sharp v. Dohme GmbH,* ECJ I-3295 (2011).
--- C-468/10 and C-469/10, *Asociación Nacional de Establecimientos Financieros de Crédito and Federación de Comercio Electrónico y Marketing Directo v. Administración del Estado* (24 November 2011).

--- C-360/10, *Belgische Vereniging van Auteurs, Componisten en Uitgevers CVBA (SABAM) v. Netlog NV* (16 February 2012).
---C-291/12, *Schwarz v. Stadt Bochum* (17 October 2013).
WORLD TRADE ORGANIZATION
Panel Report, *United States – Section 337 of the Tariff Act of 1930*, L/6439-36S/345 (7 November 1989).
---, *European Economic Community – Payment and Subsidies Paid to Processors and Producers of Oilseeds and Related Animal-Feed Proteins* (cited as *EEC -- Oilseeds*), L/6627-37S/86 (25 January 1990).
---, *Thailand – Restrictions on Importation of and Internal Taxes on Cigarettes* (cited as *Thailand -- Cigarettes*), DS10/R-37s/200, (7 November 1990).
---, *United States – Restrictions on Imports of Tuna* (cited as *US – Tuna I*), DS21/R (3 September 1991)
---, United States – *Restriction on Imports of Tuna* (cited as *US –Tuna II*), DS/29/R (16 June 1994).
---, *United States – Standards for Reformulated and Conventional Gasoline* (cited as *US -- Gasoline*), WT/DS2/R (29 January 1996).
---, *Japan – Taxes on Alcoholic Beverages* (cited as *Japan – Alcoholic Beverage II*), WT/DS8/R & WT/DS10/R & WT/DS11/R (11 July 1996).
---, *European Communities – Regime for the Importation, Sale and Distribution of Bananas* (cited as *EC – Bananas III*), WT/DS27/R/ECU (25 September 1997).
---, *United States – Import Prohibition of Certain Shrimp and Shrimp Product* (cited as *US -- Shrimp*), WT/DS58/R (15 May 1998).
---, *Canada – Certain Measures Affecting the Automotive Industry* (cited as *Canada – Automotive Industry*), WT/DS139/R and WT/DS142/R (11 February 2000).
---, *Korea – Measures Affecting Government Procurement* (cited as *Korea Government Procurement*), WT/DS163/R (adopted 1 May 2000).
---, *Korea – Measures Affecting Imports of Fresh, Chilled and Frozen Beef* (cited as *Korea -- Beef*), WT/DS161/R WT/DS169/R (31 July 2000).
---, *Korea – Measures Affecting Imports of Fresh, Chilled and Frozen Beef* (cited as *Korea -- Beef*), WT/DS161-169/R, (10 January 2001).
---, *United States – Measures Affecting the Cross-Border Supply of Gambling and Betting Services* (cited as *US – Gambling*), WT/DS285/R (10 November 2004).
---, *European Communities – Measures Affecting the Approval and Marketing of Biotech Products* (cited as *EC – Biotech Products*), WT/DS291/R (21 November 2006).
---, *China – Measures Affecting Trading Rights and Distribution Services for Certain Publications and Audiovisual Entertainment Products* (cited as *China – Audiovisual Products*), WT/DS363/R (12 August 2009).
---, *United States – Measures Affecting the Production and Sale of Clove Cigarettes* (cited as *US – Clove Cigarettes*), WT/DS406/R (2 September 2011)
---, *China – Certain Measures Affecting Electronic Payment Services* (cited as *China – Electronic Payment*), WT/DS413/R (16 July 2012).
Appellate Body Report, *United States – Standards for Reformulated and Conventional Gasoline* (cited as *US -- Gasoline*), WT/DS2/9 (20 May 1996).

---, *Japan – Taxes on Alcoholic Beverages* (cited as *Japan – Alcoholic Beverages II*), WT/DS8/AB/R; WT/DS10/AB/R WT; DS11/AB/R (4 October 1996).

---, *Canada – Certain Measures Concerning Periodicals* (cited as *Canada – periodicals*), WT/DS31/AB/R (30 June 1997).

---, *European Communities – Regime for the Importation, sale and distribution on bananas* (cited as *EC -- Bananas III*), WT/DS27/AB/R (25/September/1997).

---, *EC Measures Concerning Meat and Meat Products (Hormones)* (cited as *EC – Hormones*), WT/DS26/AB/R and WT/DS48/AB/R (16 January 1998).

---, *European Communities – Customs Classification of Certain Computer Equipment* (cited as *EC – Computer Equipment*), WT/DS62/AB/R WT/DS67/AB/R WT/DS68/AB/R (5 June 1998).

---, *European Communities – Measures Affecting the Importation of Certain Poultry Products*, WT/DS69/AB/R (23 July 1998).

---, *United States – Import Prohibition of Çertain Shrimp and Shrimp Product* (cited as *US -- Shrimp*), WT/DS58/AB/R (12 October 1998).

---, *Australia – Measures Affecting Importation of Salmon* (cited as *Australia -- Salmon*), WT/DS18/AB/R (20 October 1998).

--- report, *Canada – Measures affecting the export of Civilian Aircraft* (cited as *Canada -- Aircraft*), WT/DS70/AB/R (2 August 1999).

---, *Canada-Certain Measures Affecting the Automotive Industry* (cited as *Canada -- Auto*), WT/DS139/AB/R; WT/DS142/AB/R (31 May 2000).

---, *Canada – Certain Measures Affecting the Automotive Industry* (cited as *Canada – Automatic Industry*), WT/DS139/AB/R and WT/DS142/AB/R (19 June 2000).

---, *Korea – Measures Affecting Imports of Fresh, Chilled and Frozen Beef* (cited as *Korea -- Beef*), WT/DS161/AB/R & WT/DS169/AB/R (11 December 2000).

---, *European Communities – Measures Affecting Asbestos and Asbestos-Containing Products* (cited as *EC -- Asbestos*), WT/DS135/AB/R (5 April 2001).

---, *European Communities – Conditions for the Granting of Tariff Preferences to Developing Countries* (cited as *EC – Tariff Preferences*), WT/DS246/AB/R (7 April 2004).

---, *United States – Measures Affecting the Cross-Border Supply of Gambling and Betting Services* (cited as *US – Gambling*), WT/DS285/AB/R (7 April 2005).

---, *Dominican Republic – Measures Affecting the Importation and Internal Sale of Cigarettes* (cited as *Dominican Republic -- Cigarettes*), WT/DS 302/AB/R (25 April 2005).

---, *Brazil – Measures Affecting Imports of Retreaded Tyres* (cited as *Brazil – Retreaded Tyres*), WT/DS332/AB/R (3 December 2007).

---, *United States – Continued Suspension of Obligation in the EC – Hormones Dispute* (cited as *US/Canada – Continued Suspension*), WT/DS320/AB/R (16 October 2008).

---, *China – Measures Affecting Trading Rights and Distribution Services for Certain Publications and Audiovisual Entertainment Products* (cited as *China – Audiovisual Products*), WT/DS363/AB/R (21 December 2009).

---, *United States – Measures Affecting the Production and Sale of Clove Cigarettes* (cited as *US – Clove Cigarettes*), WT/DS406/AB/R (4 April 2012).

---, *European Communities – Measures Prohibiting the Importation and Marketing of Seal Products* (cited as *EC – Seal Products*), WT/DS 400/AB/R & WT/DS 401/AB/R (22 May 2014).

---, *United States – Measures Concerning the Importation, Marketing and Sale of Tuna and Tuna Products* (cited *as US – Tuna II*), WT/DS 381/AB/R (16 May 2012).

Kölner Schriften zum Internationalen und Europäischen Recht/ Cologne Studies in International and European Law
hrsg. von Prof. Dr. Stephan Hobe

Mingyan Nie
Legal Framework and Basis for the Establishment of Space Cooperation in Asia
vol. 25, 2016, 262 pp., 39,90 €, pb., ISBN 978-3-643-90816-2

Gabriel Orellana Zabalza
The Principle of Systemic Integration
Towards a Coherent International Legal Order
vol. 24, 2012, 392 pp., 39,90 €, pb., ISBN 978-3-643-90267-2

Johannes Fuhrmann
Der Beitrag des Libanontribunals zur Weiterentwicklung des Völkerrechts
Bd. 23, 2012, 384 S., 39,90 €, br., ISBN 978-3-643-90252-8

Stephan Hobe; Mahulena Hofmannová; Jan Wouters (Eds.)
A Coherent European Procurement Law and Policy for the Space Sector
Towards a Third Way
vol. 22, 2010, 512 pp., 49,90 €, hc., ISBN 978-3-643-10911-8

Michael Lysander Fremuth
Die Europäische Union auf dem Weg in die Supranationalität
Untersuchung der Rechtsnatur der Europäischen Union anhand der Polizeilichen und Justitiellen Zusammenarbeit in Strafsachen
Bd. 21, 2010, 392 S., 64,00 €, br., ISBN 978-3-643-10795-4

Katharina Konert
Die unterschiedliche Behandlung im Welthandels- und Umweltvölkerrecht und ihr Einfluss auf die Herausbildung eines Solidaritätsprinzips
Bd. 20, 2010, 232 S., 24,90 €, br., ISBN 978-3-643-10501-1

Maike Susanne Krewet
Wechselwirkungen zwischen dem Grundgesetz und den Primärverträgen der Europäischen Union als ihrer Verfassung
Rechtstransfer und gegenseitige Beeinflussung von selbständigen Rechtskreisen eines Mehrebenensystems am Beispiel des Grundrechtsschutzes
Bd. 19, 2009, 320 S., 29,90 €, br., ISBN 978-3-643-10455-7

Katja Wahl
Rechtsschutz gegen Individualsanktionen der UN am Beispiel der Finanzsanktionen des Taliban-Sanktionsregimes
Bd. 18, 2009, 328 S., 29,90 €, br., ISBN 978-3-643-10039-9

Stephan Hobe; Oliver Heinrich; Irina Kerner; Annette Froehlich
Entwicklung der Europäischen Weltraumagentur als „implementing agency" der Europäischen Union: Rechtsrahmen und Anpassungserfordernisse
Bd. 17, 2009, 504 S., 49,90 €, br., ISBN 978-3-643-10047-4

Jan Deuster
Ausgleichszahlungen für Dienstleistungen von allgemeinem wirtschaftlichem Interesse
Das Verhältnis von Art. 87 Abs. 1 EG zu Art. 86 Abs. 2 EG nach der Altmark Trans-Rechtsprechung unter besonderer Berücksichtigung der öffentlichen Finanzierung des Luftverkehrs
Bd. 16, 2007, 304 S., 29,90 €, br., ISBN 978-3-8258-0254-7